Building
Customer-Brand
Relationships

Building Customer-Brand Relationships

Don E. Schultz
Beth E. Barnes
Heidi F. Schultz
Marian Azzaro

M.E.Sharpe
Armonk, New York
London, England

Library of Congress Cataloging-in-Publication Data

Building customer-brand relationships / by Don E. Schultz [et al.].
    p. cm.
Includes bibliographical references and index.
ISBN 978-0-7656-1799-6 (pbk. : alk. paper)
1. Relationship marketing. 2. Customer relations. 3. Branding (Marketing) I. Schultz, Don E.

HF5415.55.B85 2009
658.8'12—dc22   2008028969

Printed in the United States of America

The paper used in this publication meets the minimum requirements of
American National Standard for Information Sciences
Permanence of Paper for Printed Library Materials,
ANSI Z 39.48-1984.

CW (p)   10   9   8   7   6   5   4   3   2   1

Contents

Preface

Who Needs Another Campaigns Book?

The first question any advertising, promotional management, or even integrated marketing communication professor will probably ask is this: Why another campaigns or capstone book? There are a lot of them out there, covering the subject from a variety of viewpoints, with a number of formats and a plethora of planning tools. So why another text with a somewhat strange title and an arguably radical format?

IS THE CAMPAIGNS TEXT A COMMODITY?

The answer is simple: Most of the current texts use the same structure and content that were developed more than thirty years ago. Building a campaign, whether in advertising, marketing communication, promotion, or whatever, from the inside out. Starting with the product or service, client or company, and then organizing outbound communication programs to sell or tell or convince or persuade customers or consumers or prospects or target markets that they should buy or try or continue to use or recommend or whatever the communication message is designed to encourage. All internally oriented—that is, using the 4Ps approach of product, place, price, and promotion to build a communication plan structured around a mix of advertising and direct marketing and sales promotion and public relations with a dollop of online, interactive, and social media thrown in to sound new and current and hip and au courant.

How do we know that? One of us wrote the first advertising campaigns texts back in the 1970s and, quite honestly, has been paid the highest of compliments as that format has continued to be used ever since.

The problem with most campaigns or capstone texts is that they are all the same and the expectations are all the same and the structures are all the same. Inside out, what the marketer wants to say to the prospect and what the marketer expects to achieve. Marketer in control. Customer or consumer as willing or unwilling, unquestioning recipient of the market's messages and incentives. Creative and content driving most of the approaches with the idea that mass communication and mass media are the solution, depending only on how you mix and match the messages and incentives.

While there is some justification for this campaigns or capstone approach, at least from the instructional view, it is becoming less and less relevant in the actual marketplace.

WHEN THE CUSTOMER GAINS CONTROL

The customer or consumer has gained control of the marketplace. Technology has given the communication recipient control of what messages are consumed, how they are accessed, in what form they are accepted, and what response they generate. Thus, the old-fashioned communication delivery model no longer makes sense for the planning, development, and implementation of marketing communication messages and programs. The customer drives today's communication marketplace—not the marketer, nor the media, nor even the event developer.

So starting with the customer or consumer and working backward to create a communication program makes infinitely good sense. That is what we have done in this text.

Building communication programs based on the media and promotional forms customers and consumers use and how they use them simplifies media planning in an increasingly fragmented marketplace.

Recognizing that consumers and customers are involved with brands, not products and services, and that they provide the linchpin between the buyer and the seller creates a whole new way to build ongoing relationships that increase in value over time. That is a significant shift from the traditional thirteen-week promotional cycle that dominates so many of the traditional campaigns texts.

Understanding measurement and accountability is critical to the approval of initial programs and absolutely vital to the continuation of any type of communication funding in today's quantitatively and marketing and management-driven organization.

Understanding that a new instructional format is needed to help students cope with the constantly changing marketplace in which they exist and in which they will develop their careers is one of the key teaching elements the professor can provide.

FOUR KEY ELEMENTS: BRANDS, AUDIENCES, DELIVERY, AND CONTENT

The format for instruction in this book is simple. In the pages that follow, we discuss four key elements that the communicator can use in developing any program for any product or service, in any market, in any culture around the world:

1. the brand;
2. the audience to be reached or with whom the dialogue must be developed;
3. the delivery forms that can be used to create and continue the dialogue; and
4. the content or brand value proposition that the marketer wants to offer to the customer or consumer.

The use of these four critical elements will allow the student or professional to understand and develop effective, efficient communication programs that can and will create long-term, ongoing relationships between the buyer and seller. Truly, that is the goal of every advertising, promotion, or communication program any marketing organization develops; and that is what you will find in the pages of this text.

The text is not for those who prefer tradition and status quo; that is, those professors or even practitioners who would like to see advertising stay advertising and direct marketing continue to be only outbound and direct. Or sales promotion people who want to continue to develop and distribute coupons and price-offs or public relations folk who want to write a press release and then move on. This text is for people who want to manage marketing communication programs as a "push" or outbound system but, at the same time, recognize that consumers and customers will "pull" or gather information about products and services through the Internet and World Wide Web from every corner of the earth. Marketing today is not either-or, it is both, and that is the key fact in understanding how customer-brand relationships are developed and maintained.

FINALLY, A TEXT THAT DELIVERS ON THE MARKETING AND COMMUNICATION PROMISE

In short, this text delivers what marketing and marketing communication have long promised but rarely provided—a customer focus. The book uses a common-sense structure and the newest and most sophisticated planning methods. It is easy to understand and apply. It includes the critical elements of measurement and accountability that too often are ignored in campaigns texts. Most of all, it fills a need for curricula and practices that recognize that the market is continually evolving and that students must learn to adapt to the marketplace, not simply regurgitate hoary concepts that are no longer relevant.

Is this text for you and your students? Only you can make that decision, but we believe it is certainly worth trying. All four authors have spent more than twenty years each teaching and training in the old, established methods. We think it is time for a change and we believe this book represents the way of the future. We hope you will agree once you see how *Building Customer-Brand Relationships* provides a totally new way to prepare your students, not just for their first job, but also for their careers.

Don E. Schultz, Northwestern University
Beth E. Barnes, University of Kentucky
Heidi F. Schultz, Northwestern University
Marian Azzaro, Roosevelt University

Building Customer-Brand Relationships

CHAPTER 1

Customers and Brands

Marketplace Drivers for All

Customers and brands and the relationships between the two are driving the twenty-first–century marketplace. Marketing organizations rely on customers, who are generally their primary source of income and profit. A number of years ago, Peter Drucker, the famous management guru, said that the primary purpose of a company is "to create a customer. . . . It is the customer who determines what a business is. It is the customer alone whose willingness to pay for a good or for a service converts economic resources into wealth, things into goods. What the customer buys and considers value is never a product. It is always utility, that is, what a product or service does for him."[1]

Brands are the primary connectors between the organization and its customers, the key ingredient in building successful relationships between the company and the people it wants to serve. Yet the industry, both practitioner and academician, seemingly know little about brands although they have been around almost as long as people. While prehistoric people did not think much about brands and branding, they practiced a crude form of identification nevertheless since different features, capabilities, and actions have always separated one person from another, for example, through dress, types of animals hunted, where they lived, their tribal rituals, and the like. As early commercial people discovered, they could use symbols or marks to distinguish the goods they made from those of other artisans, brands began to develop—for example, when the first potter marked a vessel with his thumbprint, or when the first baker hung a sign outside her hut with her family symbol, or when one village became well known for the quality of its well water. In each case, the producers were establishing their name as the source of the goods being sold or traded. History has not changed that practice. Today marketers simply have a more formalized method of differentiating and connecting people and places and products and services. That method is what we call in this text customer-brand relationships, and it is this concept that will drive the marketplace in the future, both locally and globally.

Differentiation is the key. Differentiation is what separates people. What separates organizations? What separates countries and cultures and ways of life? Companies and people are differentiated and differentiating. We will focus on company and brand differentiation in this text for it is differentiation that allows the marketing organization to separate its goods and services from all the "look alike, sound alike, taste alike" competitors and to build an ongoing relationship with customers. *Ongoing* is the key word. In a mostly transitory marketplace, con-

3

sistency, commitment, and continuity become the key elements all organizations should strive for. And all those elements can be summed up in the term *customer-brand relationships*.

The text has some simple themes. How marketing organizations can understand customers and prospects based on their differences. How marketing organizations can use brands and branding to differentiate their products and services from those of competitors. How brand communication, by being differentiated, can build the long-term and long-lasting relationships between the brand and its customers—relationships that benefit both parties. And, make no mistake, brands become ever more critical as the world moves from a marketer-controlled to a customer-controlled marketplace.

SETTING THE STAGE: KEY CHALLENGES AND REQUIREMENTS FOR BRAND MARKETERS

Today, there are four major challenges facing brand marketers—commoditization, communication, fragmentation, and reciprocity. And there is one clear-cut, overriding requirement: continuity. Continuity of relationships commonly is the result of reliability, or organizations making and keeping promises to customers, employees, distributors, shareholders, and other stakeholders. Generally, these issues are not much discussed in promotional circles—advertising, promotion, direct marketing, public relations, and the like—although they are indeed promises to the marketplace that the firm makes, promises that must be kept. We will demonstrate in this text why and how they are the real challenges for brands and how mastery of these areas will be critical in the days ahead as marketers move toward continuity of relationships with customers and away from traditional, short-term, outbound, "push" forms of marketing communication campaigns.

Commoditization and Differentiation

In today's marketplace, differentiation is critical. Once the marketer could develop a product or service with a unique feature or function and expect to have a modicum of advantage over competitors for a viable period of time. Today, however, competitors seemingly can replicate any product improvement or value differentiation almost overnight. Given the fragility of physical features or even service quality, branding today is not so much about differentiating product features or service locations as it is about creating customer value, whether that be actual or perceptual and whether delivered through marketing communication or physical differences. The key, of course, is delivering on those perceived differences in the marketplace.

Commoditization is rampant in the world today and will likely only get worse. Thus, branding becomes one of the key elements in the success of any organization. Without a strong branding program, organizations will be forced to compete primarily on price, logistics, and delivery terms, areas that are easily negotiable and that have finite values for opportunities and returns.

So what will differentiation be like in the future? Will it continue to be resident in such historic methods as innovation, research and development, and new technologies? Or will it take on new forms and features that are more closely related to the areas of marketing and communication? That is a key discussion point in this book.

Exhibit 1.1 **"Push" or Outbound Model**

Agency ➔ Media ➔ Fulfillment

Marketer ➔ Customer/Prospect

Unique Products/Offers

Messages and Incentives

Communication

Historically, organizations typically considered communication nice to have but not critically important to the success of the firm. Communication was done when times were good or when there were clearly identifiable threats or challenges. However, in between, communication was often considered an expensive toy for the marketing people and continuously subject to reductions, downsizing, or outright elimination by senior management. The fact that communication people could provide little evidence of the financial returns on their marketing communication spending only worsened the situation.

This view that communication was nonessential may have been acceptable when communication was largely a one-way street—from the marketer to its customers—and when the marketer could dictate where and how it would occur. That created the base for the traditional promotional "push" marketplace, a system where the marketer talked and the customer or prospect was supposed to listen and respond. That approach generally looked like Exhibit 1.1.

Today, however, communication is dynamic, multifaceted, and occurs whether the marketer initiates it or not. Companies can be challenged by every blogger or Web site developer anywhere in the world. Product flaws can be quickly exposed and widely publicized—witness the embarrassment brought upon the Kryptonite bicycle lock when a Web-based discussion board revealed that the expensive ($100+), supposedly secure, lock could be easily picked using a Bic ballpoint pen.[2] Or consider the furor kicked up by the Neistat brothers, Casey and Van, whose frustrations with the short-lived, irreplaceable batteries in the first-generation iPods resulted in the video "iPod's Dirty Secret," which raised challenges Apple simply had to address.[3] Management can be publicly challenged, as seen in the saga of Martha Stewart and in the ongoing labor relations conflicts for Nike and Wal-Mart. In short, marketers have lost control over the communication process they formerly thought they ruled.

Today's marketplace features both traditional, outbound or "push" communication and the new, emerging areas of customer-controlled or "pull" communication. Pull communication is generated by the customer or the audience, as illustrated in Exhibit 1.2. As shown, customers and prospects can access or acquire information about their needs and relate that to the organization and its products or services through any number of alternative customer-activated communication systems, such as the Internet, the World Wide Web, digital, and the increasingly ubiquitous social networks such as My Space, YouTube, and a host of others.

Today brand managers must be proactive in all forms of communication, both those they control directly (e.g., advertising, direct mail, events, sponsorships) and those forums where they are only a guest (e.g., blogs, podcasts). Branding is not just about advertising, a point we will return to throughout this book, but it is most definitely about strong and effective

Exhibit 1.2 **"Pull" Communication**

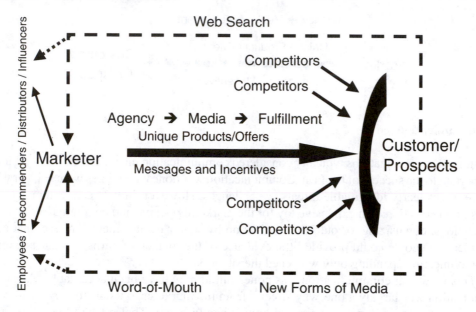

communication of all types and forms. Starbucks, the Body Shop, and Red Bull, near-iconic brands built with little or no formal advertising, have used instead powerful, pervasive communication programs to acquire and maintain their marketplace status.

So communication is critical to brands and branding. The question is what type of communication? How do organizations move beyond traditional promotional forms such as advertising, direct marketing, and sales promotion in order to combine and leverage the possibilities offered by new, interactive media forms? Those are the primary issues facing today's marketing and branding managers and their organizations.

Fragmentation

Historically, the marketplace has been the site of aggregation, consolidation, and concentration, bringing together buyers and sellers. From the earliest days, bazaars and marketplaces gathered people together to sell or trade their wares, to find products and services to fill their needs, to collect and share information, and to create social systems. This consolidation and concentration has been critical to the growth of civilization and modern economies. Yet, today, the focus is on fragmentation. A fractionalization of marketplaces. Today, the emphasis is on segments of one or only a few. On individualization. On personalization. On "me" as compared to the group. This segmentation challenges traditional branding, which is based on group acceptance and group recognition.

With the increasing emphasis on fragmentation and individualization, can the concept of branding still have value? Does branding and do brand relationships still make sense? Can they be valuable elements in the twenty-first–century organization or are they relics of the mass marketplace of the past? These critical issues for future marketing managers will be discussed at some length in the following pages.

Reciprocity

Reciprocity is a term not often heard today. In the world of "me" and "mine," reciprocity or the sharing of value just does not fit well. That is also true when it comes to traditional marketing and promotional texts. They are filled with warlike terms—capturing market share, owning a market or segment, offsetting competitors, hitting target markets, creating advertising blitzes, and on and on. In truth, we have built a marketing culture based primarily on conquest. But today not many customers want to be conquered. Instead, they want to be recognized and acknowledged.

In this text, we focus on a reciprocity model; that is, an approach in which the marketing organization and the consumer share equally in the value and benefits of the brand. This simply means that the marketer provides value and gains some return and the customer gains some value and is willing to provide a reasonable return to the marketers. In truth, this is when real brand relationships occur—when both the marketer and the customer give and receive value from their ongoing associations over time.

In our view, today, branding, which traditionally has been one-sided as we noted earlier, is in a state of transition; that is, branding and brand communication issues are discussed and defined only from the point of view of the marketing organization. Customers and prospects are still often viewed as pawns in the branding game. Too many managers believe people and markets can be manipulated and maneuvered to fit the company's needs and requirements. Branding, therefore, is often described as what the organization wants to do *to* customers, not what the organization can do *for* customers.

In this book, we will take the customer view first and translate that into practical, feasible actions for marketers. After all, it is still the marketer who has business goals to achieve, employees to pay, and shareholders to satisfy. It is still the marketing organization and its owners and shareholders who are risking their capital and resources to find ways to satisfy customer needs wants and desires, hoping that what the firm has developed will be of interest and value to the customer. So, while the customer will always come first, the view of this book is firmly on what the marketer can do to create products and services and support them with brand communications to create sustained win-win relationships with customers.

Requirement for Continuity

Modern marketing organizations have traditionally had a very short-term focus, emphasizing clever or memorable advertising or branding campaigns that quickly expire and disappear. Too often, these traditional campaign-planning approaches give little thought to the need to create long-term, enduring relationships with customers. Marketers, mistakenly assuming that customers have memories as short as the campaigns thrown at them, and do not recognize that customers have their own ways of consolidating and integrating the fragmented and discordant messages they receive over the years. Therefore, few marketers communicate their brand effectively over all points of contact, year in and year out. For every company that sagely projects an ongoing and enduring image—for example, Tiffany, BASF, General Electric, Volvo, Singapore Airlines—there are dozens like Burger King, Ford, and Motorola who seem to have had a revolving door of campaigns, messages, brand strategies, and, indeed, managers to go with them.

Continuity has two primary aspects:

1. *Continuity across all communication points*—that is, *consistency* in how the organization communicates using multiple forms of touch points. Is the direct mail effort consistent with the advertising campaign and the Web site? Is there a continuous flow of messaging, with each effort reinforcing and enhancing all other communication activities? Is there synergy between the various elements where the customer touches the brand or the brand touches the customer?

2. *Continuity over time*—that is, *constancy* of communication efforts over an extended period of time. Brands take time to develop, but, once established, can have an amazing lifespan in the minds of customers. (Think "Mikey, he likes it" for LIFE cereal; Tony the Tiger's "Grrrrreat!" for Kellogg's Corn Flakes; and Nike's "Just Do It.") Unfortunately, the almost constant churn among marketing directors has led to a revolving door of brand campaigns. Each new marketing director wants to toss out the predecessor's campaign and start fresh. The result is that customers are often confused, disillusioned, disengaged, or, most disturbing of all, simply disinterested.

GE is a company that has benefited greatly by applying the principles of continuity in its communication. Its corporate theme based on the tagline "We bring good things to life" was a paragon of consistency and constancy, running from 1979 through 2003. During these so-called Jack Welch years, GE built hundreds of TV commercials, print ads, and other communication efforts around this theme, yet each execution was fresh and compelling.[4] And while the new team under Welch's successor, Jeffrey Immelt, CEO of General Electric Company (who replaced Jack Welch, retired CEO of General Electric), moved the company to a new tagline, "Imagination at Work," there was a logical progression from the previous efforts, building upon messages of innovation, problem solving, and commitment to meeting the challenges of a changing, dynamic world. Within two years the new corporate theme not only matched the awareness level of the "We bring good things to life" approach, but brand familiarity had actually increased to 59 percent.[5]

MOVING BEYOND CAMPAIGNS TO DEVELOPING RELATIONSHIPS

The goal of this text is to move beyond the traditional advertising and promotion campaign planning approach and replace it with a more robust methodology based on building enduring relationships with customers. In the past, marketers communicated when they wanted, promoted when they wanted, all with the assumption that the customer was anxious to hear their offers and would immediately be influenced or persuaded to make a purchase. Such is clearly not the case today. Customers are selective and increasingly protective of their time and resources. Marketers must therefore take a different view of the world, recognizing customers not as targets but more closely related, almost as business partners. Thus, in this book we take the long view of building customer-brand relationships. We look at communication as ongoing, continuous, and interactive but still within the structures, forms, and formats available to the marketer and marketing organization.

The emphasis in this text is on communication planning in the broadest sense. Planning, we believe, is a very critical issue facing marketing and promotion today. Marketers must move away from the always hoped-for, but seldom achieved "big idea" to the development of an all-encompassing, customer-surrounding view of the communication world—a world where customers want to hear from marketers, not just when marketers want to talk.

Clearly, brand communication must change. The marketplace has changed. Consumers and customers have changed. Media systems have changed. Everything is in flux. That is what a pull marketplace with customer-activated and -generated communication is all about. So that is what this book is all about.

CLARIFYING THE TERMS

Brands, *relationships*, and *communication* are terms that have been bandied about in the academic and professional communities for years. Seemingly, however, there is little agreement about what they mean or how they should be used. Therefore, we start with some rather simple definitions that will help immeasurably as we move forward with our customer-brand relationship communication planning process.

What Is a Customer?

The *Dictionary of Marketing Terms*, published in conjunction with the American Marketing Association, defines a customer as "the actual or prospective purchaser of products or services."[6] Some writers further distinguish between currently active customers and those who are merely prospects for future purchases. Other writers, most typically in the consumer packaged goods field, distinguish between the direct customer (i.e., wholesalers, retailers, distributors, and other middlemen) and the ultimate consumer (i.e., those who buy the product from retail and who actually use or consume the product or service).

For our purposes in this book, we will consider customers to be individuals or organizations who have purchased or used products or services from the marketing organization in the past or who are likely to do so in the future.

However, brand building requires more than just a two-way, bilateral relationship between customers and the marketing organization. In the customer-brand relationship spectrum, a limited buyer-seller dyad approach is not appropriate nor is it broad enough in scope or in understanding. The marketplace is an interconnected group of players, all of who are acting and interacting in some way for their own and the mutual benefit of others. Marketers therefore must consider the full range of buyers, influencers, references, and other stakeholders that shape the overall customer-brand relationship.

When a marketing organization develops a comprehensive and strategic brand communication program, the customers for those communication efforts are not limited to those who buy from the organization. They include a broader range of individuals, companies, and organizations that combine to create or facilitate the ongoing relationships between everyone and everything that makes up the marketplace. They are all interconnected and all related in some way, and their interactions have an impact on all the others. Truly, it is almost impossible to separate end-users or consumers from all the supply groups, influencers, channels, and the like that make the marketplace possible.

The next several chapters will explore the nature of customers in some depth, examining customer perceptions and motivations, the cognitive processes customers bring to their purchase behavior, how organizations can go about identifying their best or most appropriate customers and prospects, and how customers relate to brands.

What Is a Brand?

There is no one single definition of a brand. At its most basic, a brand is the name, logo, or trademark of a product or organization. This narrow view is reflected in one of the most common definitions used, that of the American Marketing Association: "A name, term, sign, symbol or design or combination of them intended to identify the goods and services of one seller or group of sellers and to differentiate them from those of competitors."[7] Clearly, in this definition, the focus is on the marketer only, not the relationship between the marketer and the customer.

From a legal standpoint, brands are considered intangible assets, the intellectual property of the organization. As such, they are often considered in conjunction with other intellectual property used to support or define the brand, such as trade dress (meaning the packaging, logotypes used, corporate colors, and possibly even the product design), jingles, domain names, Web addresses, and other aural or visual elements.

From a customer standpoint, however, a brand is much more than its name or identifying elements: it is the entire bundle of perceptions, associations, and attributes that the consumer experiences when considering, purchasing, or using the brand. In recent years this view has given rise to broader and more dynamic definitions of a brand. For example, in *Creating a Company for Customers*, McDonald and his colleagues write, "A brand is an entity which offers customers (and other relevant parties) added value based on factors over and above its functional performance. These added values or brand values differentiate the offer and provide the basis for customer preference and loyalty."[8] Similarly, Ambler in *Marketing and the Bottom Line* says, "Brand, a term once used only for consumer goods, is a term that now appears in every sector. . . . Most, but not all UK, marketers now mean: Brand = Product + Packaging + Added Values. . . . The added values are the ways that the consumer thinks about the product, for example as 'cheap and cheerful,' 'innovative,' 'only for kids,' and so on. They may be psychological—the perceived quality and economic benefits, over and above those provided by the product itself."[9] These are just two examples of the new, more customer-embracing view of the brand and the relationships that occur between the two.

Kinds of Brands

Brands can be classified according to the type of product or service they represent (consumer, business-to-business, service), or the category of product (coffee, automobiles, computers), or the geographic area in which they are found (local, regional, national, global), and so on. These classifications seem to be limited only by the need of the classifier.

Brands can exist on several levels within an organization. First, at the top of the organization is the name of the company itself—the corporate brand. Below this there may be a myriad of product and service offerings that may (or may not) draw on the corporate brand for their identity. Thus, Kraft Inc. is the corporate brand of the American food giant. It offers dozens of products linked to its corporate brand identity—for example, Kraft Macaroni and Cheese, Kraft Miracle Whip, Kraft Velveeta Cheese. However, it also has many products that do not

BRANDS AND REPUTATION

The terms *brand* and *reputation* are often, but mistakenly, used interchangeably. While the two concepts have many similar characteristics, and both generally are concerned with building an image and visibility for the organization or its products or services, there are certain important distinctions.

First, a brand is grounded in its fundamental elements—name, trademark, trade dress, taglines, slogans, and so on—and is the rightful property of the organization or person who owns it. Thus, a brand may be sold, licensed, used as collateral, or otherwise disposed of as the owner sees fit.

Reputation, on the other hand, is a broader concept, generally defined as the overall estimation in which a company, brand, or individual is held by the public. Reputations are earned through the actions of the organization with its publics over time. While a good reputation is a valuable thing to have, reputations are not "owned" in the same legal sense that brands are. Thus, a reputation cannot be sold or licensed to another organization, and there are no property rights associated with reputation.

In advanced economies, both brands and reputation are accorded legal protection, but the nature of that protection is substantially different. Brands are primarily protected against counterfeiting, infringement, and fraudulent misuse that can confuse customers as to who is actually behind the brand. A brand, properly registered and trademarked, has a legal defense against another organization copying or infringing on its name, design, trade dress, or other identifying elements. While companies have legal recourse to protect their reputations, it is generally only to the extent of protecting the organization and its management from libel and slander. In most jurisdictions, truth is a complete defense against a charge of libel or slander. Thus, unflattering reports about an organization—if grounded in fact—generally carry no recourse, regardless of how damaging to the corporate brand and its reputation.

There is another important fundamental distinction between brands and reputation. Brands, as we emphasis throughout this book, are all about differentiation. Brands are built by establishing a clear promise to benefit customers and then communicating that promise in a compelling, memorable way. For example, United Parcel Service (UPS) has made "brown" mean something to customers and prospects with the line "What Can Brown Do For You?" while Tiffany is known the world over for its elegant, robin's egg blue box.

Reputations, on the other hand, reflect perceptions about the behavior of the organization and tend to run along a spectrum of good to bad. Reputations are built on certain key admirable qualities that can be shared by many organizations. For example, *Fortune* magazine uses eight criteria in its annual ranking of the world's most admired companies—innovation, people management, use of corporate assets, social responsibility, quality of management, financial soundness, long-term investment, and quality of products or service.[10] Thus, reputations are built not by establishing a unique identity but by becoming recognized as an exemplary practitioner of admirable qualities.

feature the Kraft identity, such as Grey Poupon mustard, Vegemite, Oscar Meyer lunchmeats, and Gevalia coffee. On the other hand, a company such as Nokia uses its corporate name on most of its product offerings. Models are distinguished by a number (e.g., 2100 or 6120), but there is only one brand—Nokia.

Another, related issue that often comes up is the distinction between brand and reputation. While reputation is perhaps more often associated with the top-level corporate identity, it can also impact individual product brands as well. There is more than just a semantic difference as discussed in the box.

Thus, brands come in all sizes, in all categories, and at various levels of the organization. Fundamentally, the principles of brand communication are much the same regardless of the type or level of the brand. However, as we will explore in more detail in a later section, different types of brands may have different constituencies and customer groups that must be taken into consideration in developing brand communication.

What Are Brand Relationships?

Brand relationships are those bonds that bring the buyer and the seller of branded products or services together on a continuing basis. Brands are based on the promises or commitments the seller makes to the buyer or user that in some way provide an immediate and ongoing perceived benefit. The benefit may be in the functional superiority of the product (e.g., BMW's "The ultimate driving machine") or in the emotional or psychic benefits the brand offers (e.g., Gillette's "The best a man can get" or Hallmark's "When you care enough to send the very best"). Thus, if the buyer agrees to accept the promise of the seller, the seller must deliver on the promises made. That is what creates the ongoing relationship between the two.

Brand relationships can be complex and multifaceted. Brands have relationships with many constituencies, including consumers and end users, intermediaries, influencers, suppliers, financial markets, employees, external organizations, government units, shareholders, and so on. In the next chapter we will describe in more detail how all these audiences form a network that develops, supports, and enhances the brand.

For now, the point to understand is that what differentiates a powerful brand relationship from a simple exchange between a buyer and a seller is that an ongoing value or relationship is implied in the exchange. It is not a simple, one-time purchase. Thus, a brand relationship goes far beyond the simple satisfying of a customer through product use. It is the obligation of the seller to continue to satisfy the buyer under the terms of the promises made and accepted. Thus, it is reciprocal in nature, offering benefits to both.

This continuing mutual agreement is why brand relationships are special and must be treated that way. Not every brand has a relationship with every person who buys or tries it. The relationship is reserved for a favored few on both sides who agree to participate in the ongoing relationship. In truth, most consumers have strong brand relationships with only a few special brands. Thus, brands have relationships with relatively few favored customers.

What Is Brand Equity?

Brands are unique in that they create value for both buyers and sellers. For *consumers and end users*, brands provide a range of functional, emotional, and psychic values and benefits. For one thing, they represent authenticity, providing the assurance of dealing with a known, reliable entity. They promise quality and value above and beyond price alone, and customers know the value they will receive for the price they are paying. Brands may connote luxury (Mercedes, Prada, Louis Vuitton); they may be small indulgences (M&M candies, Preference by L'Oréal); they may be a means of self-expression (Diesel jeans, Billabong beachwear). Brands often command a premium price, but not always—consider Dell computers, Wal-Mart, and other value-for-money brands.

For *intermediaries*, such as wholesalers and retailers, brands create value because they may command premium prices or because they may generate strong loyalty and drive higher volume than more weakly branded competitors. Strong brands such as Dove, Yoplait yogurt, and Pantene shampoo can drive a customer into a store or—conversely—to a competitor when the preferred brand is out of stock.

For *brand owners*, brands are the source of economic value to the organization. They help to support the pricing strategy, drive volume and economies of scale, facilitate extension to other markets or categories, create competitive barriers, and help the organization achieve loyalty and ongoing relationships with customers and intermediaries. This eventually leads to stronger financial performance, with impact on the organization's financial statements—both its income statement and its balance sheet.

Brand equity is a concept that is often misunderstood and misused by marketers and their agencies and other representatives. Generally speaking, brand equity refers to the strength and depth of the relationship that customers (and prospective customers) have with a brand, resulting in the company's ability to sustain price premiums, capture greater volume, or otherwise outperform competitors in the marketplace. In our view, there are four broad components that must be taken into consideration before a brand can be said to have strong brand equity:

• *Brand presence*: This component reflects the extent to which customers and prospects are aware of the brand, are able to recall it or recognize it, and understand the brand and its use. This is perhaps the easiest component of brand equity to achieve, as it is largely a function of investing in various forms of marketing communication. Establishing brand presence is the first order of business for new brands, but becomes less important for established brands, when the emphasis must shift to strengthening the other three components.

• *Brand identity and image*: This component comprises the values, attributes, traits, and personalities associated with the brand. Brand identify refers to those associations that the brand manager hopes or intends to establish through various promotional and communication activities. Brand image, on the other hand, refers to how the brand is actually seen by customers and prospects at a point in time. Thus, there is often a major difference in what the organization believes or feels about the brand and the experience that customers and consumers have with the brand. Achieving alignment between the desired brand identity and the actual image held by customers is one of the key challenges facing brand managers.

• *Brand commitment*: As the title of this text suggest, brands are all about relationships. Thus, a key issue is the degree of commitment that is generated among customers. How often do they return or make a repurchase? What share of wallet do they give the brand versus competitors in the category? Are they willing advocates for the brand and do they provide positive word of mouth? These are just a few of the ways in which brand commitment can be understood and measured.

• *Perceived quality*: Brands achieve strong commitment because customers believe they offer high quality for the price or time required. Quality can be measured in absolute (zero defects) or relative terms (more suitable to the customer's needs than other brands). Understanding how customers define quality and value is a critical step in meeting their needs with appropriate product and communication efforts.

Brand equity is often confused with a brand's financial value. As noted earlier, the brand is an organizational asset—in many cases, the most valuable asset the firm owns—and brand value can be measured and monitored just like any other asset. The process of determining a brand's financial value is referred to as brand valuation. As pointed out by Tim Ambler at the London School of Business, brand equity is the asset built over time through marketing activities and residing primarily in the minds of consumers, customers, and other constituents. Brand valuation, on the other hand, a measure of its estimated financial worth at a point in time, is a result of the equity the brand has established in the marketplace.[11] We will explore the goals and methodologies of brand valuation in Chapter 8.

BRAND COMMUNICATION

Having defined a few of the primary terms related to brands and branding, we next move to the issue of communication, specifically brand communication. Like branding, brand communication has a number of definitions and applications. In this text, we define communication in this way: Communication is the exchange of content and relevance between two parties. Thus, in this definition, communication can be anything that has meaning and can be shared between two parties. Communication therefore occurs only when one party comes in contact with the other so that meaning can be created and shared. In this sense, communication can take many forms and occur in many ways. The key element is that there is shared meaning, either created or exchanged between the two or more parties.

In keeping with our rather broad definition of communication, we can therefore define brand communication as any exchange of meaning that transfers the brand value understanding between the brand owner and the brand purchaser. That meaning can be based on the physical, emotional, or perceptual value of the brand no matter how it is transferred or over what time period. With this definition, it is clear that brand communication can come from the physical product or service that represents the brand, the trade dress, or images or icons that are used to identify the brand. It also could be the emotional value the brand provides the customer or any other form that would allow the transfer of meaning between the brand owner and the customer. In short, brand communication is anything and everything that connects brands and their customers. Thus, brand communication can occur as a result of outbound, push programs generated by the organization or it can come from inbound, pull information either generated by or developed by the customer or prospect. This is a broad definition, to be sure, but it is becoming increasingly relevant in the ever-increasing area of what is and should be considered brand communication.

As we shall see in later sections of this book, brand communication, whether it is push or pull, is the key element in building brand relationships. Thus, it is central to the entire methodology found in this book. We will return to this theme often in later sections.

Brand Contacts

Brand contacts are the numerous and varied ways in which a brand touches (outbound or push communication) or is touched (inbound or pull communication) by its customers or prospects.

Exhibit 1.3   **Illustration of Brand Reciprocity**

Achieving equilibrium between buyer and seller

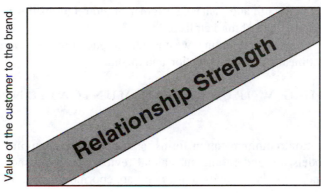

Value of the brand to the customer

Simply put, brand contacts are how brands and customers come together in the marketplace. In some cases, brand contacts are planned and developed by the brand marketer. Common examples are packaging, advertising, sales promotion, events, and sponsorships. Other brand contacts are incidental or even unplanned—for example, when a consumer observes trash from a fast food restaurant littering a forest preserve or when a friend recommends or says derogatory things about a certain brand. Thus, not all brand contacts are good and not all brand contacts are under the control of the brand owner. This pervasive nature of brand contacts makes them critical in the development of brand relationship programs, as we will note throughout this text. In fact, Chapter 10 is devoted to an in-depth exploration of how brand contacts should be understood and managed.

Creating Equilibrium: Reciprocal Brand Value

From the preceding discussion it should now be clear that brand relationships are not one-way streets. Brands are not something the brand owner creates and distributes in the marketplace, taking the profits and moving on. Nor are brands fantasies that consumers dream up in their minds. Successful brands require the cooperation and engagement of both the buyer and the seller. In short, brand relationships are based on ongoing dialogues, using both push and pull communication. As noted above, we call this common building of value by the brand owner and the brand user reciprocity. This simply means the marketer must build value into the brand for the consumer and the consumer must in turn receive value from the brand. Only if the inputs and receipts of the two parties are in equilibrium will the relationship be strong and sustainable. This concept is illustrated in Exhibit 1.3.

If the value of the customers to the brand (i.e., as determined by their purchasing actions and ability to pay the stated price) is not in balance with the value of the brand to the customers (i.e., the perceived benefits the customers receive for the price they pay)—then the relationship will be unstable and, ultimately, untenable. However, when both the brand owner and the brand consumer feel there is a mutually advantageous relationship and both profit equally from the ongoing exchange, the brand relationship will flourish in both the short and long term. It is this fine line between value delivered and value received that makes up the heart of customer-brand relationships. And that is what makes up the balance of this text: how to develop, implement, maintain, and manage customer-brand relationships in an increasingly complex and complicated global marketplace.

With this view of brands and branding, we now turn to one of the key elements in creating customer-brand relationships: communication and media.

THE CHANGING WORLD OF COMMUNICATION AND MEDIA

Clearly, communication, communication forms, and media are changing. Even the basic communication models are undergoing substantial review and adjustment. From a brand communication standpoint, the changes taking place are enormous and most likely long lasting. Yet, in many cases, marketers, their agencies, and their support organizations continue to plan, develop, and implement marketing communication programs in the same way as has been done for the last fifty years, through an outbound, marketer-controlled approach we have called push communication.

In this section, we set the stage for the new communication approach needed in the twenty-first century. We then discuss the new customer-brand relationship planning model on which this book is based.

How Has Communication Changed?

Communication is the transfer of thoughts, concepts, ideas, feelings, and the like from one person or group or organization to another. That has not changed since the beginning of time. However, the ways in which that transfer is made—what we call the communication systems—have changed, and changed dramatically.

First, the way humans in developed economies take in, process, and use information from the external world has changed. For the past 500 or so years, humans have been trained to process incoming information sequentially. That training depended on the way information was presented—that is, alphabets, books, icons, and so on in various venues—primarily through words and through learning to read and write. Reading and writing are sequential and individual; one word follows another when you are writing, and one page follows another when you are reading. You cannot do much of anything else when you are writing, although you can listen to other things while you are reading.

This sequential communication system was never challenged until about seventy-five years ago when radio burst upon the communication scene, followed by television about twenty years later. You could listen to the radio while you were also doing other things and you certainly could watch television while doing something else. But, interestingly, radio and television programming continued to be sequential and linear, just like reading, because that is how stories are generally presented, with one concept following another, and a beginning, a middle, and an end. Think how difficult it is to follow a TV show that jumps from one subject to another.

This sequential pattern, one thing followed by another, is how we have traditionally com-

Exhibit 1.4   **Mass Communication Sender-Receiver Model**

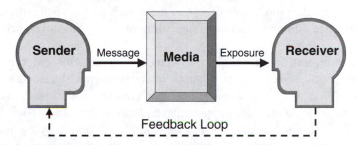

municated and why and how the traditional mass communication model shown in Exhibit 1.4 was developed. The marketer creates and sends messages through some type of medium to the receiver. Readers can respond if they care to or simply store the information away for later use. This is the model on which most current marketing communication concepts and methodologies are based. Marketers send messages to customers and prospects linearly and sequentially because that is how people were trained to accept them and how marketers were trained to deliver them.

Then, in the middle 1990s, along came the Internet and World Wide Web, soon followed by mobile telecommunication and now digital, satellite-delivered forms of interactive communication. Today, they are all around us, expanding and evolving. These new forms of communication are neither necessarily sequential nor linear. Some of the new media are clearly designed for other types of mental processing.

The big change that the electronic and Web-based communication systems introduced was not just another way of distributing sequential marketing communication messages. The new media brought back the importance of consumer multichannel processing. In other words, they enabled consumers to revive skills and talents that they were born with, but were trained out of by the traditional, sequentially developed and delivered media forms.

Humans have always been capable of multitasking or simultaneously processing information from multiple sources. That is how we survive, by being able to take in multiple warning signals delivered at the same time, converting them into danger signs, and generating life-saving responses. All the new media forms make use of these multiple processing capabilities that all humans innately possess. So, while we are excited about the new research in mono-chronic (sequential) and polychronic (parallel) processing, in truth we are merely recognizing an existing human state in which humans can multitask and parallel process various forms of information at the same time.

Some Basic Marketing Communication Planning Principles

Marketing and brand communication planning and implementation approaches, at least as we know them today, grew up around and were organized for the developing linear, outbound media systems of the time. That is, as newspapers first developed, a certain method of planning advertising developed, focused on how that advertising would be delivered through the newspaper. The same was true of magazines: a separate communication methodology developed, based on the unique properties of the magazine itself. The same was true of radio and then of television. Each medium was a bit different and therefore each demanded a slightly different way to plan, develop, implement, and measure how to use that medium. That has had a major influence on how brand communication planning has developed and how it is done even today.

As other marketing and brand communication methodologies emerged, the same thing occurred. Sales promotion, direct marketing, public relations, events, sponsorships, and so on all claimed to be a different form of marketing and brand communication, so each demanded and developed its own brand communication planning and measurement approach. Each separate. Each slightly different. Each unique—or at least considered unique by the media owner or developer and the agencies involved—in its ability to deliver marketing communication to that medium's audiences. Thus, functional brand and marketing communication-planning capabilities were developed based on the form and structure of the medium. The customers at the other end of the distribution system were no different, nor did they process the marketing communication differently. But the media form was different or was perceived to have different values.

The result is the current brand communication planning approach used today, an approach based on functional activities focused on each medium's unique properties. Functional measurement systems, none alike, try to measure only that one medium, how it is used and how it is believed consumers process information from it. All forms of media are currently planned, implemented, delivered and measured separately and independently of each other. Unfortunately, this approach is based on questionable notions. It assumes that consumers sequentially process brand communications; that is, information from each media form is accessed, processed, and stored separately and independently from the information from all other media forms. Thus, this approach completely ignores the ability of most consumers to multitask and multiprocess.

The truth is, most consumers see brand and marketing communication as bundled information packets about the company, the brand, and the offer. They see it that way because the human brain is a network, structured to aggregate and assemble various bits and pieces of information or knowledge or experience to create a conceptual whole. (More on how the brain works in Chapter 3.) As a result, the consumer's view of communication is quite different from that of the marketing organization, as shown as Exhibit 1.5.

Consumers access, process, and store information about a brand and its value based not on the communication form, but on the information's relevance and compatibility with the knowledge they already have stored away in their mind and already have related to that brand. It is a network model based on how the brain works, not a sequential model based on how marketing and brand communication is developed or delivered. We will see more of this model in Chapter 3.

If all the foregoing is true, and we will demonstrate its truth in the following section, we can only wonder why marketers continue to use brand marketing and communication approaches that are diametrically opposed to what consumers are actually doing. Again, we must look to the past to understand present practices.

A Behaviorist, Conditioned-Response Psychological Model

Why does the brand and marketing communication community hold onto the traditional planning models if the marketplace, the media, and the consumers have changed? To

Exhibit 1.5 **Consumer View of Brand Communication**

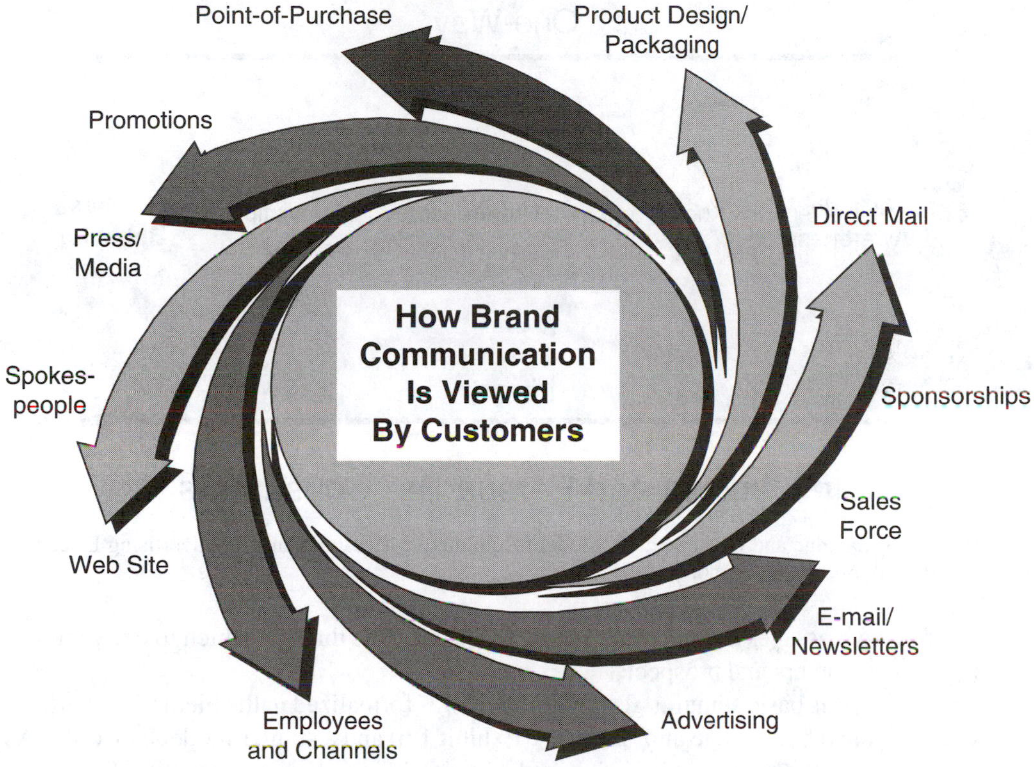

Point-of-Purchase

Product Design/ Packaging

Promotions

Direct Mail

Press/ Media

How Brand Communication Is Viewed By Customers

Spokes- people

Sponsorships

Sales Force

Web Site

E-mail/ Newsletters

Employees and Channels

Advertising

explain that, we must explain the underlying concepts that support the current marketing communication model.

When marketing communication first emerged as a major business activity in the late 1800s and early 1900s, the accepted psychological model of how consumers behaved in the marketplace was based on behaviorist psychology. The assumption was that humans operated on a conditioned response basis: that is, a stimulus-response model. This concept posited that marketers created communication programs, sent them out to consumers through increasingly efficient mass media, assumed the consumers would process the messages, and then waited for some type of consumer response. This was a marketer-controlled, outbound, sequential approach based on message frequency.

The first of these models was the famous 1920s approach called AIDA (attention, interest, desire, action). The marketer's task was to get consumer attention, build consumer interest, create consumer desire, and elicit consumer action. This approach assumed that the marketer was always in control of the system, moving the consumer through the AIDA steps by increasing distribution of media communication messages. It further assumed that consumers could be successfully influenced if the right message were developed and delivered at what was considered to be the right time. Marketers liked AIDA because they believed it gave them control over consumers. Thus, marketplace success was limited only by their ability to

Exhibit 1.6 **Hierarchy of Effects Model**

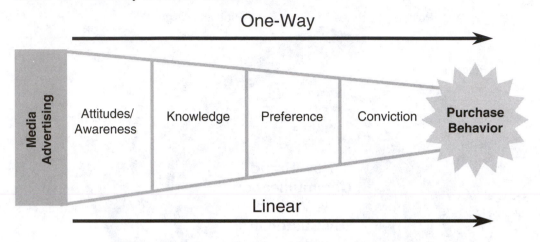

One-Way

Media Advertising | Attitudes/ Awareness | Knowledge | Preference | Conviction | **Purchase Behavior**

Linear

"Influencing and Persuading Consumers"

Source: R.J. Lavidge and G. Steiner, "A Model for Predictive Measurements of Advertising Effectiveness," *Journal of Marketing* 26, no. 6 (1961).

create effective messages and purchase media space and time through which to deliver those messages to customers and prospects.

In the 1960s, this basic stimulus-response model was formalized in the hierarchy of effects concept developed by Lavidge and Steiner[12] (Exhibit 1.6) and a similar model by Colley. As shown in the model, the marketer is assumed to control the system by inputting funds into the purchase and distribution of brand messages through various forms of media. The impact and effect of exposure to those messages move consumers through the "hierarchy," starting with awareness and ending in conviction. (The hierarchy model avoids actual purchase behavior, arguing that there are too many intervening variables to justify including purchase in the model; thus, only communication effects—the movement through knowledge acquisition and conviction stages—are actually measured.)

As shown, all consumer change is linear and one-way, essentially a marketer monologue directed to customers and prospects. And it is clearly assumed that marketplace success depends on the number and frequency of messages distributed by the marketer through the various media. The more messages the marketer sends out, the faster it is assumed the consumer will respond.

This model underlies most traditional media and brand communication planning approaches in use anywhere in the world. From this model are derived basic media planning concepts such as gross rating points, share of voice, target markets, and the like. The model is intellectually appealing. It makes "sense" since marketers like to believe they can take the consumer through some type of considered purchasing process with their persuasive messages. It is both rational and intuitive. Unfortunately, it is probably not true. The hierarchy of effects is only a conceptual model. It has never been proven in the marketplace.

The hierarchy of effects model also is based on the assumption that attitudinal change will eventually occur among those consumers exposed to the messages. This assumption makes communication effects easy to measure—for example, by survey research to determine awareness or preference or intent to buy. All these concepts have found their way into the marketing and brand communication literature and practice although almost all have little formal support. And the assumption that attitudinal change leads to behavioral change is just as tenuous.

To summarize the above discussion, historical approaches to communication planning have been based on a number of outdated or simply unfounded assumptions. The marketer was assumed to be in control. Consumers were the willing targets for the marketer's messages, and they would be eventually influenced by the number and content of those messages. A stimulus-response model suggested that if the marketer could just develop the right message and deliver it at the right time, consumers would respond. And media weight—that is, the number of messages the marketer sent out—was the basic yardstick for brand communication measurement.

These assumptions began to be seriously challenged in the early 1990s when the Internet, the World Wide Web, and other forms of interactive, electronic communication burst on the scene. What we have called pull communication systems have truly become "killer applications" that have impacted all brand and marketing communication and the planning methods being used. These are the issues and the technological changes that marketers, media, and measurement firms are still trying to get their arms around. A brief look at the changes impacting brand communication managers comes next.

How Technology Changes Brand Communication

Until the early 1990s, brand communication was developing rather nicely for marketers, agencies, and their media partners. While funds were being shifted out of advertising into the more readily measurable promotional forms such as sales promotion and direct marketing, generally the brand communication system was in place and operating, if not well, at least actively. Then, along came the electronic communication revolution brought about by the Web and interactive media forms. That is when the world changed: push communication began to be challenged by the opportunities of pull. Many marketers are still struggling with the changes these electronic forms have created.

The big change, of course, came from technology because that gave consumers ready access to the entire world of information, not just that delivered by the media or marketing organizations. Technology gave consumers a chance to talk back, ask questions, demand proof, challenge marketers' claims, but, most of all, it gave consumers choices, alternatives, and resources. This panoply of media alternatives challenged the historic limited-choice, time-specific, transportation-based models of brand communication that had always existed. For consumers, the new resources were easy, cheap, and quick. Consumers can now "Google" or "Yahoo!" anything from almost anywhere on earth—including determining whether an advertiser's claims are true, false, or mere puffery.

Today, media forms are increasingly interactive and individualistic. The iPod was just the first breeze of what has become a storm of new media forms and media delivery systems, all of which demand new views of how brand communication must be planned, developed, implemented, and measured. That new approach is now developing. It is called holistic or integrated brand communication planning.

A New View of Brand Communication

For the last 100 years, most marketing and brand communication planning has not been focused on building ongoing customer relationships. Instead, it has been focused on trying to generate short-term incremental sales of the product or service for the marketer. While marketers have given lip service to consumer focus and customer orientation, the real goal of marketing and brand communication has been to generate a quick and immediate sale. That is because most marketers' understanding of brands and branding has come from the marketing of consumer package goods—soaps, detergents, shampoos, food products, confections, drinks, and the like—which are commonly purchased, used up, and then repurchased. Since several choices were available to consumers and all products performed about the same, and since the marketer made the most money on products that were widely used and inexpensively produced through manufacturing economies of scale, most marketing emphasis has been on creating an immediate sale: that is, an immediate purchase by the consumer. The brand played a role, but the real value for consumers came from finding less expensive ways of doing mundane household chores with products that generally performed as advertised. The value for the marketer came from selling tons of the product at increasingly lower costs. In this situation, both parties won or believed they won.

Since the consumer was always returning to the marketplace, the marketer's focus was on continuous product improvement or enhancement and continuous marketplace promotion. Most marketing programs were based on some type of promotional campaign—a new look, a new package, a new ingredient, a new jingle, and a new slogan—pushed out to the consumer through mass media where tonnage was everything and results were masked by a continuously growing market. The focus was always on something new to keep the consumer interested and attentive and hopefully involved. Marketing communication developed and delivered based on what marketers wanted to say, not what consumers wanted to hear.

Today, the economy is moving beyond this marketer-in-control system that viewed the consumer simply as a marketing target. New concepts and new approaches, new ways to think about, plan, and create long-term, ongoing brand relationships with customers and prospects, will be needed. That is what the next section is about.

NEEDED: A CUSTOMER-CENTRIC, HOLISTIC VIEW OF BRAND COMMUNICATION

As long as the marketer controlled the system, an outbound, distribution-based, push messaging system made sense. Even though technologies such as TiVo and the remote control allow consumers to avoid brand communication messages, marketers today can still send out more messages than customers can avoid. However, the number of different media systems has become so great that the marketing organization simply cannot dominate them all. Recognizing this problem of media fragmentation, marketers are beginning to change their concept of brand communication.

In a consumer-driven marketplace, where consumers have choices and alternatives and can pick and acquire information and materials when they wish, the key element in brand communication is no longer how many messages the marketer can send out. The real question is how many messages the consumer receives and will accept. In other words, the marketplace today emphasizes consumer media consumption, not marketer message distribution. How consumers attend to media, how they access and process information, how they store that information away, and, finally, how they respond to the marketer's brand communication messages—these new areas for the brand marketing communication manager are critical for future success.

In today's new marketplace, traditional media-based communications such as advertising, public relations, direct marketing, sales promotion, sponsorships, events, and the host of other media forms that marketers and their media partners have developed become only one source of brand information available to the consumer. Today, in order to really understand how brand relationships can be built and maintained, the marketer must consider such opportunities as in-store; Web sites and blogs; packaging; word of mouth; consumers' personal experiences with the brand's employees, customer service, and channel partners; and myriad other communication activities and programs.

Today, it is clear, the marketer needs a holistic communication planning system that takes into consideration every brand touch point, every experience the consumer has with the brand, and every ongoing relationship the consumer develops with the brand over time. (This is discussed in more detail in Chapter 10.) It is this holistic brand communication planning process that leads to ongoing customer-brand relationships. We discuss that in the next section.

The Need for a New Brand Communication Planning Model

Given the arguments in the preceding section, it becomes clear that traditional, media-focused, marketer-oriented brand communication approaches need to be radically altered. We need to review the planning systems, perhaps altering and changing some of the previous concepts and approaches, indeed, even some of the very foundations of brand communication must be re-considered in light of the changed conditions so that we can develop approaches and tools appropriate for the twenty-first–century marketplace. We start that process here and continue it for the balance of the book.

Shifting From Outputs to Outcomes

Most current brand communication programs are focused at the tactical level, developing advertising campaigns or sales promotion programs or public relations events to generate immediate response. In other words, the brand communication planner starts with a preset or allocated budget, generally committed to a specific type of communication such as advertising or public relations or sales promotion, and then proceeds to create a message or set of messages using an available outbound delivery system. The focus is on developing the most effective messaging or promotion using commonly accepted tools and techniques that provide efficient delivery. Most marketers planning an advertising campaign immediately think about media delivery systems; when planning for sales promotion, they are immediately drawn to coupons and price-offs or premiums or prizes and whether to distribute them in-store, on-packs, or through the mail; in other words, some type of outbound media delivery or distribution system. Or, when considering public relations, marketers immediately start to think of press releases or media events pushed out to the media groups to get "ink" or "airtime" for the product or service.

The problem with this approach is that the planners too often start with the outputs to be generated, not the outcomes to be achieved. Outputs are the elements or pieces of the brand communication program and the distribution system to be used. Alternatively, outcomes are the end results or impact that the communication program will have on customers and prospects. It is this outputs-versus-outcomes challenge that creates most of the problems in building effective brand communication programs today. Thus, the challenge for the marketing organization is how to move from outputs to outcomes.

Cross-Functional Planning

If marketers do start to think about customers first, rather than communication messages and media, they soon realize that the planning of brand communication is often done by an isolated brand marketing or functional communication unit. Today, most firms are organized around functional silos that isolate the different business areas from each other. Marketing, sales, operations, accounting, logistics, and other departments are each managed separately, with little interaction or cross-functional synergy or planning. Even within the marketing area, specialists in advertising, promotion, events, and so on may be isolated from each other. Thus, they cannot plan strategies or programs together that will present a holistic brand communication for customers and prospects.

In such organizations, marketing and brand communication are isolated from operations and finance and human relations and all the other functional silos that make up the organization. With this sort of structure, marketing becomes something a group of people do, not what the organization does. In truth, it takes all the functional silos to successfully bring a product to market, develop customer value, provide customer satisfaction, and build an ongoing brand relationship. However, too often, the other functional groups do not believe that they are involved with customers or that their activities have any impact on customers and their relationship with the brand. This attitude could not be more wrong. Brand relationships are organizational relationships. That means every group and every person in the firm must be focused on developing ongoing relationships with customers. This requires a horizontal, not a vertical, view of how the company and the brand touch and respond to customers.

To succeed, the organization needs to present a united front to the customer or prospect. It must be able to deliver on the promises made to the customer and it must be able to continue that relationship over time. Thus, a holistic or united marketing and communication planning system is needed, not one that is based on functional delivery systems such as advertising or direct marketing or even online and interactive systems. An integrated program means a coordinated push and pull approach, not one that is developed and implemented piecemeal, with separate communication messages delivered through separate marketing functions.

Finding the Basic Elements

When the marketer starts rethinking brand relationships, one thing becomes clear: there are four elements on which all brand communication is based. These are (1) the customers and other audiences with whom the brand relationship is to be created and maintained, (2) the delivery systems through which brand communication will be delivered and responded to by the customer or audience, (3) the content of the brand communication message or messages,

Exhibit 1.7 **Integrated Brand Communication Model**

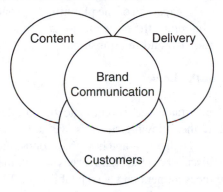

and, of course, (4) the brand that ties them all together. These three elements and the brand are truly the foundation of any type of communication program that hopes to build ongoing customer-brand relationships.

That is what this book is all about—how to move away from the details of television advertising commercials or cents-off offers or invitation lists for an event or even the identification of all the forms and formats that mention the brand in a product-placement contract. We will discuss these tactical details in later chapters, but for the moment we are going to argue that if marketers do not get the customer, the delivery system, and the content right and align them with the brand, it really does not matter how clever or cute or "breakthrough" the idea is. If no one sees it or no one responds, it fails. If the wrong audience or customer groups are selected, none of them will care. If the content or message is not attuned to the customers' needs and motivations, then nothing will happen, except the cost of the marketing communication investment will be wasted. If the three key elements are not right, no amount of creative thinking or clever activities will make the campaign successful no matter how much money is thrown at the customer. The solution is that simple but it is also that complex.

Exhibit 1.7 illustrates the integrated brand communication model on which this text is based. As shown, the outer elements—customers, delivery, and content—are all interrelated and therefore must be integrated. And the brand becomes the integrating element that ties them all together. In combination, they form the foundation for developing and implementing effective brand communication. Here, the three circles are shown with equal weight, each element contributing equally to the brand relationship. In truth, at different times, the relationship between the three elements can and should be adjusted. At certain times, for example, the identification of the correct audience will be the major task facing the organization. Once customers are identified and their needs and motivations understood, development of compelling content or effective message delivery might be more critical. As a result, the integrated brand relationship planning approach is flexible and dynamic, not static. It is a holistic approach that can be adapted to fit different requirements under different circumstances, based on the needs of both the customer and the marketing organization.

In this process, the key task of the customer-brand relationship manager is to thoroughly understand the three elements that create the relationship and then develop ongoing brand communication activities that build and enhance that relationship. While the three circles in Exhibit 1.7 represent the heart and soul of the customer-brand relationship planning approach, the key ingredient is, of course, the brand. Depending on how one looks at the illustration, the brand can be the capstone of the planning approach or the base. Whichever view is taken, the brand is what binds the three elements into a coherent whole, thus creating successful ongoing customer-brand relationships.

The Plan for the Balance of the Book

With the introduction of the integrated brand communication model, we have set the direction for the balance of the book. In the following chapters, we will explore each of the three outer circles—customers, content, and delivery—and how they contribute to the overall brand communication activity. We will discuss how the brand serves as the glue that brings these elements together. We will introduce measurement and accountability early in our discussion as a key part of the brand communication planning process. Historically, measurement and evaluation have been held to the last and often ignored. However, accountability is built into the integrated system so it plays a key part in the text. We spend considerable time on delivery systems, both push and pull, since they are often what is driving or destroying customer-brand relationships. Content or messaging comes near the end of our proposed process. That is a dramatic change from most communication planning models, where message development is generally the primary element in a communication campaign. (Think back to the AIDA model, where content is first and foremost and audiences are not even considered, being assumed to be active and interested in the communication program.) In the new marketplace, we argue that the content should fit the audience and the delivery system, so it often comes last in the development process.

In the chapters that follow, we will flesh out the integrated brand communication-planning model. We will walk through the planning process and illustrate the various steps and elements that are necessary to develop an ongoing customer-brand relationship using brand communication. So join us in the development of customer-brand relationship marketing communication. It will be an exciting trip.

NOTES

1. P. Drucker, with J. Maciariello, *Management*, rev. ed. (New York: HarperCollins, 2008), p. 98.

2. P. Torrone, "Kryptonite Evolution 2000 U-Lock Hacked by a Bic Pen," *Engadget*, September 14, 2004, www.engadget.com/2004/09/14/kryptonite-evolution-2000-u-lock-hacked-by-a-bic-pen/.

3. Neistat Brothers, "iPod's Dirty Secret," www.ipodsdirtysecret.com/.

4. P. Dusenberry, *Then We Set His Hair on Fire: Insights and Accidents From a Hall of Fame Career in Advertising* (New York: Portfolio, 2005).

5. 2005 Effie Awards Brief for Effectiveness, submission for "GE: Imagination at Work," New York Chapter of the American Marketing Association.

6. P. Bennet, ed., *Dictionary of Marketing Terms* (Lincolnwood, IL: NTC Business Books, 1995), p. 73.

7. P. Kotler and K. Lane Keller, *Marketing Management,* 12th ed. (Upper Saddle River, NJ: Pearson, Prentice Hall, 2006), p. 274.

8. M. McDonald, M. Christopher, S. Knox, and A. Payne, *Creating a Company for Customers* (London: Pearson Education, 2001), p. 171.

9. T. Ambler, *Marketing and the Bottom Line* (London: Pearson Education, 2000), p. 4.

10. *Fortune*, "America's Most Admired Companies," February 28, 2006, p. 76.

11. Ambler, *Marketing and the Bottom Line*, p. 5.

12. R.J. Lavidge and G. Steiner, "A Model for Predictive Measurements of Advertising Effectiveness," *Journal of Marketing* 26, no. 6 (1961).

PART I

UNDERSTANDING CUSTOMERS

HOW THEY THINK AND HOW THEY BEHAVE

Exhibit P1.1 **Integrated Brand Communication Model**

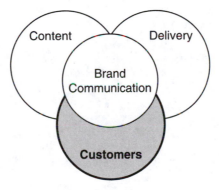

We start our exploration of how to build ongoing customer-brand relationships with an in-depth exploration of customers: who they are, how they think, what they want, and, ultimately, what relationships might be built with them. The reason? It is customers who create successful organizations, for they are the ones who generate ongoing income flow for the firm, based on their purchases and repurchases. While the products or services that the firm creates or the activities that the marketing group develops help in that value creation process, it is the customers that the company creates who really determine long- and short-term success.

While the customers of every organization are usually separate and distinct, there are generally some commonalities across disparate organizations. For example, business-to-business companies often provide somewhat different types of products and services than do consumer product firms, but it is still people who go through the consideration process, make the actual purchases, and then develop the brand relationships. So, while the companies may be different, there is one basic, underlying commonality: the entire success of the marketing company relies on people—that is, customers.

As we discussed in Chapter 1, customers are individuals or organizations who have purchased or used products or services from the marketing organization or who are likely to do

27

so in the future. However, in planning brand communication, a firm needs to consider not only the final customer—the person who ultimately makes the purchasing decision or uses the product—but also a wide, dynamic network of people who may influence purchasing and repurchasing behaviors. Thus, there are many customers for the brand communication programs that the firm launches or maintains. It is a central tenet of this text that a sound brand communication program must consider the wide range of audiences that the organization serves and understand how their perceptions, associations, needs, and motivations impact the eventual marketplace performance of the brand.

In the following chapters, we identify these "people commonalities" and then drill down into discussions of the specific and individual customers that separate one brand from another. This understanding of customer needs, motivations, and behaviors enables the company to employ brand communication programs at all levels, ranging from broad-scale mass media to more individualized communication tools and techniques. It is this understanding of customers and prospects at all levels of their relationship with the brand that distinguishes the customer-brand relationship process from other, more traditional, often internally oriented marketing and communication development programs. So we start with the importance of customer focus.

CHAPTER 2

All Marketing Starts With Customers

Our emphasis in this chapter will be on understanding the full range of recipients for brand communication programs. We will examine a variety of audiences that can impact—directly or indirectly—the building and sustenance of brand relationships with direct customers.

EXPANDING THE CONCEPT OF A CUSTOMER

If a critique of current marketing practice could be leveled across the board, it is that most marketing managers take too limited a view of who their customers are and what the marketing manager's remit is or should be. There is not just one customer or one consumer. There are multiple customers, stakeholders, and audiences, all related and all interacting to the betterment or detriment of the marketing organization and the marketplace. In short, the marketplace is much more a network of people, organizations, and activities than it is a linear inbound or outbound system. It is this broader view of customers and the marketplace interactions that truly differentiates the customer-brand relationship approach from other, traditional, more narrowly focused methodologies.

Over a decade ago, Philip Kotler wrote about the need for a holistic and comprehensive view of all the significant players in a company's environment:

> The consensus of American business is growing: if U.S. companies are to compete success-fully in domestic and global markets, they must engineer stronger bonds with their stake-holders, including customers, distributors, suppliers, employees, unions, governments, and other critical players in the environment. Common practices such as whipsawing suppliers for better prices, dictating terms to distributors, and treating employees as a cost rather than an asset, must end. Companies must move from a short-term transaction-oriented goal to a long-term relationship building goal.[1]

Good thinking on Kotler's part, but his suggestion was rarely applied by marketing organizations.

In their thought-provoking book *Creating a Company for Customers*, faculty members of the Cranfield School of Management in the United Kingdom took Kotler's view several steps further. They provide a useful, practical framework for applying an integrated view across the range of audiences, customers, and markets that an organization serves. They propose a customer-focused paradigm encompassing separate "markets" or groups of related stakeholders who influence the present and future of the organization. The key insight of this framework is

Exhibit 2.1 **The Six Communication Markets**

Source: Adapted from M. McDonald, M. Christopher, S. Knox, and A. Payne, *Creating a Company for Customers* (London: Pearson Education, 2001), p. 53.

that while marketers may focus on ultimate customers—that is, the people or organizations that share in the reciprocal value proposition discussed in Chapter 1—there is also a wide range of other participants who make the initial relationship possible and commonly have significant impact on the ongoing relationship between the marketer and the final customer. We have adapted the Cranfield model somewhat to suit this text and present it as Exhibit 2.1.[2]

As shown in the illustration, there are actually six macromarkets comprising stakeholders of various types. The astute marketing manager considers the implications of each market in developing a true customer-brand relationship strategy. Further, this six-market view also makes fairly clear when and how traditional outbound communication should be used and when the more customer-oriented pull communication programs are most applicable.

While the six markets are interdependent, they vary in importance and value to the marketing organization. We briefly describe each of the markets below to put them in the proper perspective.

Ultimate Customer Markets

The ultimate customers—consumers and end users—are clearly the hub around which all the other related markets revolve. In this paradigm we refer to customers as those individuals, groups, or firms that dig down into their wallets or bank accounts and find the resources to purchase or acquire the products or services the firm is vending and then use them.

Ultimately customers can be aggregated or segmented in any number of ways, limited only by the creativity of the marketing communication manager. We discuss aggregation approaches more fully in Chapter 7. At this stage our focus is on four basic customer aggregation methods:

- new customers to be acquired;
- existing customers to be retained at the same level of purchases or usage;

- existing customers that can be grown through creating greater volume requirements or more frequent usage; and
- customers to be migrated to higher value products or services in the portfolio.

These groupings are fairly self-evident with the exception of the last, in that the marketer tries to migrate or move customers from one level of product or service to another of greater value to either the customer or the firm. For example, consider the automobile market. The automobile maker might first try to acquire a customer by offering a relatively inexpensive model. Over time, as the customer's needs change, the marketing organization might try to move the purchaser up to a basic sedan or an SUV. In other words, the goal of the auto company would be to keep the customer in the brand marque while providing different models to fit the customer's changing lifestyle.

The key question about ultimate customer markets is the amount of emphasis the firm should place on acquisition of new customers versus the retention and growth of existing customers. Organizations must have new customers simply to survive. Existing customers move on, retire, change their needs and wants, or simply pass from the scene. But it is the existing customers and their purchases that make it possible for the firm to acquire new customers. Without the consistent, ongoing income flows from present customers, there would be no way to develop new products, expand to new markets, or meet new needs. Thus, the challenge of every organization is how to balance the organizational focus between maintaining existing customers and acquiring new ones. We will say more about this in later chapters.

Intermediary Markets

For most marketing organizations, intermediary markets are critical because they are composed of the distribution channels that bring the manufacturing or marketing firm's products or services to the final users or consumers. Intermediary markets include retailers, distributors, wholesalers, resellers, and the like. These are often considered "interim customers" or "middlemen" by manufacturers since they must be sold to and convinced to support the brands the marketing organization is offering in order for the organization to reach the ultimate end user. Retailers are the primary direct clients of many organizations and the focus of most selling activities. Such organizations may do little or no direct selling to end users and consumers (i.e., the ultimate customers discussed above) and therefore rely almost entirely on intermediary customers to distribute their goods. In some cases, because of the functional organizational structure of the firm, sales and marketing are often in conflict. The sales group is commonly the primary communicator with the intermediary customer and thus believes that its activities take precedence. Marketing argues that unless the firm communicates with the final consumers as well, it will have little overall success. This lack of clear direction as to which group takes precedence in the organization's communication activities—the intermediary customers or the ultimate consumers and end users—can create internal challenges for the communication planner. It also raises the question whether push or pull communication programs should take precedence.

One of the challenges of brand-relationship management is understanding that while intermediary customers are critical to the ongoing success of the firm, these groups do not, by themselves, generate income flows for the brand. Rather, they funnel funds from the purchasing consumer back to the marketer. Retailers such as Target, Wal-Mart, and Neiman Marcus, for example, do not produce income flows for the manufacturer. They only serve as a conduit between the manufacturer and the end-user buyer. It is important for the marketer to keep this fact in mind. Often the brand-relationship can be influenced by the intermediary market, but the intermediary is not the only factor in the customer-brand relationship chain.

Another challenge in managing intermediary markets is that many of these organizations are also trying to build relationships between themselves and the ultimate consumers. Retailers want the consumer to buy from them, not really caring which manufacturer's brand the consumer purchases. The manufacturer, on the other hand, does not care which retailer the consumer frequents, only that the consumer purchases the manufacturer's brand. This ongoing tug between the manufacturer and the retailer makes the management of intermediary markets extremely challenging.

Ideally, the brand-relationship chain should include a strong combination of values for the manufacturer, the retailer or channel, and the end user or consumer. In order to maintain the relationship among all three, they should be in balance and reciprocal. This is likely the most difficult challenge in many of the customer-brand relationships the manager must develop.

Supplier Markets

Suppliers come in many types, varieties, and formats. In some cases, they supply the raw materials or ingredients that enable the marketer to produce the final product or service that is of benefit to the end user. For example, farmers grow the crops that are used in food processing and by restaurants suppliers. Energy producers provide the power to run the plants and factories to make the products or services. Technology companies provide software programs that enable the marketing organization to be more efficient and therefore more capable of responding to customers' needs. The suppliers in today's complex, interrelated, global marketplace are many and varied, and generally critical to the ongoing support of the organization that is trying to build a long-term brand relationship with its customers.

However, suppliers are not limited to just providing raw materials. Some suppliers provide the resources that allow the marketing organization to maintain good customer relationships. For example, they may provide ongoing customer service, manage the database, or even provide short-term employees, such as retail clerks or warehouse people, who help the firm meet its varying levels of demand. Thus, a marketing organization needs to take a broad view of its suppliers.

In some instances, alliance or trading partners are suppliers, too. They may provide a portion of the end product or the ongoing support the organization needs to serve its customers. For example, Xerox Corporation has document centers located in the offices of a number of large global companies. Xerox workers and machines provide the printing, collating, and documentation their clients require, on-site. Another example is UPS, which has ongoing supplier agreements with several firms to provide the logistical systems that allow them to be global organizations without investing their own resources in duplicating what UPS can easily supply.

Suppliers obviously have an important role in assuring quality inputs to the manufacturing or service delivery process. Beyond this, however, they also can be strategic partners in developing brand communication, often funding a portion of the budget. For example, Dell

Computers promotes the fact that its computers carry Intel microprocessors—and receives co-op funds from Intel to underwrite a portion of its own brand advertising.

Again, in the supplier market, we see the need for both push (outbound) communication to suppliers and pull communication programs (e.g., Web sites and Internet systems) that supplier markets can access and use.

Referral Markets

Generally, there are two broad types of referral markets. One is the existing customer base of the marketing organization. The brand relationship that the marketing firm has built up with these customers over time encourages them to speak on behalf of the marketer to others in their industry or to advocate to friends, associates, social networks, and the marketplace in general through personal contact, blogs, and the like. We might consider these customers as members of the extended sales force for the company. They know the marketing organization; they have used its products and services and have some type of ongoing relationship with the marketer. Thus, they not only have a vested interest in seeing their own customer-brand relationship increase but also believe that others would benefit from having the same experience with the marketer. Often, these referral sources or markets occur through word of mouth, which is often considered the most effective type of marketing available.

The other type of referral market is often called a third-party reference. Commonly, these are knowledgeable individuals or organizations that are relied on by new buyers or new-to-the-market customers seeking information on who might be the best supplier for them and their needs. These individuals may be consultants or business advisers, such as accountants or lawyers, or trade association executives who are believed to have expertise in the area or knowledge about the particular market in which the buyer has an interest. These referents may be rewarded in some way for their knowledge and expertise, commonly through some type of "arm's-length" consultative relationship. Some of the most rapidly growing referral markets are the online social network systems, such as MySpace, Facebook, and YouTube, where people with common interests share their experiences and knowledge.

Influencer Markets

Influencer markets can have a positive or negative impact on the marketing organization since they commonly influence organizational or market or public opinion about the organization, its products or services, or its operating capability. For example, financial analysts and capital suppliers have a large influence on the current and future operations of the organization since they influence shareholders and competitors. Likewise, governments and regulatory organizations, community groups, nongovernmental pressure groups, and environmentalists can have a major impact on the organization's ability to build long-term brand relationships with customers and prospects.

The news media are also a key element in this area of influencer markets. What the media reports and how they report it has much to do with the ongoing perception of customers and their relationships with the brands they use. The media are often critically important in developing or maintaining the reputation that organizations rely on so greatly for success.

In short, the influencer market is critical to the marketing organization, but often is neglected in the development of ongoing customer-brand relationships until it is too late. The influencer market is one that needs to be managed proactively, not reactively.

Internal Markets

Internal markets are the last on our list but certainly not the least important. In fact, they may be the most important market of all, next to the ultimate customers. Internal markets are made up of those individuals, work groups, departments, internal teams, and others that are directly engaged in the ongoing operation of the marketing firm. They are often the most important market for they are the ones that actually create and maintain the brand experiences and relationships that the firm has with end users and final customers.

Internal markets are complex for two reasons. First, every employee and every department within an organization is both an internal customer and an internal supplier. This bifurcated relationship is difficult for many organizations to handle, since managers must provide high-quality inputs of care and concern for the employees and their work situations while ensuring that the employees treat customers in ways that always build on or continue the brand relationship. Balancing these two demands requires attention, skill, and capabilities that organizational managers simply do not possess or are not encouraged to utilize.

The second challenge of the internal market is that, commonly, employees do not report to nor do marketing people have direct supervision over many of the people who are delivering the all-important brand experiences; that is, the things that develop long-term customer-brand relationships. These groups include personnel in operations and logistics, information technology, customer service, technical support, finance, and all the other departments that influence and impact how customers are treated and the brand experiences they receive. These personnel often have totally separate management groups that have little or no relationship with the marketing and branding managers. Thus, the marketing manager must work with the other department heads and unit managers to encourage a customer focus and the delivery of consistent, well-designed customer brand experiences. As we have seen earlier in this chapter, the organizational structure of the firm often challenges even the most dedicated employee to be customer-focused and to continuously deliver positive brand experiences.

Much of this ability to involve and include the internal markets in the successful customer-brand relationship depends on how well the organization communicates with employees and associates. It is here that marketing and communication managers should be able to assist other department heads in developing effective, ongoing communication programs that stress the importance of building customer-brand relationships—no matter what level of actual physical contact with customers, intermediaries, influences, suppliers, or referral sources the employees have. In truth, the internal market commonly has the most influence in all these areas, but the employees are often the ones overlooked when it comes time to develop customer-brand relationship programs.

Taking an Integrated View of the Six Markets

Of course, for every product or service, the role and impact of these six customer markets are different. Likewise, the need to develop proactive and compelling communication plans for specific groups may vary according to circumstances at different times. Under certain conditions, the internal market may be more important than the referral market, or the sup-

Exhibit 2.2 **Assessing Current and Desired Emphasis by Market**

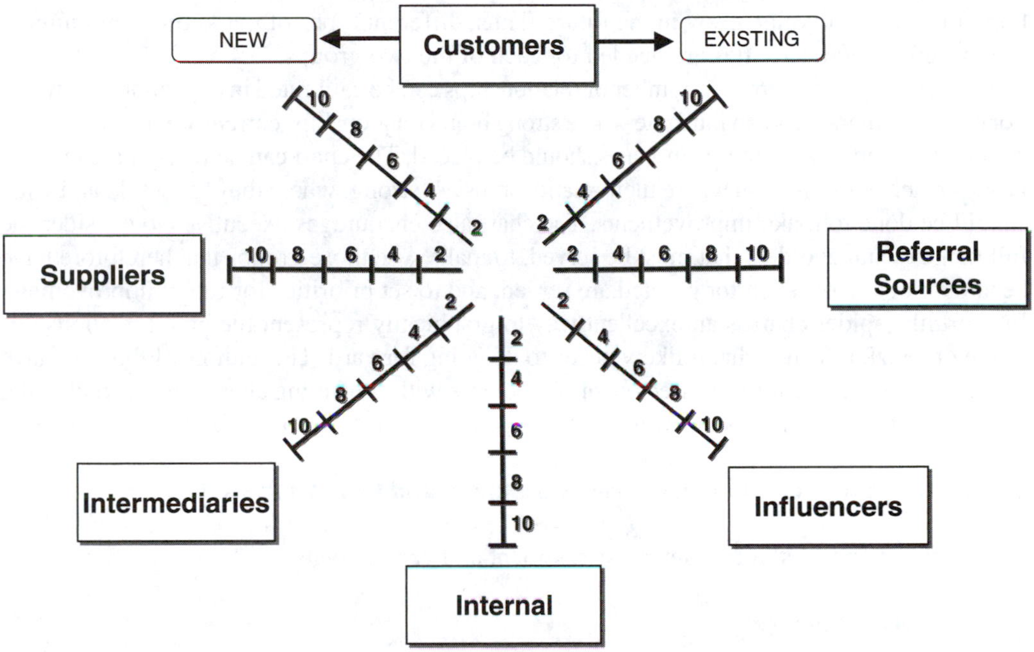

Source: Adapted from M. McDonald, M. Christopher, S. Knox, and A. Payne, *Creating a Company for Customers* (London: Pearson Education, 2001), p. 53.

plier market may more important than the intermediary market. For example, a well-trained, dedicated customer service team may be more critical to the long-term success of a privately held firm than the short-term valuation a financial analyst may put on the company. Both are clearly important. But it is the immediate pertinence and degree of importance of each that really drives the communication planning process. It is also clear that various types of communication programs may be required. In some instances, traditional, outbound, push communication may be called for. In others, where customers have developed their own needs and requirements, the availability of pull programs such as Web sites, the Internet, and mobile communication forms may be more appropriate. Given the multiple markets and multiple customers with which the organization is engaged, the marketer needs some type of process to sort out that value. We provide a tool for this purpose in the next section.

VISUALIZING CUSTOMER RELATIONSHIPS

The faculty at the Cranfield School of Management has developed a simple but very effective tool for considering and relating the value of various customer groups to the marketing organization. This "spider chart" depicts the networked interconnections that make up the relationships between and among the marketing organization and its customer bases. Exhibit 2.2 is the framework for the spider chart, where each of the six markets discussed above has been located.

We have made one change in the six-market concept. "Customers" (the central unit in Exhibit 2.2) has been divided into two groups: existing customers (those customers the company is presently serving) and new customers or prospects. Obviously, prospects are different from existing customers. Prospects are to be acquired. Existing customers are to be retained and hopefully see their value grow in the future. Thus, different types of marketing communication programs and activities are needed for each of the two groups.

Using this spider chart, any number of relationships can be calibrated in any number of ways. For example, marketers can illustrate where strong brand relationships currently exist, where they are lagging, and where future emphasis should be placed. The chart can help disparate internal groups reach consensus on where their relationships are strong, where they are weak, and what should be done to make improvements. The chart also encourages executives to consider the full range of stakeholders that must be served, to make sure those groups that heretofore have been overlooked or taken for granted are served, and to set priorities for future improvement. In short, the spider chart is an excellent way to graphically represent the brand relationships of the organization and what it likely needs to do going forward. The authors of this text have successfully used an exercise based on this framework with consulting clients and in conducting executive education classes in North America, South America, Europe, Australia, and Asia.

Conducting a Spider Chart Exercise: Assessment and Gap Analysis

This exercise consists of two steps—assessment and gap analysis.

Step One: Assessment

In the first step, executives from the organization are asked to rate each stakeholder group on two questions, using a scale of 1 to 10.

1. How important is each group to the future success of your organization? (10 = "highly critical")
2. How effective is your organization currently in marketing and communicating with each audience? (10 = "highly effective")

In answering these questions, the executives must consider a number of factors:

- Have we treated each stakeholder audience as a source of potential value?
- Have we overlooked possibilities to improve or leverage relationships among some audiences?
- Where have we traditionally focused our efforts?
- Should or could marketing and communication efforts be expanded?

Exhibit 2.3 illustrates the spider chart developed by a group of senior managers from a communications technology company. This firm made and marketed devices for personal communication, selling their products through dealers, their own retail outlets, and the Web. While the company had grown in recent years and received generally high satisfaction ratings from their customers, there was concern about how the company could maintain its position against increasingly powerful competitors.

In the diagram, the solid line around the outside represents how the managers rated each of the key stakeholder markets. Current and prospective customers were rated at 10, highly critical

Exhibit 2.3 **Communication Device Manufacturer: Self-Assessment**

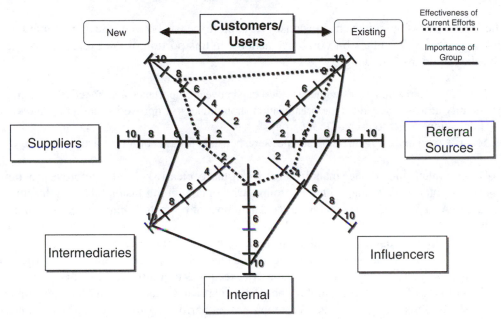

Source: Adapted from M. McDonald, M. Christopher, S. Knox, and A. Payne, *Creating a Company for Customers* (London: Pearson Education, 2001), p. 53.

to the organization's future, as were intermediaries. However, as the managers discussed the issues they faced, they decided that employees were virtually as critical as the end users and dealers. Referral sources and influencers were deemed of moderate importance, and the supplier group was considered less critical to the company's future than the other stakeholders.

The dotted line in the center of the diagram represents the managers' assessment of the effectiveness of the current communication activities directed to each of the stakeholder groups. In the previous years the organization had directed extensive marketing initiatives toward its current and prospective end users, with considerable success. Thus, the executives gave themselves relatively high marks among both customers and users, especially among existing customers for whom the company had implemented innovative customer retention programs. The group also felt that programs directed to referral sources, influencers, and suppliers were moderately effective.

The big revelation, however, came regarding communication activities directed to intermediaries and internal audiences. Communication to these two critical groups was deemed the least effective. In fact, the discussion revealed that the organization had several long-standing problems with their dealers, including inconsistent communication, tangled processes, and conflicting pricing. Further, the company had done little to communicate to its employees about how to serve customers and dealers, and thus employees had little understanding of their role in meeting customer expectations. This was a revelation for some of the executives, since the firm had previous given little attention to the role employees played in delivering value to customers. In fact, many of the communication problems with dealers stemmed from inadequate training and communication to employees.

Step Two: Gap Analysis

The second part of the spider chart exercise is to explore the gap between the two sets of ratings and begin to develop plans for corrective actions. In this portion of the exercise, managers are asked to do the following:

1. Identify the three audiences with the widest gap between importance and effectiveness ratings.
2. Identify at least three steps the organization should take to improve its marketing and communication efforts to each of these groups.
3. Identify who in the organization should be responsible for executing the action steps.

   The communication device manufacturer, for instance, clearly needed to improve programs directed to intermediaries and internal groups, while maintaining historical strengths among end users. As a result, the executives initiated a number of projects to improve dealer relationships, including a review of the firm's ordering and billing processes, credit approval processes, and overall pricing policies. Critical to this review was a training program to help employees, especially those who dealt with dealers, understand their role in the marketing process. The firm tasked the communication and human resources executives to jointly develop this program.
   As is obvious from these examples, the spider chart can be used for any number of planning tasks by illustrating the changing importance of various customer groups over time. It is a tool that can be easily mastered by the brand relationship team and understood by all types of audiences.

THE CHALLENGE OF ACHIEVING CUSTOMER FOCUS

We now move to a discussion of how to encourage the firm to become more customer-focused, the seemingly elusive goal of almost every marketing organization in the twenty-first century. Senior management promotes customer focus to shareholders. Marketing managers try to achieve it internally. Employees wonder what it is and why it is important. Stock analysts base their recommendations on it. Yet few if any organizations are able to achieve customer focus consistently and effectively.
   Customer focus, as we use it here, is a simple concept but extremely difficult to implement. The marketing organization identifies groups of customers it wants to serve and then proceeds to develop products and services that fill the needs and wants of those customers. In this section, we explore how organizations can achieve higher levels of customer focus. To assist them, we provide a tool to help make that transition possible.
   We start first with why customer focus is so difficult in today's marketing organization.

Supply Chain Versus Demand Chain

As a broad generalization, most organizations can be differentiated as to whether they employ a "supply-chain" or "demand-chain" business model. The two alternatives are illustrated in Exhibits 2.4 and 2.5.
   The firm employing a supply-chain business model focuses primarily on creating value

Exhibit 2.4 **Supply-Chain Approach**

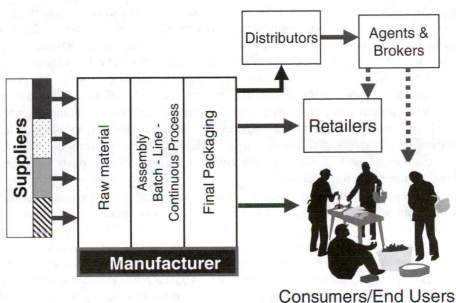

Exhibit 2.5 **Demand-Chain Approach**

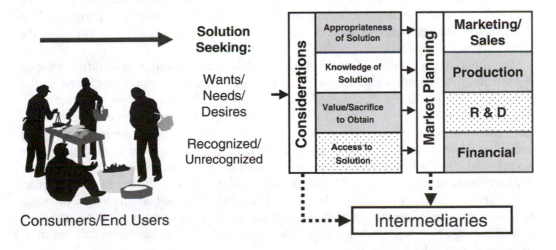

inside the organization, which it then pushes out to customers and prospects. As shown in Exhibit 2.4, the company develops very efficient manufacturing, logistics, and distribution systems internally with the cooperation of suppliers. Those internal processes allow it to take a mass-market approach, providing products or services at the lowest possible cost to the broadest range of consumers possible.

Supply-chain organizations believe they create value internally and need little or no input from customers or consumers. The company believes that it knows what customers want or would like, primarily, good products at low prices with broad distribution. Some companies delude themselves into thinking that customers are not very smart and that the marketing organization knows more than they do and thus can supply anything it can make or invent. These types of companies put relatively little reliance on understanding customers and their needs or motivations. Thus, most "marketing" efforts are not really marketing at all; they are essentially sales activities, attempts to get rid of what the firm has decided to make. The focus is on the company trying to persuade customers and prospects to buy the products it has either manufactured or acquired or the offerings it has developed in the facilities it controls. Consumer product companies, automobile manufacturers and "big box" retailers are examples of this business model, as are many technology, telecommunications, manufacturing, and energy organizations. Clearly, in this model, the primary communication tool is the delivery of outbound messages—that is, push messages—to target markets the firm has selected.

The other end of the business model spectrum is represented by organizations that use a demand-chain approach. As shown in Exhibit 2.5, those organizations start with customers and prospects, their needs, requirements, wishes, and wants. The company then aligns its business structure and capabilities to fit those identified customer requirements. Thus, research, understanding, and knowledge about customers permeate the entire organization. The focus is on understanding customers first and then developing customer-specific products and services to fit their needs. Dell Computers and Amazon represent this type of business model. Dell will build a computer to fit the needs of each and every individual who contacts the company. Amazon focuses on an increasing array of high-quality products with excellent service and true customer focus. In this business model, customers and prospects come first. Thus, a combination of push and pull communication is commonly required—pull to understand what customers want and need, and push to advise customers how to acquire the value propositions the firm has developed.

These two diametrically different business models illustrate why it is so difficult for an organization to become customer-focused. In a supply-chain business model, no matter how hard the organization tries, it is difficult, if not impossible, for it to put customers first. What comes first is what the organization does or manufactures or distributes. Everything is geared to making the organization work as efficiently as possible. Customers and prospects can either take the offerings the firm has developed, find another supplier, or do without. The supply-chain firm believes what it is doing is best for the firm and, hopefully, there are some benefits for the customer as well. These types of organizations have little or no need for marketing or even customer knowledge. Thus, they place little value on building long-term brand relationships with customers. Customers come and go. As long as the price and distribution proposition is strong enough, these firms believe the customer will accede to their business model and they will be successful.

In the demand-chain business model, customer focus is inherent. Knowing and understanding customers is what the organization is all about. Thus, these firms are able to develop long-term, ongoing relationships with their customers. In fact, these kinds of companies create the ingredients necessary for customer-brand relationships as a natural part of doing business.

Therefore, the first step in developing a customer-focused organization is to understand the business model the company employs. If it is a supply chain, customer focus is generally difficult, though not impossible, to develop. If the firm is based on a demand-chain business model, it will be much easier. Not simple, but certainly easier.

The Four Ps

Becoming customer-focused is difficult for many marketing organizations simply because of the training many managers have undergone, either through university education, professional programs, or on-the-job training. The problem? Almost all marketing training for the past sixty or so years has been based on the 4Ps: product, price, place, and promotion. Almost every marketing text written in the past fifty years has been based on this simple mnemonic. This "marketing mix" has evolved into the "marketing mantra"—easy to remember, easy to use, but certainly not customer-focused.

In the 4Ps process, marketing people are encouraged to develop marketing programs based on an analysis of the product, pricing, place or distribution, and promotion. The 4Ps marketing methodology forces the marketing manager to think about what the company or organization does, how it wants to go to market, what communication tools it wants to use, and so on. In short, the 4Ps provide an internal, organization-based view of marketing, not an external, customer-based view of what is needed.

The inherent assumption in the 4Ps model is that if the marketer gets the product, price, place, and promotion right, customers will magically appear. While this works in some markets, it is increasingly clear that the internal view simply does not work very well anymore. Customers have too many choices and too much market and product information to be held captive by any marketing organization.

When we reflect back a bit, we can easily see how the 4Ps evolved out of the supply-chain business model. Get your product right. Get your pricing right. Get a good location or develop a solid distribution channel. Do a bit of advertising and promotion, and success will naturally follow. Simple. Easy. Clear-cut. And, all controlled by the marketer. No wonder marketers love the 4Ps system. It assumes they have total control over the marketplace and the consumers, who are simply targets to be manipulated.

True, the 4Ps system worked, particularly in the middle of the twentieth century. Customers and prospects accepted what the marketer said through the mass media because they had little access to information, limited methods of travel, little knowledge of price or pricing in other markets, and no other resource or choice. This period, from about 1950 to 1985, is often called the "golden years of marketing" because the market worked the way the marketer wanted it to and almost every marketing plan and program found willing customers, eager to buy and continue buying. Consumers were hungry for new products and services, and retailers and manufacturers were anxious to supply them.

But today commoditization reigns supreme in almost every product category. In many markets, there are more retailers and manufacturers than there are consumer demands. Pricing is inconsistent and generally declining. Plus consumers are simply overwhelmed with the cacophony of promotional offers directed toward them. In short, marketers are becoming more aggressive and consumers are becoming more resistant. The 4Ps are no longer the right marketing model.

But if the 4Ps are no longer relevant, what should marketers do?

THE SIVA SYSTEM

One approach is the recently developed SIVA (solutions, information, value, access) system now being adopted around the world. The SIVA system is a demand-based way for the organization to become customer-focused simply by using a different type of planning process. In the SIVA system, the marketer starts with customers, rather than products or services. The research and marketing groups determine what customers really want, need, or would like to have. Using this information, the marketer then matches products or services to customers' needs. Since SIVA starts with customers, there are no preconceived notions about what type of brand communication program should be developed. Instead, appropriate push or pull communication programs emerge naturally from the analysis of the customers' needs.

SIVA is simply a reconceptualization of the marketing approach from the customer's view. (Incidentally, "Siva" is an alternative spelling for "Shiva," the Hindu god of destruction and re-creation. He destroys in order to create something better. SIVA destroys current planning models in order to provide a better solution.) There are four key elements to SIVA based on the four key questions customers generally ask when considering or buying a product or service. A brief description of the SIVA process follows, along with an example of how it might be used.

S Is for Solutions

> Customer question: How can I solve my problem or what is the solution to the need, want, or desire I have?

This is the key question marketers must answer in order to build ongoing customer-brand relationships. Helping customers solve problems or find solutions to existing or emerging needs is the essence of the SIVA approach. The 4Ps start at the wrong end, with the product or service, not with the issue or question the customer faces. SIVA starts with an understanding of the solution desired and then fits the products or services to that need. Most marketers seem to be obsessed with developing new products or new uses for old products, rather than identifying and filling customer requirements. SIVA starts with questions, not with answers—a radically different way of developing marketing programs.

Once the best solution to the customer problem is determined, the next step is to let the customer or prospect know about the solution. The argument is therefore made that the element of promotion in the traditional marketing mix should be destroyed in its present form and re-created as information.

I Is for Information

> Customer question: Where can I learn more about the solution being offered to my problem?

The current marketing and marketing communication spectrum inundates customers and prospects in a sea of messages, visuals, sound bites, and icons, most of which are essentially irrelevant because they focus on flogging products, not solving customer problems. For example, it has been estimated that Americans are exposed to more than 3,000 advertisements per day, most of which they now try to avoid. Customers do want information, but it must be relevant information, available or delivered through their media choices with varying levels of customization in ways that are convenient for them, not just efficient for the marketing organization.

The challenge for the marketer, of course, is determining what type and level of information customers want and need. Again, there is a clear need for both push and pull communication programs going forward. Given those requirements, one of the key elements of any customer-brand relationship has to be an understanding of what information customers actually want and need and how they would like to obtain that information. That understanding, of course, involves the two prime elements of the customer-brand relationship approach, content and delivery. We will deal further with these two areas in many of the following chapters.

Once the information is obtained by the customer or prospect (note: we did not say "disseminated by the marketer," a radical concept in and of itself), the value of the information must be delivered to or made available for the customer or prospect to access or acquire. Here, we propose replacing the third P, price, with value, the next key element in the SIVA model.

V Is for Value

> Customer Question: What is the value of the solution being proposed, does it solve my problem, and what will be my total sacrifice to get that solution?

Today, most consumers want to obtain a solution or a solution bundle or even a solution experience. They do not necessarily want the product or service that supports the solution; they want the experience or solution the product or service can provide. Thus, in SIVA, we think in terms of value—the value of the solution, the value to the customer, not just value to the marketer. That in itself is another dramatic shift from the 4Ps process.

Of course, value can be delivered only at some cost. Thus, value is balanced by the sacrifice the customer or prospect must make to receive the solution being offered. More than 100 years ago, economists said value was best defined as pleasure minus pain or satisfaction minus sacrifice. Price is one way of looking at sacrifice, but it is not the only one. When only price is considered, the increasingly important nonprice elements of value, such as saving of time, gaining of prestige, and delay of unhappiness, disappear. Thus, to really build ongoing customer-brand relationships, the marketer must provide a valuable solution that includes a winning price-value relationship for the consumer as well.

Once the best solution has been identified and the most useful information offered in a timely manner and determined by the correct balance in value—that is, benefit minus cost—the marketer can now provide the total solution, the entire bundle the customer is seeking. So, in replacing the final P, or place, by the SIVA process, the marketer provides access—giving customers the solution on their terms: what they want, when they want it, where they want it, and how they want it. This of course, includes the rapidly increasing area of pull communication—information on the customer's, not the marketer's, terms.

A Is for Access

> Customer Question: Where can I find the solution being offered?

Today, instead of thinking in typical supply-chain business model terms of "getting the product to the customer," marketers using the SIVA approach should think in terms of service businesses that are obsessed with bringing the solution to the customer. Think Coca-Cola, whose prime goal is never to be more than an arm's length away from a customer. Thus, Coca-Cola is everywhere.

Today, the question is less about what type of logistical system (often the heart of a supply-chain business model) the marketer can build and more about what type of distribution system the consumer or customer wants to access. Thus, the question in the customer-brand relationship model is no longer about place but about how the marketer can provide the fastest, easiest, least expensive (not just in financial terms but in time as well) access to the product or service, alone or in combination with other products or services that promote and provide the best consumer solution. Those are the types of approaches that will build ongoing customer-brand relationships.

In the SIVA approach, in essence a replacement for the traditional marketing mix advocated by the 4Ps, the marketer acts as a server or co-creator of customer value, not just as supplier. The goal is to provide the ideal combination of solution, information, value, and access for each market segment identified. Defining, designing, and delivering these combinations constitute the marketer's key challenges. Clearly, doing it from the customer's point of view can only improve the odds of success. That is why the traditional marketing approach, always pushing out messages or incentives to target markets, is no longer always appropriate. Various forms of pull communication are required, as we will discuss in later chapters.

The question naturally arises: is SIVA just another clever marketing mnemonic device that reiterates what marketers are already doing or have done in the past? We argue that SIVA supports and builds on the true marketing concept—finding customer needs, wants, or desires and filling them at a profit to the marketing organization—because SIVA offers a radically different way to think, plan, and develop customer-brand relationship programs.

Southern LINC Puts SIVA Into Practice

Southern LINC, a division of the Southern Company, grew out of a set of tools and technologies originally developed by Motorola, the technology company. The company chose to replace an aging dispatch system used by its electrical utility operating companies in the southeastern United States with something better.[3]

Recognizing the need for a highly reliable communication network for the utility operations, the company chose to build a mobile communication system using Motorola iDEN technology, which combines two-way radio, cellular phone, paging, and Internet access through one integrated handset. Since the new technology would provide considerably more capacity than the operating companies required, Southern LINC was charged with marketing the additional capacity to other business and government users within its four-state region. Southern LINC officially launched commercial services across the region in 1996.

Like many other technology-driven organizations, initially Southern LINC focused on the products and services it provided, not on the customer benefits that the service delivered. Like most other telecommunications organizations, Southern LINC was organized and operated on functional lines. While the functional managers generally worked well together horizontally, Bob Dawson, the CEO, felt the organization was missing something. Although the organization held an annual meeting where all functional groups came together to plan the coming year, the focus was still on trying to sell what Southern LINC had to offer.

Starting in 1998, Julie Pigott, the vice president of marketing, began to organize an annual planning meeting around team-building and cross-functional team interactions. That brought the top managers of the firm together to create a common ground for product and service development and delivery. However, Dawson and Pigott still felt the organization was missing a customer orientation.

At the 2003 meeting, the group of managers attending was introduced to the SIVA framework. In the opening sessions, the managers of the various functional groups were immersed in the approach as the model for their future planning. The impact was almost immediate. Rather than talking about product improvements and enhancements, the managers began to talk about customer needs. What were they? How were they currently being met? By whom, if not Southern LINC? What did the organization need to do to solve customer problems and provide solutions? "We began to look for ways to provide what customers wanted and needed, not to just find new or different or better ways to tell prospects about the nifty new features that Southern LINC was developing," said Rodney Johnson, the vice president of sales and distribution. Customer problems and solutions became the topics of discussion during the intensive, three-day planning program.

One of the key elements coming out of the 2003 planning meeting was a consensus that, in spite of all the improvements Southern LINC had made in product offerings, customer service, and network capacity, the company was falling short of where it needed to be. The dominant theme running through all the discussions was "we have to make it easier for customers to do business with us."

The managers worked through the components of the SIVA process one by one. Starting with customers, they identified the solutions that customers wanted. Next, they determined the information customers wanted Southern LINC to supply and the form and manner in which those customers wanted it available and delivered. Then, the managers looked at value, not in the sense of cost-benefit but in terms of customer experiences. What was Southern LINC doing that solved customer problems or customer concerns or questions? The total customer experience became the beacon for the Southern LINC managers, more than the network or system or reliability of the service. By looking at customers first, Southern LINC managers began to imagine new ways in which they could expand and extend their services. Of course, access became a key issue. The focus was not just what service Southern LINC wanted to provide or how Southern LINC wanted to reach its customers and prospects; the focus now became how the customers wanted to access the information and material they needed from the organization, how they wanted to be served, what type of relationship they wanted.

In short, SIVA provided the framework that Southern LINC managers needed to truly understand their customers. Best of all, SIVA promoted a horizontal planning system in which marketing became a task performed by the entire organization, not just a group of functional marketing managers.

The SIVA approach was a success at Southern LINC. It helped a technologically driven company move from a product and service focus to a customer orientation. It brought the organization together horizontally. From a management view, it helped the middle managers identify the changes that need to be made. It allowed them to identify, value, and prioritize the recommendations they now present to senior management for funding. Most of all, SIVA provided the catalyst for a very strong and capable organization to move to the next level of marketing thinking by building a better model. It allowed Southern LINC to escape the restraints of the internally focused methodology of the 4Ps and adopt the customer-oriented SIVA approach better suited to the realities of the twenty-first-century marketplace.

Summing Up

With this view of the importance of customer focus, the six-market approach to expanding the marketer's view of customers, and the introduction of two new planning tools, the spider chart and the SIVA system, we have laid the groundwork for a new view of customers and how customer-brand relationships might be built. In short, we have provided the thinking tools all marketing and communication managers need to meet the challenges of the twenty-first–century marketplace.

The next stage of the customer-brand relationship methodology becomes much more action-oriented. We start the next chapter with a discussion of how the marketing organization might identify the customers or customer groups it wants to serve. Those decisions are often based on which customers the organization can serve, not just those it would like to serve. A firm might want to serve the high-end real estate market, but only have run-down tenements in declining neighborhoods as its product offering that would severely limit their alternatives. Obviously, the firm's strategy makes little economic or marketplace sense. No matter how customer-focused the firm is, there simply is not a marketplace match. This matching procedure, the key to success in a customer-brand relationship, will be discussed next.

NOTES

1. P. Kotler, "Total Marketing," *Business Week Advance, Executive Brief* 2 (1992).

2. M. McDonald, M. Christopher, S. Knox, and A. Payne, *Creating a Company for Customers* (London: Pearson Education, 2001), p. 53.

3. C.S. Dev and D. Schultz, "Get Results with the New Marketing Mix," *Marketing Management* (March/April 2005).

CHAPTER 3

Developing Customer Insights

Having established a framework for thinking about the customer-brand relationship, we now turn to a closer look at customers themselves. Customers are one of the three components of the brand communication model, along with delivery channels and content (see Exhibit 3.1).

In this chapter, we look at the decision-making process and some of the internal and external influences on customers' behavior. Chapter 4 examines in more detail recent research on the role of emotion and brain processes in decision making. In Chapter 5, we revisit the various customer groups introduced in Chapter 2 and discuss their needs and influences more completely.

THE CONSUMER DECISION-MAKING PROCESS

How do customers go about making decisions about the brands they buy and use? The components and complexity of the decision-making process depend on the individual customer's familiarity with the product category and the brand, as well as the importance of the decision in the customer's life or career. John A. Howard developed a model that depicts three decision-making processes, with choice of process determined by the depth of the consumer's existing relationships with the brand and the product category under consideration.[1] The model is shown in Exhibit 3.2.

In each case, the decision-making process is sparked by problem recognition, wherein the current state differs from the ideal. In habitual decision making, the problem can be as simple as running out of toothpaste. In extended decision making, it could be the situation of the soon-to-be college graduate who will be starting a job in sales and needs to buy a car for the first time. Problem recognition is associated with particular brands in habitual decision making since in this scenario the consumer has a past relationship with the brand. The decision, then, is generally whether to repurchase the brand bought the last time or to make a change. In both limited and extended decision making, the consumer's relationship with the brand may be either weaker or nonexistent, in which case problem recognition may have less to do with brands and more to do with broader product categories.

Having recognized that problem recognition has occurred, the information search begins. This is a very important stage for the marketer, one that has been greatly affected by some of the societal trends noted earlier. Internal information search involves extracting brand and category messages from long-term memory. What do I already know about this category? What brands have worked for me in the past? Which brands have been recommended to me by friends or have I been urged to stay away from? What have I seen or heard about this brand

Exhibit 3.1   **Integrated Brand Communication Model**

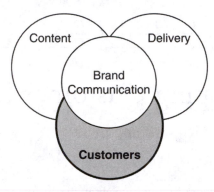

Exhibit 3.2   **Consumer Decision-Making Model**

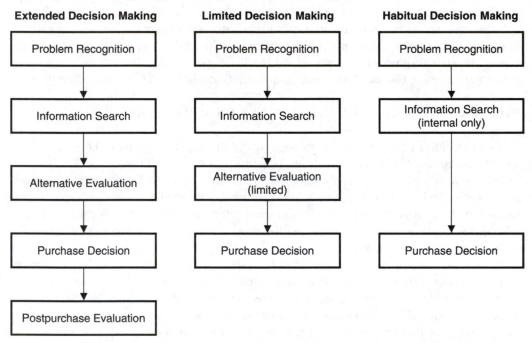

Source: Adapted from J.A. Howard, *Consumer Behavior: Application of Theory* (New York: McGraw-Hill, 1977).

in the media or from friends or associates? What is the nature of my own relationship with those brands—positive or negative, weak or strong? These questions hint at how information is stored in memory, a topic we will discuss in detail in Chapter 4.

If the existing relationship is weak and brand information in memory is lacking, the consumer turns to external search. This is active search for more information. It can certainly involve communication controlled by the marketer—ads, sales promotion offers, the brand's Web site—but also can involve sources outside the marketer's control, such as word of mouth, favorable (or unfavorable) news stories, and Web chat rooms where other consumers dissect the brand. As has been discussed earlier, today's consumers know that there is no shortage of information sources, and they expect to be able to find brand information quickly and easily.

One of the primary sources of brand knowledge for a consumer is the consistent level of quality and services provided by the brand. With a brand, consumers know what they can expect from one usage situation to the next. As that relationship between the consumer and the brand is established and reinforced over time, the brand name becomes a type of shorthand for all the associations of information, features, and benefits tied to the brand. To start that process of building the connections to the brand, basic information about the brand needs to be readily available. Failure to make the information that the customer needs and wants available will almost certainly prevent the relationship from being established, which will in turn cost sales. Thus a key requirement for the planner is to identify the likely places consumers will go for information on the brand and make sure the needed information is available and easily accessed. The availability of this information is a critical aspect of any brand promotion program.

In the habitual decision-making process, the work is now done. The consumer buys the brand that has been used before, reaffirming the relationship with that brand. Perhaps the reason behind the choice is as simple as that, the strength of the existing relationship. Or the decision may have been made because of an incentive being offered or a recommendation from an external or internal source. Either way, the decision is quick and positive. And as long as there has not been a noticeable slip in quality or increase in price since the last time the customer bought the brand, something that changed the nature of the previous relationship, that is the end of the decision-making process.

Habitual buying is easy for the consumer and works to the advantage of marketers, whose goal is to maintain market share and hold on to current users. The easiest decision to make is not to make a change; inertia can be a powerful force driving brand success. While this non-thinking behavior is not the best basis for a relationship (brand or human), it can certainly work to the benefit of the brand marketer.

For those brands trying to gain share, increase sales, or attract new customers, breaking consumers' existing habits can be quite challenging. In their book *What Sticks: Why Most Advertising Fails and How to Guarantee Yours Succeeds*, Rex Briggs and Greg Stuart argue that 37 percent of all the money spent on advertising in the United States is wasted. The book is based on the authors' work with thirty top U.S. companies, studying how consumers responded to their advertising messages. One of the key points Briggs and Stuart make is that a substantial amount of message exposure is necessary to truly influence consumers' buying behavior.[2]

To effect long-term brand change, a marketer must first get consumers' attention and then shift people from habitual decision making into limited decision making, where they will consider new information and reevaluate the choices available. Too many marketers fall into the trap of using sales promotion incentives to spark brand change. Doing so influences the consumer merely on this purchasing occasion, not on future decisions; once a customer has become promotion sensitive, the decision next time will likely favor whichever brand is offering the best deal at that point. A brand decision based on sales promotion alone is like a personal relationship based only on appearance. It may work for a while, but in the long term, there is not much to keep the relationship alive.

If the brand decision is not habitual, information search is followed by alternative evalu-

Exhibit 3.3   "Moving 101"

Moving 101

COURSE DESCRIPTION: Move to College

OBJECTIVES:

Bring all of your essential items
Pack smart
Survive moving day
Get the school year off to a great start

COURSE MATERIALS:

Box labels and markers
Sturdy packaging tape
Protective materials like packaging peanuts and bubble cushioning
Strong moving boxes in a variety of shapes and sizes

When it's time to start the school year, many college students simply pack up the family car and head out. This works fine for those within driving distance of their school, but for students who live across the country or overseas, the only choice is to ship their possessions. With more than 4,300 locations across the country, The UPS Store is a natural choice for many college-bound students. At this one-stop shop, families and students can find a variety of moving supplies for those easy-to-pack items like clothes and bedding. For fragile objects or electronics, students may want to rely on the experts at The UPS Store to pack and ship their items directly to their dorm or apartment.

Source: www.upsstore.com/shipshape/mov101.html.

ation. This is the comparison stage, where the consumer weighs conflicting information and decides which attributes are most important. Consider the description of "Moving 101" for The UPS Store in Exhibit 3.3. Problem recognition is sparked by the need to get a lot of really important items to campus to equip the dorm room. If the student is a freshman, it is the first time he has had to deal with this problem. If he is a returning student, he may have shipped things home at the end of the last school year, or this may be the first time he has accumulated so many belongings that the car just cannot handle the load. In any case, this is probably a limited decision-making situation.

Internal information search generates a list of options: bring less stuff to school and buy new items there to replace what was left behind; attach a trailer to the car bumper or a carrier to the roof; use the U.S. Postal Service; use a dedicated shipping service. Today, there are a multitude of options available for most products and services, information on which is available through a few keystrokes from Yahoo or Google. The UPS Store wants the student to go with a shipping service, specifically with UPS. The "Moving 101" description, found on the Web site for The UPS Store, is designed to encourage that decision, in part by emphasizing a number of attributes that might be important in making the decision. The description mentions convenience and risk reduction as well as help with packaging. The alternative evaluation stage involves comparison of possibilities on key attributes. The difference between alternative evaluation in limited and extended decision making lies in the number of attributes considered, number of possibilities evaluated, and how the evaluation occurs. Choosing a shipper will generally be much simpler than choosing an automobile. Think about the difference in the nature of those relationships; a consumer's relationship with her car is generally reinforced daily through repeated use, while she uses a shipper much less frequently. She wants that shipper to provide quality service whenever she uses it, but the relationship is much less intense than with her automobile.

Once the preferred brand is identified out of the alternatives considered, purchase takes place. Generally, the purchased brand will be the preferred brand, but that is not always the case. Marketers spend large amounts of money on point-of-purchase communication in an attempt to change decisions at the point of sale. (Those incentives are much more likely to be effective in either habitual or limited decision making than in extended decision making because of the intensity of evaluation that has already taken place.)

The final stage in the process is post-purchase. Here the consumer evaluates whether the choice made was the right one—that is, did the brand deliver as promised or expected? If the experience with the brand is as expected, or better than expected, a relationship can often be established or reinforced. The positive experiences will be stored in memory, burnishing the consumer's associations with the brand. If the usage experience is negative or not as good as expected, dissonance will occur as the consumer second-guesses the decision. If the dissonance is severe enough, it may spark new problem recognition and the process begins again. That brand will likely be eliminated from the consumer's consideration set in the future, and any associations stored in memory will be negative. With the variety of brand choices available in most product categories, a brand that does not deliver will probably never get a second chance with that consumer, and the brand may also suffer if the consumer serves as an influencer on other people's brand choices. In either case, satisfaction or dissatisfaction, new information has been added to memory as a result of the decision-making process, and it will be there to be used the next time.

The marketer has a powerful opportunity to influence the post-purchase evaluation process. Obviously, product performance, the brand's ability to actually deliver the value promised, is critical. But so is the marketer's continued communication with the consumer after the sale. How responsive is the marketer to consumers' questions or concerns through customer service representatives, a comprehensive FAQ section on the Web site, and the like? What kind of ongoing communication does the marketer engage in with the consumer? Are there regular updates on product improvements, price savings on future purchases, or new features provided through email, bill inserts, or other means? Is the consumer offered incentives to repurchase or continue use? All of these are means of building and maintaining a relationship, not just making a sale.

The means of ongoing communication need not be complicated. Chico's, a women's clothing and accessories retailer, invites customers to join its preferred buyer group. Members receive a Chico's catalog in the mail about every six weeks. The catalog includes a savings coupon whose value is tied to the member's purchasing volume. This is a relatively simple, cost-effective way for Chico's to demonstrate its appreciation for its customers while at the same time encouraging additional sales. The customer's sense of an ongoing relationship with Chico's should encourage positive evaluations of the brand after and in between purchasing occasions.

Exhibit 3.4 **Maslow's Hierarchy of Needs**

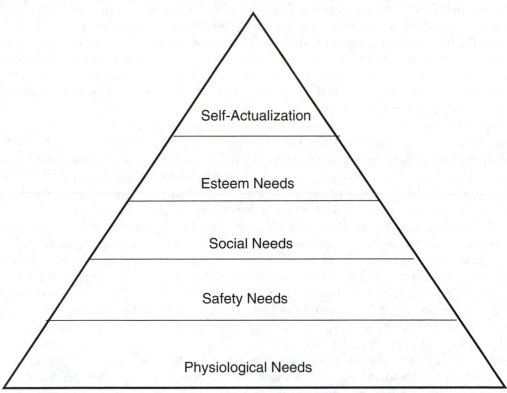

Source: Adapted from A.H. Maslow, *Motivation and Personality*, 2nd ed. (New York: Harper & Row, 1970).

INFLUENCES ON CUSTOMER DECISION MAKING

The decision-making process described above seems fairly straightforward. What then explains why two people with similar demographic, geographic, socioeconomic, and even psychographic characteristics can behave quite differently in terms of brand choice and product use, developing widely different relationships with the same brand?

As noted above, a variety of internal and external factors can influence customers' decision making. We review these factors in further detail here. These are elements that marketers should keep in mind both when planning the communication program and when attempting to determine the relative success or failure of various relationship elements.

Problem Recognition and Motivation

What causes a customer to purchase a product in the first place or to make a brand switch away from a previously used product? One important factor is motivation, the internal drives that influence behavior. Perhaps because motivations are hard to explain, felt but not generally articulated, they have been the subjects of much research. One fundamental approach to examining motivation is the hierarchy developed by Abraham Maslow (see Exhibit 3.4).[3]

Maslow posited five levels of motivations, moving from most basic to most refined. At the lowest level are *physiological needs*, the drive for shelter, sustenance, the basic elements that make it possible to survive. In Western culture, it is unusual to see marketing communications messages focused on physiological needs simply because they have already been satisfied for most people. When an appeal is made to physiological needs, it is often expressed in fundamental terms. For example, Gatorade's slogan "Is it in you?" implies that the product contains basic ingredients that are essential to keep the body functioning after the exertion of sports.

At the next level are *safety needs*, the drive to feel protected, safe, and sheltered. A number of product categories frequently deal in safety needs: for example, insurance, smoke detectors, and automobile tires. For these types of brands, the relationship with the customer emphasizes protection: we (the brand) will help to keep you and your family safe. Because the flip side of safety is danger and risk, marketers of these types of products must be careful in crafting messages. They want customers and potential customers to feel enough risk so that they will consider purchasing the product, but not so much risk that they are frightened and react negatively to the message. For example, some years ago, a Prudential Insurance television ad campaign depicted people who had nearly died in accidents or medical emergencies. Grateful that they had received "a second chance," these survivors said that one thing they had done as a result was to buy more insurance. The ads were arresting, but the degree of danger in them created negative reactions. The risk shown in the commercials, which generally depicted people coming near death in an accident, was very upsetting to many viewers. Prudential's next campaign showed joking, humorous angels escorting people up to heaven via escalator, with the message that these people were all carefree because they had plenty of insurance. That message was much more palatable to prospective customers, possibly because of the humor, but also because the images were much less realistic than those in the previous, frightening campaign.

Similarly, Volkswagen ran a campaign emphasizing its cars' safety features. The ads in the campaign showed people driving their VWs while engaged in the kinds of typical conversations that happen in automobiles after a dinner out or on the way home from school. Suddenly, that commonplace conversation is interrupted by a car crash. The next scene shows the car's occupants standing outside the car; they are obviously unhurt, although the car itself is smashed. The juxtaposition between the casual conversation and the crash itself is attention-grabbing; the message that a Volkswagen is engineered to protect its passengers comes through strongly, but in a way that is not overly threatening. The situations shown in the ads remind viewers that an accident can happen to anyone at any time, so it is best to be prepared by driving a car that provides good safety features.

The third level of Maslow's hierarchy is *social needs*, the motivation to be part of a group, to fit in. This motivation forms the basis of many persuasive campaigns, where brand use is shown as the path to winning friends. In a sense, being friends with the brand is the path to winning other friends, just like the use of My Space, YouTube, or other online services. While many messages focused on social needs use positive imagery, this motivation also can be used to show the possible negative consequences of not using the brand. Head & Shoulders shampoo used a long-running campaign that showed people scratching their heads, with the voice-over "That little itch could be telling them you have dandruff." The other people in the ads inevitably grimaced and shied away from the poor afflicted dandruff sufferer. Who would want to associate with someone who had dandruff? Social needs are an implicit message in many brand communication campaigns, particularly those for brands that are used publicly, where others will know what brand choices the consumer has made. Using the brand equals belonging to the group of people who have chosen that brand.

Esteem needs are the fourth level of the hierarchy. A person motivated by esteem is driven by the desire to feel superior to others. Many luxury products use messages based in esteem needs, where brand usage is a badge of honor and a mark of superiority. For example, Moet & Chandon Champagne uses "Be Fabulous" as its slogan. The reference is to the person drinking the champagne, who is fabulous by association because of drinking Moet & Chandon. E*Trade appeals to prospective online investors with the message "Be Smarter Than the Average Bear. Or Bull." Investors who use E*Trade are smart investors, smarter than others. Brand use brings esteem.

The final level of Maslow's hierarchy is *self-actualization*. At this level, a person has no concern about fitting in or being superior, but is motivated by the desire for self-improvement, being the best you can be for yourself. The U.S. Army's long-running campaign, "Be All You Can Be," was a powerful self-actualization message. Just how powerful may be shown by the relative ineffectiveness of the campaign that followed it, "An Army of One." Dealing with the esteem level rather than with self-actualization, "An Army of One" suggested that a soldier could succeed without the support of anyone else; it was a message of isolation. "Be All You Can Be," on the other hand, did not set the soldier apart from others; the ads emphasized teamwork, showing individual soldiers improving their skills, but doing so along with other soldiers. "Be All You Can Be" was a message of self-fulfillment, but not in opposition to the achievement of others.

Maslow's hierarchy of motivations is usually depicted as a triangle, with physiological needs at the base and self-actualization at the top. Interestingly, many brand planning models and other marketing concepts also have been presented as triangles. Maslow's influence has been quite far-reaching, and thinking about which level of the hierarchy the brand's relationship with customers currently focuses on, and whether it might be possible to move that relationship to a higher level, is a useful endeavor for any brand planner.

We will look at motivation in more detail in Chapter 4, with particular attention to the interplay between motivation and emotion.

Information Search and Perception

Perception processes affect how we take in, store, and respond to information contained in a variety of sources, including persuasive messages. An understanding of perception processes can help the marketer with both message design and media placement.

Every day, customers encounter far more persuasive communication messages and incentives than they can possibly process. This is the case even when consumers are overtly seeking information as part of the decision process. Perception processes help them organize and make sense of the myriad of messages. The first process, *selective exposure*, has to do with seeking out or avoiding messages. While many messages cannot be avoided (or at least, that is what the marketers hope), customers can choose to leave the room during television commercials, use their TiVo to skip commercials, watch programs on DVD and avoid the ads altogether, change the station or mute the volume during radio ads, flip quickly through the ad pages in magazines, and the like. The consumer's increasing ability to avoid mass media advertising messages is one of the greatest challenges facing marketers today.

Sometimes, the decision to avoid a message can be based on an existing strong brand relationship. Think about political advertising and various types of advocacy messages, such as newspaper articles reporting on candidate press conferences. People will tend to read the articles about those candidates they like most, to reinforce their positive attitudes, while ignoring or discounting reporting about those they like least. The same process can happen with brand messages.

Just because a message is not avoided does not mean it will merit attention. That is where the second perception process, *selective attention*, comes in. Having seen or heard a message, customers consciously choose what to pay attention to. They make choices every day about what print ad copy they will actually read, what Internet banners they will click on, what television spots they will watch closely.

The choice is further influenced by the fact that most consumers today are engaged in multitasking when using traditional mass media. They read a magazine while watching television, do housework or office work with the radio on, work on their computer while the television is on, and carry on multiple conversations through instant messaging. If it was ever realistic for marketers to assume that consumers were paying full attention to their messages, that time is clearly past. The increasing evidence of the decline in the effectiveness of mass media advertising has led to increasing emphasis on techniques such as event marketing, sponsorships, and in-store promotion. The former has been shown to engage targeted consumer groups much more effectively than advertising; the latter at least reaches customers when they are in a purchasing situation and have few distractions.

The challenge of how best to capture customers' attention for the marketer's message also has changed traditional thinking about push versus pull marketing programs. Generally, *push* means that the marketing organization develops products and services and pushes them out toward the consumer or prospects using various outbound programs. For example, the traditional marketing mantra of the 4Ps—product, price, place or distribution, and promotion—assumes that if the marketer gets those right, customers will show up at the marketer's door.

Alternatively, pull marketing assumes that the customer controls the marketplace and is able to select from a broad array of products or services. Thus, the customer contacts or sources information from the marketing organization or other places and pulls that information or material or whatever is required together to make a purchase decision. It is this shift in the consumer's marketplace power that really differentiates the two approaches. Assuming, though, that the customer has indeed paid attention, she must then interpret the message. *Selective comprehension* is the process of making sense of the message. While marketers certainly want customers to pay attention to and understand their message, the possible compounding factor is how the message interpretation may occur. If a customer has a strong relationship with the brand based on regular past use and then sees a message for a competitive brand, it is quite possible that she will interpret that message negatively, despite the marketer's original intent. People interpret messages based on what they already know and believe. That is one key reason why the best predictor of future behavior is past behavior. If the brand delivers value for the customer and does so consistently (which, after all, is one of the essentials of branding), then it should be very difficult for a competitive brand to force a change in that behavior. We look at comprehension more fully in the next chapter.

The last of the perception processes is *selective retention*. Since consumers may not be able to act upon persuasive communication messages immediately, the information must be stored in memory for future use. Selective retention determines which messages the customer chooses to remember and make part of her brand schema. Peter and Olson defined a schema as "an associative network of interrelated meanings that represent a person's declarative knowledge about some concept."[4] We will look at the concept of the brand schema in more detail in Chapter 4.

What can a marketer do to try to make sure that messages are seen, given attention, correctly interpreted, and remembered? There are several basic strategies. The first is to select an appropriate target audience and learn what factors motivate its members and what media they use. Knowledge of the target's media use in a customer-driven marketplace is very important. Two university professors, Martin Block and Don Schultz at Northwestern University, working with a commercial research house, BIGresearch, have illustrated the concept of media consumption.[5] Simply put, the number of messages that a marketing group distributes is not as important as the number of those messages that are received or consumed by the intended audience. Clearly, message consumption is driven by many factors, but the amount of time spent with the media form has much to do with the success of any form of promotional communication. Understanding media consumption is a critical task for the twenty-first–century communication planner. There is also little doubt that message relevance aids in comprehension and retention; customers are far more likely to give attention to messages that address their problems, speak to their issues, and focus on satisfying their motivations.

The physical characteristics of the message also can aid in navigating the perception processes. Television and radio spots that are louder than surrounding programming can command attention (positive or negative, depending on whether or not audience members find this annoying), as can print ads that use bright colors or large visuals. Use of popular celebrities also can aid in getting attention, although their presence may overshadow the main message, causing problems in both comprehension and retention. Similarly, pop-up ads and interstitals online can force consumer attention through their interruption of the primary message, although the associated irritation factor also can cause problems. More effective are targeted links tied to the content of the page the consumer has chosen to view; consumers may even consider such links as positive forms of added value provided by the primary Web page.

Alternative Evaluation and Attitude Change

Customers typically choose not from among all brands in a category but instead from a subsegment of brands, what is often called the consumer's "evoked set." The evoked set is the group of brands that the customer finds acceptable and, in many cases, interchangeable. In most instances, this is the group of brands toward which the customer has a positive attitude. The ease of communication and information sharing online has led to the rise of communities of interest focused around brands. Online groups cover everything from hobbies and life interests to political action groups and self-improvement discussion sites. The most common and currently the most vibrant of these types of groups are My Space, YouTube, and the like.

If customer research suggests that competitive users have negative, or even neutral, attitudes toward the brand, a campaign focused on attitude change may be necessary. There are at least four attitude change strategies that may be effective: linking the product to a desired goal or

Exhibit 3.5 **One-A-Day Women's package showing company's sponsorship of breast cancer research fundraising efforts.**

event, adding an important characteristic, changing perceptions of the brand, and changing perceptions of the competition.

Linking the product to a desired goal or event can change attitudes if the desirability of the goal becomes associated with the product. Consider the many brands that have created linkages to breast cancer awareness and breast cancer research support. The list of corporate donors to the Breast Cancer Research Foundation includes Estee Lauder, the International Housewares Association, Macy's, Target, Ann Taylor, Saks Fifth Avenue, Wilson Sporting Goods, Bloomingdale's, Coach, Danskin, One-A-Day Women's, General Mills, Godiva, and Lord & Taylor, among many others.[6] By contributing to this cause, the marketers show their concern for those afflicted with breast cancer and their families. Consumers may consequently view the company and brand favorably, using the brand's support of the breast cancer cause as a reason to select this brand over others. Exhibit 3.5 shows a One-A-Day Women's multivitamin package highlighting the company's commitment to breast cancer research.

The critical element in the attitude change strategy of adding an important characteristic is the word *important*. Companies frequently add product features that are of little consequence to consumers; as a result, those new features have little effect on product sales. But when an important characteristic is added, something that consumers value and see as useful, that move can have a strong effect on the brand's success. For example, Crystal Light's repackaging of its beverage flavoring powder product into small pouches suitable for adding to a bottle of water added a useful difference to that brand.

Changing fundamental perceptions of the brand is quite difficult and poses a tremendous challenge to marketers. This attitude change strategy is generally used only when the marketer's research has shown that customers' negative attitudes are so strong that they must be addressed directly. Hardee's Thickburger campaign is an example of a message designed to change perceptions of the brand. In the early stages of this campaign, Hardee's messages acknowledged that the product had been seen as, at best, second-rate. The chain even characterized itself as "the last place you'd go for a burger." The introduction of the new Thickburger, made with 100 percent Angus beef and significantly larger than the old Hardee's burger, was partially a case of adding an important characteristic. But the promotional program went further and attempted to completely change Hardee's image, moving away from an old reliance on the use of flame-broiling to an approach that positioned the chain as the place for macho, primarily male, appetites.

While Hardee's effort was quite successful in revitalizing the chain's sales,[7] not all attempts to change brand perceptions work so well. Hormel's canned meat product, Spam, has tried for years to revitalize its image. As Spam's core customer group (World War II veterans and their families) aged, the company's sales slipped. The marketing challenge became how to make Spam relevant and acceptable to a younger generation. Spam developed a series of communication programs focused on changing brand perceptions. One featured a blind taste test, where customers were given food products made using Spam, such as Spam pizza, and reacted with pleased surprise when they learned what the main ingredient was. Another described Spam as its own food group in the well-known food pyramid. Another series of ads touted the virtues of the "Spamburger hamburger," slices of Spam pan fried and served hamburger-style on a bun. While merchandise carrying the Spam name has become very popular[8] and the Spam museum in Austin, Minnesota, attracts many visitors each year, sales of Spam itself have remained flat.[9] The brand name has attained a cult following, but more as a symbol of kitsch than a preferred brand of food product.

The final attitude change strategy, changing perceptions of the competition, is also difficult. If the brand's message is too heavy-handed, the brand may be seen as a bully rather than a strong contender. In an effort to avoid that result, brands that seek to change perceptions of their competitors often will use humor or have consumers make the comparison themselves. Consider Quizno's attempt to compete directly with Subway. The ads featured consumers comparing a Subway sub with a similar Quizno's sub. The Quizno's sub was piled high with meat, while the meat in the Subway sub was barely visible. The consumers in the ad expressed their preference for the Quizno's sandwich. Interestingly, this campaign was almost a direct lift from a classic 1980s campaign in which Wendy's worked to change perceptions of its competition. The centerpiece of that campaign was an ad featuring a little old lady peering at a burger from another fast food chain and asking, "Where's the beef?"

HOW CONSUMERS LEARN

When marketers apply an attitude change strategy, they are often trying to teach consumers something new about the brand, hoping that the new knowledge will lead to a change in brand beliefs and perceptions and a resulting change in either the strength or the nature of the customer-brand relationship. There are several paths to learning that are relevant for persuasive messages.

Classical Conditioning

Anyone who has taken a basic psychology course knows the fundamentals of classical conditioning from the study of the experiment conducted by Ivan Pavlov. In that experiment, a conditioned stimulus (a bell) was paired with an unconditioned stimulus (food). Each time the dogs in the experiment were given food, the bell was rung. Over time, the dogs' response (salivation) to the unconditioned stimulus of food also became associated with the ringing of the bell, to the point where the mere ringing of the bell would cause the dogs to salivate.[10] That is classical conditioning.

The idea of association created through repetition was adopted by mass media advertising planners to develop guidelines for "effective frequency." The traditional rule of thumb in media planning was that consumers needed to see an advertisement at least three times before it would begin to affect their thinking about the brand. More recent research, particularly that by John Philip Jones,[11] has refuted this idea as overly simplistic. Interestingly, the research that media planners claimed as the basis for the theory, a study conducted by General Electric's Herbert Krugman,[12] actually did not say that three exposures was the magic number, but instead talked about varying consumer reactions to each message exposure.

How does classical conditioning apply in the marketing setting? Simply put, the brand marketer selects a conditioned stimulus that the target audience responds to favorably. That conditioned stimulus is then associated with the brand (the brand is the unconditioned stimulus) in the hope that the existing positive feelings toward the conditioned stimulus will be transferred to the brand itself. The conditioned stimulus can be something overtly positive; that is a partial explanation for why marketers will pay millions of dollars to use a particular celebrity in their advertising campaigns. It also can be a subtler pairing. For example, showing the brand in a warm, family setting may create positive emotions about the setting that will then transfer to the brand.

Classical conditioning is often based on borrowed interest; the focal point of the message is the recognizable, favorable conditioned stimulus and the brand is secondary. Relying on borrowed interest is always risky. Customers may remember the celebrity or the setting or the familiar song used in the ad, but fail to recall what brand was being promoted. In that case, the money spent to secure the rights to use that person or music was wasted. In order for classical conditioning to work well, the association between the conditioned stimulus and the brand must be constantly reinforced; it also helps if there is a logical fit between the two stimuli. Consider the work of basketball superstar Michael Jordan as a celebrity endorser. Which brand(s) come first to mind? Most likely, it is those brands that themselves have some sports connection. (Here is a partial list of the brands endorsed by Jordan when he was at the height of his career: Oakley sunglasses, Rayovac batteries, Wheaties cereal, Gatorade sports drink, Ballpark franks, Hanes underwear, Nike, Coca-Cola, Wilson sporting goods, McDonald's, Upper Deck trading cards, WorldCom communications.[13]) That is not to say that Jordan did not benefit the nonsports brands that he endorsed, but it probably took more time to establish a memorable positive association between those brands and the basketball star.

Similarly, Chrysler spent a great deal of time and money to produce a series of commercials featuring Celine Dion. In the ads, Dion sang a song created specifically for the Chrysler campaign to launch the upscale Pacifica model. The association was not effective; the Pacifica launch did not meet Chrysler's expectations and overall sales of Chryslers fell.[14] Apparently, either consumers could not make the connection between the French-Canadian Dion and Chrysler, or the notion of a luxury Chrysler model was not appealing.

Marketers who decide to pursue a classical conditioning approach to create positive associations with a brand must be very selective in the choice of conditioned stimulus. Many red-faced marketers paid large amounts of money for a celebrity endorsement, only to see that celebrity soon go from famous to notorious. Perhaps no marketer has been more unlucky than Pepsi. Within the span of a few years, Pepsi had endorser problems with both Michael

Jackson and Madonna. In the former case, the then-superstar Jackson had a mishap when his hair caught on fire while shooting an elaborate Pepsi commercial that drew negative attention.[15] Five years later, Pepsi paid handsomely to put Madonna under contract and to produce a commercial using the music and some of the video scenes from her song "Like a Prayer." The commercial debuted during the televised Grammy Awards presentation; the next day, the actual music video for "Like a Prayer" was released. The religious imagery in the video (some of which also appeared in the Pepsi commercial) sparked widespread criticism, to the point where Pepsi never aired its commercial in the United States again. (It did run in Europe, where criticism was much more muted.)[16]

Despite these kinds of problems, when classical conditioning does work, it can work very well. Consider the wide range of sponsors who sign up each year to have their brands associated with particular NASCAR drivers. The popularity of stock car racing and the strong, loyal fan followings enjoyed by top drivers make NASCAR a very attractive venue for brand associations. And studies have shown that NASCAR sponsors benefit from more than just positive attitudes created by association. Seventy-two percent of male NASCAR fans say they make a conscious effort to buy the brands that sponsor their favorite driver.[17] While both race attendance and television ratings for NASCAR slipped during the 2006 season, including a drop of 10 percent for ratings for the final chase for the Nextel Cup,[18] the sport's core audience appears to still be engaged. The expansion of television coverage of NASCAR races in 2001 allowed people outside the core audience to experience the sport by watching more televised races and consequently gaining more knowledge about drivers, sponsors and the like; those who were not captured by the spectacle then began to tune out, possibly leaving only those with a true relationship with the brand.

It is that core group that the brands associated with the winner of the NASCAR 2006 Nextel Cup Challenge, Jimmie Johnson, are trying to reach. Johnson's lead sponsor was Lowe's, but his winning Chevrolet car also carried the logos of 3M, Gillette, Kobalt, Gatorade, Levi Strauss, Gargoyles Eyewear, Tylenol, XM Satellite Radio, Sunoco, and MotorSports Authentics, among many others.[19] While Lowe's derives the greatest benefit in terms of visibility and name recognition (during races, NASCAR announcers refer to cars interchangeably by their number, driver name, or lead sponsor, i.e., "the Lowe's car"), all the sponsors associated with Johnson's win should benefit.

Sponsorships in general, and sports sponsorships in particular, are a major component of many marketers' promotional programs. According to *Promo* magazine, U.S. marketers spent $13.9 billion on sponsorships in 2006; worldwide sponsorship spending was $33.8 billion.[20] In sponsorship, rather than creating their own stand-alone event, the marketer associates the brand with an existing event with which the desired customer audience already has a relationship. Sponsorships of Little League and professional sports teams, concert tours, fairs and festivals, even art exhibits, are all hot commodities. For the sponsorship to have the greatest positive effect, the link between the brand and the sponsored event or entity must be logical and believable. In addition to the marketing benefits gained for the brand, the growth in sponsorships has also greatly benefited the many organizations and entities that have been able to maintain and even expand their operations due to sponsorship support. The knowledge that their favorite team or organization is able to survive thanks to the support of sponsors can create tremendous customer goodwill toward the sponsoring organization. Exhibit 3.6 shows the number twenty NASCAR racing car sponsored by The Home Depot.

Exhibit 3.6 **The Home Depot sponsors this NASCAR racing car as a way to reach its target audience of men interested in home improvement projects.**

While the connection between racing and home improvement supplies may not be obvious, The Home Depot is likely hopeful that the two entities, NASCAR and its stores, appeal to the same audience.

Operant Conditioning

Classical conditioning is not the only approach to learning used by marketers. Operant conditioning involves learning through reinforcement, either positive or negative. When Target or other retailers send customers coupons keyed to their past purchasing behavior, that is operant conditioning. The coupons are a reward for the past behavior of shopping at Target. Receiving the reward should make the consumers think that much more favorably of Target, encouraging them to shop there again in the future, not only to redeem the coupons, but also to qualify for future rewards.

Sales promotion techniques such as coupons can be used effectively in this way to provide tangible rewards for desired shopping behavior. The risk the marketer runs in this approach is overdoing the rewards to the point where consumers will shop at that retailer only when they have a coupon to use. A better strategy might be to offer a mix of reward types, where not every reward involves a simple price savings on a specified brand only. For example, grocery retailer Kroger mails (or emails, depending on the customer's preference) offers that are tied to the customer's past purchasing behavior (Exhibit 3.7). Kroger's mailers carry messages such as "You are unique, so are your savings!" and "Your customized coupons inside!" The customized coupons include a mix of savings offers on specific brands the customer has purchased

Exhibit 3.7   **Kroger Mailer**

Dear Beth Barnes,

Thank you! Many people shop with us, but few are as loyal as you. To show our appreciation, we've teamed up with some of your favorite brands to bring you extra BEST-CUSTOMER-ONLY savings on products you can use.

Your coupons were picked just for you. We hope they make your next shopping trip especially rewarding. Remember, the more you use your shopper's card, the better we can help you save.

Thanks again for being such a great customer and enjoy the savings!

Sincerely,

John P. Hackett

John Hackett
President, Kroger Mid South

P.S. Don't miss your valuable coupons below!

in the past as well as offers intended to modify behavior. One such offer might be a coupon for savings in the Kroger meat department offered to a customer who buys from that department only occasionally. Another offer might be for savings on grocery purchases when the customer transfers prescriptions to Kroger instead of using another pharmacy.

Vicarious Learning

In vicarious learning, people learn by watching. Marketers most often use this approach to learning when they show the brand being enjoyed by a person or a group of people to whom they assume the target audience can relate. If that person who looks like me, or behaves like me, or has a job like mine, can benefit by using the advertised brand, perhaps I can, too. Vicarious learning, the most subtle of the three learning approaches discussed here, is usually operating at some level in any advertisement that takes a slice-of-life approach, depicting the brand in a realistic setting.

Successful vicarious learning works through identification. The consumer sees something in either the person depicted as using the brand, or the brand use situation, that resonates with his own personal experiences. As a result, there is a feeling of comfort and familiarity. Because the consumer can picture himself in that same situation, he should be more likely to be open to establishing his own relationship with the brand. Clearly, this is a subtle, but powerful, form of learning.

The power of vicarious learning underlies Dove's "Campaign for Real Beauty." This global campaign began in 2004, following results of a survey that showed that very few women regarded themselves as beautiful and that most regarded true beauty as something they could not hope to attain. The ideal of real beauty was the "perfect" models shown in advertising for all sorts of products, but particularly for beauty products. Dove's approach was to begin a series of ads featuring women of varying shapes, sizes and complexions, but all labeled as "beautiful." The campaign has evolved to include educational and self-esteem programs for young girls, supported through the Dove Self-Esteem Fund. Through its efforts associated with the Campaign for Real Beauty, Dove is trying to offer an alternative to the images most often associated with beauty products in the hope of offering a counterbalance to the vicarious learning inspired by those traditional images.[21]

Motivation, perception processes, attitude change, and learning are all internal factors that affect consumer decision making. That is, they are things intrinsic to the individual customer and so can vary greatly from person to person. Consumers are also influenced by a host of external factors. We review some of those next.

ENVIRONMENTAL INFLUENCES

Customers are greatly influenced by the environment in which they live and work. Some environmental influences are so broad and sweeping that they tend to be taken for granted. But these influences affect what symbols are understood by the consumer, what concepts are considered acceptable, and what brands are considered.

Culture

Culture is one such pervasive influence. People's attitudes and opinions are influenced by the values of the culture in which they grew up. We often hear comments, both positive and

Exhibit 3.8   **Accenture Homepage**

negative, about the exporting of American culture. What exactly does the term *American culture* mean? In a political sense, American culture translates to democracy, which might evoke the value of individualism. Other positive values typically associated with American culture include hard work, perseverance, and achievement.

All those values are brought to bear in the campaign for management consulting firm Accenture. Accenture's communications feature champion golfer Tiger Woods out on the course, with the tagline "Go on. Be a Tiger." Woods is known for his individualism, his work ethic, and, of course, his remarkable success. Accenture's Web home page, www.accenture. com, featuring Woods, is shown in Exhibit 3.8.

There are two interesting points to consider about Accenture's campaign. First, while the company is U.S.-based, it operates in markets around the world. So, to the extent that the "Go on. Be a Tiger" message can be said to embody American values, Accenture itself is exporting American culture (more on that below). Second, the choice of Woods' as a spokesperson emphasizes another, growing aspect of both American and international culture, the importance of multiculturalism. As has been widely documented, Woods' father was African-American and his mother was from Thailand; Woods has referred to himself as "Cablinasian," reflecting that he has "a blend of Caucasian, black, Indian and Asian" within his heritage.[22]

Given Accenture's services, its audience is businesspeople, and relatively senior businesspeople at that. Accenture clearly expects—or at least hopes—that the values embodied by Tiger Woods's success will translate across cultures. Certainly, Woods's success has been significant enough that he is recognizable in many countries. Thus, Accenture assumes there will be a local acceptance for his values as well.

American culture also places value on youth: looking young, feeling young. While in some cultures, age is venerated, in the United States the focus tends to be on fighting off age as long as possible, as shown by the messages for most skin care products, Botox cosmetic, and many vitamins, just to name a few. When Danny Ocean, George Clooney's character in *Ocean's 12*, realizes that some of his gang members think he is older than he really is, there is true horror in his voice when he asks, "Do I look like I'm fifty?" For all the talk in magazines targeted at older readers about fifty being the new forty, there is a clear bias toward youth in the U.S. culture. Marketers are easily able to exploit people's fear of looking and feeling their actual age, let alone looking or feeling older than they actually are!

Convenience and the desire for instant gratification are other mainstays of U.S. culture. The emphasis on these goals has led to the rise of instant everything: meals microwavable in minutes, drive-through pharmacies, even faster ATM service. According to JP Morgan Chase, the average time per ATM transaction in the United States is forty-two seconds. If forty-two seconds seems too long to wait for cash, the firm offers its customers a service called Chase QuickChoice that cuts the average time to just twenty-four seconds. To use QuickChoice, customers register on Chase's Web site to establish their ATM withdrawal preferences; their pre-sets are then automatically accessed and applied when they use a Chase ATM.[23] Only in a convenience-driven, time-oriented culture would there be a need to streamline a process that initially takes less than a minute.

There are, of course, also more positive values associated with U.S. culture. The desire to help others, for example, is frequently tapped into by marketers, particularly nonprofit firms attempting to raise funds or other kinds of support for those in need, and by manufacturers who associate their product with charitable causes. An appreciation for nature and an emphasis on family ties are other positive aspects of American culture. All these offer opportunities for marketers to associate their brand with outcomes valued by customers within the culture.

The influence of culture and the variability of cultural values are factors that need to be carefully considered when an organization is making the decision on how to market a brand globally. In some instances, there may be enough similarities across target markets to make a global campaign (appropriately translated) effective. For example, it is not uncommon for airlines that do a great deal of international business and that cater to business travelers to use a global campaign throughout the countries where they fly. British Airways, Qatar Airways, and Korean Airways are among the airlines that have taken a global approach. In other instances, there may be so many fundamental differences in values related to the brand that developing a successful unified campaign will not be possible. This is often the case with food products because both preferred tastes and the experience of preparing and eating food can vary greatly between cultures.

Subcultures

The preceding discussion may imply that the U.S. culture (and, by extension, other cultures) is monolithic. This is not the case. Within the overall culture are many, many subcultures, based on a variety of demographic, psychographic, and socioeconomic characteristics. These subcultures also can offer opportunities for marketers, in terms of both brand development and messages about those brands.

One obvious basis for subcultures is ethnicity or race. Consider the large number of media vehicles (and accompanying advertisements) targeted toward Spanish-speaking Americans and immigrants. The list includes cable television networks, radio stations, newspapers in major cities, and magazines.[24] The Hispanic subculture has received a great deal of attention from marketers thanks in part to statistics; the 2000 U.S. Census indicated that Hispanics were the fastest-growing ethnic group.[25] The group also won marketing attention because of other research that showed that Spanish was the dominant language in many Hispanic households.[26] Thus, for many marketers, the Hispanic subculture represented a promising opportunity: a large group of consumers, comfortable with a different language, worthy of targeting with messages designed specifically for them.

U.S. marketers' experience with the Hispanic subculture has been largely positive.[27] Marketers' experience with another important subculture has been more mixed. For every success story involved in targeting African-American consumers, there seems to have been a misstep. First, black leaders complained, with some merit, when noticeable marketing dollars began to be diverted to Hispanic marketing.[28] Hispanics were suddenly getting the kind of attention that advertising agencies specializing in marketing to African-Americans had been advocating unsuccessfully for years. The notion that the language difference was a valid reason for this attention was regarded by many blacks with skepticism at best, suspicions of racism at worst. The suspicion was compounded by poor judgment on the part of some major marketers. For example, a campaign for Toyota's RAV4 showed a black male consumer with a big grin and a gold outline of a RAV4 on one of his front teeth. The move generated a great deal of negative backlash, leading to both an apology and a new diversity initiative from Toyota.[29]

Another subculture gaining growing attention from U.S. marketers is the gay, lesbian, bisexual, and transgendered (GLBT) group of consumers. Recent studies by OpusComm Group,[30] Harris International,[31] and others have shown that this group has considerable disposable income, always a draw for marketers. The GLBT group is similar to the Hispanic subculture in the sense that a variety of media vehicles are targeted specifically for this group, making it relatively easy to reach them without too much exposure to straight audiences. That may be an important consideration for risk-averse marketers who want to tap into the buying potential of this group but at the same time not offend their straight audience. The Disney Corporation, for example, has faced considerable public relations problems over this issue, including threatened boycotts by members of conservative religious groups.[32]

Psychographic-based subcultures include fans of particular sports (think about the wide range of sports attire and memorabilia available), hobbyists (pay a visit to the scrapbooking area of your local crafts store), and people devoted to spirituality (messages directed at Christians around Easter, for example). One of the intriguing aspects of U.S. culture, and that of a number of other Western nations, is the notion of overall national unity overlying a tolerance for many, many subcultures. Depending on the particular brand being marketed, a subculture appeal may be more powerful, and more appropriate, than a message that taps into the values of the larger culture.

Social Class

The dichotomy in American thought noted above may be most evident when it comes to discussions of social class in America. While the U.S. market does not have the rigid social class distinctions seen in some countries (for instance, there is no clearly identified aristocracy as is found in some European countries), social class, or the perception of social class, clearly plays a role in many persuasive messages. The esteem motive in Maslow's hierarchy is very often expressed in brand campaigns in words and symbols that denote social class distinctions. Many luxury products would not exist were it not for the parallel existence of an upper class in society that not only can afford such things but also places sufficient value upon them to justify their purchase. The "American Dream" embodies the notion of improvement, of making it possible for a family's children to live a better, richer, more prosperous life than the generation before. People cannot aspire unless there is something to aspire to, and that motivation can be quite powerful. The strength of this motivation may partly explain the popularity of reality shows such as *American Idol* that give "average" persons a shot at fame and fortune.

The Claritas company's PRIZM classification system groups consumers into one of sixty-six segments based in large part on socioeconomic characteristics. The names of many of the PRIZM segments have obvious social class connotations: Upper Crust, Blue Blood Estates, Country Squires, Money and Brains. Marketers profile their customer base using the PRIZM system to learn more about their customers and to get ideas on how to develop more persuasive messages to influence them.[33]

Social class is a significant enough element in American society that the *New York Times* devoted an eleven-part series to an examination of the topic in 2005.[34] The *Times* definition of social class includes four factors: education, income, occupation, and wealth.[35] Among the statistics in the series: 0.1 percent of the nation's taxpayers (the very top group) accounted for 8.0 percent of the nation's reported income in 2001, while 19.5 percent of the nation's taxpayers (the very bottom group) accounted for 2.5 percent of the nation's reported income.[36] Exploring social class, and the effects of social class, from a variety of perspectives, the *Times'* series is well worth reading by marketers.

Reference Groups

Reference groups bear some relationship to the notions of subcultures and social class, but they are a more personal, individual form of external influence on behavior rather than an overarching societal influence. Reference groups, as the name might suggest, are any group of people to whom one refers for cues on behavior. Those behavioral cues can include pressures for brand choice, which is why reference groups are an important concept for marketing communicators. There are several types of reference groups.

Aspirational Groups

Aspirational groups are groups to which the consumer does not currently belong, but would like to join. An attorney in a small firm might aspire to belong to a larger, more prestigious firm in town. To put herself in the position to make that move when the opportunity arises, she might shop at the same stores as that firm's partners, attend the same industry conferences, read the same trade journals, eat at the same restaurants—in short, behave like a group member prior to actually joining the group. A similar phenomenon can often be seen with college students as they approach graduation. As the world of work becomes more and more real to them, their behaviors, including brand choice behaviors, begin to change. The soon-to-be graduate might upgrade his wardrobe, purchase a new car, and even change his cell phone ring tone and answering machine message, modeling his behavior after the behavior of people in the group he aspires to join. While much of the direct brand influence of aspirational groups comes from observation, marketers also can tap into it by depicting successful-looking people using the brand or by becoming the "official brand" of whatever membership group exists that might confer a positive association.

Disassociative Groups

Disassociative groups are the opposite of aspirational groups; they are groups the consumer wants nothing to do with. As a result, the consumer will strenuously avoid using products used by members of the undesirable group. Think back to the various cliques in your high school (or at work, if high school memories have faded). What role did brands play in signifying group membership? The key brands may have been related to apparel, music choices, and the like—visible product choices that identified someone as part of a particular group and not part of other groups. For example, the kids in the marching band may have dressed differently than the athletes, who may have dressed differently than the "slacker" kids. As you might suspect, when certain groups cause problems, the marketers whose products are associated with those groups may get negative publicity. For example, many news stories about "Goth" teens after the Columbine, Colorado, school shootings in 1999 mentioned how the teens dressed, giving parents advice as to fashion cues to look for in their children's wardrobe if they had concerns about their children associating with other students with a profile similar to that of the Columbine shooters.[37]

Membership Groups

Membership groups are the formal and informal groups to which a consumer belongs. Formal groups include fraternal organizations, nonprofit organizations, alumni organizations, civic clubs, and the like: groups in which there is an actual recognition of membership. Involved group members behave in certain ways and participate in certain activities, and particular brand choices may well be involved, such as preferred brands' affinity credit cards and the like. Informal groups can be even more powerful; these are groups such as friends and co-workers, people the consumer associates with regularly and who influence brand choice either through overt peer pressure or more subtle word of mouth or modeling. Computer-mediated social networks such as Facebook and MySpace are also examples of membership groups.

A marketer who is seeking to map out the network of ways in which a prospective customer might be reached should always consider reference groups in that exercise. Identifying the various groups to which a person belongs, or aspires to belong, can guide media placement and message construction. Many forays into guerrilla marketing have been designed specifically to tap into the power of reference group influence, especially informal group influence in social settings. In their book *Under the Radar: Talking to Today's Cynical Consumer,* Jonathan Bond and Richard Kirshenbaum describe their agency's efforts to help clients take advantage of guerrilla marketing in social settings, including work done for Hennessey Cognac, which cosponsored bar-based events with *Cigar Aficionado* magazine.[38]

Families and the Family Life Cycle

Families are a very particular, and often very powerful, form of reference group. Unlike most of the other types of reference groups mentioned above, people do not choose to become part of a family; they are born into that group. (Obviously, choice is involved when it comes to marrying into a family, but the influence of the in-law family is generally much less than that of the birth family.) As children grow up and begin to establish their own independence, their brand choices often mirror those they grew up with. New roommates sharing an apartment, for example, may argue over the "right" brand of staples such as peanut butter, toilet paper, or laundry soap, arguments sparked by the fact that the roommates grew up using different brands. Not only is previous brand experience a powerful influence, but also brands in such staple categories may themselves connote "home." In these cases, it may not be too much of a stretch to say that to question someone's brand choice is to question their entire upbringing!

Of course, independence is also often coupled with rebellion, and one very visible way to rebel is to make brand choices, or product category choices, that are at odds with what one's parents did. If the parents have always bought domestic cars, their child's purchase of a car from a foreign manufacturer might be an act of rebellion—perhaps not an overt rebellion (unless the parents work in the domestic car industry), but a subtle rebellion nonetheless. An adult child's choice of brands that are different from those he grew up with may well be a conscious or subconscious declaration of independence from family influence.

The family life cycle concept maps out the stages that families, and people in families, move through over time. The family life cycle is useful both as a guideline for targeting decisions in many product categories and for the insights it offers into motivations and message types most likely to be at play.

While there are many conceptions of the family life cycle, one developed by Mary C. Gilly and Ben M. Enis should be useful in illustrating how this mapping works. The Gilly and Enis family life cycle groups families based on the age of the head of household (under 35, 35 to 64, or older than 64), whether there are one or two adults in the household, and whether there are children in the household. A consumer under the age of 35 would be in either the Bachelor I stage, the Young Couple stage, the Full Nest I or II stage, or the Single Parent I or II stage. A consumer aged 35 to 64 might be in the Bachelor II, Childless Couple, Delayed Full Nest, Full Nest III, or Single Parent III stage. A consumer older than 64 would be in either the Bachelor III or Empty Nest stage. The differences in the nesting and single parent stages have to do with the age of children: youngest child under 6 years old in category I, youngest child 6 or older in category II, and all children older than age 6 in category III.[39]

Obviously, a 28-year-old in the Bachelor I stage has different brand needs and interests than another 28-year-old in the Young Couple stage, and both have different needs than a 28-year-old in the Full Nest I stage. So the family life cycle moves beyond simple age-based demographics to a richer means of looking at how family structure might affect buying behavior.

SUMMING UP

This review of the decision-making process and some of the internal and external factors that influence consumer decision making provides a basic framework for thinking about challenges facing the brand. Marketers cannot build a relationship between the brand and the customer unless they understand that customer's motivations, perceptions, and attitudes and have a sense of the external factors that might influence the customer's decisions. With this framework in place, we turn next to a closer examination of the process of communication, particularly the role of emotion in decision making, which has often been found to be a key ingredient in communication success.

NOTES

1. J.A. Howard, *Consumer Behavior: Application of Theory* (New York: McGraw-Hill, 1977).

2. R. Briggs and G. Stuart, *What Sticks: Why Most Advertising Fails and How to Guarantee Yours Succeeds* (Chicago: Kaplan, 2006).

3. A.H. Maslow, *Motivation and Personality*, 2nd ed. (New York: Harper & Row, 1970).

4. J.P. Peter and J.C. Olson, *Consumer Behavior and Marketing Strategy*, 3rd ed. (Homewood, IL: Irwin, 1993), p. 68.

5. Paper presented at ESOMAR WAM Conference, Geneva, June 2004.

6. Breast Cancer Research Foundation, "Our Corporate Partners and Corporate Donors," www.brcfcure. org/partners.html.

7. E. Peterson, "Anatomy of a Better Burger: Eric Peterson Analyzes the Elements That Add Up to Hardee's Bigger Burgers," *Chain Leader* (August 2005): 41.

8. M. Del Franco, "Redesigns: Hormel Spices Up Its Spam," *Multichannel Merchant* (March 2000).

9. *National Provisioner*, "Lunchmeat Manufacturers on the Attack to Regain Market Slippage," August 1999, p. 80.

10. Nobelprize.org, Educational Games, Nobel Prize in Medicine, "Pavlov's Dog," http://nobelprize.org/ educational_games/medicine/pavlov/.

11. J.P. Jones, *When Ads Work: New Proof That Advertising Triggers Sales* (New York: Simon & Schuster, 1995).

12. H.E. Krugman, "Why Three Exposures May Be Enough," *Journal of Advertising Research* 12, no. 6 (1972): 11–14.

13. R.S. Johnson, "The Jordan Effect," *Fortune*, June 22, 1998, pp. 124–138.

14. J. Halliday, "Chrysler Forms Task Force After Flubbed Pacifica Launch," *Advertising Age*, November 24, 2003.

15. R. Morgan, "The Michael Jackson Explosion: Will Pepsi Be Able to Beat It?" *Adweek*, February 6, 1984.

16. S. Battaglio, "Pepsi Didn't Pull Madonna—It's Giving Her a Breather," *Adweek*, March 13, 1989.

17. L. Clarke, "NASCAR Is Shifting Gears: Younger, More Polished Drivers in Vogue as Sport Seeks to Remake Its Image and Satisfy Sponsors," *Washington Post*, June 9, 2001.

18. R. Thomaselli, "Caution Flag Flies for NASCAR as Ratings Slip," *Advertising Age*, November 27, 2006.

19. Jimmie Johnson Sponsor List on Lowe's Team Racing, www.lowesracing.com/jimmie/sponsors.

20. A. Scott, "Goal Tending," *Promo*, April 1, 2006.

21. Dove, "Campaign for Real Beauty Mission," www.dove.us/#/CFRB/arti_cfrb.aspx[cp-documentid=7049726]/.

22. "Woods Stars on Oprah, Says He's 'Cablinasian,'" *Lubbock Avalanche-Journal*, April 23, 1997, www.lubbockonline.com/news/042397/woods.htm.

23. B. Capps, "Chase Seeks Competitive Edge in Speedy ATM Transactions," *Advertising Age*, November 20, 2006.

24. S. Yin, "Look Who's Tuned In," *American Demographics* (October 2002): 9.

25. E. Cose, "Our New Look: The Colors of Race," *Newsweek*, January 1, 2000, p. 28.

26. *Broker* magazine, "Hispanic Americans: A Potent Market Force," December 1, 2002, p. 6.

27. K. MacArthur, "Fanta: Stuart Kronauge," *Advertising Age*, November 13, 2006, p. S-3; J. Neff, "Wal-Mart Retools Stores With Hispanics in Mind," *Advertising Age*, October 2, 2006, p. 43.

28. C. Hayes, "Crossing the Color Line," *Black Enterprise*, June 2002, p. 199.

29. *Adweek*, "The Lowest Moments in Advertising: The Most Offensive, Most Tasteless, and Downright Dumbest Ads of the Last Decade," June 9, 2003.

30. W. Buchanan, "More Same-Sex Couples Want Kids; Survey Looks at Trends Among Homosexuals," *San Francisco Chronicle*, April 25, 2006.

31. E. Iwata, "More Marketing Aimed at Gay Consumers; Companies Covet Their Buying Power," *USA Today*, November 2, 2006.

32. Ibid.

33. Claritas.com, "PRIZM® NE: The New Evolution in Segmentation," www.claritas.com/claritas/Default.jsp?ci=3&si=4&pn=prizmne.

34. The entire series, "Class Matters: A Special Section," www.nytimes.com/indexes/2005/05/15/national/class/.

35. *New York Times*, "How Class Works," May 15, 2005, www.nytimes.com/indexes/2005/05/15/national/class/.

36. *New York Times*, "The Wealthiest Benefit More From the Recent Tax Cuts," June 5, 2005, www.nytimes.com/indexes/2005/05/15/national/class/.

37. K. Flynn, "Black Trench Coats Not Necessarily Tied to Cults, but to Social Isolation," *Rocky Mountain News*, April 21, 1999.

38. J. Bond and R. Kirshenbaum, *Under the Radar: Talking to Today's Cynical Consumer* (New York: Wiley, 1998).

39. M.C. Gilly and B.M. Enis, "Recycling the Family Life Cycle: A Proposal for Redefinition," in *Advances in Consumer Research*, ed. A.A. Mitchell, 271–276 (Ann Arbor, MI: Association for Consumer Research, 1982).

CHAPTER 4

How Customers Think

The *Encarta World English Dictionary* defines "relationship" as "the connection between two or more people or groups and their involvement with each other, especially as regards how they behave and feel toward each other and communicate or cooperate."[1] Our concern here is with creating and sustaining relationships between customers, companies, and brands. To do that successfully, marketers need a basic understanding of how customers think. How do people acquire, manage, and react to information on brands and brand usage situations? How can marketers create and manage the connection between their brand and their various customer groups?

In this chapter, we review recent research from several observers of customer behavior, as well as some older models designed to map out customer responses. This collection of resources should provide some indication of how customers think when they go to market and how a marketing organization might influence or at least understand their thought processes enough to create and sustain a strong relationship between the customer, the firm, and the brand.

One very important point to consider is whether the targeted customer actually wants a relationship with the brand. Clearly, few, if any, customers are interested in establishing or maintaining a relationship with every brand that they use; in some cases, there may be customers who are not interested in maintaining relationships with any brand at all. Every day people receive hundreds of brand offers through the multitude of communication channels they use or to which they are exposed. Credit card offers, magazine subscriptions, Web-based service offers, special events, sponsored activities and on and on . . . all seeking to catch attention and establish a relationship between the customer and the brand. The majority of those offers are either ignored completely (emails deleted without being opened, envelopes or flyers thrown in the trash) or given only cursory attention before being discarded. Most of these offers were presumably directed to their recipients because something about those customers' demographics, past behavior, or media use suggested to the marketer that they might indeed have an interest in the product or the brand value proposition being offered. If that is the case, how many less targeted, mass media messages fall far short of the desired effect of initiating a relationship?

The marketer's goal is always to create and sustain a relationship, sometimes for the short term, but hopefully for the long term as well. The customer's goal is commonly not the same. Customers generally have many options to satisfy their needs and wants. Building a relationship with a particular marketer's brand, with all the energy that entails, may not be the most appealing option based on the particular customer's interests, past experiences, and

Exhibit 4.1 **Multiheaded Model**

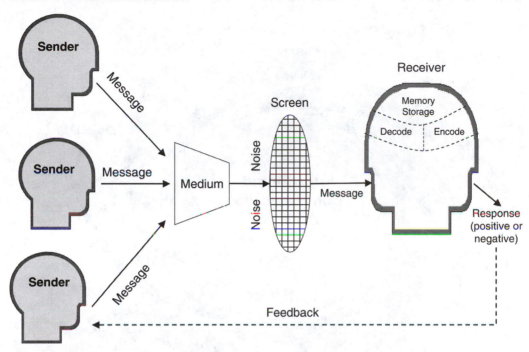

Source: Adapted from D.E. Schultz and S.I. Tannenbaum, *Essentials of Advertising Strategy*, 2nd ed. (Lincolnwood, IL: NTC Business Books, 1989), p. 32.

specific motivators. Marketers cannot hope to influence the decision process if they do not first understand the steps customers use in making brand decisions. That means how brand information is taken in, assessed, and applied.

THE COMMUNICATION MODEL

In the basic model of communication first discussed in Chapter 1, Exhibit 1.4, a sender sends a message to a receiver, assuming minimal interference (noise). The sender hopes to get feedback from the receiver, ideally positive feedback. The overlapping circles in Exhibit 1.4 labeled "field of experience" are crucial to communication success. A field of experience is the background both the sender and receiver bring to the communication interface. In order for effective communication to occur, there has to be some shared field of experience between the two parties. The influences on consumer decision making described in Chapter 3 are among the factors that contribute to the receiver's field of experience, meaning that the more the planner knows about the customers, the more likely an effective message can be crafted.

The process gets somewhat more complicated when we switch from interpersonal communication to marketing communication. As shown in Exhibit 4.1, suddenly there are multiple senders, a medium that carries the message, and the receiver's perceptual screen through which the message must pass. Note that different senders are all competing for the receiver's attention, as is the surrounding matter associated with the medium itself (news stories, en-

Exhibit 4.2   **Customer View of Brand Communication**

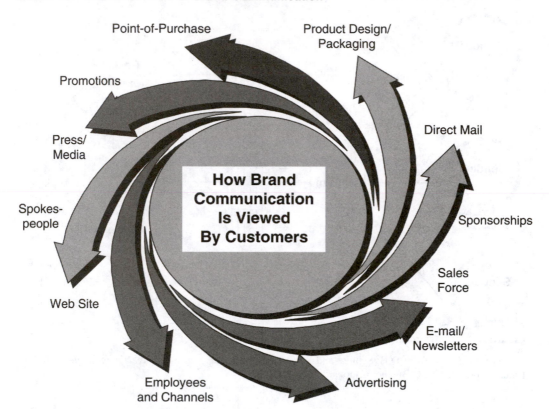

tertainment content, traffic in the case of a billboard, and the like). For the communication to be effective, the receiver has to somehow sort through all this.

These concepts, methodologies, and approaches made a great deal of sense in the traditional, outbound marketplace of the 1980s and 1990s. As we illustrated in Chapter 1, however, consumers, in many cases, now have control of the marketplace. Given the new technology forms, consumers can control when, where, and in what way they want to either accept or access information from the brand marketer. In the customer-controlled marketplace, reproduced in Exhibit 4.2, consumers have a multitude of resources, channels, and facilities to acquire information or material about the product, service, or brand, and all those resources compete for the consumer's attention. How does that process work?

Information Processing

Information about the brand comes from the marketer (the sender) in any combination of messages and incentives sent through a range of persuasive communication forms, from the customer's own use of the brand, or from other external sources such as media articles or comments of friends and family members and even formalized social networks. If the information gets through the customer's perceptual filters (gets noticed, gets paid attention to), it goes into short-term memory. If the information is considered important enough (relevant to the customer's current or potential needs, interesting, appropriate for that person's income level, etc.), it moves into long-term memory. Then, the information can be pulled back out of memory when the time comes to make a brand decision. This stored information is what makes up much of the mental network: that is, the schema, for the brand. The process, as we describe it, sounds relatively simple, but it is actually quite complicated. There are potential problems at every step along the way that can keep the message from being seen or heard, keep the information from being interpreted in the way the marketer wants it to be, keep it from being remembered, and keep it from being accessible at decision-making time.

People working in the media and media planning area, whatever the form of persuasive communication being used, spend tremendous amounts of time trying to determine the right place to put the message or the right way to deliver the incentive so that it reaches the desired audience at a time when the intended receiver will be receptive. This part of the brand communication process is discussed extensively later in this text. For now, we will just note that message delivery must be effective before any consideration can be given to how consumers might react to the message.

Previously, we argued that the most critical ingredient in successful communication is the proper identification of the right audience followed by the question of delivery. Our premise is that if the right audience is not selected initially and if some method of getting messages or incentives to that audience is not clearly identified, it makes little difference how powerful the creative product is or how strong the brand value proposition. Reaching and touching customers and prospects are the two key issues in the twenty-first–century marketplace.

Assuming that the media people have done their job and the message reaches the desired consumer, can anything go wrong now? If the strategists and database analysts did not choose the appropriate value proposition, the message will not be relevant and the audience will not give it any attention. Even if the value proposition is right, there may be other competitors for attention at the time the message is being delivered. The opportunity for any particular message to get through the consumer's perceptual screen increases with product and message relevance. Thus, the message's vitality becomes critical.

The Elaboration Likelihood Model

Many models of communications effectiveness assume that the consumer is paying close attention to the message. Such purposeful communication involves consideration of the message and the arguments being made in support of the brand. But we know that careful attention to persuasive marketing messages is not the norm. Petty and Cacioppo's elaboration likelihood model (ELM) maps out what happens under both the purposeful and lower-attention scenarios[2] (Exhibit 4.3). The left-hand column in the model shows what Petty and Cacioppo term the central route to persuasion. This is purposeful communication, where the message recipient has both the motivation and the ability to carefully process the message. If successful, this type of communication can lead to long-term, sustained attitudinal change and can ultimately influence behavior. The right-hand column shows peripheral processing. This is what happens when the consumer's interest is low or other factors affect the ability to process the message. Here, cues other than the message itself take over. While this type of processing can cause attitude change, such change is relatively short-lived and unlikely to affect the behavior of the person in the long run.

Consider the Rayovac batteries sales promotion tie-in to the movie "Wall-E" shown in Exhibit 4.4. A consumer who regularly purchases Rayovac batteries would probably view this piece

Exhibit 4.3   Elaboration Likelihood Model

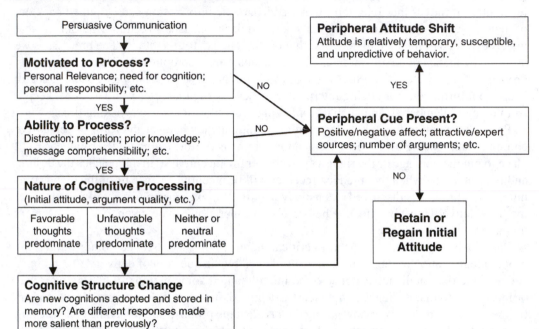

Source: R.E. Petty and J.T. Cacioppo, *Communication and Persuasion: Central and Peripheral Routes to Attitude Change* (New York: Springer, 1986).

following the guidelines for central processing. The free "Wall-E" rolling toy offer would be an inducement to buy Rayovac, but probably secondary to the satisfaction the customer would receive from the previous product usage. Other consumers considering this offer might need to buy batteries on their next shopping trip, are not particularly brand loyal, and are looking for an incentive to help make a brand choice. For those shoppers, the incentive of receiving the toy (for them or a child in their household) would be the primary motivation under peripheral processing. It is also easy to imagine other consumers seeing this piece who are not Rayovac users and do not have an immediate need for batteries, but who are fans of the movie. For them, the presence of the Wall-E character could prompt purchase of Rayovac batteries. In each of the latter cases, the likelihood is a one-time purchase, not long-term commitment to the brand.

Long-Term Memory

Consumers are often exposed to marketing messages at times when they are not actively seeking information or not in a situation where they need to make brand decisions. In those

Exhibit 4.4   **Rayovac Wall-E Tie-in Offer**

instances, movement of information into long-term memory is particularly important. Writing in *The Advertised Mind: Ground-Breaking Insights Into How Our Brains Respond to Advertising*, Erik Du Plessis, a marketing researcher, provides a psychology-based model of the brain (Exhibit 4.5). Some of this should look familiar from our earlier discussion. The model shows both the short-and long-term aspects of memory, as well as some intermediary factors. The "central executive" is the guiding force that makes sense of the entire process. The "filing and retrieval system" is the organizing system for storage of the many, many inputs the brain receives. The "supervisory attentioning system" is a sort of scanner that filters through all the possible inputs in the customer's environment and selects for attention those that are relevant to that customer.[3] For information to move from short-term memory into long-term memory, it must get past the central executive and the supervisory attentioning system. To do that, it must spark the positive emotional response needed to get attention and then be relevant in some way so as to qualify not only for attention, but also for interpretation. Information that makes the cut is filed into long-term memory, there to be retrieved back into short-term memory when needed.

THE MIND OF THE MARKET

Gerald Zaltman's *How Customers Think: Essential Insights Into the Mind of the Market* emphasizes the critical role of the unconscious. This is not a rehashing of subliminal advertising; instead, professor and marketing executive Zaltman makes a thoughtful argument that the majority of influences on consumer behavior take place at an unconscious level. He defines "the mind of the market" as the interaction between decisions made consciously and unconsciously by marketing managers and the consumers they seek to influence. In other words, he argues that much marketing communication value is co-created by interactions between the marketer and the customer.

Zaltman's discussion refutes six marketing truisms about how customers take in and think about information that have come from traditional methods of market research. He argues that consumers do not "think in a well-reasoned or rational, linear way"; that they cannot "readily explain their thinking and behavior";[4] that it is not practical to look at the mind, brain, body, and social effects as separate elements in influencing consumer decision making; that consumers' memories are faulty and cannot be relied on to explain past decisions; that

Exhibit 4.5   **Du Plessis Model**

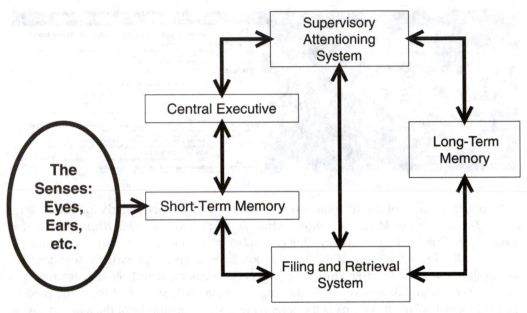

Source: Adapted from Du Plessis, *The Advertised Mind: Ground-Breaking Insights Into How Our Brains Respond to Advertising* (London: Kogan Page, 2005).

consumers do not think only in words, as most traditional marketing research assumes; and that consumers will more often than not interpret marketing messages differently than the message creator intended. These six points provide a framework both for considering how people think and also for identifying appropriate research methodologies to guide relationship development. We will explore the latter area in more detail in Chapter 6, but for now we look more closely at Zaltman's ideas on the role of the unconscious and the mind-brain-body-society relationship.

The Unconscious

Zaltman draws on research from many areas in making the case that "at least 95 percent of all cognition occurs below awareness, in the shadows of the mind while, at most, only 5 percent occurs in high-order consciousness."[5] Cognition is the process of creating knowledge, building from perceptions and received information. It is not enough simply to know that something exists; it is also important to make some judgment about the thing, which means that some beliefs or connections have been established in the mind. So, Zaltman's argument is that people are not truly aware of how they come to know what they know; only a small part of the activity of creating knowledge comes through making connections happen in a perceptible, noticeable way. There are processes going on in the unconscious all the time; people simply do not become aware of them until something happens to require application of that information. This argument helps to explain seemingly impulsive behavior, the ability to make quick decisions in a crisis, and also why, in a market research situation, consumers can claim with all good intentions that they will probably buy the product being studied when it goes on sale in the local store, but never follow through and actually make that purchase.

The concept of simultaneous media consumption mentioned in Chapter 3 is also relevant here. This concept simply means that some people have the capability of processing incoming information in parallel; that is, they can focus on one activity or event while still monitoring what is going on around them. For example, many teenagers can be online with their computer with the radio blaring away while they are flipping through a magazine and talking on a cell phone. They are processing all these activities and events at the same time. Some are in the foreground, while others are in the background, but the teens have trained themselves to shift back and forth between several activities at the same time. Another example is a business executive's continuous monitoring of a Blackberry or other mobile device while sitting in an important meeting.[6] Some researchers have called this phenomenon "continuous partial attention," which seems to describe what increasingly is happening in the lives of many consumers. This capability to simultaneously process various types of media messaging and content has a major impact on how media planning must be developed in the future, as we will see in later chapters.

The unconscious is the storage area for past experiences and the learning that has come with them. Memories of past experiences are "engrams." Zaltman describes an engram as an "electrochemical etching,"[7] a characterization that evokes an interesting mental picture. Imagine your brain cells overwritten with millions of these etchings; the longer you have been alive and the more experiences you have had, the greater the number and variety of etchings. Practically (and scientifically), you cannot be aware of all these etchings all the time. Many are stored in your long-term memory and can be used later to make decisions; others never make it past short-term memory and are lost to you. One very important, but very difficult task in market research is to discover what etchings consumers have related to the brand and to the company that provides it.

The engrams in long-term memory that can be called up easily are known as explicit memories. Zaltman cites research that suggests that, while explicit memories are important, implicit memories are even more powerful in guiding decisions. Implicit memories are engrams that are housed in the unconscious. The influence of implicit memories can be sparked by cues such as visuals, words, odors, anything that triggers a memory of a past experience.

A radio campaign for Finesse hair care products uses this idea. As a recognizable snippet from an old song plays, the voice-over announcer makes the connection between the music of that particular era and the hairstyles that were popular then. The songs change from commercial to commercial to fit with the particular era being discussed. To the extent that the music evokes memories of where consumers were at that time, how they looked, and how their hair looked, the campaign seeks to spark positive memories. The overall message is that Finesse products (a brand that was introduced in 1982) served consumers' needs well then and still can today.

Most messages are not as overt in their ties to past memories. Instead, marketers choose images, colors, music, and words they hope will resonate with their intended audience and tap into existing positive memories. For example, the mountain camping visual in the Suzuki Grand Vitara ad (Exhibit 4.6) may spark memories of a similar mountain camping trip, a mountain vacation that did not involve camping, a camping trip to a different locale, or family vacations in general. The image is specific enough to add meaning to the text in the copy, but general enough to connect to a range of consumers.

Exhibit 4.6   **Suzuki Grand Vitara**

Malcolm Gladwell has written two books that explore concepts related to the research cited by Zaltman. In *The Tipping Point*, Gladwell describes the concept of "social epidemics," that is when small changes, often barely noticeable as they occur, suddenly spark major changes or shifts in marketplace trends. Ideas, concepts, perceptions build up imperceptibly until they reach "the tipping point," where either their relative mental weight pushes a person (or people) into action or some other element or spark sets off the action.[8] The concept of social epidemics helps to explain how brand and music crazes catch on, when a brand tried by just a few people seemingly becomes an overnight phenomenon.

Consider the case of Webkinz. Webkinz are stuffed animals, manufactured by Ganz, that come with a code number. The Webkinz recipient (often a preteen child) logs onto the Webkinz Web site, enters the code, and acquires a virtual pet to care for online that looks just like the stuffed animal. In the online Webkinz world, the child can earn points to use to buy the virtual Webkinz a house, furniture, clothing, food, and many other items.[9]

The Webkinz product line was introduced in 2005, and Ganz had sold 1 million of the stuffed animals by 2006, with demand so high that many stores had multiple back orders for the toys. At some point after their introduction, kids' word of mouth spread and the Webkinz became a very hot commodity. In some places, children were so engrossed in the toys that Webkinz were banned from schools.[10] Webkinz offered a way for tweens to participate more fully in the online world they saw their older siblings and parents frequenting, and the combination of that draw and the cute appeal of the tangible stuffed animal may have been what pushed Webkinz over the tipping point.

In *Blink: The Power of Thinking Without Thinking*, Gladwell describes the process that the mind goes through in reaching an almost instant conclusion about new people, places, and situations. He argues that the brain sorts through the available information very, very quickly and makes what he claims are very important, often very accurate, decisions.[11] The strength of those decisions and inferences made "in the blink of an eye" may lie in their not being over thought, but instead in a simplifying and cutting through extraneous material to get to the heart of the information needed to make the quick inference.

Mind-Brain-Body-Society

Zaltman argues that "culture and biology go hand-in-hand."[12] Social norms influence how the brain processes and stores information, particularly which engrams make it into long-term memory and what other engrams they get connected to there. These social norms, which include many of the cultural elements discussed in Chapter 3, influence the outcome of the types of quick decisions Gladwell discusses in *Blink*.

Consider the Evian ad in Exhibit 4.7. This message was used in a variety of media formats in London around the winter holidays. The message, "Detox with Evian," made little sense to a group of American students on a study-abroad trip. In fact, they initially assumed that the bottle depicted in the ad was a wine or champagne bottle; only on closer inspection did they realize that it was bottled water. In the United States, the word *detox* is associated with a rigorous, supervised purging of illicit drugs from the body and has no association with bottled water. But *detox* has a much broader meaning in England, where it connotes adopting a healthier lifestyle. The Evian messages were intended to reach people who had overdone their holiday drinking and were thinking about a New Year's resolution to cut back. In that context, bottled water made perfect sense, and the use of the Evian bottle in a setting that might normally show a wine or liquor bottle became understandable. Once the context was explained, the American students' brains could easily make the intended connections. Without that social context, however, the ad made no sense.

THE FILING SYSTEM

How, exactly, is all this information stored? Erik Du Plessis draws on biological research to present a fairly detailed discussion of the physical construction of the brain, particularly neuronal systems, the connections between individual brain cells (neurons). Engrams, a person's memories, are stored "in the sensitivities between the neurons."[13] Connections, called synapses, build up between particular neurons over time, linking them together. The more often two or more neurons have been linked in the past, the more likely they will link again

Exhibit 4.7 **Evian**

in the future. Those linkages form the customer's impressions and memories; as Du Plessis notes, the assorted linkages lead to "the Gestalt effect: the whole is more than the sum of the initial components."[14]

Think about that assertion as you look at the Women's Voices ad in Exhibit 4.8. Women's Voices is an advocacy group organized to increase voting by single women. First, just look at the visual. What is going on? Why are all those women gathered together? It is a diverse group, at least in appearance. What might the various women have in common? Then read the headline. Does that affect your interpretation of the picture? The reader's reaction to both the photograph and the information in the ad is likely to be very different depending on the reader's own gender and past voting experience. A single woman eligible to vote in a national election for the first time might find the ad much more interesting, and empowering, than a married, middle-aged man who has voted in the last several national elections.

There are certainly several interpretations and reactions possible. But, the way you, the reader, summarized the elements in this ad has to do with the neuronal systems in your brain. Different interpretations are possible because different people have different memories and experiences that activate different connections between their neurons. What those differences might be is a challenge for the brand communication planner.

Marketers are far less interested in differences in interpretation than in similarities. They have to be, unless all messages are going to be customized for the individual consumer, and

Exhibit 4.8 **Women's Voices**

This year, we're voting.

Too often, women decide not to vote.

We're busy. And sometimes, we think we don't have enough information.

But this year, there's too much going on to sit back and let somebody else decide what's best for you and your future.

Whether it's Iraq, your health care or your job — think about what's important to you.

Then talk to your friends, your family. And if you need more information, look online at www.OntheIssues.org to find out which candidate is right for you.

Make a Choice. Make a Difference. Vote!

Paid for by Women's Voices. Women Vote. Online at www.WWWV.org
OnTheIssues.org ©2006 The Speakout Foundation

**Women's Voices.
Women Vote.**

Source: Women's Voices, www.wvwv.org/assets/2007/10/24/wvwv2_2_.pdf.

that is generally not cost-effective, certainly not for widely used products which have a broad base of users and prospects. Zaltman discusses this need using the framework of "networks of abstract understanding that constitute part of our mental imagery."[15] When multiple consumers share similar networks of understanding, "consensus maps" emerge. A consensus map is a schema shared by groups of consumers who are homogeneous in some way.

Neuronal systems, consensus maps, and schemas are all ways of considering how consumer thinking takes place. The key element in each case is connections—what is linked to what else in the brain. Linkages of largely positive elements spark positive emotions, which should create sustainable relationships between the customer and the brand. The job of the marketing communication professional is to learn what linkages exist and how they are associated with the brand. The marketer can then work to enhance the positive linkages and minimize the negative ones. The goal, of course, is to create, build, and foster the relationship between the brand and the consumer.

For example, one of the biggest brand success stories in recent years has been Apple Computer's introduction of the iPod. As of April 2007, Apple had sold over 100 million iPods; the iTunes online store's sales to consumers of song downloads reached 5 billion songs in June 2008.[16] Apple did not invent portable music—remember the Sony Walkman (among others)? But Apple took the technology, put it into a package that was wildly attractive to consumers, and then promoted it so effectively that the company was in first place on *Business Week*'s list of the best performers in 2006, and its advertising agency, TBWA\Chiat\Day, was named both *Adweek*'s U.S. Agency of the Year and *Advertising Age*'s Global Agency Network of the Year (for parent TBWA Worldwide) in 2005.[17]

What was it about iPod that made it so appealing to so many people, many of whom paid several hundred dollars for the product? (The iPod Shuffle, which holds "only" 240 songs, sells for under $100, but the rest of the iPod family costs over $100.)[18] In terms of the decision-making process outlined in Chapter 3, iPod probably required limited decision making for most buyers, who were already music fans, familiar with the available options for listening to music on the go. For these consumers, the introduction of iPod sparked real problem recognition. It was not so much that the current choices were bad, but iPod was clearly so much better. It was smaller, sleeker, easier to use, and it looked really, really good. An early review hailed the "care and concentration" Apple had put into the iPod design, describing it as near "perfection."[19] The look of iPod, its visible difference from the other choices available, caused an emotional reaction—that all-important first step toward success. The appeal was so strong that many people quickly made the decision to get an iPod, applying the snap decision-making process described by Gladwell in *Blink*.

Once the word about iPod started to get out, people who were intrigued with the product could easily perform an external information search. The product was reviewed in countless magazines and on many Web sites, including Apple's own site. As for internal search, while part of that was a review of other options for portable music, it is very likely that for many consumers, the synapses and engrams associated with Apple in general were quickly activated. While Apple's computer products tend to consistently generate only a low market share, Apple's cool quotient has far outpaced sales. For consumers old enough to remember the heady days in 1984 when Macintosh was introduced with Super Bowl ads that are still used as shining examples of creativity, iPod was "cool Apple" all over again. (While iPod may be thought of as a young person's product, it also has a following among the younger range of the baby boomers, who well remember the Macintosh "1984" ad and its successors and who can relate to Apple's cofounder and president, Steve Jobs.) The cool factor also tapped into the social needs level of Maslow's hierarchy—owning an iPod also makes the user cool. And owning a really high-end iPod might even nudge the customer into the esteem level of the motivation hierarchy.

As for alternative evaluation, as noted earlier, iPod was clearly better than its competition on many attributes. While price was a sticking point for some would-be buyers, it was really the only initial concern. For most people, iPod was the clear winner in any comparison, and there was very little dissonance after purchase. Apple's goodwill with customers held up even when many of the company's computers were affected by a problem with bad batteries, manufactured by Sony, that were subject to overheating and even catching on fire. While the situation was a public relations and manufacturing blow for Sony, Apple itself emerged relatively untouched.[20] Apple's relationship with its iPod customers allowed the company to overcome the battery problem with a minimum of difficulty.

Pretty quickly, it seemed as though iPods were everywhere. Apple and other companies developed iPod accessories; Apple introduced line extensions with the iPod Shuffle, the iPod Nano, even a U2 iPod that focused on that band's music, which had been featured in early iPod advertising. iPod sales grew by 469 percent between 2003 and 2004 and by 213 percent between 2004 and 2005; growth for 2006 was estimated to be "only" 60 percent.[21] By 2008, sales growth had slowed further, to only 1 percent growth during the first three months of that year[22]; but as noted above, the total number of iPods sold to consumers continued to generate robust sales for Apple's iTunes. (It is important to note that many marketers are happy if they can hold sales constant, let alone grow.)

The magnitude of iPod's success suggests that something was at work beyond just a high-quality, technologically advanced product. For all the rational arguments in favor of buying an iPod, there are many more, and stronger, emotional arguments, and those are the likely explanation for the incredible sales of the brand. The schema in Exhibit 4.9 shows possible associations a customer might have with iPod and Apple. While some of those associations concern physical features of the product (and a few are negative), many more are emotional connections. For many iPod users, owning an iPod means they are on the cutting edge, they are independent, they are cool, and they are in control. How can other companies hope to compete effectively against that promise, even with a similar product?

Apple is not the only company benefiting from the creation of emotionally charged customer-brand relationships. Motorcycle riders love their Harley-Davidson bikes so much that they dress in branded attire and tattoo the brand's logo on their bodies.[23] Starbucks customers will go out of their way to get that chain's coffee and other products. We could easily compile a long list of brands that have created strong attachments with their customers. Actually, this list is published. New York-based marketing consultancy Brand Keys annually develops recognition of these loyalty-based products and services. In association with *Brandweek* magazine, a "Brandweek Customer Loyalty Awards Powered by Brand Keys" is published annually. The list ranks brands in different product categories based on how satisfied customers are with the brand and how close it comes to their ideal product for that category. (We should note here that the 2006 listing does not include the motorcycle, chocolate, or automotive categories, but it does provide brand rankings in thirty-four categories, including coffee and wireless phone service.)[24]

The work of Brand Keys, like the research discussed by Gladwell, Zaltman, and Du Plessis,

Exhibit 4.9   **iPod Schema**

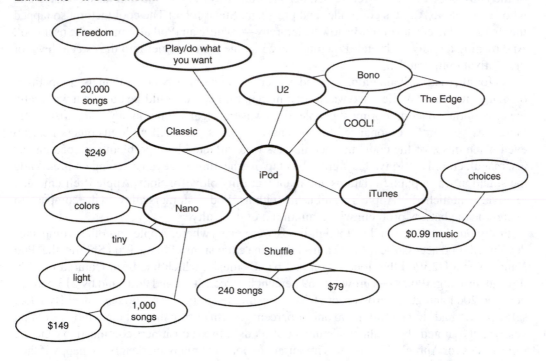

relies heavily on emotional cues and tapping into consumers' unconscious thoughts. Robert Passikoff, Brand Keys founder and president, writes that "consumer engagement, decision-making, and loyalty are principally emotionally driven."[25] Passikoff ties the importance of emotion in part to the lack of true differentiation among most brands in most categories. With few rational differences, emotionally based differences become the driving factor in brand attitudes and brand choice.

BIOLOGY AND EMOTION

In *The Advertised Mind*, Du Plessis argues for the primacy of emotion in decision making. As he puts it, "Emotion feeds into, shapes and controls our conscious thought."[26] Du Plessis's book offers a compelling explanation of why it is so important for consumers to like ads—that is, to experience a positive emotional response to them. Many advertising research studies have found that liking the ad predicts brand preferences, purchase intentions, and actual purchase, but De Plessis goes beyond that basic finding to explain why a positive emotional response is important.

Du Plessis reviews research and thinking from a variety of fields to build the case for the primacy of emotion. In his words, "*Advertising does not first get attention, and then create an emotion. Advertising creates an emotion, which results in attention.*"[27] Why? Because emotion is instinctual, not a learned behavior. The instinctual reaction always occurs first; it is how human brains are wired. Another reason we suggest is that delivery, not content, is key in today's marketplace.

People are not able to react without regard to emotion, even in situations that would seem to call for strictly rational decision making. Du Plessis, like Zaltman, writes about the important role of the unconscious, where the instinct of emotional reaction occurs: "Emotion not only shapes our unconscious reactions; it also feeds into, shapes and controls our conscious thought about brands, products and services." That is because, unless the communication message sparks an emotional response, it will not be noticed. Messages that are not noticed cannot be remembered, and messages that are not remembered cannot influence conscious behavior. So establishing an emotional response is the critical first step in the process of influencing conscious thought. However, just any emotional response will not do. Du Plessis is quick to point out that the communications message needs to generate a positive emotional response: "We are all programmed to seek out the positive, and shun the negative."[28] Advertisements that confuse, irritate, embarrass, or anger the consumer will not be effective in creating long-term positive behavior. Although Du Plessis's focus is on advertising, his findings are likely to apply to all forms of brand communication.

MORE ON MOTIVATION

Motivation researchers have also focused on the importance of emotion. While the Maslow model discussed in Chapter 3 is widely used, Maddock and Fulton posit a different motivational hierarchy that may be useful when thinking about the role of emotional responses related to particular brand choices.[29] They argue that emotional appeals based on basic motivations are a key element of successful advertising because of the need to appeal to the right side of the brain, where both emotional responses and long-term memory are contained.

Maddock and Fulton's motivational framework is far more elaborate than Maslow's basic model. Their hierarchy, shown in Exhibit 4.10, includes eleven levels derived from five groups of motives. The groups are orientation motives, survival motives, and then individual motives related to adaptation, expectation, and play. Orientation motives have to do with being oriented to and working within one's surroundings. The importance of orientation has been shown in studies of people who have undergone lobotomies; they often lose their sense of place and time, and they have trouble interacting with others.[30] Survival motives have to do with overcoming challenges. According to Maddock and Fulton, survival motives are quite strong, although generally not consciously perceived by consumers. Interestingly, the survival motives include the first two levels in Maslow's hierarchy, physiological needs and safety needs, underscoring their fundamental importance.

The individual motive of adaptation is about fitting in with the surrounding world. It has some similarities to the social needs level in the Maslow hierarchy, but covers a much wider range of elements involving people's need to feel at home where they live and work and in their interactions with others. Expectation deals with hopes for the future, how a person's life and work will turn out over time. Lastly, play has to do with enjoyment and release of tension, getting the most out of life.[31]

Maddock and Fulton's motivational hierarchy orders the eleven levels from weakest to strongest effects. The weakest motivation in their scheme is orientation to circumstances, the influence of the situation in which consumers find themselves. Consumers seek to minimize the effects of their circumstances in order to ease pressures. Many communication messages, particularly those for pharmaceutical products, show the product as a means to help the customer overcome unwanted circumstances, a way of reasserting control.

Exhibit 4.10 **Maddock and Fulton's Hierarchy of Motives**

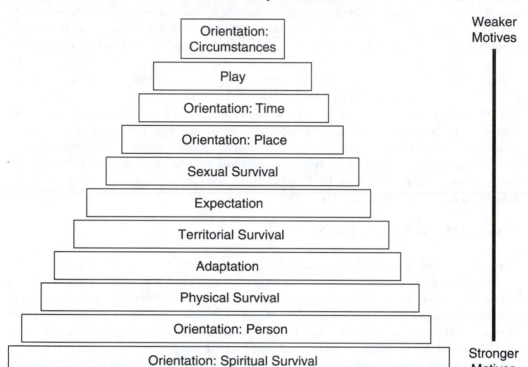

Source: Adapted from R.C. Maddock and R.L. Fulton, *Marketing to the Mind: Right Brain Strategies for Advertising and Marketing* (Westport, CT: Quorum, 1996).

The next level in Maddock and Fulton's hierarchy is the play motivation. A wide variety of leisure-themed brands focus on the enjoyment that product usage can bring to the customer, as in the Jeep Grand Vitara ad shown earlier. Play is followed by orientation to time, which can be forward-looking but is more often focused on looking back fondly to simpler times. Nestlé has developed a Web site for its Nestlé Crunch Candy Bar at http://forthekidinyou.com. It incorporates elements of both the play and orientation to time motivations by encouraging adult consumers to view the brand as a way to recapture some of the fun of childhood.

Maddock and Fulton identify orientation to place as the next strongest motivation. This is the desire to escape to somewhere more exotic than the everyday, an appeal used by a wide variety of travel and entertainment brands. Such appeals to escapism can easily lead to daydreaming, accessing many engrams in the brain.

Sexual survival follows orientation to place. Sexual survival has to do with gender expression and the consumer's self-identity. It is followed by expectation and then by territorial survival. Territorial survival deals in security and career advancement. Adaptation is the fourth strongest motivation. All of these are areas frequently tapped into by brand communication campaigns. To the extent that a brand can help to define or reinforce the customer's self-identity, the likelihood of developing a strong relationship with that brand increases. The same is true for brands that position themselves as essential to the customer's career aspirations and the like.

The three most powerful motivations are physical survival, orientation to person, and spiritual survival. Physical survival corresponds closely to Maslow's physiological needs, adding an element of safety. Orientation to person combines elements of esteem and self-actualization, focusing on the consumer's self-perception. Finally, spiritual survival involves elements of social needs, but framed more positively as the connections people have with others and with society.[32]

Maddock and Fulton offer a wide range of examples of the application of their motivational hierarchy in advertising. The gist of all the examples is that consumers are driven by emotion in making decisions and that the marketer's job is to identify which motive or motives best match the brand in order to build the relationship. Tapping into the identified motives should lead to successful communication that sparks the desired behavior in the consumer. Identifying the relevant motives can pose quite a challenge because most, if not all of them, are housed in the right side of the brain, the unconscious mind, and are difficult for consumers to access when being questioned using traditional research methods. We will review some techniques for identifying key motivations in Chapter 6.

THE FCB GRID

Are all decisions really driven by emotion? Richard Vaughn, when director of research at the Foote, Cone and Belding (FCB) advertising agency, developed a model for categorizing decision making that takes into consideration many of the factors discussed in this chapter and Chapter 3. Vaughn's model assumes that emotion may be a contributory factor, but not always the major force. The FCB grid categorizes brands based on whether the customer's decision-making process is driven primarily by reason or primarily by emotion and whether the customer's involvement level with the brand is high or low. The grid is shown in Exhibit 4.11.

The elements of "learn," "feel," and "do" in each of the quadrants have to do with the assumed process of communication. "Learn" is a cognitive component, where the customer learns of the brand and its benefits. "Feel" is an affective component, where positive or negative attitudes emerge in an emotional response to the brand. "Do" is a behavioral component, where action (product trial, purchase) occurs. In the high-involvement, thinking quadrant, the consumer must learn about the brand in order to develop an emotional response that will then lead to the desired behavior of purchasing the brand. In the high-involvement, feeling quadrant, the emotional response comes first, and only in the case of positive emotions will the consumer bother to learn about the brand.

The FCB grid suggests that the role of emotion varies depending on product type and involvement level. As we discussed in Chapter 3, involvement has to do with how relevant the brand is to the consumer's life, the importance of the purchase decision, the perceived risk associated with the decision, and the like. To apply the grid in brand communication development, the marketer needs to look at the brand from the customer's perspective, determining whether the decision making associated with the product is primarily rational or primarily emotional and then assessing whether this decision is likely to be high- or low-involvement for the consumer. That will determine which quadrant applies and where the emphasis of the messages and incentives developed to promote the product need to lie: on providing information (learn), on tapping into emotional responses (feel), or focusing on prompting immediate

Exhibit 4.11 **FCB Grid: How Advertising Works**

THINKING ⟶ FEELING

HIGH INVOLVEMENT	
INFORMATIVE (THINKER) CAR-HOUSE-FURNISHINGS- NEW PRODUCTS	**AFFECTIVE (FEELER)** JEWELRY-COSMETICS-FASHION APPAREL-MOTORCYCLES
MODEL: LEARN-FEEL-DO (Economic?)	**MODEL:** FEEL-LEARN-DO (Psychological?)
Possible Implications	**Possible Implications**
TEST: Recall Diagnostics **MEDIA:** Long Copy Format Reflective Vehicles **CREATIVE**: Specific Information Demonstration	**TEST:** Attitude Change Emotion Arousal **MEDIA:** Large Space Image Specials **CREATIVE**: Executional Impact

LOW INVOLVEMENT	
HABIT FORMATION (DOER) FOOD-HOUSEHOLD ITEMS	**SELF-SATISFACTION (REACTOR)** CIGARETTES-LIQUOR-CANDY
MODEL: DO-LEARN-FEEL (Responsive?)	**MODEL:** DO-FEEL-LEARN (Social?)
Possible Implications	**Possible Implications**
TEST: Sales **MEDIA:** Small Space Ads 10-second IDs Radio; POS **CREATIVE**: Reminder	**TEST:** Sales **MEDIA:** Billboards Newspapers POS **CREATIVE**: Attention

Source: R. Vaughn, "How Advertising Works: A Planning Model," *Journal of Advertising Research* 20, no. 5 (1980): 31.

behavior (do). In other words, the FCB grid can help to identify the best approach to starting a relationship between the customer and the brand: by appealing to the mind, the heart, or a sense of action.

In applying the FCB grid relative to iPod, for example, based on the schema presented earlier, we could certainly make the argument that the purchase of an iPod is a high-involvement, feeling decision. Placement of iPod in that quadrant of the grid suggests the need to focus on an emotional response first, which is what the image-oriented advertising produced for the brand. The strong word-of-mouth buzz it generated provided additional support. The cognitive aspect of learning was accomplished through product reviews in technology publications, detailed product specs available on Apple's Web site, and explanations from salespeople in electronics stores. Stores that featured the product as a loss leader or offered other deals on the brand provided the behavioral push to get iPod into the hands of many, many customers. Emotion led the way in driving decision making, but cognition also played a role.

In terms of Maddock and Fulton's motivational hierarchy, iPod certainly appeals to a sense of play. It also likely speaks to orientation to place, sexual survival, and spiritual survival. The personal musical world an iPod user enters often provides a sense of escape, at least temporarily, from everyday cares. Apple's campaign for iPod also gave the brand very strong ties to self-expression, both in the basic use of the product and in the choice of music the user puts on the iPod. And the more that iPod became perceived as a cool, must-have brand, the more brand usage became linked to being connected with one's peers, an important aspect of spiritual survival. The range of motivations associated with iPod underscores the primacy of emotion in purchasing decisions related to the brand. And while portable music and MP3 players had been around before Apple introduced iPod, iPod's visual appeal caused the *Blink* reflex that quickly pushed the brand over the tipping point.

SUMMING UP

A marketer who intends to create relationships with customers and influence their behavior must first understand how customers think in general and then how they think about the marketer's brand and competitive brands as well. As much as possible, marketers need to try to get inside and understand their customers' subconscious mind. Tools such as Maddock and Fulton's motivation scheme and the FCB grid can help marketers better understand the responses they observe and in turn use that understanding to improve their communications with customers.

The bottom line: every decision a customer makes has an emotional element. Marketers must make sure that the relationship they seek to build between the customer and their brand is based on emotional ties, not just practical reasoning. We will explore this idea further in the next chapter when we consider what the various types of customers want from a brand and any type of relationship with that brand.

NOTES

1. *Encarta World English Dictionary* (New York: St. Martin's Press, 1999), p. 1514.

2. R.E. Petty and J.T. Cacioppo, *Communication and Persuasion: Central and Peripheral Routes to Attitude Change* (New York: Springer, 1986).

3. E. Du Plessis, *The Advertised Mind: Ground-Breaking Insights Into How Our Brains Respond to Advertising* (London: Kogan Page, 2005), pp. 27–29.

4. G. Zaltman, *How Customers Think: Essential Insights Into the Mind of the Market* (Boston: Harvard Business School, 2003), pp. 7, 9.

5. Ibid., p. 50.

6. D.E. Schultz and J.J. Pilotta, "Developing the Foundation for a New Approach to Understanding How Media Advertising Works," Worldwide Audience Measurement 2004—Cross Media Conference Papers, ESOMAR WAM Conference, June, 2004.

7. Zaltman, *How Customers Think*, p. 167.

8. M. Gladwell, *The Tipping Point: How Little Things Can Make a Big Difference* (New York: Little, Brown, 2000).

9. Webkinz, www.webkinz.com.

10. B. Tedeschi, "Fuzzy Critters With High Prices Offer Lesson in New Concepts," *New York Times,* March 26, 2007; *Grand Rapids Press*, "Cute, Cuddly Webkinz the Rage Among Tweens," November 26, 2006; T.G. Fox, "Toy Animals Being Squeezed Out; Administrators Tell Parents That Webkinz Aren't Allowed at School," *Hartford Courant*, March 20, 2007.

11. M. Gladwell, *Blink: The Power of Thinking Without Thinking* (New York: Little, Brown, 2005).

12. Zaltman, *How Customers Think*, p. 33.

13. Du Plessis, *Advertised Mind*, p. 53.

14. Ibid., p. 53.

15. Zaltman, *How Customers Think,* p. 88.

16. T. Wasserman, "In Search of the Next iPod," *Brandweek,* June 20, 2005, p. S8; "100 Million iPods Sold," Apple, April 9, 2007, www.apple.com/pr/library/2007/04/09ipod.html; "iTunes Store Tops Over Five Billion Songs Sold," Apple, June 19, 2008, www.apple.com/pr/library/2008/06/19itunes.html).

17. P. Burrows, "#1 Apple Computer," *Business Week,* April 3, 2006, p. 68; N. O'Leary, "U.S. Agency of the Year: TBWA\Chiat\Day," *Adweek,* January 10, 2005, p. 16; E. Hall, "TBWA Proves Its Network Mettle," *Advertising Age,* January 10, 2005, p. S4.

18. Apple.com, "The iPod Shuffle," http://store.apple.com.

19. S.H. Wildstrom, "iPod: The Designers Got This One Right," *Business Week,* January 21, 2002, p. 16.

20. *Los Angeles Times*, "Battery Recall Swamps Sony Production," October 25, 2006.

21. M. Veverka, "Beyond the iPod: Mac Attack," *Barron's,* June 17, 2006, p. 20.

22. K. Allison, "Macs Surge Shields Apple From Recession Fears," *Financial Times*, April 24, 2008, p. 26.

23. D. Lazarus, "Image Is Everything—No, Wait, Profit Is," *San Francisco Chronicle*, November 24, 2006.

24. Brand Keys, "2006 Brandweek Customer Loyalty Awards Powered by Brand Keys," www.brandkeys.com/awards/clif06.cfm.

25. R. Passikoff, "If You Can't Change Your Fate, Change Your Attitude," *Chief Marketer,* March 11, 2006, www.chiefmarketer.com/attitude_marketing_03112006/index.html.

26. Du Plessis, *Advertised Mind*, p. 4.

27. Ibid., p. 84, emphasis in original.

28. Ibid., p. 107.

29. Ibid., pp. 106, 5, emphasis in original.

30. R.C. Maddock and R.L. Fulton, *Marketing to the Mind: Right Brain Strategies for Advertising and Marketing* (Westport, CT: Quorum, 1996).

31. Ibid., pp. 144–145.

32. Ibid., pp. 35–36.

33. Ibid., pp. 64–65.

CHAPTER 5

Identifying Customer Needs, Wants, and Desires

Having reviewed the importance of understanding what factors influence customers' purchases and how customers take in and process information, we can return to consideration of the six customer groups introduced in Chapter 2. One basic decision for marketers is on which group or groups they should focus their communication efforts. In many cases, that decision might seem straightforward. After all, the marketer responsible for an existing brand might be expected to easily identify the ultimate customers, intermediaries, suppliers, referrals, influencers, and internal markets involved in that brand's performance. But identification and strategy are not the same. Except in the rare case where the marketer has unlimited resources, decisions must be made on with which groups to communicate, what messages to convey, and with what frequency. In this chapter, we offer guidance on identifying the groups to select, and we outline the factors that should be considered as they affect each group.

THE NEED FOR TARGETING

The starting place is usually a fairly simple question: Why not simply communicate with all six markets as frequently as possible? As suggested above, resources are generally the key variable. Simply put, the greater the number of people and business entities that must be addressed, the greater the cost. The challenge, of course, is that the size of the group is not always directly related to its value to the marketing firm; the value of the audience is not just the number of people in it. While some savings can certainly be realized through economies of scale, most firms, faced with choices about on which groups to focus communication, must decide which groups to either communicate with less often or perhaps even ignore.

However, beyond the resource question is the issue of return-on-investment (ROI) or return-on-communication-investment (ROCI). Which groups or subsets of groups offer the greatest potential for response to the communication messages? Which groups must the marketer communicate with in order to maintain existing relationships and which groups offer the greatest potential for improved relationships? Answers to those questions drive decisions about communication within and among audiences. Exhibit 5.1 illustrates the six-market concept introduced earlier. This chapter provides detailed considerations related to each of the markets.

Exhibit 5.1 **The Six Communication Markets**

Source: Adapted from M. McDonald, M. Christopher, S. Knox, and A. Payne, *Creating a Company for Customers* (London: Pearson Education, 2001), p. 53.

Ultimate Customers

In the case of the ultimate customer market, unless the firm is operating in a situation with no competition, some level of ongoing audience communication is generally needed, if only to retain current users. However, not all current users may need, or merit, the same level of communication. Instead, it may be desirable or even necessary to dis-aggregate the present user market in some way—that is, to subdivide the large ultimate customer group into smaller segments, with different communication goals assigned to each. Market segmentation is a well-established concept in mass or push marketing. The basic premise underlying segmentation is that smaller groups that share particular characteristics or interests will tend to react similarly to messages. By tailoring messages to the smaller group, instead of trying to develop one message that will appeal to a broad, undifferentiated group, greater returns can be realized—an important consideration to keep in mind.

Segmentation is something the seller does. Marketers try to identify groups they want to communicate with, groups they think are important. Segmentation needs to be thought of separately from aggregation, which is what customers do. Customers aggregate or come together themselves by their behaviors; thus, they create the value that marketers only identify. Clearly, behavioral aggregation is what must form the basis for the segmentation practiced by the marketer.

In some cases, a marketer may choose to focus on just one narrowly defined group. Such a *concentrated* approach is a way to conserve resources through specialization. The opposite strategy is to try to attract the greatest number and variety of customers—an *undifferentiated* approach. Neither is particularly common (although many brands have started out practicing a concentrated approach). Instead, most companies offer multiple brands in order to appeal to multiple audiences.

Exhibit 5.2

Pantene Needs-Based Segmentation

Segmentation basis	Pantene product
Needs	
Volume	Sheer Volume
Curl production	Hydrating Curls
Smoothness	Smooth & Sleek
Thickness	Full & Thick
Moisturizing	Daily Moisture Renewal
Color protection	Color Revival
Simple process	Classic Care
Shininess	Ice Shine
Damage control	Restoratives
Race/Ethnicity	
Black	Relaxed & Natural
Hispanic	Extra Liso
Demographics	
Hair color	Pro-V Expressions (formulas for blonde, red, brunette, and gray hair)

Marketers who take this approach, communicating with multiple groups with messages (and, often, brands) tailored to each group, are said to practice a *differentiated* approach. In many cases, the basis for the development of the different messages or different brands is the varying needs of customer groups. Consider, for example, Pantene Pro-V hair care products, a Procter & Gamble brand. The Pantene Pro-V hair care line has multiple formulations, including formulations specifically for two demographic groups, black women and Hispanic women (see Exhibit 5.2). The product line is built primarily around varying customer needs based on the chief benefit sought. Each product is focused on one of those segments; the consumers within the segment are similar in terms of the specific benefit they view as most important in the choice of a hair conditioner (prolonged color life, curl, volume, etc.).

Benefit-based segmentation is one of the most common means of segmenting consumer markets. While benefit segmentation is concerned with the interaction between the brand user and the brand itself, other segmentation approaches focus solely on characteristics of individuals. These include demographics (segmentation based on population statistics such as age, gender, ethnicity, marital status, household size), geographics (segmentation based on region of the country, type of area lived in, city size), socioeconomics (segmentation based on income level, education level, disposable income), and psychographics (segmentation based on lifestyle, including attitudes, leisure activities, values). Of these, marketers tend to rely most heavily on demographics. One reason is that, in the absence of other, more detailed information about customers, demographic information is relatively easy to use because it is the easiest to acquire, whether directly from the customer or through third-party suppliers. Another reason is that most media vehicles define their audiences primarily in terms of demographics; thus, mass marketers' media choices are generally driven by the need to match the demographics of the target customer group to the demographics of the media vehicle.

While the segmentation process can aid in identifying viable target audiences, it does not provide much assistance in building and nurturing relationships with the people in those audiences. Because segmentation works by lumping people together into groups, it can lead to a focus on sweeping generalizations about the group as a whole rather than an understanding of and appreciation for the specific concerns of the individuals who make up the group. The types of segment descriptions that many mass marketers have traditionally relied upon are far more general than the descriptors that are possible when the marketer has access to a customer database and uses that database information to understand the behavior of either individual consumers or smaller groups within the overall customer base. It is at that level of analysis and evaluation that inferences can begin to be drawn about the issues discussed in the previous two chapters.

In the past, a marketer might have defined the target audience for the brand primarily (or even solely) on the basis of a limited number of factors—for example, "women aged 25 to 44 with household incomes of $35,000 or more, living in suburban areas." The problem with such a description is the tremendous variability within that group. A twenty-five-year-old woman and a forty-four-year-old woman might have very few things in common, even if their incomes are similar. Two twenty-five-year-old women might be very different from each other as well. While the description above is certainly more focused than characterizing the brand's audience as "all women," it is still not particularly useful.

This sort of broad target definition grew out of the reliance on demographic-based descriptors mentioned earlier and the need to match target audiences to media audience descriptions. Today, not only can marketers gather more specific, richly detailed information on customers that go well beyond demographics, but the opportunities for increasingly personalized media choices have increased as well. Hopefully, that combination of factors will lead to a decline in the use of general, demographic-only segmentation.

We argue that effective segmentation must be based on identification of similar behaviors and audience characteristics that can be observed as they are related to the brand. Such an approach starts with the aggregation that customers perform themselves through their own actions. Consider the four possible strategies with regard to the ultimate customer markets that were mentioned in Chapter 2: acquisition, retention, growth, and migration. All are behavior-based. Ultimate customers targeted for acquisition are people who are not now using the brand. Instead, they either are using a competitor's product or are not currently involved in the product category. If they are customers of a competitor, the marketer needs to determine why they have chosen to use the competitive brand in order to develop strategies to get them to switch to the marketer's own brand. If the customers are not now purchasing in the product category, the marketer needs to determine what other type of product they are using to satisfy their needs and develop a strategy to convince them of the value of the category and, specifically, the marketer's brand within that category.

For example, LG Electronics targets both cell phone users and MP3 users with its "Chocolate," a device that functions as both a cell phone and an MP3 player and also contains a camera and navigational technology (Exhibit 5.3).[1] In promoting Chocolate, LG Electronics is attempting to both acquire customers from other brands and migrate current customers to the more extensive and most likely more expensive services available with Chocolate. The device's multiple uses might also attract prospective customers who are not currently using either a cell phone or an MP3 player. Again, it is important to note that LG Electronics' promotional push for Chocolate is based on benefits and user behavior, not general demographic categories.

In the case of retention, growth, and migration, marketers are dealing with customers

Exhibit 5.3 **Print Ad for LG Electronics' Chocolate**

currently using the brand. A customer database will provide detailed information on their past behavior with the brand: how often they have bought it, where they purchased it, how much they paid, and what form of payment they used. That behavioral information can aid in developing strategies to either reinforce current behavior (retention) or change behavior (growth and/or migration). Because behavior is what marketers are seeking to influence, behavior logically must be the foundation for any relevant segmentation strategy.

What about the other forms of segmentation that have traditionally been used? Are they now worthless? Not completely. Knowing customers' demographic, geographic, socioeconomic, and psychographic characteristics can help a marketer better understand what might be motivating their behavior. It can certainly help in crafting messages that will be relevant to the particular group. These bits of knowledge can usually help to explain the behaviors that marketers have observed. In the case of an acquisition strategy, the best prospect is often someone who is similar to a current customer, so knowing current customer demographics,

Exhibit 5.4

MRI's Cat Food Comparison (in percent)

	Purina Tender Vittles	Whiskas Homestyle Favorites
Age group distribution		
18–24	6.7	6.8
25–34	14.0	16.3
35–44	18.3	23.1
45–54	27.8	16.1
55–64	17.4	19.5
65+	15.8	18.0
Census region		
Northeast	28.1	18.6
South	36.4	49.3
North central	21.4	16.1
West	14.2	15.9
Child in home	38.9	29.7

Source: MRI+, Spring 2005 Product Report.

geographics, and the like may help in developing a profile of most likely prospects. Our position is not that these traditional descriptors are no longer valid, but that they are helpful only when used to describe segments that have first been defined by brand-based behavior.

Wal-Mart has developed customized product mixes based on customer segment profiles, focusing on six groups. Two are ethnic groups, Hispanics and African-Americans; one is based on lifestyle, "empty-nesters/boomers"; one is the affluent socio economic group; and two are geographically based, suburban and rural customers.[2] Although the segments selected for this strategy are based on traditional descriptors on the surface, the real reason for using this segmentation is that each group exhibits different buying behaviors and so can be better served by a product mix that responds to its behavioral differences.

In pursuing an acquisition strategy, several resources may be used to determine which segment or segments on which to focus. In the case of consumer products, both the Simmons Market Research Bureau and Mediamark Research, Inc. (MRI) offer syndicated research products that identify current brand users by demographics, geographics, socioeconomics, and media use. These services are discussed in detail in Chapter 11.

Simmons collects data on individual adults (ages 18 and up), teens (ages 12 to 17), "tweenz" (8 to 14), youths (6 to 17), kids (6 to 11), Hispanics, households, and gay, lesbian, bisexual, and transgendered consumers. Simmons's studies cover more than 8,000 brands with 460 product categories. Data are available in a variety of formats, including Choices3, a software package that allows subscribers to create custom analyses based on the individual marketer's needs.[3]

MRI collects data on 6,000 brands in more than 450 product categories. MRI's focus is the adult market, eighteen years old and up. Its specialized products include a study of the affluent market (people with incomes of $70,000 or more), a teen study, a Business Influencer Study and a Home Influencer Study, both of which focus on technology products. MRI's data are available to subscribers online using the MRI+ software package.[4]

Simmons and MRI data can be used to profile users of competitive brands. Both companies offer classifications based on volume of product usage, so some behavioral data beyond basic purchasing is available. These data are also helpful in identifying the media habits of brand users. Exhibit 5.4 shows demographic data from MRI+ comparing characteristics of home-makers who buy Purina's Tender Vittles cat food for their pets and those who buy Whiskas Homestyle Favorites. The data show that, compared to Whiskas customers, Purina customers are more likely to be middle-aged, live in the Northeast, and have children living at home.

The U.S. Census Bureau offers a wealth of free data that can be useful in profiling both consumer and business markets. The Census Bureau's Web site, www.census.gov, includes estimates and projections across a wide variety of categories. It provides detailed information on the North American Industry Classification System (NAICS), a recent scheme for classifying companies in the United States, Canada, and Mexico by industry type. NAICS replaces the old Standard Industrial Classification system that was unique to the United States. It also adds 350 new industries to the list of those to be tracked by the Census Bureau. A similar, product-focused listing, the North American Product Classification System, is under development; updates on that process are also available on the Census Bureau Web site.[5]

Census Bureau data are useful in quantifying the size of various market alternatives. This can aid in forecasting and in evaluating the potential of various markets by providing comparable statistics for opportunity analysis.

Intermediary Market

The intermediary market requires a regular flow of information. Retailers, distributors, whole-salers, and resellers are focused on the profitability of their own businesses. Any changes in terms of sale, delivery methods, and the like, whether permanent or part of a short-term promotional incentive, must be communicated quickly and efficiently. Intermediaries should also be aware of what types of communications are being directed at ultimate customers so that they can plan for changes in consumer demand and adjust their own promotional programs accordingly. Intermediaries should never learn important brand information third-hand; this implies that the brand organization does not view the intermediary as important or a valued partner. With competitive brands constantly jockeying for improved or increased shelf space or display positions, brand marketers cannot afford to weaken the brand's position with intermediaries. After all, it is often the retail sales clerk who is the most visible illustration of the brand message and the brand promise.

Some of this information can be conveyed through impersonal means—Web site postings, faxes, or broadcast emails. Depending on the nature of the relationship between the intermediary and the brand, it is often best if some of the communication takes place face-to-face, commonly delivered through the company's sales force.

Although one-size-fits-all was once a common approach to intermediary marketing, account-specific efforts are now far more common. In an account-specific approach, the marketer puts together a customized promotional program for a specific retailer, distributor, wholesaler, or other intermediary, tailoring the program to the intermediary's own goals and customer mix. Thus, the marketer may be working with a number of retailers simultaneously, with each retailer receiving support from the marketer appropriate to that retailer's particular needs. This makes the communication planning process quite complex. For the Canadian launch of Sunsilk hair care products, Unilever developed fourteen different account-specific

Exhibit 5.5

"Best" Customer Matrix

Marketer driver	Key "best" customer characteristics
Profitability	Buys under terms that are most favorable to company; does not require deep discounting, greater than average sales force attention, or special delivery terms
Volume	Buys in large quantities; buys more frequently than average
Distribution cost control	Located in close geographic proximity; does not require special shipping terms
Market share	Willing to enter into exclusive deals; resistant to competitive attention

promotions, ranging from a customized magazine for one retailer to an account-specific direct mail piece sent to another retailer's customers to store-specific movie advertisements in yet another retail chain.[6] This degree of intermediary customization helped to ensure each retailer's cooperation in the brand's launch and increased the retailers' own commitment to supporting the Sunsilk brand.

Behavior-based segmentation is also an important tool for developing communication strategies for intermediary markets. "Best" customers generally merit more frequent and more personal communication than customers that are not as strong in performance, although there are some legal issues in developing this type of approach. In the U.S. market, for example, the same degree of price discount must be made available to all retailers in the same class of trade—that is, all retailers who generate a similar level of sales. While the details of the particular program developed can differ, the bottom-line terms must be equivalent. The definition of "best" depends on how brand success is defined. See Exhibit 5.5 for an example of some of the possible ways to define "best."

Obviously, there are a variety of ways to define "best" customers. The definition chosen will vary depending on circumstances. What is important is to select a definition, use it to segment the intermediary base, and then enrich the segment definition with behavioral data that will make it possible to develop and enhance a relationship with the customer and to refine communication strategy development.

A complicating factor in dealing with intermediaries is that a customer can also be a competitor. In 2006, a national U.S. consumer survey found that five Wal-Mart brands ranked in the top ten of customers' preferred brands.[7] That makes Wal-Mart a major competitor for other manufacturers' brands at the same time the retailer is a major, perhaps primary, intermediary trading partner. Coca-Cola chose to change the distribution strategy it has used for years, distributing PowerAde to Wal-Mart warehouses instead of through the company's traditional system of direct store deliveries from local bottlers. The change was made out of concern that if Coca-Cola did not yield to Wal-Mart's wishes, Wal-Mart would develop its own competitive product.[8] Even a major marketer like Coca-Cola cannot afford to upset or irritate a key customer such as Wal-Mart. Wal-Mart claims that 85 per cent of Americans shop in its stores at least once a year,[9] making it an integral part of most consumer products' distribution strategies, and often meriting its own communications strategy and dedicated sales force.

Other intermediaries may lack Wal-Mart's dominance, but they are an important element in a brand's ultimate success. Imagine trying to sell an office supply product without distribution in Staples, OfficeMax, and Office Depot or launching a would-be best-selling book that is not available through Barnes & Noble or Amazon.com. Large accounts such as these must be treated with care, making a consistent flow of information and personalized communication important elements of the marketer's strategy.

Intermediary markets can be segmented on the basis of sales volume, number of employees, geographic location, or class of trade. As with ultimate customer markets, behavior is a critical consideration. Important behavioral elements include speed of meeting financial obligations, receptivity to brand-originated promotional programs, length of relationship with the brand, and brand placement practices. For new brands seeking initial intermediary partners, business directories, trade journals, and research on competitors' distribution practices are possible starting points in identifying intermediary prospects.

For example, a food producer looking to sell its products to the food services industry might review trade publications such as *Food Arts*, *Food Engineering*, *Food Processing*, *Frozen Food Age*, and *Prepared Foods*. All are specialized publications focused on that particular industry. There are also must-visit Web sites such as www.foodservice.com, www.foodservice411.com, and www.foodservicecentral.com. Depending on the producer's product, an even more narrowly focused publication might be appropriate reading, such as *Pig International, Poultry International, SeaFood Business*, and various narrowly focused Web sites.

The same strategies discussed for ultimate customers apply: acquisition, retention, growth, and migration. Unless a firm has saturated the brand's distribution system, locating new intermediaries to expand distribution may be a sales force concern. Expanded distribution can introduce the product to new ultimate customer segments, realize economies of scale in shipping, and increase brand visibility. Prospective intermediary partners will be most interested in the brand's performance in current retail outlets, the location of competitors carrying the brand, and customized marketing programs offered as incentives to consumers to pick up the brand if it is stocked.

Aveda personal care products are sold through dedicated retail stores—Aveda Experience Centers—but also through company-owned Lifestyle Salons and Spas and independent salons and spas. For example, there are twenty Aveda outlets within a hundred miles of Lexington, Kentucky: seventeen concept (independent) salons, one lifestyle salon, and two retail stores. There are also twenty outlets within the Chicago area: thirteen concept salons, three lifestyle salons, three retail stores, and an Aveda Institute, a teaching program for intermediaries.[10] Other markets offer a similar array of choices for this nationally distributed product line. In addition to these company-affiliated outlets, other beauty salons and spas may also carry some of the Aveda line. And customers can order directly from the Aveda Web site. In making the decision whether to add the Aveda product line, the owner of a prospective concept salon would want to know what other concept salons stocking the Aveda line are in the area, the volume of business they do, how many Web orders come in from the salon's geographic area, and what kind of promotional support the salon can expect to receive from Aveda.

Retention will always be a consideration, most particularly in highly competitive markets where trade sales promotion spending is heavy. Ale-8-One is a ginger-flavored soft drink, available in regular and diet varieties, distributed in parts of Kentucky, Indiana, and Ohio. Ale-8-One, which was first sold in 1926, competes for customers and shelf space with much larger soft drink brands. While Ale-8-One is distributed by Coca-Cola, the brand maintains its independence.[11] The product's status as a cult favorite helps in maintaining distribution, but the arrangement with Coca-Cola is also important in retaining intermediary partners.

Growth strategies are particularly important for brand marketers seeking to increase their product's in-store presence vis-à-vis competition; getting a retailer to carry more varieties of the brand or more sizes can lead to increased shelf space and greater in-store visibility. Kraft Foods' Crystal Light line of beverages and powdered mixes includes seven flavors of Crystal Light On the Go (small packets to be mixed with bottled water), fifteen flavors of powdered mixes in traditional scoop-out packages, seven flavors of single-serve bottled drinks, and three flavors of multiserve bottles.[12] The On the Go and multiserve bottles are relatively new additions to the product line, giving the sales force something new to offer retailers and a way to perhaps gain additional shelf space for the Crystal Light brand.

Migration can sometimes be achieved by offering particularly attractive intermediary partners exclusive rights to carry the firm's high-end, high-margin products. Procter & Gamble gave the English retail chain Tesco exclusive rights to Procter & Gamble's Physique hair care products for the first nine months of the brand's distribution.[13] Doing so likely meant that other P&G brands would also get a boost in promotion within Tesco stores and in Tesco advertisements.

Supplier Market

Like intermediaries, suppliers should never be taken by surprise; that is, keeping suppliers informed of the marketer's activities and operations, particularly providing advance notice of any significant changes in direction, can help to maintain effective working relationships. However, while most brand managers are very well aware of the importance of maintaining relationships with intermediaries, the same level of concern does not always apply to suppliers. Perhaps that is because many suppliers tend to deal most closely with the manufacturing end of the business rather than marketing or because suppliers of business services tend to be regarded more as interchangeable vendors than as business partners. We argue that supplier concerns must be an important consideration in developing communication strategies.

While the identities of a firm's suppliers may be invisible to ultimate consumers, the impact those suppliers have on ultimate customer satisfaction is enormous. Consider the case of frozen food manufacturer Stouffer's. For its line of Lean Cuisine (a line of frozen entrees with reduced fat and calories) Paninis, suppliers include the sources of the ingredients for the four sandwiches and the materials for the outer packaging and the inner grill tray that makes the sandwiches edible after microwaving. If any element from any supplier is below final customers' expected quality levels, it is Stouffer's reputation (and future sales) that will suffer most directly in the marketplace, not the reputation of the supplier.

Sometimes the identity of the supplier is all too clear. In 2000, Ford Motor Company battled Bridgestone/Firestone when Ford's Explorer SUV was linked to a number of rollover accidents. Ford blamed the problem on its tire supplier, Bridgestone/Firestone, saying the fault for the accidents was with the tires, not the Explorer's design. The tire company argued that Explorers would have rollover problems no matter what tires were on the vehicles due to a design flaw.[14] Both companies were subject to recalls and lawsuits; Bridgestone/Firestone replaced nearly 6.5 million tires.[15] The accusations and counteraccusations forced American drivers to think seriously about whose tires were on the new vehicle they were considering buying. The automakers' supplier choices, and perceptions of those suppliers, suddenly became far more important than in the past. The sniping that went on between Ford and Bridgestone/

Firestone certainly did not improve consumers' perceptions of either company, highlighting what can happen when manufacturer or supplier relationships deteriorate.

In many cases, brand manufacturers are a supplier's intermediaries, so the same considerations discussed above apply to communication from the supplier to the manufacturer. But communication must flow in the other direction as well. No supplier wants to read in the trade press that a manufacturer it works with is increasing prices shortly after that manufacturer has negotiated a new contract with more favorable terms from the supplier. While such news is unlikely to be welcome under any circumstances, hearing about it from a third party is less than ideal. While it may seem trite to advocate following the Golden Rule in such circumstances, thinking about how a given decision will affect all the brand's markets is usually the best course to follow in developing communication plans.

Much of the communication between marketer and supplier may take place through automated systems. Enterprise resource planning (ERP) systems are a technology tool designed to help firms streamline their operations, particularly with regard to business partners. ERP systems track processes, including order processing, automating steps in the system to speed up transaction times and allow for better tracking.[16] Although there have been many useful developments in this area and improvements to the early ERP systems, many attempts at implementing ERP systems have not been successful. Recent research has shown that the human element is still critical,[17] underscoring the need for competent communication to manage the relationship between supplier and manufacturer.

When selecting and/or evaluating suppliers, many of the key considerations are linked to the supplier's product's role in producing the brand. What level of volume can the supplier handle comfortably? What processes does the supplier have in place to ensure consistent quality? How will the supplier's geographic location affect the ability to deliver components and services in a timely manner?

The importance of proximity is easily demonstrated by a look at the marketing communications firms serving the U.S. automotive industry. Detroit, Michigan, is home to the offices of a number of major U.S. advertising agencies. Most of those offices were started specifically to service automaker accounts. Having the agency in the same town, instead of an airplane flight away, made for improved communication and better working relationships, at least initially. With improvements in communication, immediate geographic proximity may not be as critical as it once was, but it is still an important consideration in the choice of suppliers.

Recognition of the importance of supplier proximity is not limited to brand marketers. When the state of Ohio lost out to Indiana as the location for a new Honda automotive plant, Ohio moved quickly to offer incentives to various automotive parts suppliers to get them to build plants in Ohio to supply the new Honda location.[18] Ohio's reasoning was clear: both Honda and the parts suppliers would benefit from proximity, and Ohio might be able to make up for some of the potential revenue lost when Honda chose Indiana by attracting parts suppliers instead.

Supply chain experts argue that firms must have flexible backup plans in place in preparation for possible supply chain disruptions due to natural or human-caused events (such as terrorist attacks, SARS-type epidemics, or uncertain demand projections).[19] This advice certainly makes sense in terms of protecting relationships with intermediaries and ultimate customers; however, to prevent such decisions from appearing to have been made arbitrarily, it is important that the suppliers involved understand the reasoning behind decisions on use of substitute suppliers, redundancies, and scenarios when different suppliers might be brought into the mix.

Both the concept and role of suppliers are undergoing some change as manufacturers and service providers look for ways to differentiate their offerings from competition. Two New York City condominium developments emphasize that a company's associates can say a great deal about the business. A condominium being developed in the Columbus Circle neighborhood is using famed New York toy retailer F.A.O. Schwarz to equip its playroom. Another development, 20 Pine: The Collection, will feature décor by Armani/Casa.[20] In both cases, the choice of supplier confers prestige on the builder and has the potential to enhance the builder's product for the end target group of potential residents.

The bottom line when dealing with supplier markets: Do not take them for granted. Yes, the suppliers need the marketer as a customer. But the marketer also needs the suppliers in order to serve its own ultimate customers. Regular attention to communications with suppliers can go a long way in preserving and enhancing relationships.

Referral Market

Business-to-business advertising experts often cite the strength of case histories as a persuasive communication tool. Knowing that someone else, an independent voice, has had a good experience working with a particular organization or using a product or service reduces perceived risk and increases comfort levels in the present and potential markets. Hence the importance of the referral market, particularly through word-of-mouth referrals from current customers.

Management of referral markets has become an important aspect of business for many companies. Internet chat rooms are an increasingly powerful source of product information, both for the ultimate consumers who participate in the discussion and for brand marketers who monitor what is being said. For example, Del Monte tracks chat room discussions to gain insight into how pet owners feel about their animals, which can guide product development and promotion.[21]

Promotional programs encouraging existing customers to make a referral to a friend are common in both consumer and business markets. Catalog companies offer incentives to their customers to provide contact information for friends who might want to receive the catalog. Online neighborhoods MySpace and Facebook encourage referrals to get new users. Companies use referrals to identify prospects and reward current customers, who may receive discounts or other recognition for successful referrals.

The power of positive referrals is important enough to constitute the focus of an entire book, *The Ultimate Question: Driving Good Profits and True Growth,* by Fred Reichheld. The title question is the likelihood of recommending a particular company to a friend or business associate. People who would recommend a company are termed "promoters"; those who would not are "detractors." The book and a companion Web site, www.bain.com/theultimatequestion/home.asp, offer a model for determining net promoter scores, which are the company's number of detractors subtracted from the number of promoters. Companies with high net promoter scores tend to be leaders in their product categories.[22]

John Goodman, CEO of TARP consulting firm, argues that customer referrals and word-of-mouth advertising can be managed effectively by tracking four items: (1) the number of referrals made by a satisfied customer, (2) the degree to which opinions and perceptions affect the company, (3) the proportion of people who act based on the referral, and (4) the percentage of new customers attracted.[23]

The best way to get referrals, not surprisingly, is to provide an outstanding product and excellent service. Goodman cites a study conducted for the investment market showing that providing information, offering consistently good service, and creating personal connections all contribute to a customer's likelihood of recommending the investment provider to someone else.[24] Other referral sources include a broad range of professional service providers such as doctors, lawyers, accountants, and architects. These are the most common types of referral groups for many customers.

In addition to current customers, third parties can serve as referral sources. College career centers and college faculty and staff members, for example, play an important role in guiding students toward internship sites and career opportunities. It is not unusual for firms that need a steady stream of new employees to cultivate relationships with key faculty and staff members at feeder campuses to encourage them to direct suitable students toward the company. Segmentation decisions here are relatively simple: identify the programs that have produced successful current employees, and target those same programs for future hires. Geography obviously plays a role, but so does preparation obtained through the curriculum, propensity of the program's students to have done internships or gotten other practical experience while in school, and the like.

In considering communication strategies for the referral market, the starting point must be to try and put oneself in the ultimate customer's place. Where is the prospect most likely to encounter existing customers? Some marketers develop events designed both to bring diverse customers together to maintain the relationship between the customer and the brand and to encourage referrals that might result in growth or migration.

Jeep provides a link from its Web site, www.jeep.com, to a Yahoo! Groups listing of 647 discussion groups associated with Jeep, including groups specific to the CJ, Cherokee, Liberty, and Wrangler models. The basic Jeep group has nearly 4,000 members.[25] The 2006 Jeep Jamboree included events at thirty-two locations across the United States. The Jamborees are off-road trail rides, and only Jeep vehicles can participate. A typical Jamboree begins on a Thursday evening and runs through the following Sunday morning. Jeep owners may bring non–Jeep-owning friends and family members along for the experience.[26] These are just a few examples of a number of programs Jeep runs to keep current customers satisfied and maintain existing relationships, but also to provide forums for current owners to interact with prospective Jeep owners.

As you might expect, Jeep is not alone in doing this, but its program is particularly well developed. The high levels of product involvement in the automotive category make it more likely that customers will participate in such events. High involvement products are not the only beneficiaries of such approaches, however. The Hormel Corporation attracts large numbers of consumers to its annual festival celebrating Spam luncheon meat, appropriately titled the Spam Jam![27]

Influencer Market

The influencer market plays an important, often critical, role in most brand decisions. As noted in Chapter 3 in our discussion of external influences on consumer behavior, key influencers include personal influence groups, such as family members, friends, and coworkers, as well as marketing communication–related influencers, such as opinion leaders, financial analysts, government agencies, and the media. Because influencers of both types are often sought out by the other customer groups, their role in brand decision making cannot be overemphasized. This is particularly true in situations where specific acquisition, growth, or migration strategies are being pursued. Those are all cases where behavior change, rather than behavior reinforcement, is the goal. Because behavior change requires a movement away from the status quo, those are the situations where it is likely that the views of others might be sought.

The importance of family influence and personal reference groups was discussed in Chapter 3. Marketers certainly recognize the increasingly critical role word of mouth (positive or negative) from personal influencers plays in today's customer decision making. For this reason, much of the work done with the marketing communication–related influencers is intended to impact or play off of the personal influencer relationship.

Opinion leaders are people others view as expert in a particular area; they can be personal influencers, but play a somewhat specialized role due to their presumed brand knowledge. Because they are assumed to know more about the brand and the category than the average person, their opinion is considered more important and more likely to influence behavior. Opinion leaders tend to seek out specialized information on the topics that interest them, so publicity efforts aimed at specialized publications or insider newsletters are often used as ways to reach opinion leaders with information on new products and product improvements. The assumption, and hope, is that they will in turn pass this information along to other prospective customers who consult them for their expertise.

Identifying opinion leaders is not an exact science. Consequently, some marketers have chosen to communicate product innovations more broadly in an effort to tap into other influencer groups. For example, pharmaceutical manufacturer Glaxo Smith Kline took the approach of encouraging its sales representatives and other personnel to engage friends, neighbors, and family members in conversations about pharmaceutical products and the pressures of costs and governmental regulations on business area. The company implemented its grassroots campaign in Missouri in 2005, and employees made 15,000 presentations to a variety of groups.[28]

The Glaxo Smith Kline strategy recognizes that anyone who has adequate information can be an influencer. Thus, the most important strategic goal is to build that concept into any communications effort with the influencer market, whether the group is a grassroots organization or a more formal type of influencer. Glaxo Smith Kline built its specific strategy on the basis of social networks.

Social network theory looks at the importance of interpersonal influences and communication on the formation of attitudes and, ultimately, behavior. The closer the relationship between people, the more likely, and stronger, the influence.[29] The individuals who make up a social network are termed nodes, which are connected by ties.[30] The families whose children attend the same school are a social network. Each family is a node; all the families are connected, but the ties between some of the nodes are stronger than between others due to reinforcement through a range of connections—for example, some families attend the same church or their children participate in the same after-school activities. Glaxo Smith Kline's approach was to encourage its employees to communicate within their existing social networks; in other words, the importance of interpersonal influence drove the strategy.

Web sites such as MySpace and Facebook operate on the basis of social networks. Participants identify friends who are allowed access to more data in the individual's Web profile than the casual user. A number of marketers, recognizing the power of the online social networks, are moving to place brand messages within the framework. Microsoft and Facebook have an agreement that allows Microsoft to sell all of the ad space (banners and any other form of advertising, including pop-ups and the like) on Facebook; Google has a similar deal with MySpace.[31]

Chase is a financial services company that offers a wide variety of services, including banking, loans, credit cards, and insurance. Chase is one of many companies using the social network links on Facebook to attract college students to its financial products by offering incentives to join the Chase banking network.[32] What remains to be seen is whether the users of these social network sites will respond favorably to branded messages or whether they will instead view them as intrusive and out of place on a site where they go to catch up with friends in a nonthreatening environment. In the latter situation, brands promoted on these sites may see negative consumer backlash instead of the positive buzz they are hoping to create.

Much of the work done by public relations professionals, whether internally or in an agency setting, recognizes the importance of more formal influencer groups. These include the financial community, government agencies at all levels, and the media. Edelman, one of the leading global public relations firms, offers its clients a variety of areas of expertise in dealing with the financial and investment community. These include corporate governance consulting (fine-tuning internal operations and communicating those changes to media and the investment community), investor relations (communications with the investment community and financial media), litigation support and crisis communication (protection of corporate reputation), executive positioning (personalizing the face of the company), and transaction communications (information surrounding mergers, restructurings, and IPOs).[33]

One example of a type of company needing financial public relations expertise is the publicly traded companies that are required to provide particular types of information to their stockholders on a regular basis. Financial relations personnel at such firms spend much of their time developing quarterly reports, annual reports, and other publications targeted both at current and prospective stockholders. The publications provide detailed financial information that individual customers can use as a resource in evaluating their own relationships with the company and discussing their investment strategy with family and friends and with financial professionals. The first case would be a personal influence: the customer might recommend the company's stock to a friend or colleague. The second case would be a marketing communications–related influence: the financial adviser and customer would refer to one of the group's publications as an information source. A range of annual reports is available online through Report Gallery (www.reportgallery.com). It is useful to spend some time reviewing a sample of annual reports to get a sense of the vast amount of information presented in this format. Annual reports and other financial relations documents are also distributed to the influencers in the investment community, professionals to whom both casual and serious investors will turn for advice and counsel.

Government relations is another critical area of focus. While all government agencies have the potential to affect a firm's business, certain agencies are particularly important for the influencer role they play. For example, decisions by and reports from the Food and Drug Administration (FDA) and Federal Trade Commission (FTC) affect perceptions of particular brands and entire product categories. The FDA's Web site (www.fda.gov) contains information on FDA investigations and decisions in many product categories. Past hot topics include contact lenses, weight loss products, and online purchases of medication. Much of the information on the site is also communicated to the media through press releases, broadening public knowledge of products that have been found to have problems. Similarly, the FTC's Web site, www.ftc.gov, has a section for consumers alerting them to potential scams and product problems.

Public relations professionals working in government relations try to manage their clients' relationships with government regulators, minimizing damage and making sure their clients' brands are treated fairly. Another leading public relations firm, Burson-Marsteller, offers its clients government relations services that include lobbying expertise to influence legislative decisions, assistance working with trade associations that speak and act on behalf of industries, and help working with governments outside the firm's home country.[34]

The influencer role of the media cannot be overstated. Both traditional and new media serve as critical sources of information customers use in comparing brands, developing brand attitudes, and making brand choice decisions. Publicity efforts rely on getting media outlets to carry stories to both business and consumer markets. The best-written, best-researched press release is ineffective if the media does not pick it up. As with so much of what we have discussed, building relationships and offering a reliable source of sound information are critical to success here. Ideally, a firm wants its chief executive officer to be the person who is always quoted when a major story breaks involving the product category. It wants its brand to be the category exemplar reporters use in talking about new product developments. It wants to be the subject of favorable podcasts and the brand generating the most buzz in key blogs.

Fleishman-Hillard International Communications, yet another leading public relations firm, recognized the importance of media relations in both traditional and newer outlets when it developed its "Next Great Thing" (NGT) initiative. As described on the firm's Web site: "The NGT group will constantly introduce new products and services to help FH clients maintain a level of continual activity, integration, and immersion with their marketing messages. Additionally, the group will seamlessly bring together media relations, channel marketing, peer-to-peer, and nontraditional communications across all message distribution channels."[35] NGT includes the use of blogging and wireless communications to reach and influence various customer markets. It recognizes that while information search is more important than ever, sources of information are changing and vary across customer groups. Media influence has not lessened, but the increase in media choices available to customers has increased the complexity of the media relations aspect of marketing and public relations.

Internal Market

The final market group to be discussed is the internal market, the firm's own employees. This group is as important as the customer group. If employees are uninformed or unmotivated, the brand will ultimately suffer. Unfortunately, this market is perhaps most similar to the supplier market in that it is often taken for granted by marketing and brand managers and not kept as well-informed as it should be. However, doing so is a serious strategic error. As with suppliers, a person buying a company's product at the grocery store may not know anything about the employees of the firm that made that product. But the actions of those employees are integral to how satisfied the buyer will be with the brand.

Besides the obvious role employees play in producing and marketing the brand (there is no product for people to buy without assembly line workers or the sales force) and providing the service that creates the brand (consider the role of housekeeping and room service personnel and bellmen in creating the image of a luxury hotel), employees matter in other ways. Part of a firm's reputation and, consequently, part of the brand's reputation is the image the firm holds in its community. That image is largely created by the actions of individual employees as community citizens. What is their level of involvement outside the firm? Are they perceived as making contributions to the community? How do they speak of the firm outside—favorably or unfavorably? Employees make the company human; people prefer to buy products from companies they feel good about, and employee actions are integral to corporate image creation.

The Edelman Trust Barometer, an index created by Edelman Public Relations, surveys 2,000 opinion leaders in many countries to assess their perceptions of the importance of trust as a decision-making factor. In the 2006 survey, U.S. respondents rated "rank-and-file employees as more credible spokespersons than corporate CEOs (42 percent vs. 28 percent in the U.S.)."[36] The study found that the people who tended to be viewed as most trustworthy were those perceived as having the most regular day-to-day involvement with the brand, such as those on the assembly line for a manufactured product. (The television commercials for Post Cereals that feature Post Cereal manufacturing employees are an example of a campaign using close-to-the-brand spokespersons.)

So an important first step is to make sure that all employees are reasonably informed and satisfied with their company knowledge. Once again, information is a key component of satisfaction. Hearing about major changes in company policy or new initiatives only after they have been announced to the press can make employees feel undervalued. In one large firm, the president routinely communicated important information or identified problems that would affect employees through email sent late in the day, often after regular working hours. Employees did not object to the use of email as the communication device; almost everyone in the firm had access and used email as their primary communication tool. The objection was to the timing, which often seemed deliberate, a way to be able to say "but we told you about this," even though the telling generally came too late. This might seem a small thing, but over time, such small issues can combine to create critical disconnections between corporate management and employees.

Because of the importance of employee communications, many large firms have established employee relations departments that specialize in managing the communication between management and line employees. Employee relations is now a recognized field of professional study within the organizational communications area of some universities. Employee relations tools include newsletters (print or electronic), intranets, employee satisfaction surveys, and even incentives for employees to suggest ways the firm can be improved. Companies covet high ratings on *Fortune* magazine's annual list of the "100 Best Companies to Work For." In 2006, the number one firm on that list was Genentech, a San Francisco-based biotechnology company where 95 percent of the employees are also stockholders.[37] At just over 8,000 employees, Genentech is classified as a medium-sized firm. The best-performing large firm, number two on the 2006 list, was Wegmans Food Markets, a supermarket chain in the Northeastern part of the United States. Wegmans has nearly 32,000 employees. *Fortune*'s example of the care Wegmans takes of its employees was a move to bring all full-time employees of two new Wegmans stores to the company's headquarters in Rochester, New York, for a kick-off speech from Wegmans' CEO Danny Wegman. The company is praised for the family atmosphere it creates and maintains.[38]

Exhibit 5.6

Fortune's Twenty-Five Best Companies to Work For, 2006

Rank	Company	Job growth (percent)	Company size	U.S. employees
1	Genentech	20	Midsized	8,121
2	Wegmans Food Markets	7	Large	31,890
3	Valero Energy	5	Large	16,582
4	Griffin Hospital	2	Small	1,049
5	W.L. Gore & Associates	6	Midsized	4,537
6	Container Store	16	Midsized	2,857
7	Vision Service Plan	−2	Small	1,915
8	J.M. Smucker	−13	Midsized	2,930
9	Recreational Equipment (REI)	9	Midsized	7,443
10	S.C. Johnson	0	Midsized	3,404
11	Boston Consulting Group	17	Small	1,261
12	Plante & Moran	9	Small	1,356
13	Quicken Loans	60	Midsized	2,951
14	HomeBanc Mortgage	9	Small	1,342
15	Whole Foods Market	18	Large	33,248
16	Edward Jones	3	Large	29,197
17	Republic Bancorp	−9	Small	1,190
18	Baptist Health Care	0	Midsized	4,003
19	Alston & Bird	3	Small	1,509
20	Kimley-Horn & Associates	24	Small	1,777
21	QuikTrip	6	Midsized	7,819
22	American Century Investments	0	Small	1,778
23	Qualcomm	23	Midsized	7,562
24	David Weekley Homes	18	Small	1,361
25	Cisco Systems	8	Large	26,644

Source: Fortune 100 Best Companies to Work For, 2006, http://money.cnn.com/magazines/fortune/bestcompanies/full_list/.

Notes: U.S. employees include part-timers as of time of survey. Job growth is full-time only. All data based on U.S. employees.

Many of the firms on the "100 Best Companies" list have very low employee turnover. They attract good people, and they have programs in place to hold onto them. Consider the potential impact that simple metric may have on the quality of the products and services offered by these firms. When people are comfortable in their jobs and confident in what they are doing, they make fewer mistakes. And their own positive attitude about their work environment cannot help but be communicated to the people they interact with, both inside and outside the company. (See Exhibit 5.6 for the top twenty-five "Best Companies.")

What about the role of the company in the community? A growing number of firms make community service a priority within the company, including providing their employees with incentives to get involved in community service. Southwest Airlines calls its community service program Share the Spirit. It includes such activities as Adopt-a-Pilot, where school students use a variety of skills to track and write about a particular pilot's travels; ongoing sponsorship of an annual camp for child burn patients; ongoing sponsorship of Ronald McDonald houses; and various specialized programs in the cities Southwest flies to all across the United

Exhibit 5.7 **Spider Chart for Automotive Company**

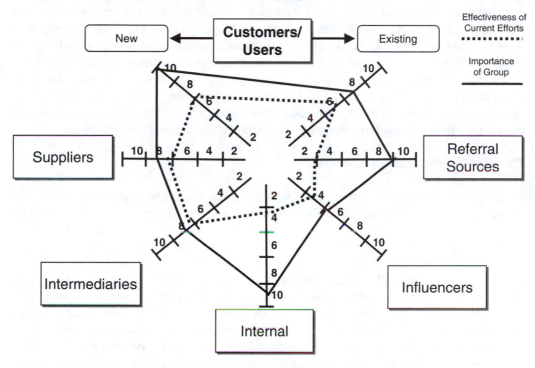

Source: Adapted from M. McDonald, M. Christopher, S. Knox, and A. Payne, *Creating a Company for Customers* (London: Pearson Education, 2001), p. 53.

States.[39] Southwest supports its employees' community activities, which not only enhances the corporate image, but also increases the employees' satisfaction with their employer.

MANAGING COMMUNICATION AMONG THE SIX MARKETS

As noted at the outset of this chapter, in an ideal world companies would have abundant resources so that all six market groups would receive maximum attention and consistent, ongoing communication. Realistically, that is usually not possible. So how does a manager go about deciding which audience to focus on and which deserves only passing attention? Spider charts, key audience leaders, and scorecards are three methods that can help managers with this task.

Using the Spider Chart

In Chapter 2, we introduced the spider chart, a simple graphic tool that allows all six or more potential audiences to be identified, valued, and measured on the same chart (see Exhibit 2.3). By showing all the potential audiences and then rating them in one or several ways, the spider chart makes the challenge of proper allocation of resources less onerous.

Exhibit 5.7 shows a spider chart that maps out the challenges facing a U.S. automotive manufacturer. The chart indicates key areas where the manufacturer might place more attention: employees (frequent, large layoffs have hurt U.S. automotive firms' relationships with their employees); customers (Toyota is poised to take the position of world's leading auto manufacturer); referrals (as sales decline, personal recommendations decline); and influencers (for company stock, for example, brokers may not make it a recommended buy). However, the manufacturer's relationships with intermediaries (car dealers) and suppliers (manufacturers of the component parts of the vehicles) remain reasonably strong because those markets are particularly dependent on the manufacturer's continued success. Spider charts can be based on specific, identifiable information or, often, on consensus management judgment.

The Key Audience Leader Approach

In addition to the spider chart, there are other useful tools that can be employed in this strategic management process. One example is the idea of a key customer or key audience leader (KAL). This is simply the identification of a person or group within the organization who is most familiar with the audience for whom the marketing communication program and, thus, the relationship are being built. The reason for this KAL approach is simple. The marketing group, no matter how well versed in audiences and audience understanding, does not generally have ongoing contact with many of the external or even internal audiences. However, the investor relations group, for example, is regularly in contact with the various members of the financial community, such as analysts, financial writers, and editors of financial publications. Thus, the investor relations people would serve as KALs for these important groups. This does not mean that the investor relations people take on the role of marketing or communication, only that they serve as internal consultants to the people who develop the formal communication programs. KALs can generally be identified for each of the six audiences described in this section simply by determining which internal group has the most contact or the best relationship with each specific audience.

The Value of Scorecards

Customer scorecards are electronic systems that allow the marketing and communication groups to keep track of and manage the investments and returns being made against various customer groups or audiences. Commonly, they are based on some type of ROI model that illustrates how well the communication program is working. Scorecards are an outgrowth of the quantitative systems developed using the Six Sigma methodology (an approach that uses data to track quality levels in an organization's operations) or the balanced scorecard approach as developed by Kaplan and Norton.[40]

Six Sigma is now used in many types of industries; one of the early champions of the process was Jack Welch at General Electric. Six Sigma is about improving quality by minimizing defects and building and improving relationships. The system focuses on identifying factors customers find most important, improving delivery to the customer, examining processes, looking at issues from a customer perspective, building consistency, and designing processes to meet customer needs.[41]

Balanced scorecards are a management methodology designed to ensure that all elements in the organization's activities are given equal weight and that no type of activity is given more emphasis than another. Thus, the term *balanced scorecard* suggests that all elements in the management of the organization must be considered if the firm is to be successful.

Customer scorecards are used in tracking the firm's relationship with key customer groups. Behavior-based metrics are developed for each group, and then performance is measured against those metrics on an ongoing basis. The scorecard can be used not only to track the company's own self-assessed performance, but also to allow different external and internal customer groups to regularly grade the company from their own perspective.

SUMMING UP

Decisions about which customer groups to focus on and how to define target customers within those groups are among the most important ones to be made in developing brand campaigns. Marketers cannot make any informed decisions related to delivery or content until they know which customers will be the focus of the brand communication efforts.

It is critical for the brand communicator to identify and understand the needs of ultimate customers, intermediaries, suppliers, referrals, influencers, and internal markets or other markets or groups and to be able to prioritize them in terms of importance. In order to do that effectively, the brand communicator needs to know as much about each market as possible. We turn next to the types of research marketers use to learn more about their customers and the motivators behind successful brand-customer relationships.

NOTES

1. LG Electronic's Chocolate, www.verizonwireless.com/b2c/.

2. A. Zimmerman, "Thinking Local: To Boost Sales, Wal-Mart Drops One-Size-Fits-All Approach," *Wall Street Journal,* September 7, 2006.

3. Simmons Market Research Bureau, www.smrb.com.

4. Mediamark Research, Inc., www.mediamark.com.

5. U.S. Census Bureau, www.census.gov.

6. A. Bourdeau, "Rocket Launcher," *Strategy,* August 2006, p. 16.

7. S. Reyes, "Study: Wal-Mart Private Brands Are Catching On," *Brandweek,* August 21–28, 2006, p. 9.

8. W. Hoffman, "Coke: Wal-Mart Is It," *Traffic World,* June 19, 2006, p. 1.

9. Zimmerman, "Thinking Local."

10. Aveda, www.aveda.com.

11. Ale-8-One Bottling Company, www.ale8one.com.

12. Kraft Foods, www.kraftfoods.com/crystallight/CL_products.htm.

13. A. Wilkinson, "Tesco Strikes Exclusive P&G Launch Deal," *Marketing Week,* January 24, 2002, p. 5.

14. K. Naughton and M. Hosenball, "The Focus Shifts to Ford," *Newsweek,* October 9, 2000, p. 38.

15. T. Aeppel, "Bridgestone Unit Widens Tire-Recall Effort," *Wall Street Journal,* July 24, 2006.

16. C. Koch, "ABC: An Introduction to ERP: Getting Started with Enterprise Resource Planning (ERP)," CIO.com, www.cio.com/research/erp/edit/erpbasics.html#erp_abc.

17. J. Ettlie, V. Perotti, D. Joseph, and M. Cotteleer, "Strategic Predictors of Successful Enterprise System Deployment," *International Journal of Operations and Production Management* (2005): 953–972.

18. *Lexington Herald-Leader,* "Ohio Fishing for Parts Suppliers," July 15, 2006.

19. J. Katz, "Be Flexible," *Industry Week,* September 2006, pp. 14–15.

20. E. Mala, "Luxury Buildings Crave High-End Brand Alliances," *New York Sun,* November 22, 2006.

21. S. Reyes, "Del Monte Dogs Blogs to Fetch Pet Trends," *Brandweek,* August 7–14, 2006, p. 12.

22. F. Reichheld, "The Ultimate Question," www.bain.com/theultimatequestion/home.asp.

23. J. Goodman, "Treat Your Customers as Prime Media Reps," *Brandweek,* September 12, 2005, pp. 16–17.

24. Ibid.

25. Yahoo! Groups, Search Results for Jeep, http://groups.yahoo.com/search?query=jeep.

26. Jeep, www.jeep.com/jeep_life/events/jamborees/sample_itinerary.html.

27. Hormel, http://media.hormel.com.

28. M. Arnold, "Stepping Up to the Plate," *Medical Marketing and Media,* February 2006, p. 38ff.

29. A. Rindfleisch and C. Moorman, "The Acquisition and Utilization of Information in New Product Alliances: A Strength-of-Ties Perspective," *Journal of Marketing* 65, no. 2 (2001): 1–18.

30. S. Downes, "Semantic Networks and Social Networks," *Learning Organization* 12, no. 5 (2005): 411–418.

31. R. Guth, "Microsoft Nabs Facebook Deal in Reach for More Online Ads," *Wall Street Journal,* August 23, 2006.

32. *Wall Street Journal,* "Ad Notes," August 15, 2006.

33. A full description of Edelman's financial services is available at www.edelman.com/expertise/practices/financial/.

34. A full description of Burson-Marsteller's government relations services is available at www.burson-marsteller.com/pages/functional/government/.

35. Fleishman-Hillard, "NGT (Next Great Thing)," www.fleishman.com/capabilities/products_services/next_great_thing.html.

36. "'A Person Like Me' Now Most Credible Spokesperson for Companies; Trust in Employees Significantly Higher Than in CEOs, Edelman Trust Barometer Finds," Edelman.com, www.edelman.com/news/showone.asp?ID=102.

37. "Fortune 100 Best Companies to Work For, 2006: Genentech," CNNMoney.com, http://money.cnn.com/magazines/fortune/bestcompanies/snapshots/558.html.

38. "Fortune 100 Best Companies to Work For, 2006: Wegmans Food Markets," CNNMoney.com, http://money.cnn.com/magazines/fortune/bestcompanies/snapshots/1558.html.

39. Information on Southwest's many community service projects is available at www.southwest.com/about_swa/share_the_spirit/share_the_spirit.html.

40. R.S. Kaplan and D.P. Norton, "Transforming the Balanced Scorecard from Performance Measurement to Strategic Management: Part I," *Accounting Horizons* 15 (2001).

41. General Electronic, "Key Concepts of Six Sigma," www.ge.com/en/company/companyinfo/quality/whatis.htm.

CHAPTER 6

Finding Customer-Brand Connections

As we have discussed earlier, one of the important aspects of the dynamic interactions between customers and brands today is the wealth of information accessible to customers and prospective customers through a multitude of sources ranging from online search engines to the ability to share information on social networks. Marketers also have more information on customers available to them than ever before. The collection, organization, and analysis of information play a critical role for the marketing organization. In this chapter, we review some of the common methods marketers use to collect customer and market information.

Information is key, even for newly emerging brands in nascent categories. No brand marketer is comfortable making decisions in a vacuum, and even so-called gut decisions usually have some basis in hard data or at least in perceptions of what the data would suggest if available. While changes in information technology and consumer behavior have prompted some changes in how research is conducted and the specific techniques used, the basic need for research has not changed. We discuss the major sources below.

SECONDARY DATA

The starting point for any brand decision making is to look at what information is already available. This previously collected information is referred to as secondary data. It may come from the company's own files or from outside sources.

When identifying and sorting through secondary data, marketers should examine at least four topic areas in order to develop or refine a strategy for the brand. They are the brand itself, the competition, the marketing environment, and the customer. As this book has already suggested, we view customer-related research as the most important and will save it for last here because we will review it in the greatest depth.

The Brand

The critical question to be answered regarding the brand is what, from the customer's point of view, differentiates, or could differentiate, this brand from others. What is the brand's value proposition; that is, the promise being made to the customer? To begin to answer that question, it is important to understand the brand inside and out. When, how, and why was it created? What enhancements have been made to it over the years and what prompted those changes? Where has it been distributed and how has it been priced?

The answers to these questions are important for at least three reasons: a thorough knowledge of the brand and its history (1) can avoid future mistakes or missteps; (2) may identify attributes and/or benefits that have not yet been the focus of marketing efforts and that might be appealing to customers; and (3) can give some indication of what associations with the brand customers may have stored in long-term memory.

Sources of Brand Information

We have discussed customer sources of brand information previously. For the brand planner, the initial point for collecting brand information is generally the company's own records. Past annual reports, marketing plans, promotional literature, and other documents can help to map out the brand's history. Communication planners who are already working with the brand will have access to these materials. In the case of a new brand introduction, some of the materials will be unknown and others proprietary. Yet all publicly traded companies are required to produce an annual report. Many companies now provide links to their current and past annual reports on their Web site; AnnualReports.com also provides a free directory of annual reports available online. This site is searchable by company name, stock symbol, alphabetically, exchange type, industry, and sector.[1]

When reviewing an annual report, it is important to keep in mind that the intended audience is the investment community—that is, stockholders and the analysts who influence stock purchases. Thus, the emphasis in the annual report will typically be on financial data rather than marketing strategies. Still, annual reports contain a great deal of useful information that can give an important perspective on the brand or potential new brand.

For example, Kellogg's 2005 annual report describes the success the company had in taking the Special K Challenge from its roots in Venezuela to Kellogg's markets around the world, with the result that Special K became Kellogg's largest world brand.[2] (Customers participating in the Special K Challenge eat Special K cereal for two meals a day as a means of diet control.) The annual report reviews Kellogg's key business strategies related to its core businesses of cereals and snacks. The report also describes Kellogg's commitment to social responsibility and the company's core values, important elements for internal and external audiences beyond stockholders and the consumers who purchase and eat the company's products.

Because marketers want to understand their brand through customer eyes, the trade and popular media are also important sources of brand information. Articles in newspapers and business publications can shape the opinions of suppliers, intermediaries, influencers, and referral sources as well as customers. Articles in consumer publications and mentions in electronic media can be important information sources for consumers. Many companies maintain a clipping service (traditional or electronic), either internally or through a vendor, to track mentions of the company and its brands in the media. These services monitor a wide variety of sources, both print and electronic, and retrieve all mentions of the company. A review of the clippings file for the last several years can reveal important insights into how the brand is perceived externally.

Marketers can also access a number of electronic information databases to search for information in newspapers, magazines, and television and radio transcripts. ABI-Inform indexes more than 1,800 business-related publications and provides full-text access to many articles. This index is easily searchable and offers ways to limit the search to the most current information. LexisNexis Academic Search is another electronic database. It provides articles from a wide variety of newspapers and other publications. Like ABI-Inform, most citations are full text, and there are tools to focus the search. Readers' Guide Retrospective, an electronic version of the Readers' Guide to Periodic Literature, provides access to articles in consumer publications.

These electronic databases are available through most college libraries and many large public libraries as well. Such widespread access to this information means that most of the secondary research that marketers might need can easily be found through an online session or two.

The Competition

Ideally, it is important to learn as much about the competition as about the brand itself. Obviously, proprietary competitive data may be beyond the brand manager's reach, but learning as much as possible about competitive brands' strategies and business practices will be quite valuable.

There are at least two reasons to gather data about the competition. First, the marketer's brand is in competition with these other brands for a space in the customer's mind and a share of their business. The marketer needs to understand how the customer views competitive brands compared to the marketer's own brand. What types of associations do customers have with those brands? What attributes and benefits are most pertinent? How have those competitive brands segmented the customer market? Second, a competitive focus makes sense from a business point of view. Where are competitors most vulnerable? Where do they stand with regard to the supplier and intermediary markets? What weaknesses can be exploited?

One of the most important decisions in researching the competition is to determine exactly who the key competitors are. Take, for example, Kodak photographic film. On a basic level, Kodak's competition is Fuji photographic film and other, smaller brands and private labels. But, as in many product categories, technological advances have greatly affected the photographic industry. Kodak film also competes with digital cameras in all their various forms (including cell phone cameras), and that competition is far fiercer than any challenge put up by other companies making traditional film products. As prices of high-quality digital cameras decline and intermediaries provide easy access to digital prints, the market for film is becoming increasingly limited.[3]

Focusing only on the directly competitive film brands would result in missing the key challenge to Kodak's business. To reiterate our common theme, the marketer must define competition as the customer defines it. What are the appropriate and/or acceptable substitutes for the brand? Those are the brand's competitors, whether or not they fit neatly into conventional marketing categories.

Sources of Competitive Information

Information sources for competitive data are largely the same as those for data on the marketer's own brand. It is also useful to purchase the competitor's brand, if possible, and to test it in use, the way a consumer would. What differences are apparent between that brand and the target brand? If there are differences, how or why might they be important to prospective customers? Another important source of competitive data, certainly in regard to understanding how competitive customers use those brands, is a careful examination of major competitors' marketing communication materials. What messages are being conveyed in competitors' advertisements and publicity materials? What incentives are competitors offering to their customers? What tone or personality is conveyed through the competitor's Web site?

TNS Media Intelligence provides several products that offer information on where competitive brands are spending their advertising media dollars. Stradegy™ tracks 2.2 million brands in nineteen types of media, including Hispanic media. Ad$pender tracks allocations in eighteen different media types and also provides category and parent company reports; five-year trend data are also available to assess changes in media strategy.[4] (An academic version of Ad$pender is available to colleges and universities.)

The Marketing Environment

Forces outside the company's control can affect brand communication strategy. Constant monitoring of governmental action at the local, state, regional, and national levels is essential to track changes in policy or legislation that might affect the firm's ability to market its product effectively.

For example, U.S. wine lovers and owners of small wineries must contend with varying state regulations on whether and how wine can be shipped directly to customers from wineries outside the customer's home state. Some states place no restrictions on such shipments, some allow shipments only under limited shipping methods, and others ban such sales entirely. The issue has been the subject of a U.S. Supreme Court case, but state-by-state differences persist.[5] A marketer working for a winery would need to keep track of pending court cases, legislative issues, and the trend of consumer sentiment on this issue.

Governmental actions have such a critical effect on firms' business practices that most large companies employ lobbyists, either internally or through a public relations agency, to track and influence legislative decisions. Smaller companies that cannot afford their own lobbyist often rely on trade associations to provide such services. For example, the American Advertising Federation, acting on behalf of its member agencies and advertising practitioners, routinely lobbies in favor of legislation supporting advertising and against any proposals that would restrict a firm's promotional activities, including advertising. Recent efforts have included arguing against proposed restrictions on outdoor advertising and tighter regulation for direct-to-consumer advertising of prescription medications.[6]

Another important area to monitor through secondary research is the other external forces that might affect the company's ability to market its product effectively. Think of the large number of firms whose livelihood is affected by the price of crude oil. Obviously, gasoline companies, auto manufacturers, and retail gasoline operations keep a close eye on this pricing, but so must manufacturers of plastics products, many types of cosmetics, and even petroleum jellies like Vaseline! Recent concern about global climate change has made many consumers more aware of the impact of their actions and the products they buy on the environment. A number of Web sites allow individuals to calculate their "carbon footprint" (their yearly carbon dioxide creation) and then provide suggestions on how to reduce that impact. Many of the suggestions have to do with use of specific types of products or services.[7] If this school of thought continues to develop, marketers may begin including information in their promotional communications materials and on their product packaging on how their product affects carbon dioxide production. That is a factor outside the company's direct control, but one that might well affect its future business.

Sources of Marketing Environment Information

The best way to identify changes and potential changes in the marketing environment is to keep up to date on business and consumer news. Many news and trade publications include regular reporting on emerging trends. "Trendspotting" is considered a legitimate business these days; for example, Burson-Marsteller lists trendspotters as a resource in its work with "e-fluentials," its term for online influencers.[8] Similarly, BIGresearch provides its clients with results of a monthly Consumer Intentions and Actions™ survey that tracks trends among 8,000 consumers.[9] The challenge is not to be caught by surprise in the wake of a trend, but instead to anticipate trends.

The Customer

Secondary research on customers generally consists of examining syndicated research sources and reviewing work published in news sources. A number of research organizations conduct regular studies of customer buying behavior for different market segments and provide those data on a subscription basis. Trade publications frequently produce special reports on key customer groups; for example, *Advertising Age* runs regular features on the Hispanic market, and its sister publication, *American Demographics*, profiles different consumer market segments in each issue.

The firm's own customer database is an excellent source of secondary data. In addition to the information in the database itself, third-party information providers may be used to supply more detailed data through matching the customers in the firm's file to those in the third-party provider's database. Experian, a firm providing data and analysis services in a number of categories, offers one product that can help identify what brands in a given product category various customer segments are purchasing. Experian offers this "share of wallet" service as one of its targeting products.[10]

While a detailed discussion of analytical research techniques that can be used in assessing database information is beyond the scope of this book, there are several useful resources in this area. *Direct Marketing Analytics Journal*, published yearly by the Direct Marketing Association, publishes a variety of articles on data analysis techniques. Bruce Ratner's *Statistical Analysis and Modeling for Database Marketing: Effective Techniques for Mining Big Data* reviews many of the basic statistical techniques essential to database analysis.[11] *The New Direct Marketing: How to Implement a Profit-Driven Database Marketing Strategy*, by David Shephard Associates, includes a number of chapters on statistical analysis techniques.[12] In addition to these publications, the Direct Marketing Association (www.the-dma.org) offers frequent seminars on analytical techniques.

Summary of Secondary Data

Marketers can often obtain a fairly detailed picture of the brand's situation, the competition, the marketing environment, and general consumer trends through secondary research. With the movement of many commonly used secondary sources to the Internet, such data are far more easily accessible than was the case even a few years ago. However, as with any Internet-based research, source knowledge and credibility are key. Users must always be careful to review the source of any information that will be used to develop strategy. Is the source unbiased? If not, what are the likely inherent biases and how might they affect the validity of the information? The number of legitimate sources available online continues to grow, but vigilance is still needed to sort out misleading information.

PRIMARY RESEARCH

Once secondary research has established the parameters under which the brand's marketing program will need to operate and provided general guidance on customer matters, there often remain questions that cannot be answered by any other means than going directly to customers and prospective customers. That is when primary research comes into play: the marketer will gather information specific to the particular situation facing the brand. This can be done either through studies developed specifically for the particular brand situation and funded wholly by the marketer (either internally or by using an outside research firm) or through using syndicated research sources, where costs, and results, are shared across a number of companies. In the latter case, no proprietary information is shared. Syndicated research makes it possible to gather information from many more respondents than can usually be afforded in a custom study.

While some types of primary research can be put into place relatively quickly, doing so involves important trade-offs. We will discuss those methods below, but first, we look at the recommended, systematic process of designing and implementing a quantitative primary research study. Important questions concern what will be studied, who will be contacted, and how contact may be made.

While many organizations are involved in establishing and monitoring policies for primary research, one—the Advertising Research Foundation (ARF)—is of particular interest given our focus. ARF's comprehensive "Guidelines for Market Research," issued in August 2003, are intended to systematize research processes for marketers. The eighty-three-page document details recommended practices and considerations in a number of areas; those related to developing the research plan are reviewed here.

Study Design

The type of research done must obviously fit the data needs. What is the objective of the research? Given that objective, what is the best means of gathering data that will answer the questions? ARF guidelines discuss two broad types of research objectives, strategic and tactical. Examples of strategic studies include "segmentation studies; market studies; brand equity studies; behavioral tracking of market share or media; and many qualitative projects, particularly when conducted as part of segmentation projects."[13] Strategic studies can augment information gathered through secondary research to give a clearer picture of the overall market situation with regard to customers. Tactical research studies tend to focus on narrower areas of inquiry. Some common types of tactical studies are "copy tests; ad tracking studies, media studies; product tests; service evaluations; customer satisfaction studies; pricing studies;

simulated test markets; test market audits; or a variety of other research approaches employing experimental designs."[14] A questionnaire designed to find out how current customers rate the brand relative to competitive brands would be an example of a tactical study.

In determining what type of research approach to use, validity, timing, and costs are key concerns. Validity has to do with accuracy: is the research, in fact, measuring what it is intended to measure, so the results of the study can be used with some confidence? If the marketer is concerned with brand perceptions, but fails to ask about the leading competitive brand, the results will provide only a partial picture of customer attitudes. If the subjects of the research study include a number of people who are outside the target market for the brand, their attitudes may not be representative.

Timing is also related to data relevance; an overly complicated study that takes several months to generate results may be outdated by environmental changes that take place during the course of the study. For example, if a competitor introduces a new product feature part way through data collection, previous results on customer attitudes may well be inaccurate in the new context.

Costs are influenced by data collection mode, study design, and number of respondents involved, among other factors. Cost considerations may reduce validity; cheaper is not always better and in research often leads to sloppy study designs and inaccurate findings.

An additional consideration that is related to all three of these factors is the trade-off between realism and control. A wide range of influences can affect customers' perceptions of brands, including marketing communications messages, in-store conditions, and influence of family members on decision making. Stopping customers in a shopping mall and bringing them into a room to watch television commercials may provide focused evaluation of the ads, but it is not a realistic re-creation of how most commercials are viewed. Controlled experiments offer many benefits to researchers, but realism is not one of them. Depending on the objectives of the research study, control may need to be sacrificed for realism. For example, if the objective is to learn if members of the target market find a particular commercial amusing, a controlled experiment may work just fine. If the objective is to see if the commercial will not only amuse but also prompt purchasing, a more realistic research structure may be necessary.

Choosing Respondents

Finding people, particularly the "right" people (i.e., target audience members), to participate in marketing studies is increasingly difficult. According to studies cited in the ARF guidelines, typical response rates for most research projects are about 20 percent, with only 13 percent cooperation in telephone surveys.[15] Those percentages are frightening for researchers trying to collect useful data for clients. The ARF recommends several ways to improve response rates:

- Carefully train interviewers
- Monitor a sample of interviews
- Anticipate and address privacy concerns
- Give respondents as much information as possible to encourage participation
- Offer incentives for participation
- Keep questionnaires as brief as possible[16]

Exhibit 6.1

Research Considerations for Different Populations

Group	Target definition	Target issues	Getting cooperation
Consumers	Problematic for new products or product categories.	If using lists to develop sample, care needed in list selection.	Offer incentives; use in-person or phone to reduce refusals; emphasize confidentiality.
Customers	May need usage time frame for identification.	Customer lists are typical sampling frame, but may raise questions from those contacted if not notified in advance about research study.	Provide opportunity for direct pass-along of comments and complaints if requested.
Business-to-business	Both broad company choices and selection of respondents within the firm must be defined.	Consider multiple respondents: decision makers, influencers, etc.	Will likely require compensation. Important to notify in advance and possibly schedule an interview.
Employees	Census of employees or sample? If unionized, will need union leadership agreement.	Need to know lines of reporting for respondents to identify place within the organization.	Cooperation more likely if employees believe the data will truly be used to make improvements. Confidentiality extremely important.
Children	Age of targeted respondents will determine survey format and design.	Young children need short surveys.	Incentives very helpful. Permission of parent or guardian required for children aged sixteen or younger.
Multiculture	Is selection based on race, ethnicity, nationality, or some other factor?	Care needed in selection; sample design based on geography can be very biased.	Cultural and racial sensitivity in question design and fieldwork very important.

Source: Derived from Advertising Research Foundation, "Guidelines for Market Research," August 2003, pp. 63–73.

The ARF guidelines discuss a number of types of research participants and offer suggestions for dealing with each of these groups. Exhibit 6.1 summarizes some of those suggestions.

Sampling and Sample Terminology

Except in the case of a true census, research is usually conducted among a small group of people whose opinions are considered to represent those of the larger population. In order to draw an accurate sample, the researcher must first define the population; in most cases, this will be the target market definition the firm has developed for its brand. As noted in our earlier discussion of segmentation, we believe that target market definitions should include behavioral elements. This makes particular sense in terms of research population definitions: people who have used the brand in the past would probably be asked different questions than people who have never used this brand.

The sampling frame is the group of sampling units used to approximate the research population. If the target market is men aged eighteen to twenty-four who use Axe body products three or more times a week, then the sampling unit would be eighteen-year old men, nineteen-year old men, and so on. Since men in this age range can be found in large concentrations on college campuses, the sampling frame might be a student directory at a large university, or young men shopping in supermarkets and drugstores near college campuses, or the like.

But which eighteen- to twenty-four-year-old men will be selected from the sampling frame? Chances are it will not be practical, in terms of time or costs, to attempt to interview every man listed in the college directory. Instead, a smaller group will need to be chosen. If that selection follows certain guidelines, the chosen sample can be considered representative of the larger group within some specified error parameters. Such a sample is considered a "probability" sample. If, instead, the researcher just talks to a group of his friends who are male Axe users from eighteen to twenty-four, they may provide some interesting insights, but cannot be considered representative of other eighteen- to twenty-four-year-old male Axe users. Instead, they are a "nonprobability" sample.

There are a number of approaches that will result in a probability sample. If names are drawn at random from the college directory, that would be a simple random sample. If every fifth (or some other constant increment) name is chosen, that is a systematic random sample. If the directory names are first grouped by age, so all eighteen-year-olds are in one group, all nineteen-year-olds in another, and so on, and then selections are made randomly within each group, that would be a stratified random sample. Other approaches are possible, but these examples should provide a basic idea of how the process works.

How big a sample is needed? The answer depends on what is being studied, how much time is available, how large the research budget is, and how precise the results of the study need to be. In general, more is better—the closer the sample size to the true market size, the more accurate the findings will be. However, one of the reasons for doing sampling is to be able to make projections to a large population from a relatively small sample group. Nielsen uses a sample of a few thousand households to estimate television viewing for the entire U.S. population.

The college directory used in our Axe example is one possible source of respondents. The firm's own database could also be used, or random digit telephone dialing, mall intercepts, or recommendations from experts. There are special considerations when conducting the research study online; because online research is becoming so popular, we will discuss it separately later in this chapter.

Research Instruments

Questionnaires are a popular research device; they provide the opportunity to ask a series of structured questions in a format that makes it easy to compare answers across research respondents. Common types of questionnaires include paper surveys that are either self-administered or administered by an interviewer, telephone surveys, and online surveys. In marketing research, questionnaires usually allow for respondent anonymity, and special measures are needed when respondents are minors.

Questionnaires are generally designed to move from general to specific topics. Demographic information should be requested last unless it is needed to qualify an individual as an appropriate respondent. For example, respondents may be more likely to answer a question about their annual income if they have already invested time in answering a series of questions about the product category and brand rather than if the income question is one of the first they encounter.

Questions must be carefully worded to avoid bias and the likelihood of leading respondents to desired answers; in the case of multiple-choice questions, the researcher must make sure that all possible answer choices are available or offer "other" or "none of these" as a possible choice. If the answer to one question affects what question the respondent should answer next, such skip directions need to be made as clear as possible. Many potential problems with questionnaires can be avoided through careful design.

Overly long questionnaires are one reason for low response rates. Here are the ARF's guidelines for desired questionnaire length:[17]

Screening interviews	2–3 minutes
Telephone interviews	20 minutes
Mall intercepts	30 minutes
Door-to-door	30 minutes
Mail	20 minutes
Internet if invited via email	15 minutes
Internet pop-up intercept on site	5 minutes
Internet pop-up intercept at new site	10 minutes

Questionnaires must always be pretested, both to identify the time requirements for the respondent and to identify any problems with question wording, question order, and the like. Finding a problem with a question only after the survey is in the field can result in much wasted effort, driving up costs and delaying the completion of the research study.

Fielding the Study

Once the sample has been drawn and the questionnaire has been developed and tested, the study must be put into place. If the survey is to be self-administered (that is, the respondents answer questions on their own, without an interviewer's assistance), it must be placed online or paper copies must be made and distributed, along with a mechanism for return of finished surveys. If interviewers will be involved, they must be carefully trained to administer the survey without adding any bias or confusing respondents. The ARF points out that using interviewers with demographic characteristics similar to those of the desired respondents is likely to increase response rates.[18]

Not everyone selected for the sample will ultimately participate in the survey. Some people who are contacted will refuse to participate at all or will stop the interview before it is completed, some people cannot be contacted despite repeated tries, and some will turn out not to meet eligibility criteria after all. It is important that interviewers keep careful records of the status of each person in the original sample, because that information will be needed to calculate the overall response rate for the study.

An important note on those people who are contacted but either refuse to participate or end the interview early: they are completely within their rights to do so. The Respondent Bill of Rights adopted by the Council for Marketing and Opinion Research (CMOR) in 1998 appears in the box below; its tenets guide all legitimate market research conducted in the United States. Other countries have similar codes.

CMOR RESPONDENT BILL OF RIGHTS

What Your Rights Are If You Are Interviewed

Your participation in a legitimate marketing or public opinion research survey is very important to us, and we value the information you provide. Therefore, our relationship will be one of respect and consideration, based on the following practices:

- Your privacy and the privacy of your answers will be respected and maintained.
- Your name, address, phone number, personal information, or individual responses will not be disclosed to anyone outside the research industry without your permission.
- You will always be told the name of the person contacting you, the research company's name, and the nature of the survey.
- You will not be sold anything, or asked for money, under the guise of research.
- You will be contacted at reasonable times, but if the time is inconvenient, you may ask to be recontacted at a more convenient time.
- Your decision to participate in a study, answer specific questions, or discontinue your participation will be respected without question.
- You will be informed in advance if an interview is to be recorded and of the intended use of the recording.
- You are assured that the highest standards of professional conduct will be upheld in the collection and reporting of information you provide.

Marketing and opinion research is an important part of our democratic society, allowing people to express their views on political and social issues, as well as on products and services.

Source: The Council for Marketing and Opinion Research (CMOR), 1998. See www.CMOR.org.

Processing the Data

Once data collection is completed, the data must be put into a format for aggregating the responses. In the case of either telephone or online surveys, this will already have occurred during data collection—interviewers doing telephone surveys typically enter respondents' answers into a computerized program, and then those answers go into some sort of spreadsheet program to facilitate analysis. For in-person or mailed interviews, the responses must be entered into the analysis program in a separate step. In some cases, decisions will have to be made as to whether respondents can be retained in the research study if numerous questions were unanswered or wrongly answered (for example, if a respondent was asked to identify a sole preferred brand but instead specified several brands). Consistency is the key concern here; whatever rules are applied must be used for every respondent.

Presenting Findings

The results of the research study should be presented simply and accurately, with all limitations identified. For example, if a particular question was skipped by a number of respondents, that should be indicated in the study report. Given that many important strategic decisions are made based on research results, it is critically important that those using the research know how the questions were asked and of whom, and are aware of any problems encountered during the study.

Online Research

It has become very popular to conduct both quantitative and qualitative research online. For survey research, the online environment offers benefits such as tremendous flexibility in questionnaire design (including the use of audiovisual elements), convenience of answering for respondents, speed of data collection, and easy download of responses into a form that can be analyzed. Respondents' perceptions of anonymity and data security also make the online environment attractive for studies targeting populations that can be hard to reach through other formats, such as the gay, lesbian, bisexual, and transgendered population.

The biggest drawback to using the Internet to conduct market research is that online populations can never produce true random samples.[19] There is no comprehensive list of Internet users (for any population), so comparisons cannot be made to a known population distribution. That does not mean that surveys conducted online have no value—quite the contrary. It simply means that the limitations of online research must be kept in mind when evaluating the results of those studies.

A number of firms are now active in conducting online research studies for clients. Taylor Nelson Sofres PLC (TNS) conducts research in seventy countries, including running the National Family Opinion panel in the United States.[20] National Family Opinion has been conducting panel-based research since 1946; a recruited panel of consumers participates in a variety of surveys yearly. The panel research allows for fast and easy access to respondents who meet particular demographic characteristics and who have agreed to take part in research studies. Panelists receive email invitations to participate in particular surveys and are awarded points for their participation. Points can be redeemed for cash or prizes or donated as cash awards to selected charities. Survey participation also qualifies participants for raffles and other prize drawings.[21]

Online surveys can take advantage of the Internet's audio and video streaming capabilities to show commercials for comment, provide constant access to product descriptions, and randomly shuffle question order to avoid bias of order effects. A number of companies provide software to construct online surveys using a wide variety of question types, making survey design and posting easier than ever. SurveyMonkey is one such example. It offers clients a wide range of survey features that include both design elements and results downloads.[22]

One word of caution: perhaps because of easy access to the range of survey-building and hosting software, online surveys seem to be everywhere. The anonymity of the Internet offers security to research respondents, but also means that survey administrators cannot know the characteristics of people responding to surveys and have no means of verifying that people's demographic (or purchasing) characteristics are what they say they are. While there are always risks that respondents are providing false or mistaken data in any type of research, the much greater anonymity of the Internet in comparison to face-to-face or telephone interviewing exacerbates the problem. Marketers who decide to use online surveys as part of their primary research should consider establishing a Web site that can be accessed only by respondents who have been invited to participate through email or some other means, where prequalification as part of the desired target audience is possible. Just posting a survey and opening it to anyone who happens to be online is asking for trouble in the form of spurious responses from people without a real interest in your brand.

QUALITATIVE RESEARCH

While surveys and other types of quantitative research can be very helpful for identifying customer trends and some types of behavior, it can be difficult to get at motivations for behavior through a list of closed-ended questions. Qualitative research has long been popular as either a precursor to quantitative studies or on its own as a means of probing customers' knowledge and perceptions more deeply than is usually possible through quantitative approaches. Qualitative methods can be used for both strategic and tactical studies; while respondent numbers are generally lower (sometimes much lower) than with quantitative studies, the depth of information obtained is often worth that trade-off. Qualitative research has grown in importance as marketers increasingly believe that emotions have much to do with consumer purchases. Qualitative research seems much more effective in getting at the basic reasons and motives for consumer decisions.

Observation Research

A trained researcher can often learn a great deal from watching people shop or actually use a product. In the shopping scenario, an observer can record how many different brands a shopper considers within a product category, which product labels she takes the time to read, how many different brands' labels she reads, the length of time she spends in a particular section of a store, and the like. This information can lend insight into the type of decision making occurring (habitual decisions will take less time than limited decisions) or the influence of others on brand choice decisions (a mother shopping for breakfast cereal with her children may buy different items than if she is shopping alone), to name just a few possibilities. This information can also affect marketers' package design decisions, shelf space allocation, and so on.

Imagine the insights that could be gained if an observer spent time watching people cook in their own kitchens. How and where are knives, pans, and measuring utensils stored? What kitchen gadgets are most useful in preparing a dinner for guests? What types of products are staples in the cook's pantry? What brands? While a marketer could certainly ask a person these questions in an interview, actually seeing what items are used and how they are used may provide much more useful information for creative strategy development.

Observation research is widely used in fields such as psychology and anthropology. Its migration into marketing research has come, in part, from the emergence of account planners, a position in advertising and planning agencies that combines traditional research, strategy, and creative inclinations. Account planners are said to represent the voice of the consumer within campaign development, and one way to think like a consumer is to watch consumers in action, interacting with the brand.

In *Truth, Lies and Advertising: The Art of Account Planning,* account planner Jon Steel describes the research that his agency, Goodby, Silverstein & Partners, did to win Sega's video game account. Planners sat with children in their bedrooms while the children and their friends played video games. As Steel explains, "The combination of their own surroundings and their own friends (as opposed to the strangers who are usually required for most focus groups) made them much more relaxed, and for teenage boys, they really had quite a lot to say."[23] The insights revealed by this approach formed the basis of the strategy and probably could not have been discovered through other research methods.

Focus Groups

Focus groups are widely used for both strategic and tactical research. A focus group brings together up to twelve people for a discussion of the category, the brand, advertising executions, whatever the topic of interest might be. The group is led through a focused discussion by a trained moderator, who is careful to make sure that all group members participate without dominating the discussion. People are usually recruited for focus groups based on similarities. Given our emphasis on behavioral segmentation, one focus group might be made up of frequent users of the brand, another of occasional users, and a third of users of the primary competitive brand. The point of the focus group is to explore attitudes and perceptions through social discussion. A conversation among peers can yield far richer insights than answers to a typical survey.

Focus groups are another tool in the account planner's arsenal. According to Merry Baskin of Account Planning Group, "Moderating your own groups is by far the best way of coming to grips with your target audience, putting yourself in their shoes and seeing the world from their perspective. It also gives the planner a confidence and an authority he/she wouldn't otherwise be entitled to. It means you are both a psychologist and an interpreter"[24]—psychologist because part of the moderator's job is to probe the meaning behind seemingly random comments; interpreter because the moderator/planner will later use the information from the focus groups to recommend strategies that will capitalize on the insights gained.

An agency developing a new image-oriented advertising campaign for a major university tested rough executions of television and print advertisements using focus groups. A variety of groups were convened, including current students, alumni, administrators, faculty and staff, opinion leaders, and "average" citizens. The focus group moderators explored perceptions of the university among each group, reactions to the proposed ads, and relative rankings of the ads. The series of focus groups recognized that the proposed campaign would have several target audiences, each of which might well have widely differing perspectives on the ads and the university itself. The focus group discussions allowed participants to react not only to the ads, but to fellow group members' reactions to them, which led to livelier discussion and more detailed explanations of likes and dislikes than would have been the case if the ads had been tested through one-on-one interviews.

The social nature of focus groups in some ways mimics word-of-mouth advertising. The ideal for most brands is to generate positive buzz—word of mouth that takes on a life of its own and builds the brand up far more positively and forcefully than could be accomplished by any media campaign. If a particular brand, creative concept, or sales promotion idea can get a group of focus group participants buzzing, that marketer has clearly done a good job of identifying and responding to real consumer interests. Similarly, concepts that fall flat and generate only negative comments are failing for a reason and should probably be shelved rather than salvaged.

Depth Interviews

Depth interviews are a type of one-on-one qualitative study that uses a basic survey format, but also allows for more varied question types, more in-depth discussion, and greater follow-up to try and get at the reasons behind answers. In *Qualitative Communication Research Methods*, Thomas R. Lindlof and Bryan C. Taylor explain some of the purposes of the qualitative depth interview. They advocate using story-telling and other methods to truly understand the interviewee's perceptions and experiences, finding out what words and phrases are commonly used in talking about the brand and brand experiences, learning about elements that cannot be seen through observation, and asking about past experiences.[25]

Depth interviews often employ a range of "projective techniques," approaches that ask respondents to project their own feelings and perceptions onto the brand in a variety of ways. Projective techniques include storytelling, where the respondent is given a scenario involving the brand and asked to relate a story about that situation; sentence completion, where partial sentences having to do with brand characteristics or brand usage are provided and the respondent must fill in the blank; brand obituaries, where the respondent is asked what accomplishments an obituary written on the "death" of the brand would highlight; bubble drawings, where the respondent is shown a cartoon depicting the brand in a situation and asked to fill in the bubbles with appropriate dialogue; and personification, where the respondent is asked to describe the brand as a person. Many other projective techniques can also be used; these examples merely suggest the range of possibilities.

To marketers who have not had experience working with projective techniques, these ideas may seem somewhat silly. However, these methods can reveal amazing insights into the emotions and imagery people associate with a brand. For example, consider in-depth interviews with cell phone users. Would a Verizon customer highlight the same things in an obituary for Verizon that a T-Mobile customer would bring up in talking about Verizon? What makes a Verizon customer different from a T-Mobile customer? Those differences may well show up in storytelling or personification exercises.

Depth interviews allow the researcher to get beyond simple yes and no answers to questions to probe the reasons behind those answers. Say a survey respondent indicates that a potential new product is of no interest to him, even though he frequently buys that type of product. With a survey, the marketer knows only that the interest is not there; when that respondent's answers are aggregated with those of other respondents, if the majority say the new product holds no interest, the idea will likely stop there. What the survey does not reveal is *why* there was no interest. A depth interview, with the opportunity for follow-up questions, allows the marketer to find out.

Summary of Qualitative Research

While qualitative research does not provide hard statistics and the ability to project the answers of a sample population to a larger group as can be done with quantitative studies, the insights gained through closer contact with fewer respondents can yield very valuable information. Many successful brand campaigns have been developed through qualitative research ("Got Milk," for one—profiled in *Truth, Lies and Advertising*) or through a combination of qualitative and quantitative methods. Qualitative research can be quite helpful at both the start and end of the research process.

For example, focus groups can be used initially to identify customers' key concerns about the brand and what words and phrases they use in describing those concerns. That information can then be used to develop a quantitative survey, including question choice, question wording, and range of answer options. Once the quantitative results have been analyzed to identify the prevalence of various perceptions, message concepts developed to address those perceptions can be tested in depth interviews to see if the new messages are successful in altering negative perceptions or in reinforcing existing positive perceptions.

RELATIONSHIP RESEARCH

In recognition of growing marketer interest in assessing success at building relationships between customers and brands, there are now firms that specialize in providing both syndicated and custom research to measure this success.

Net Promoter (www.netpromoter.com) helps companies determine who their brand's promoters and detractors are and then track what those people are saying about the brand. Promoters are brand advocates, people "so enthusiastic about a firm or brand that they not only increase their own purchases, but also refer their colleagues or friends."[26] Detractors, on the other hand, have had a bad experience with the brand and actively discourage others from using it.[27] Net Promoter offers a way to quantify the effects of each group. Its Net Promoter Score subtracts the percentage of detractors for a brand from its percentage of promoters. A company whose customers are all extremely happy would have 100 percent promoters. The Net Promoter Score is believed to be a key indicator of likely company growth. Companies that have many promoters who recommend them to other prospective customers will grow much faster than those with few promoters and/or many detractors. Net Promoter lists top-performing companies on its Web site; a list of some of those brands is shown in Exhibit 6.2.

A company's Net Promoter Score can be assessed using research products from Satmetrix Systems, a provider of Customer Experience Management research applications.[28] Satmetrix Solutions offers specialized software, support, and consulting services to help its clients fully understand their customers' perceptions and needs related to the brand and the company.[29] The thinking underlying the Net Promoter Score concept and approaches to collecting the necessary data are described in *The Ultimate Question: For Opening the Door to Good Profits and True Growth*, a book by Fred Reichheld of Bain & Company, the codeveloper of Net Promoter.[30]

Exhibit 6.2

Net Promoter List

	Winners		Sinners	
	Highest (percent)	Promoter	Highest (percent)	Detractor
Airlines	63	Southwest	34	Northwest
Rental car	53	Enterprise	28	Avis
			28	Dollar
Car brands	74	Saturn	49	Mercury
Full-service brokerage	64	AG Edwards	36	Merrill Lynch
Retail banks	66	Commerce Bank	45	KeyBank
Cell phones	42	SBC	56	Quest/US West/MCI-WorldCom
Credit cards	94	USAA	55	Providian
Wintel PCs	62	Dell	33	Acer
Health insurance	47	AFLAC	60	Health Net
Life insurance	72	USAA	49	Aetna Cigna
Property & Casualty Insurance	83	USAA	40	CAN
Shipping/Delivery	66	FedEx	22	Airborne
Department stores[a]	59	Target	55	Macy's
Do It Yourself stores[a]	70	True Value	50	Ace
Drug stores[a]	55	Walgreens	54	Osco
Grocery stores[a]	81	Costco	28	Safeway

Source: The Net Promoter Database built by Satmetrix, Q1 2001–Q1 2005.

Notes: [a] represents data from a survey sponsored by Bain & Company performed in Q4 2004.

The percentage scores represent the percentage of brand users who rate the brand highly minus the percentage of brand users who rate the brand poorly. A brand that had only happy users have a score of 100 percent.

Young & Rubicam, a marketing communications agency, uses its BrandAsset Valuator to assess the strength of its clients' brands and those of their competitors. The BrandAsset Valuator investigates more than 35,000 brands from forty-four countries on dimensions of differentiation, energy (the brand's ability to adapt), relevance, esteem, and knowledge.[31] Based on extensive consumer questionnaires, brands within a product category can be placed on a matrix relative to their strength (differentiation and relevance) and stature (esteem and knowledge). For example, in 2006 results for the Australian market in video games, Sony Playstation was ranked highest on both brand strength and brand stature, while Sega was rated lowest on both areas (although higher on stature than on strength).[32]

Another relationship measure is the Taylor Nelson Sofres Conversion Model. This technique assesses customers' commitment to a brand, with commitment defined as "the likelihood of repurchase based on what's in the consumer's mind."[33] The Conversion Model groups current customers into one of four levels of commitment and noncustomers into one of four levels of availability. Commitment levels range from entrenched, the strongest level, to convertible, the weakest level. Availability levels range from available to strongly unavailable. The questionnaire used for the Conversion Model takes under five minutes to administer and has been used for more than 300 product categories in multiple countries.[34] The Conversion Model Web site (www.conversionmodel.com) includes a number of case studies showing applications of the model in different product categories and to answer different types of marketing questions.

Net Promoter, the BrandAsset Valuator, and the Conversion Model are just a few examples of syndicated research (some with custom services available) that can be used to probe customer perspectives on brands in order to develop more complete understanding of the strength and nuances of the customer-brand relationship. These and similar services are applying traditional research methods in new ways to gain insight into customers' thinking.

SUMMING UP

If planning is to start with the customer, then marketers must know as much as possible about customers, beginning with their behavior regarding the brand, but also including their perceptions of the brand, the sources of those perceptions, the depth of the perceptions, the ways that the brand fits into their lives, their motivations for using the brand, their attitudes toward the brand and the company, their perceptions of competitors; the list of useful information is endless. Effective planning starts with effective research, which starts by formulating useful research questions: what does the marketer really need to know right now to make decisions? Can those questions be answered through analysis of existing data (secondary research)? If not, what type of primary research will be most useful? Are there syndicated services that can provide the necessary answers, or is a custom study required? If the latter, should it be a quantitative study, a qualitative study, or some combination? The important thing is to get the answers to these questions from the brand's customers, not simply to make assumptions about how customers feel. Successful customer-brand relationships demand mutual understanding, and research is the marketer's best tool to develop and enhance the relationship.

NOTES

1. AnnualReports.com, www.annualreports.com.

2. Kellogg Company, *The Tiger Inside*, Annual Report, 2005, p. 4.

3. W. Bulkeley, "Kodak's Loss Widens as Revenue Declines 8.8%; Making of Digital Cameras Will Now Be Outsourced; More Job Cuts Are Planned," *Wall Street Journal,* August 2, 2006.

4. TNS Media Intelligence, "Media Intelligence for Advertising Agencies," www.tns-mi.com/prodAd-Agencies.htm.

5. Free the Grapes! News, "Direct Shipping News Headlines," www.freethegrapes.org/news.html.

6. American Advertising Federation, Government Affairs, Legislative Activity, "Outdoor Advertising Alert," August 14, 2006, and "Urgent Action Request—DTC Advertising," September 5, 2006, www.aaf.org/default.asp?id=164.

7. Examples may be found at Conservation International (www.conservation.org) and Carbon Footprint (www.carbonfootprint.com).

8. Burson-Marsteller e-fluentials®, "Trendspotters," www.efluentials.com/Efls1/resources/trendspotters.jsp.

9. BIGresearch, Complimentary Top Line Findings, www.bigresearch.com.

10. Experian, Marketing Solutions, "Targeting: Reaching the Right People with the Right Message," www.experian.com/direct_marketing/targeting.html.

11. B. Ratner, *Statistical Modeling and Analysis for Database Marketing: Effective Techniques for Mining Big Data* (Boca Raton: CRC Press, 2003).

12. David Shephard Associates, *The New Direct Marketing: How to Implement a Profit-Driven Database Marketing Strategy,* 3rd ed. (New York: McGraw-Hill, 1999).

13. Advertising Research Foundation, "Guidelines for Market Research," August 2003, pp. 13–14.

14. Ibid.

15. Ibid., p. 17.

16. Ibid., pp. 18–19.

17. Ibid., p. 36.

18. Ibid., p. 48.

19. Ibid., p. 76.

20. Taylor Nelson Sofres corporate fact sheet, www.tns-global.com/corporate/.

21. National Family Opinion, MySurvey.com, http://mysurvey.com/aboutus.cfm.

22. SurveyMonkey, www.surveymonkey.com.

23. J. Steel, *Truth, Lies and Advertising: The Art of Account Planning* (New York: Wiley, 1998), p. 131.

24. M. Baskin, "What Is Account Planning? (and What Do Account Planners Do Exactly?): A Revised Millennium Definition," Account Planning Group, 2007, www.apg.org.uk/about-us/what-is-planning.cfm.

25. T.R. Lindlof and B.C. Taylor, *Qualitative Communication Research Methods*, 2nd ed. (Thousand Oaks, CA: Sage, 2002), p. 173.

26. Net Promoter, "Promoters," www.netpromotor.com.

27. Net Promoter, "Detractors," www.netpromoter.com.

28. Satmetrix, "Solutions," www.satmetrix.com/solutions/overview.htm.

29. Satmetrix, "About Satmetrix," www.satmetrix.com/company/overview.htm.

30. F. Reichheld, *The Ultimate Question: For Opening the Door to Good Profits and True Growth* (Boston: Harvard Business School, 2006).

31. Young & Rubicam, "Our BrandAsset Valuator," www.yr.com.

32. George Patterson, Young & Rubicam, BrandAsset Valuator, 2006 Results, www.brandassetvaluator.com.au/.

33. Taylor Nelson Sofres, Conversion Model, "What Is the Conversion Model?" www.conversion-model.com.

34. Taylor Nelson Sofres, Conversion Model, "Frequently Asked Questions," www.conversionmodel.com.

CHAPTER 7

DATA

Using the Database to Separate Good and Bad Customers

From the preceding four chapters it should be clear that having substantial information about those people or organizations with whom the marketer wants to build a customer-brand relationship is a key element for success. By being able to identify customers and prioritize them; by understanding how customers think and how they process, store, and use information; by knowing or at least understanding what customers want, need, and desire; and, most of all, by understanding how that information can be gathered, assimilated, and used, the marketing communication manager can develop strategies and programs that will lead to powerful, ongoing customer-brand relationships. The challenge for marketers is to turn the millions of bits and bytes of data they have on customers and prospects into useful, well-informed insights that enhance brand communication efforts. Simply gathering hoards of audience or customer data points is not enough. To be useful, customer information and knowledge must be managed with as much care and thought as any other corporate asset. In fact, customer information and knowledge may be among the most valuable assets the organization possesses, but it is often underleveraged. Too often customer data a fragmented, isolated in various parts of the organization, and accessible only with great difficulty by the managers who could put the information to profitable use.

Because customer information is typically stored electronically in computerized databases, this chapter will focus on a managerial view of how all these valuable bits and bytes can be gathered, managed, analyzed, and applied to provide real customer insight so that effective, ongoing customer-brand relationships can be built and maintained.

We do not intend, however, to submerge readers in a mass of statistical analysis, relationship paradigms, and computer programming methodology. This chapter is designed to be user-friendly, to provide a practical, nontechnical, and managerially oriented grounding in data and databases. In our view, a general understanding of a customer database, how it is organized and how it might be used, is what is really critical to building long-term customer-brand relationships. We will leave the technology to the experts on whom marketers will want to draw on a regular basis.

To start, there are a few things managers need to know about data and databases. A database is simply an electronic storehouse for business or customer information from which information can be extracted and analyzed as needed. Ideally, the database is structured so that mangers can find exactly what they need, use the information or combine it with other bits of captured or stored data, and then return it for others to use in the future. Thus, the database is a shared value for all managers in the organization. It is not a private cache that a person or group of people could or should control or to which access is limited to only a favored few. A database is only as good as the information that is shared across the organization.

In too many instances, unfortunately, databases have been reserved and controlled for the convenience of the database builders and information technology managers, not for marketing people who could apply the data to build better relationships with customers and prospects. Fortunately, those days of database mystification are being replaced by programs and approaches focused on user accessibility. That change allows marketers with limited technical capabilities to engage with and use the data.

In this chapter, we will develop a managerial perspective on how data are gathered, managed, disseminated, and applied to business operations. Our intention is to enable marketers to become sufficiently fluent and facile in the use of basic customer database analytical tools so they can communicate their objectives and needs to an analyst or database manager without resorting to an advanced statistical text. We start first with a brief description of the varieties of internal and external customer information that may be contained in a database and how these data can be integrated, consolidated, and applied to managerial tasks. That discussion is followed by some relatively simple data manipulation methodologies dealing with audiences, customers, and prospects. And, finally, we will provide some tools and techniques that can be used to determine the value of a customer or group of customers. Along the way, we will provide examples of how customer data can be used to develop well-defined, customer-based, effective brand communication programs.

WHAT MARKETERS KNOW ABOUT CUSTOMERS: TYPES OF CUSTOMER DATA

Most organizations have enormous amounts of information about their customers, although it is often dispersed in a variety of locations across the corporation and even among outside suppliers. Chapter 6 delved deeply into the types of customer data that can be developed and stored through various types of primary and secondary market research activities. However, other, internally generated sources of information may exist within the organization and are also valuable in developing customer insight. For example, Exhibit 7.1 illustrates the internal data sources commonly maintained by organizations in departments as disparate as sales, marketing, research, customer service, technical support, and even accounting.

Likewise, different business units and subsidiaries may develop their own databases without regard to the data collected or stored within sister units or other parts of the organization. Thus, it is not uncommon for a large corporation to have dozens, if not hundreds, of databases containing various types of information on customers and prospects that is known only to them. Thus, the organization commonly has much more information than it knows about or can use simply because it has not been organized into a customer-focused database. Often, finding the available customer data within the firm is the first task in building a customer relationship. Much of this information comes into the firm as a result of business operations. The most common types of information are the names and addresses of existing customers, their service history, the warranties they submit, the rebates they request, the financial records of purchases and payments, and the technical support they have requested. These data are

Exhibit 7.1 **Capture and Storage of Data in Multiple Areas of the Organization**

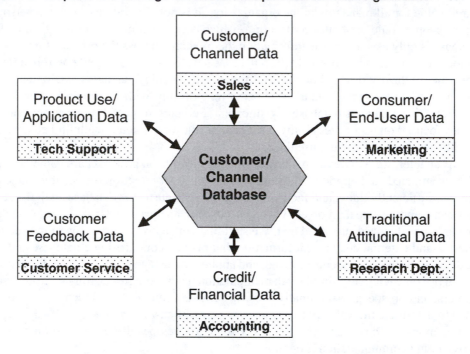

often held in separate databases created and managed by siloed groups throughout the firm. Some of this information may be easily accessed and aggregated if the files are compatible and use a common format or code structure. However, more often data gathered by different departments or business units for their specific purposes are in a different form and format than the other databases within the same firm. This may make it difficult or impossible to get a "single view" of a given customer; that is, a view reflecting the totality of what is known about that customer and his or her interactions with the organization. Another problem is that the marketing staff is sometimes denied access to nonmarketing data or able to access it only with great difficulty and delay. Thus, in many organizations, the first hurdle in database management is finding, aggregating, and aligning the various data sources so that managers can develop a complete, concise, and useful understanding of the business and its audiences in order to build customer-brand relationships.

Dimensions of Customer Data

So far we have discussed externally generated data that result from primary and secondary market research, as well as data that arise internally as the result of customer interactions with the business. Another way to look at the data gathered on customers is to consider two additional dimensions of customer data—measured versus implied data, and observable versus projectable data, as depicted in Exhibit 7.2. All types of data play a role in shaping customer insight, but it is useful and necessary to understand the nature—and the limitation—of each.[1]

Exhibit 7.2 **Observable Versus Projectable Data**

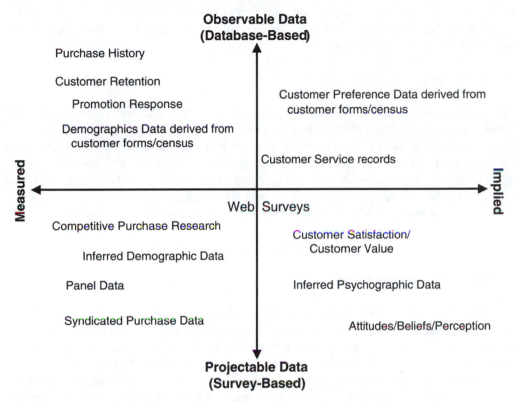

Source: D.E. Schultz and H. Schultz, *Leveraging Customer Information: Driving Strategic Direction and Marketing Profitability* (Houston: American Productivity and Quality Center, 2000).

Measured Versus Implied Data

Measured data are concrete information reflecting the actual behaviors of customers; for example, the number of customers who bought a given product during a certain time period, the number who responded to a direct mail promotion, the number of nights someone stayed in a hotel, or the percentage of magazine subscribers who renewed their subscription. Implied data, on the other hand, are typically gathered through survey methods or through episodic customer contacts and comments.

Implied data are generally more qualitative and less structured information, often based on a sampling of customers or prospects. Brand awareness, brand preference, and similar forms of attitudinal research often fall under the category of implied information, as do such qualitative research methods as focus groups and one-on-one interviews. Since implied data are usually gathered on a relatively small sample of customers and prospects, they are often too difficult to standardize, match, or append to one primary customer database. Thus, implied data are typically not linked to actual customer records, but are sometimes used as the basis for scoring customers according to certain characteristics that they may share. For example, a marketer may not have direct knowledge of a particular customer's lifestyle. But by using census data (zip code) and incorporating implied data from a firm conducting psychographic research, marketers may categorize families within a certain zip code as "Blue Bloods" and in another zip code as "Blue Collars."

Observable Versus Projectable Data

Observable information is based on actual, traceable customer behaviors and data (e.g., purchases, usage, age, and marital status, provided by customers or surrogates). It can include hard data, such as the number of items purchased, but it may also include customer-volunteered soft data, such as a preference for an aisle seat or a low-fat meal on an airline. By contrast, projectable data are based on information gathered through surveys and other sample-based techniques, which is then projected to the entire universe of customers or prospects. That is, if 55 percent of survey respondents are college graduates, and if the sample was properly balanced to the overall customer population, then a marketer can project that approximately 55 percent of the entire customer base has graduated from college.

Challenge of Data Integration

As can be seen from the discussion so far, organizations often have many types of customer information available to them, usually located in multiple files within the organization. Thus, the key task in any customer-brand relationship-building program is to find the right information, wherever it may reside, and find a means to integrate it to achieve a holistic, meaningful view of customers and prospects. The challenge is further complicated by the fact that some types of data have inherent characteristics that make it more or less feasible to undertake integration. Additionally, different tools may be used to link data with very different characteristics. For example, highly measurable and observable data are often captured and stored in databases. Therefore, it is likely they can be linked through methods such as extraction, name matching, or other automated means. Data that are implied and projected, on the other hand, cannot be easily "matched" to a database. However, they can be used to profile, score, or otherwise tag records within the database that match certain criteria. Generally, data with similar characteristics and sources are easy to integrate and link, while those using very different methodologies are often more difficult. However, even where data cannot be actually physically linked using software or other technological means, it is possible to use the insight or learning of one data source in order to shape or improve the exploration of another. This is the essence of how organizations seek to leverage their available knowledge assets to build customer-brand relationships.

LEVERAGING CUSTOMER INFORMATION: A FRAMEWORK

In a study of customer data integration practices conducted for the American Productivity and Quality Center, Schultz and Schultz developed a framework depicting how organizations best utilize and integrate the various sources of customer knowledge that they possess or can access.[2] That framework is shown in Exhibit 7.3. The three key elements of the framework

Exhibit 7.3 **Framework for Leveraging Customer Information**

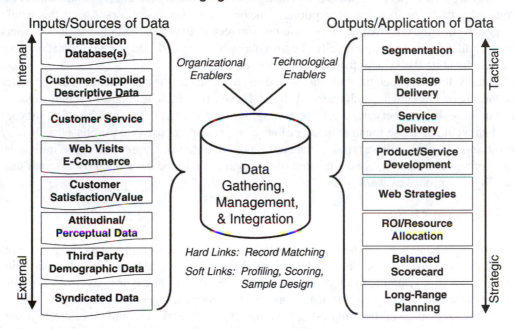

Source: D.E. Schultz and H. Schultz, *Leveraging Customer Information: Driving Strategic Direction and Marketing Profitability* (Houston: American Productivity and Quality Center, 2000).

are (1) inputs, the various sources of customer information, (2) outputs and applications, or how the data are applied for marketing and organizational management, and (3) the tools and mechanics used to manipulate and move data around to create new combinations and groupings that lead to better customer insights.

Sources of Customer Data

Shown on the left side are some examples of the sources and forms of data that an organization might maintain or to which it might have access. In the exhibit, the data inputs are arranged from bottom to top from external (data that the marketing organization would acquire from an outside vendor or other supplier) to internal (data that the company would gather and maintain itself, such as company records of customer purchases, transactions, service visits, and supply interactions).

At the bottom of the graphic are examples of external sources of data—syndicated data and market-wide information gathered by third party organizations. These types of data generally describe an entire market or segment of a market. Typically, that includes very broad, general information such as demographics, geographics, or psychographics about various customer groupings (e.g., urban versus rural, education level, "soccer moms"). This type of information is commonly gathered by external suppliers, organized, and then sold or rented to marketers for their own use or to enable them to develop further analysis. Research data services such as Simmons, NFO, and R.L. Polk represent this type of syndicated data.

Moving up the spectrum, we come to data gathered by the organization to understand customers' attitudes, values, and perceptions of the brand and its competitors. Again, this would largely be implied information that is assumed (projected) to reflect the thinking of customers with similar attributes. Additionally, the firm may gather, record, and store information from customers at its Web site or through customer service points.

Finally, the most specific of all customer data are those that the customer actually provides or that are part of known purchase transactions. These would include details of actual inquiries or purchases by product category, price, timing, and the like. The best examples of these types of data would be those found in hotel, airline, or supermarket customer purchase/use loyalty programs. Typically, these types of data are captured, organized, and held by the individual marketing organization, although some of this material may be developed by external data intelligence groups as well.

Applications of Data

On the right-hand side are the ways the data outputs can be applied to marketing activities within the organization. As shown, these capabilities are arranged from top to bottom to indicate a spectrum ranging from the highly tactical activities of brand or marketing managers to the more long-ranging and strategic concerns of senior management.

At the tactical level, the simplest application of customer data would be to create a segmentation or aggregation scheme, as will be discussed in the next section. Additionally, customer data can be used to improve the relevancy of brand communication by sending customized messages to different customer segments. It can also be used to support customer service activities, so customer representatives have complete information about a customer's history in front of them during a service call. In the somewhat longer term, customer data and insight are invaluable in shaping new or improved products, developing new services, or seeing which segments respond best to new offerings or messages or features on the corporate Web site. At the most sophisticated level, the data held in the database can be used as part of the organization's balanced scorecard or dashboard, tracking such key metrics as customer retention, revenue per customer, number of products sold or held per customer, and so on. And, finally, customer data can and should be a central input into the long-range, strategic plans of the firm. For example, by analyzing and understanding long-term birth trends, the firm might be able to create new businesses or new technologies in anticipation of the market rather than simply reacting to those customers once they are identified.

Data Gathering, Management, and Integration

In the middle of the illustration, between the inputs and outputs we have just described, are found the actual database(s) and the analysis engine or data manipulation structure. This is where the complications of database management occur and where technical expertise is commonly needed. This is where the data analysts apply their skills in managing the available data to generate more sophisticated information on the intended customer. Here, the analyst uses various forms of statistical analysis such as correlation and regression analysis—ANOVA and CHAID—to create new customer groupings or to develop a better understanding of the identified segments that enables the database manager to do the data gathering, manipulation, management, and integration of various types of data. Typically this analysis of this type, using these methodologies takes two forms. The first is hard linking of data between two or more databases, whereby records are matched according to name, account number, or other formula, The second, when exact record matching is not possible, is soft linking—that is, applying inferred data through a scoring mechanism by matching and creating profiles for certain customer behaviors or characteristics, or structuring samples used for research so that they can be related back to the specific segments from which they were drawn.

Most importantly, this step is where the statistical analysis or "data tumbling" occurs. We will discuss some common and powerful forms of data analysis later in this chapter.

One final point: at the top, feeding into the database analytical engine, are two other factors that determine the organization's ability to integrate customer knowledge. On the left are the organization enablers. These are the managerial structures, internal alignments, cross-functional teams, corporate culture, and other elements that assist the entire organization in bringing all the needed data together to conduct the proper analysis. On the right side are the technological enablers. These are generally the data management programs, processes, software, and the like used to manage and manipulate the data to provide the answers that the marketing manager or the firm is seeking. When these two types of enablers are combined, a useful, usable, and relevant database program generally can be developed.

While database integration is an interesting challenge and one that most marketing organizations face, the technical aspects are well beyond the scope of this text. Our focus will not be on how to delve into this process. There are a number of other books and references that can assist in the development of a customer/channel database. It is sufficient here to say that, in our experience, most marketing organizations have sufficient data on audiences, customers, and prospects from which to build very successful analytical tools that can provide customer insights to guide customer-brand relationship programs. So it is not a lack of data, but rather a lack of data access and incompatible formats that are often the biggest barriers preventing organizations from realizing the full potential of their customer information assets.

How Much to Invest in the Database

At this point, the question often arises about the depth, complexity, and content an organization needs in its database. The answer can be as simple as a spreadsheet holding the names and addresses of customers who have purchased in the past or as sophisticated as a powerful data warehouse linking dozens of subsidiary databases in a comprehensive customer relationship management (CRM) system. While the costs of computer hardware and software have decreased dramatically in recent decades, the development and management of customer databases still demand an enormous investment of money, time, and managerial attention for most organizations. Therefore, it is critical that the organization fully and realistically assess its database requirements prior to installing the equipment and programs. Some years ago, Targetbase Marketing developed a managerial view of databases in terms of what an organization really needs to build ongoing relationships with customers. That is illustrated in Exhibit 7.4. The Targetbase approach correctly relates the size and complexity of the database to two other factors—the value that individual customers might represent to the firm and the types of data-driven marketing programs that would be used as a result of database capabilities.

Exhibit 7.4   **Managerial View of Database Requirements**

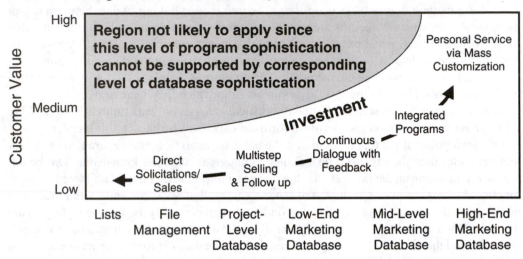

Sophistication of Database Technology

Source: D. Schultz and J. Walters, "Measuring Brand Communication ROI" (New York: Association of National Advertisers, 1977), p. 160.

Customer Value

The value of an individual customer is determined, at least in part, by the product category and the nature of the customer-brand relationship. For example, toothpaste marketers have many thousands of consumers, but each one represents a relatively low dollar value. Additionally, the relationship with the customer is fairly straightforward and does not include a need for repeated support and customized communication. Airlines, on the other hand, have a very different relationship with customers. The value of each transaction is substantially higher, and the customer may communicate with the airline in many ways and at many points in time. In short, there is much more information to be maintained on an airline customer than on a buyer of toothpaste, and much more financial incentive for the airline to capture, store, and manage this information. Determining customer value will be discussed later in this chapter, but for now the basic idea should be clear.

Data-Driven Marketing Programs

The other key investment variable is how the data are to be applied in marketing programs. If the data are to be used simply for contacting customers or prospects for purposes of a sales solicitation, then a simple name and address list may be sufficient. However, as the customer contact program becomes more complex, so do the costs of developing and maintaining the supporting database. Thus, if a continuous, integrated, multicontact communication program is needed, then a more elaborate (and expensive) database will be required. At the highest end would be programs supporting highly personalized and customized communication, such as might be the case with the airline example used above.

The key is for the organization to balance its database needs and expectations against the required sophistication and investment, with an eye on how the investment can potentially pay out in improved and enhanced customer-brand relationships. The technology should enable the appropriate level of marketing capabilities, and the level of expenditure in the system should be driven by the potential payback. Too often we see the reverse—the technology installed with little consideration of how it can or will be utilized to enhance customer value and strengthen customer loyalty or brand relationships. This commonly leads to suboptimal outcomes. On one hand, a company could overinvest in technology that is not truly justified given the value of the firm's customers and the programs that are to be directed toward them. Or, just as damaging, the company might underinvest in a system that cannot deliver the level of sophistication or capabilities required to support ongoing, complex relationships with high-value customers.

At this point, we can begin to develop certain database concepts that will help marketers gain understanding and insight in their relationships with customers.

USING AND ANALYZING CUSTOMER DATA

Of much more interest than gathering and storing data is what is done with that data to help construct effective customer-brand relationship programs. For that task, marketers need to understand some of the analytical tools and techniques that turn bits of raw data into compelling customer insights. We will start with a brief discussion of some basic concepts that will help neophyte marketing managers acquire a general understanding of the analytical tools used in database analysis.

Common Statistical Analytical Tools Used in Database Analysis

As indicated earlier, this is not a book on data or databases although we will rely heavily on the use of customer data in developing customer-brand relationships. But since databases are becoming so common and the use of data analysis so critical in gaining customer insights, the marketing or communication manager needs at least a working knowledge of statistical analysis simply to understand what and how data are manipulated.

Three analytical techniques are commonly at the core of any type of statistical analysis. These are cross-tabulations, correlation analysis, and regression analysis. Each is discussed quite briefly in the section below to provide a working knowledge of what they are and how they are used.

Cross-Tabulations

Cross-tabulations are simply tables that have been created by comparing one factor by another. For example, a marketer might compare the number of customers in a database by age breaks—for example, those under 24, those 25 to 49, and those over 49 years of age. More complex tables can be created by cross-tabbing those age breaks by income categories—for example, annual income under $34,999, annual income $35,000 to $49,999, and annual income over $50,000. Thus, the marketer could create discrete groups of target customers by age and income—individuals 25 to 49 with incomes under $34,999, individuals 25 to 49 with incomes between $35,000 and $49,999, and so on. These would then be the age-income cross-tabs created from the database.

Correlations

Correlations represent how closely variables or data points in the database are related. That is, can we predict one variable or data point from another variable or data point? In the cross-tab illustration above, if there is a high degree of relationship between age and income of customers—that is, if age goes up and income goes up at the same rate—the two variables are said to be correlated: they vary together. If age goes up and income stays the same or goes down, the two variables are not correlated. Correlation is a valuable tool since if there are strong correlations among variables in the database, it can be assumed that when only one variable is known, the general nature of the other can be inferred.

Regression Analysis

Regression is a statistical technique used to predict the value of one variable from another. Where correlation simply seeks to identify the relationship between one variable and another, regression is used to predict the value of a second variable by knowing the distribution of the data points of the first data set. By constructing a line that best represents the direction or vector of the data points in the variable, it is possible to estimate the value of a second variable. For example, a manager might plot the age and income of 100 customers on a chart. The x-axis represents age and the y-axis income. The manager then draws a line of best fit between all the points on the graph. This line will indicate if age and income are positively related (the plotted line goes up) or negatively related (the line goes down) or unrelated (the line is flat). Using the regression line, the manager can then predict the future value of other customers simply by knowing either their age or their income. Thus, knowing a customer is thirty-seven years old will yield an accurate estimate of his income. Regression analysis is a key element in any type of database usage.

While data analytics can become very statistically complex, most database manipulation generally involves one or more of the techniques just discussed—cross-tabs, correlation, and regression. More details on these and other statistical or analytical techniques can be found in any social statistics text.

With this basic understanding of how data in a customer database are analyzed, we can move on to discuss how the use of those analytical tools can provide customer insight.

Using Data to Aggregate Customers by Their Behavior

One of the first tasks in understanding and using the data is to find ways to either separate the audiences so that relevant and cost-efficient content and delivery programs can be created. Exhibit 7.3 showed that the most basic tactical output of database analysis is some type of segmentation scheme. So we start there.

Segmentation means that the customer market for the product or service is broken into smaller, mutually exclusive groups or units that have some common elements or relationships. For example, families with children have different needs than households consisting of a single

Exhibit 7.5   **Segmentation and Aggregation**

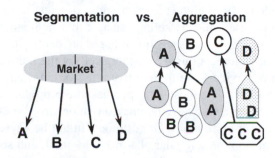

individual or families without children. By identifying smaller groups of people with common needs, wants, or desires, desires being those things which are essentially aspirational, the marketer can identify much more specific delivery systems to reach them and develop much more relevant messages that might interest them. This strategy is substantially more effective than trying to find one common medium or message that would appeal to the entire range of the population. Thus, segmentation or market separation is one of the most basic of all marketing activities.

Traditionally, segmentation was done using broad, readily available demographic or geographic information, largely because media organizations profiled their audiences along these dimensions. In the 1970s and 1980s it also became common to segment customer groups along psychographic lines, which reflected somewhat more complex data based on socio-economic status and lifestyle characteristics. Despite the widespread use and popularity of these approaches, however, they are not necessarily the most effective means of developing a successful customer-brand marketing program.

As shown in Exhibit 7.5, there are two ways of organizing customers or prospects and placing them in common interest or need-related groups. The first is traditional segmentation using implied data that have been attributed and projected to the population of prospects. This occurs when the marketer creates the segments or groups customers and/or prospects based primarily on how the marketer believes the product or service to be offered should be used. This approach is often used when the marketer has little specific information about the individual customer's needs or wants. Thus, the marketing approach is to rely on some type of surrogate measure in place of customer knowledge.

Therefore, the marketer relies primarily on demographic attributes such as age, sex, income, education, and geography to group people into likely prospects for the product or service. The marketer makes assumptions about people's interest in the product or service to be sold and thus develops marketing approaches that attempt to interest those people in the offering. At its worst, this approach reflects the supply-chain business model discussed in Chapter 2. The company has made the product or developed the service; now it must find people who might want or need it. In other words, the marketer creates the segments based on common assumptions and available knowledge of the audience or customer, without having very much information on specific people or groups of people.

The alternative and, in our opinion, by far the more effective method is to create the segments based on actual customer behaviors. That is what is called the aggregation approach, shown on the right side of Exhibit 7.5.

Aggregation simply means that the marketer observes and, through various methods, captures the marketplace behavior of both customers and prospects. Based on the behaviors of marketplace purchasers or users, the marketing manager then aggregates them into groups—Group A, Group B, and so on. Thus, aggregation is based on identifying like-behaving groups of people. For example, customers might be aggregated by the number of times they have purchased the product or service—one time or five times or ten times and so on. Using our simple graphic, Group A could be those who purchased the product only one time, while Group B might represent those who have purchased two or three times, and Group C those who have purchased four or more times. Or customers might be aggregated by where they purchase—in a discount store, in a regular pharmacy, by mail, and so on. Or by how they purchase two products together—milk and cookies or bread and tuna or fast foods and snack items. Thus, the customers sort themselves into segments or groups based on their purchasing behaviors, not some surrogate for those behaviors.

A well-recognized example of this type of aggregation is the composition of the market for Harley-Davidson motorcycles. Harley owners are an eclectic group ranging from eighteen-year-olds scraping to make the payments on their bikes to wealthy retirees who make cross-country journeys on luxury machines. The key ingredients are their behaviors, which are supported by their lifestyles and attitudes. Typical segmentation approaches using age, income, sex, education, and the like mean little in identifying Harley customers or prospects. It is the Harley lifestyle that separates users from nonusers and certainly separates them from the four-door sedan owners. In other words, the Harley owners self-identify with the machine and all the imagery that comes with it. All Harley-Davidson really has to do is to count the noses of those owners that have bought into the concept and provide resources and facilities to keep them in the franchise.

Traditionally, it has been difficult for marketers to develop aggregation schemes because they lacked customer knowledge, particularly behavioral data. Today, behavioral data is increasingly available and, most important, usable. Thus, in the following chapters, we focus on the use of behavioral data where possible in developing customer-brand relationship programs. We have found behavioral data to be ever so much more powerful than the traditional attitudinal data that have historically been used. Yet attitudinal information does have its place. Typically, in the development of a customer-brand relationship program, the attitudinal data are used to help explain the observed behaviors rather than trying to predict them. That is the primary difference we will stress in this text.

Given the capabilities of databases today, we recommend defining target customer groups first according to their measurable behaviors and then using other types of demographic, geographic, or attitudinal data to help explain or describe the group. Furthermore, we recommend that the behaviors be analyzed according to value-driven characteristics in order to assist the organization in determining its best or most valuable customers and prospects. For example, a common approach is to understand those customers who purchase the product most often or in the greatest quantities and then incorporate nonbehavioral information to further understand the needs, motivations, and geographic, demographic details of each group.

The reason we put so much emphasis on aggregating customers by behaviors is that we believe this is the cornerstone of creating a measurable and accountable framework for marketing communication. A marketer who knows what a group of customers currently does—buys the marketer's product once a month and spends about $25, for example—can then set specific, measurable objectives for the communication program. The aim may be to encourage the customer to buy more often, use the product more frequently, use it in greater volume, or display some other defined behavior that will generate increased value. Once the communication program is launched, the marketer can measure if the marketing objectives were achieved. This topic of measuring the outcomes of brand communication will be examined in great detail in later chapters. For now, suffice it to say that much depends on having good behavioral benchmarks upon which to build the metrics.

The primary requirement in a reciprocal customer-brand relationship is that the customers must willingly provide data to help the marketing organization develop more useful and valuable customer-brand relationship programs, and the marketing organization must use that data to meet the needs of the customers, not just to try to sell them additional products. As this sharing occurs, more and more customer behavioral data become available and more and better marketing communication delivery and content are developed. That is really the purpose of a customer-brand relationship approach.

VALUING CUSTOMERS AND PROSPECTS

As has been discussed, one of the most important uses of a customer database is the ability to aggregate like-behaving customers or prospects so that proper customer-brand delivery vehicles can be identified and relevant communication messages developed. A key element in this process is determining how a customer or prospect might be valued; that is, how much the individual is worth to the organization. Clearly, in a behavior-based marketing approach, different consumer behaviors have different values to the marketing organization. A customer who purchases only when the product is on sale or being promoted may have a far different value than a customer who buys at full price with full profit margins on an ongoing basis. Marketing organizations want to attract the most profitable customers possible since they provide the profits that reward shareholders for their financial risk in supporting the firm. Thus, the financial value of a customer or prospect must be known if the marketing firm is to make the most effective use of its marketing and communication investments. Generally, that means developing some type of financial customer-brand value estimate.

Probably the easiest technique is to simply sort customers by how much they spend. Usually, something like 20 percent of the customers will account for 80 percent or so of the company's revenue or profits. This is a well-established principle in statistics known as "Pareto's rule." Applied to marketing, it holds true across most categories of products and services. Thus, the financial value of a customer (or group of customers) is based on the income flows the customer creates for the brand marketer through ongoing patronage. As a result, the real success of the marketing firm is determined by when and how often the customer votes for a favorite brand by making purchases. And, hopefully, those purchases are ongoing, the true definition of a customer-brand relationship.

To determine past, present, or future customer value, the marketer needs a method of estimating customer financial value and profitability. Exhibit 7.6 illustrates an approach widely used in marketing both consumer and business-to-business products.

Four factors determine how much a customer may be worth to the brand:

1. *Penetration* (P): the number of customers the organization has as a percentage of the total number of customers in the category—that is, all who buy from all providers. Thus,

Exhibit 7.6   **Determining Customer Financial Value**

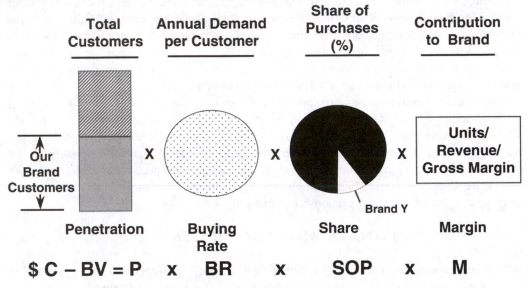

$$\$C - BV = P \quad \times \quad BR \quad \times \quad SOP \quad \times \quad M$$

if there are 100,000 buyers of replacement ink cartridges within a given region and 40,000 of them buy the marketer's brand at some time or another, then the penetration rate for the brand would be 40 percent.

2. *Category buying rate* (BR): the average demand for the product or service per customer within a given time period. For example, if the customers within the region typically buy a total of twelve ink cartridges a year per person per machine owned.

3. *Share of purchases* (SOP): the proportion of total customer purchases that come to the marketer's brand. This is also often referred to as "share of wallet" or "share of requirement." Thus, of the twelve cartridges that each customer buys, on average, each year, how many of these are the marketer's brand? Does the marketer capture a third of the customer's purchases? Or is the customer strongly loyal, giving the marketer virtually all of the purchases?

4. *Contribution to margin* (CM): gross margin for the product or service in question. By studying not only the number of items purchased, but also the margin on those items, the marketer can develop a financially based view of customer value. By margin we mean the profit before corporate expenses involved in the sale of the product. This type of calculation, i.e., determining or counting the customer's purchases in units and then multiplying by the gross margin, as shown in the illustration. This also allows the marketer to factor in such things as various sales promotion activities, which often succeed in driving volume up, but may also drive total profitability down by increasing costs or reducing margins.

By using this customer valuation approach, the marketer can estimate the value of any customer and, by aggregating like-behaving customers, can develop multiple levels of relevant marketing communication programs. This approach is one of many ways in which customer value can be determined. In the next section, we briefly discuss some additional customer valuation methodologies using specific examples.

Exhibit 7.7 **"Best Customer" Profile**

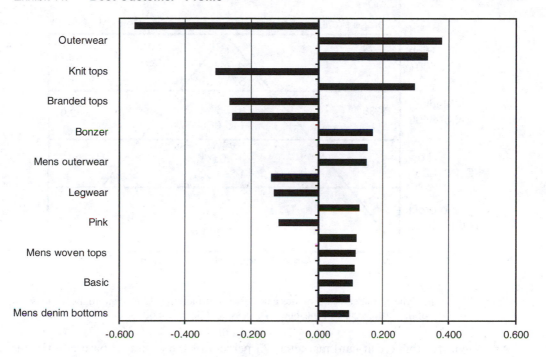

Some Examples of How to Value Customers and Prospects

The simplest form of customer valuation is to use the available customer data to gain an understanding of their buying behaviors. Some fairly simple models can provide a wealth of customer knowledge and insight. Exhibit 7.7 illustrates how aggregated data from customer purchases in a small department store chain were used to obtain a better understanding of the purchase history of "best customers" (defined as the top 10 percent of customers in terms of their annual purchases from the department store).

In this retail example, the top 10 percent of the customers in this department store chain are much more likely to purchase their outerwear and dresses in the department store than they are to purchase lingerie or knit tops. This type of analysis can then be used to dig further into the data to try to understand why some product lines are purchased and others are not. Even at this level, however, the department store managers have learned that "best customers"—that is, highest-spending customers—do not shop the store evenly or completely.

Additional analysis can move beyond the customers' volume of purchases to calculate or estimate which customers are profitable and which are not. Exhibit 7.8 illustrates how customer data, using the approach described earlier in customer valuation—that is, by determining the customer's profitability as illustrated by the methodology as shown in Exhibit 7.6 where volume or number of units were multiplied by gross margin to determine the value of a customer—can be used to help marketing organizations understand the differences between profitable and nonprofitable customers. Drawing on its customer database, a credit card marketer constructed the following customer analysis chart.

Exhibit 7.8 **Credit Card Marketer Example**

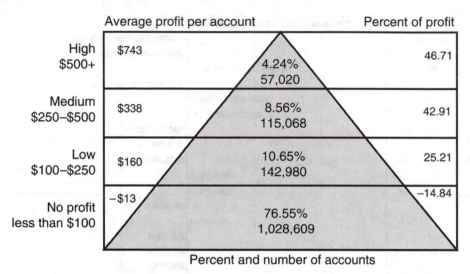

Percent and number of accounts

Notes: 77 percent of the customer base provides a negative contribution (–15 percent) to the business on average; 23 percent of the customer base contribute in excess of 100 percent of profit (115 percent).

As shown, for this credit card marketer, 23 percent of the customer base contributes more than 100 percent of the firm's profits. In fact, only 4.24 percent, or less than 50,000 of the more than 1 million customers this credit card organization serves, provides nearly half of the total profit. This type of analysis, when related to marketing activities, can help the organization increase its focus on the best customers and reduce the waste that is likely occurring among a vast majority of customers to whom the company is probably marketing too heavily, given the response rates being achieved.

While these are two of the most common types of data and data analytics used today, some organizations have gone much further in their use of customer behavioral data. Tesco, a supermarket chain headquartered in the United Kingdom, has developed one of the most sophisticated data and data analytic approaches anywhere in the world. Its basic approach is to encourage shoppers, now more than 12 million in the United Kingdom, to use their "Club Card" every time they shop at Tesco. Presently some 80 percent of customer purchases are captured through the program, for which Tesco provides customers with quarterly reward and incentive coupons and cash. As a result of the customers' willingness to share their purchasing behavior, Tesco has been able to identify and aggregate more than 30,000 like-behaving customer groups or segments for which specific marketing programs can be developed. Today, Tesco uses its customers' shopping behavior to determine what products to stock in its stores, what range of brands to offer, what pricing approach to use, and so on. In short, Tesco lets customers identify what they want through their shopping behaviors. More important, however, is the fact that Tesco listens to and responds to its customers based on the shopping information they provide. Today, Tesco is the most successful supermarket chain in the world, and, much of its success can be directly attributed to its use of its customer database and its customer data analysis.

Exhibit 7.9   **Managing Customers as Investments: Drivers of Customer Profitability**

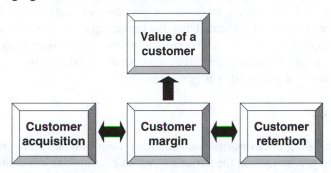

Source: E. Anderson, C. Fornell, and D. Lehman, "Customer Satisfaction, Market Share, and Profitability: Findings from Sweden," *Journal of Marketing* 58 (July 1994).

With this brief description of how marketing firms are using customer data to build longer and stronger customer-brand relationships, we next move to a broader view of customer analysis and evaluation.

THE ISSUE OF CUSTOMER PROFITABILITY

To this point, in our data analytics, we have viewed customers primarily on the basis of their "income flows" to the organization; that is, how many dollars they give the marketing organization in exchange for the products and services they purchase. That view fits very well with the reasons why organizations invest funds in customer-brand relationship programs, as discussed in Chapter 2. There, we said that marketing organizations invest resources for only four reasons: to acquire new customers, to maintain present customers, to increase the value of present customers, or to migrate customers through a product portfolio. With the data found in a marketing database, we can extend and expand that concept to move beyond income flows to the most current view, which is summed up in the phrase *customer profitability*. (We illustrated the concept of profitability with the credit card company in Exhibit 7.8. Here, we provide more detail).

Profitability goes beyond simply measuring the number of units the customer purchases or the frequency of those purchases. We move to the idea that customers must be profitable if the marketing organization is to succeed. By profitability, we mean that customers must produce more income than the cost to serve them. But, like any other investment the organization makes, that profitability is not best determined in the short term or on a unit-by-unit basis in spite of the corporate pressure to do so. Marketers need some new concepts of customer valuation and profitability in order to create ongoing profitable customer-brand relationship programs. Writing in the *Journal of Marketing,* E. Anderson, C. Fornell, and D. Lehmann summarize the different metric approaches.[3]

As shown in Exhibit 7.9, the true financial value of a customer and, therefore, the value of a customer-brand relationship is based on three factors: (1) the customer acquisition cost, (2) the margin generated from the income flows when the customer purchases and repurchases the product or service, and (3) a deduction for the cost of retaining the customer over the time of the relationship. The challenge, of course, is in developing and tracking these relevant income flows and costs. However, profitability is often beyond the control of the marketing or communication manager since it involves complex financial analysis. While this analysis is possible, it is much more sophisticated than the present discussion will allow. A number of relevant texts and other resources can be consulted in this area. It is enough at this point that the manager knows that customer profitability is a desirable goal to strive for and understands the concepts of how that profitability is generated.

SUMMING UP

With this understanding of customers and audiences, their makeup and value for customer-brand relationship programs, and the various forms of customer research and databases, the marketer is now ready to identify the delivery systems that might be used to reach customers, along with the most appropriate content for marketing messages and incentives.

Before moving to the development of these tactical areas, however, marketers must first determine, based on their customer insight and knowledge, how they will measure the results of their marketing and communication programs. While such measurement is normally held to the end of traditional communication processes, we have found it much more useful to consider measurement right after gaining an understanding of customers and prospects. So Chapter 8 discusses measurement and Chapter 9 is devoted to determining the appropriate amount to invest in customers and customer groups in order to achieve the marketing organization's goals—in other words, the budget.

NOTES

1. Material in this section has been extracted and adapted from D.E. Schultz and H. Schultz, *Leveraging Customer Information: Driving Strategic Direction and Marketing Profitability* (Houston: American Productivity and Quality Center, 2000).

2. Ibid., p. 21.

3. E. Anderson, C. Fornell, and D. Lehmann, "Customer Satisfaction, Market Share, and Profitability: Findings from Sweden," *Journal of Marketing* 58 (July 1994).

PART II

ACCOUNTABILITY

MARKETING'S
BIGGEST CHALLENGE

One of today's most critical issues in marketing communication is accountability. Accountability, as defined here, means being responsible for and managing the funds and activities involved in the development and implementation of a customer-brand relationship program.

Marketing and communication accountability is critical for all firms, large or small, global or local, since all have limited and finite resources of time, money, people, capabilities, and the like. Resources must, therefore, be identified and allocated in ways that provide the greatest value for both the marketing organization and its customers and prospects. It is, therefore, the responsibility of the customer-brand relationship manager to invest the firm's resources wisely so they provide the most value to customers and optimal returns to the marketer.

Because accountability, which is commonly driven by some type of measurement and evaluation system, is so important, it must be one of the key considerations of any marketing or communication manager. Too often, though, because these activities generally occur at the end of the marketing or communication process, they are often forgotten, overlooked, or simply ignored. It seems the marketing communication manager just "never quite got around to it."

Such is not the case in customer-brand relationship accountability. That is because the base for any reciprocal relationship is the creation of shared values (see Chapter 1). Thus, the drive for reciprocity requires the manager to determine the value that the customer has received from the marketing organization and its brands as well as the value derived from the process and the customer. Therefore, measurement is a key element in the development of customer-brand relationships and one that drives the entire approach.

Because accountability and measurement are so critical to the ongoing success of customer-brand relationships, we place them at the start of the process, not at the end. The reason? You must know where you are going before you start the journey. That is why measurement and accountability are here, to get the attention they deserve.

A ROAD MAP TO SUCCESS

The first task in accountability is to determine how the marketing organization will measure success. It is the entire organization, not just the marketing communication manager, which must make the measurement decisions. All the other managers in the organization, including top management, must agree as to what is or has been a successful customer-brand relationship program. In short, what yardstick will the firm use to measure success?

Clearly, getting consensus on the measurement methodology and tools to be used is not an easy task, but it is a most important one. Concentrating on what returns will be obtained for both the marketing organization and the customer moves the managers away from considering merely how much they will spend to what the organization and the customer will receive as a result of the marketing communication program. In other words, the focus moves from outputs—what the firm did—to outcomes—the results of the activities. We will return to this theme of outcomes versus outputs several times in the next two chapters because it is a key concept in accountability.

Another reason why gaining consensus on a measurement yardstick is not easy is because there are so many available alternatives. For example, some functional managers will argue for attitudinal measures—what customers and prospects remember and understand about the company, the brand, the advertising, and the like. Other managers will focus on the financial returns—how much money was invested in building customer-brand relationships and how much return the marketing organization generated. Some will want to measure short-term success—the immediately measurable impact on the customer and the customer-brand relationship over the next or past few months. Others will demand longer-term measures, suggesting that building customer-brand relationships takes time and effort and results may not be apparent for several years. It is this lack of agreement on what constitutes success for both the marketer and the customer that creates many of the challenges in measurement and accountability.

THE THREE PATHWAYS MODEL

In Chapter 8, we present the three pathways model of the various ways customer-brand relationship success can be measured. The firm will have to determine which pathway or pathways are most relevant for the customer-brand relationship the firm is trying to build. The challenge of the pathways model is that each of the pathway measures does just what it says it will do and measures what it says it will measure. In addition, each pathway does the job quite well. But each pathway is different and each provides a different view of organizational success. That is why building consensus among managers for success measures at the beginning of the process is so critical.

After establishing the measures of success, we then move back to determine how much the organization can or should invest in building customer-brand relationships. For that task, in Chapter 9, we present a discussion of customer-brand relationship investment strategies.

With the next chapter on success measurement and the following chapter on investment strategies as background, we then move on to the delivery systems and content methodologies that make up the other two circles of the three-circle integrated model introduced in Chapter 1.

CHAPTER 8

Customer-First Planning

From the Outside In

Historically, many marketers have not been concerned about the results of their efforts; that is the business outcomes achieved through marketing programs. Rather, they have focused on creating new slogans, ad campaigns, mailings, or events—what we call outputs. Being primarily tactical in their approach to marketing communication, especially with customer-brand relationships, these managers failed to consider that measurement played a key role in the field. That is only natural. When the marketer starts with a traditional marketing approach, generally some form of the 4Ps (product, price, place, and promotion), the natural tendency is to focus on the content of the messages or product descriptions or ringing praise for the product and the firm. The goal becomes how to "deliver" or "distribute" those messages to customers and prospects. Thus, the goal of this type of product-focused measurement and accountability was merely to determine how many messages were delivered and who heard or saw, understood or accepted the messages sent out by the marketing organization. It was an outbound-only system. If the marketers delivered their messages at a reasonable cost, the job had been done; they did not worry about response. Ergo, the development of new messages, new visuals, new jingles, and so on was much more interesting to the marketing or communication manager than the results of what was done yesterday or last week or last year. Sadly, that has historically been the marketing and communication process. Although we may challenge it now, there was a reason why that outbound approach developed.

THE HISTORICAL BASE FOR CURRENT CUSTOMER-BRAND RELATIONSHIP MEASUREMENT

In the early days of marketing, right after World War II, which had been immediately preceded by a global economic depression in the 1930s, almost anything an organization brought to market sold quickly. There was so much pent-up demand that firms focused much more on filling the supply chain than on marketing the product or acquiring new customers. And since most products sold so rapidly and the market was growing exponentially with the huge influx of new family formations and the resulting children, what we now call the "Baby Boomers," there was little concern for ongoing relationships with customers. If a customer was not happy with the brand or the marketer, there was always another right behind to take their place. Thus, marketers became accustomed to investing relatively little effort in retention marketing programs while, at the same time, gaining substantial returns. As a result, measurement of marketing results was not very high on the priority list, and development of accountability systems simply did not matter to marketing and communication managers.

Therefore, until the mid-1960s in the United States, accountability and measurement were largely ignored. Mass production, mass consumption, mass marketing, and mass communication ruled and a booming market covered up many of the inadequacies of unsuccessful marketing and communication programs. Because business was good and the market was growing, even though at the same time it was becoming more complex and differentiated, marketing organizations were content to simply measure the distribution of their marketing efforts—how many magazine advertisements were distributed, how many radio commercials were broadcast, how many direct mail pieces were posted, how many sales calls were made. It was a marketing distribution model, pure and simple. The marketer talked, and, it was assumed, the customer listened . . . and generally responded.[1]

The development of this approach was easy to understand. Marketing and communication were built on a base of assumed customer behaviors derived from behavioral psychology and mass communication theory.

Behavioral Psychology

Behavioral psychology posits that humans can be conditioned to respond to external stimuli. That conclusion was based on experiments conducted on animals by Pavlov, Skinner, and other psychologists.[2] These psychological experiments showed that with sufficient repetition of a consistent stimuli or message, animals could be trained to respond in ways the experimenter wanted. In the case of Pavlov, the test subjects were dogs, while Skinner used pigeons. Marketers assumed that this conditioned behavior response could be transferred to people as well—that consumers would respond in the same way the test animals did. A marketer who sent out the same advertising message enough times could influence and manage the purchasing behavior of customers and prospects. That assumption is the source of the media concepts of reach and frequency.[3]

Further, following the work of other psychologists, marketers began to convince themselves that changes in consumer attitudes or feelings about a product, a company, or a brand would eventually lead to a change in consumer behavior toward that brand. Thus, a consumer who was "taught," through various forms of marketing communication, that a certain brand was the best available would develop a positive attitude toward the brand and at some point in the future try it . . . and keep on buying it, provided there were sufficient marketing and communication activities to keep the brand top of mind. That is where the concepts of positioning, unique selling propositions, and the like developed.

We can thus summarize the basis of most historical marketing and marketing communication approaches:

Marketing stimulus → *consumer response*
Consumer attitudes → *consumer behaviors*

Mass Communication Theory

Mass communication theory supported these behavioral psychology concepts and added some additional ideas as well. The primary contribution of the mass communication field was the model of outbound communication systems:

Marketer → message → medium → receiver (consumer)

In this model, the marketer controlled the message and determined the medium to be used and the receiver (i.e., consumer) to be reached. The consumer simply accepted and responded to those messages.

The Hierarchy of Effects Model

Based on these two concepts, it is easy to see how marketing communication measurement developed in the middle of the last century. It was summed up in the Hierarchy of Effects model introduced in Chapter 1. This model was, in essence, an amalgamation of the two concepts of behaviorist psychology and mass communication theory. In the hierarchy of effects model, the marketer is always in control of the system. The marketer determines the content of the messages to be delivered, the medium to be used, and the number of messages to be distributed. The more messages the marketing organization sends out, it is assumed the faster the consumer will move through the process on the way to some type of purchasing behavior.

The primary problem with the concept is that there is still no relevant evidence to show that consumers respond better or more quickly to increased levels of advertising or marketing communication stimuli. That certainly seems true in a marketplace where consumers are inundated with marketing and communication messages of all kinds. In addition, there is little credible evidence showing that attitudinal change about a product or service will result in some type of behavioral change, such as purchase or use. While traditional marketing and communication approaches seem intuitively correct, there is still scant tangible evidence to support them.

Unfortunately, the Hierarchy of Effects model continues to be only a theoretical concept since it has never been proven in the marketplace.[4] While it is reasonable and useful, it cannot really be used to achieve the primary goal of most marketing organizations today, to connect investments in marketing and communication to financial returns to the organization. We will see that more clearly when we begin our discussion of the three pathways model.

THREE CHALLENGES

Until the middle of the 1970s, because measurement was not critical and there was general acceptance of the communication effects approaches, such as the hierarchy of effects model, marketers were content to assume that measuring communication effects of their marketing programs was sufficient to provide marketing accountability. As long as the behaviorist psychological models were accepted, all was well. However, marketers eventually faced three challenges.

The Challenge of Behavioral Data

A major technological change occurred, however, when supermarkets in the United States began to capture the sale of individual products through UPC codes and point-of-sale register technology and to relate those sales to individual consumers through the use of frequent shopper cards. That technology allowed marketers to connect actual sales responses to the marketing communication activities that had been used. These, in turn, could be statistically related to identify what probably influenced the consumer's behavior. As a result, the entire world of advertising and marketing communication changed. By knowing that the individual product was purchased by a specific household and that the primary variable in the mix was the marketing communication, either in the store or sent into the household, the marketer, for the first time, could actually connect expenditures on various forms of marketing communication to actual consumer behaviors—that is, sales. That link allowed the marketing firm to begin estimating the return on investment of the marketing program. This goal had long been desired but was now achievable. Importantly, that same process could be used to evaluate all types and forms of marketing communication, from media advertising to sales promotion to in-store displays and so on.[5]

Behavioral data—that is, what customers actually do in response to certain marketing communication activities—thus began to challenge and, in some cases, replace the traditional attitudinal data based on what people could remember about the marketing communication to which they had been exposed. And because behavioral data could be connected to marketing and communication investments, the marketer could begin to create closed-loop, financial investment and return systems. So another measurement system developed, that of short-term financial returns generated by investments in various types and forms of marketing and communication activities. We will see this approach in Pathway 2 in the three pathways model.

The Need for Long-Term Measures

The missing element in many marketing communication measurement or evaluation approaches has been any way to measure or estimate the impact of various activities over time. While all marketers know that long-term effects are important, they have opted to develop measurement systems primarily to determine the immediate or short-term effects. This choice has been driven to a certain extent by marketers' reliance on the double-entry accounting systems that usually have relatively short time horizons. As brands have become more important in the overall marketing and communication arena, and since they are generally considered to be long-term investments by the marketing firm, demand for new marketing and communication measurement forms has increased. Clearly, some type of longer-term measure is critical in the development and measurement of customer-brand relationships. Some progress has been made in brand measurement in the last few years. That will be illustrated in Pathway 3 of the three pathways model that follows.

With this brief background and explanation of what constitutes accountability and measurement in customer-brand relationships, only one more background element is needed before we begin to work through the three pathways model. That is the challenge of time and time frames.

The Challenge of Time in Accountability and Measurement

Time is a critical factor in any type of accountability and measurement approach. It is particularly important in the development of customer-brand relationships. Relationships typically develop and grow over time. Thus, they are radically different from traditional marketing activities that are commonly focused on exchanges—that is, product or service purchase and use that may or may not result in any long-term relationship between the two parties.

Clearly, organizations need both short-term and long-term sales and profits. That means they need both short-term and long-term customers. Some customers will never be interested in a long-term relationship with the organization or the brand. For example, a baby eventually outgrows the need for diapers and a teenager generally matures past the acne-medication stage. There may have been strong relationships during the time of the product need, but, in essence, they only last for a limited period of time.

Other brands and organizations create long-term, ongoing relationships with customers such as automobile owners or cosmetic users or credit card holders. The challenge facing the marketing relationship manager is to determine whether the product is a candidate for a long-term relationship with the customer. This decision will identify the need for a specific type of accountability and measurement system.

For purposes of accountability and measurement, we have arbitrarily divided the measurement systems into two forms: (1) short-term measures, which generally cover the current fiscal year of the marketing organization, and (2) long-term measures, which provide returns or relationships that span two, three, or more years. Clearly identifying the marketing and communication activities that are expected to provide short-term and long-term returns to the organization is a critical ingredient in accountability. The marketing manager must therefore identify which activities should be measured with a short-term yardstick and which should employ a longer-period measure.

The challenge, of course, is that almost all current marketing and communication measurement models and methodologies have been developed as short-term tools. Changing this mind-set is often one of the major challenges facing the manager in setting up the proper accountability system. Part of the problem is the campaign mentality that pervades the marketing communication field. The marketing organization typically plans in terms of four-, eight-, or thirteen-week sales and promotional "campaigns," often supported by marketing communication activities of the same length. Thus, most marketing programs are short-term and assumed to be exhausted after they have appeared in the marketplace. Customer-brand relationships are long-term, however. Therefore, in developing suitable customer-brand relationship measurement systems, the manager must take into account both the long-term and short-term impact of the activities.

With this short-term, long-term issue in mind, we can now move to the discussion of the various methodologies that can be used to measure or estimate the value of a customer-brand relationship program.

THE THREE PATHWAYS MODEL OF CUSTOMER-BRAND RELATIONSHIP MEASUREMENT

As mentioned earlier, there are a number of methodologies for tracking, measuring, and evaluating the outbound marketing and communication efforts of the firm.[6] These methodologies vary widely in purpose, scope, definition, and outcome. In this chapter, our focus is on three primary forms of measurement: (1) attitudinal, (2) short-term incremental sales, and (3) brand value added. While there are many variations of these three primary approaches, these essentially summarize the overall outbound methodologies that have been developed and are currently in use.

We note here that the measurement systems all take the view of the marketing organization

Exhibit 8.1   Three Pathways Model for Measuring Brands

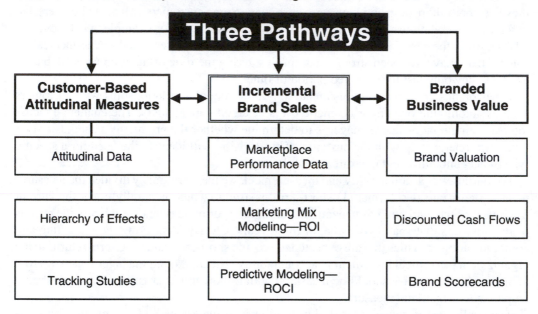

as the originator, implementer, and evaluator of the marketing and communication programs. This view is typical and reflects the ongoing challenge of developing and managing reciprocal customer-brand relationships. Thus, the three pathways are described from the marketer's point of view in this chapter. We will develop alternative views in other chapters that deal with the value that customers and prospects receive from the marketer's activities. In the following sections, however, the discussion is primarily on identifying and explaining the measurement and accountability options for outbound communication programs available to the manager. More important, however, the following discussion provides a guide to when, where, and how to apply each of the pathways to meet the accountability goals.

The three pathways model illustrated in Exhibit 8.1 represents the three primary methods of measuring, tracking, and evaluating the impact and effects of outbound marketing and communication programs on customers and prospects over various periods of time. Each pathway has distinct goals and management information objectives. The challenge, as mentioned earlier, is identifying and gaining consensus among all organizational managers as to which pathway is most applicable to the overall goals of the company.

Within each pathway, a number of analytical tools and approaches can be used to determine the success of the customer-brand relationship program. Before discussing the methodologies, however, each pathway is briefly described.

Pathway 1: Customer-Based Attitudinal Measures

Pathway 1 consists of quantitative and qualitative measures and means to determine the customer or prospect's awareness, knowledge, preferences for, and intent to purchase the product or the brand. (Note the close relationship between these approaches and the hierarchy of effects model discussed earlier.) The most common approach is to measure current brand perceptions, knowledge, understanding, and the like and then to connect them to the marketer's communication programs and then to track changes in those factors as they occur over time. These changes are then related to the customer-brand relationship programs conducted in the marketplace, where successes and deviations are noted.

Pathway 2: Short-Term Incremental Brand Sales

Pathway 2 provides measures of the short-term, incremental sales generated as a result of the customer-brand relationship programs employed. These are hard numbers—that is, the number of units, dollars, or other measurable financial factors. They are based on various methods of tracking the actual purchasing behaviors of customers or prospects in the marketplace in the short term, which we have previously defined as the current fiscal year. For example, one measure might be how many units or dollars the consumer spent on the firm's products and services this year versus last; another measure might track how many customers switched from the competitor's brand to the studied brand during a promotional period. Measures in this pathway are, therefore, primarily financial, as they seek to relate what the organization spent on marketing and communication to the volume or dollar value of purchases that customers made during the same time period. This is what is commonly termed the return on investment of marketing and communication spending. Little attention is given to the long-term effects or impact of the customer-brand relationship program in this pathway.

Pathway 3: Branded Business Value

Pathway 3 measures the financial value of the brand to the firm over the long term. With some modifications, this same measurement can be used to determine the value of customers or prospects to the firm as well. For the most part, measures in this pathway treat the brand as an organizational asset in which investments can be made and returns achieved. Those returns are measured in the long term, with five years being the most common span. The basis for most of these measures is some type of discounted cash flow that the brand or the customer brings to the firm. Typically, these measures provide a valuation or appraisal of the brand to the organization with the assumption that similar connections can be made between the firm's brand or brands with longer-term customer-brand relationships. If the customer-brand relationship is defined as the customer's loyalty to the brand or the firm, then brand income flows can act as a surrogate for the customer-brand relationship that is being created or managed by the brand owner.

With this general framework in mind, the various tools and processes found in each of the pathways can now be discussed. As will be seen, each pathway offers a number of specific methodologies that can be provided by a variety of external vendors. We will not delve into the specifics of each of the approaches but will provide an overview of one methodology that generally represents that specific pathway.

PATHWAY 1: CUSTOMER-BASED ATTITUDINAL MEASURES

Pathway 1 is called customer-based attitudinal measures since it attempts to measure how customers and prospects feel about the brand, the organization, or the specific products or services being marketed. The premise is that customers must have positive feelings toward the marketing organization and its products to justify their current and ongoing support. The measures used in Pathway 1 therefore are generally designed to identify the awareness, knowledge, preferences, likes, and dislikes that customers and prospects hold about the product and brand and, therefore, its value to them. This first pathway is the most closely related to traditional marketing, advertising, and communication measurement techniques and is thus the most widely used.

The Underlying Premises of Pathway 1

As previously discussed, the measurement approaches used in Pathway 1 stem from the assumptions of behaviorist psychology and mass communication models discussed earlier—that is, that consumers' attitudes, opinions, and beliefs drive their purchase behaviors. The stimulus-response model and the idea that consumer attitudes eventually lead to consumer purchase behaviors permeate the approaches and methodologies. Thus, the principle questions underlying Pathway 1 are whether the marketing organization has successfully developed, delivered, and created or modified the attitudes, opinions, and beliefs of the customers and prospects whom the firm has defined as its target market. If so, it is assumed that the marketing and communication activities have been successful.

Clearly, the hierarchy of effects model from the 1960s permeates Pathway 1. Most measurement systems attempt to track the movement of customers and prospects along the continuum from awareness to knowledge to preference and so on, relating that movement back to the marketing and communication programs. However, the measures generally stop short of purchase behavior, relying on the argument that there are simply too many intervening variables to make any direct connection between attitudinal change and actual purchase behavior even though this connection is implicitly assumed in the hierarchy of effects model. This inability to connect attitude change to behavioral change is often cited as the greatest weakness of this pathway.

The Development of Customer-Brand Attitudinal Measures

In spite of this missing behavioral link, Pathway 1 is by far the most widely used method of measuring marketing and communication effects and concurrently implied customer-brand relationships. Much of the value of this pathway comes from the development of the concept of customer brand equity or what has been termed the future earning power of the brand. This concept was developed in the early 1990s by David Aaker and later expanded by Kevin Lane Keller.[7] Keller defines "customer-based brand equity" as "the differential effect brand knowledge has on the customer response to the marketing of that brand. Equity occurs when the consumer has a high level of awareness and familiarity with the brand and holds some strong, favorable and unique brand associations in memory." The basic premise that underlies this view is that customers determine and drive the value of the brand. That is, customers essentially create the image of the brand on a personal level, based on the way they take in the brand information and then assemble and retain that information for themselves. Therefore, to determine the level of customer equity, or value of the relationship, the marketer must measure the attitudes, opinions, and beliefs that customers have acquired, captured, and attached to the brand in their own minds over time.

Keller's underlying assumption is that if strong, favorable, and unique associations about the brand are held by the customer, those associations will at some point lead to favorable customer behavior toward the brand, such as purchase, trial, continued use, and so on. Interestingly, Keller and others who support this view are hesitant to connect these consumer attitudes to actual brand purchases. Thus, in Pathway 1, there is no real way to connect the financial investments made by the marketing organization to market-level behaviors by customers. If the marketing organization can accept this concept of customer-brand equity as a measure of the customer-brand relationship being created and accept this approach as a nonfinancial methodology, then Pathway 1 is a relevant measurement or accountability methodology. If measures of financial returns are required, Pathway 1 falls short.

Current Status of Customer-Based Brand Equity Measures

As might be expected, over the sixty or so years since the hierarchy of effects concept was developed, a number of approaches have been developed to understand, measure, and track customer attitudes over time. Many major advertising agencies and market research organizations have developed proprietary models or methodologies to measure or track consumers' attitudinal change over time. Three widely accepted models are Millward Brown's Brand-Dynamics, the Y&R Brand Asset Valuator, and the TNS (Taylor, Nelson, Sofres) Conversion Model.

Generally speaking, most of the approaches are based on defining and tracking levels of awareness, familiarity, and attitudinal change over time. While there are differences in nomenclature, methodologies, and output, all have the common goal of measuring changes in consumer attitudes, opinions, and beliefs that result from brand communication programs. A brief summary of Millward Brown's BrandDynamics model, which is typical of the methodologies found in Pathway 1, appears in the next section.

The BrandDynamics™ Model

Exhibit 8.2 illustrates the output of Millward Brown's BrandDynamics model. As shown, it is based on a hierarchical methodology designed to measure customer or prospect attitudes, opinions, and beliefs about the brand and the product or service. Customers and prospects are surveyed and asked questions designed to identify the strength of the relationship between the customer and the brand. Five levels of relationship are identified. Each level is defined by multiple questions capturing the most important dimensions of that aspect of the relationship, and each depicts a stronger connection between the customer and the brand. The five levels are Presence, Relevance, Performance, Advantage, and Bonding, with Bonding being the most powerful relationship of all.

By measuring customer attitudes over time using the BrandDynamics methodology, the marketer can see changes in the relationship between the customer and the brand. Additionally, it is often possible to trace those changes to various marketing and communication activities. The BrandDynamics approach also compares the marketer's brand with competitive brands to provide a comparison of customer perceptions. This type of brand relationship information can be very valuable to the marketer in adjusting or adapting the customer-brand relationship marketing and communication programs in the marketplace to meet or offset competitive threats.

The usefulness of the BrandDynamics approach is that the marketing organization can see

Exhibit 8.2   **Millward Brown's BrandDynamics Model**

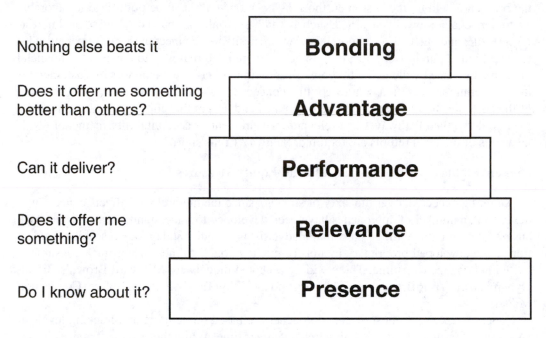

Nothing else beats it — **Bonding**

Does it offer me something better than others? — **Advantage**

Can it deliver? — **Performance**

Does it offer me something? — **Relevance**

Do I know about it? — **Presence**

Source: Millward Brown; used with permission of TNS.

where the brand relationship is improving and where it is declining. Those measures generally provide guidance to the manager in where to change, adapt, or enhance the marketing and communication activities being delivered in the marketplace.

Summary of Pathway 1: The Three Pillars of Customer-Based Brand Equity Measurement

In summary, most methodologies used in Pathway 1 are based on three pillars of measurement.

1. The Pathway 1 accountability approaches are based on the following assumptions:

- Customers create brand equity for themselves based on the attitudes, opinions, and beliefs they create about the brand for themselves over time.
- This brand equity is created by the observations, exposures, and other brand contacts developed and communicated by the marketing organization.
- Thus, the marketing organization can, through its messaging and marketing activities, directly impact the level, type, and strength of the brand associations held by the customer.

2. The Pathway 1 measurement approaches assume that strong feelings or associations with the brand will, at some point, result in positive brand behaviors such as purchase, repurchase, switching brands, and so on.

3. The Pathway 1 approach also assumes that marketers can determine the impact of their marketing communication programs by measuring changes in customer attitudes, opinions, and beliefs. Thus, positive changes can be determined, and, in some way, these changes can be related back to the activities of the organization, based on the assumption that those organizational activities contributed to the positive changes that occurred.

Inherent in these types of customer-based brand metrics is the understanding that changes have occurred in customer attitudes, opinions, and beliefs that can be quantified in some way. As discussed earlier, the measures generally stop short of linking communication measures to actual customer behavioral measures such as sales or repurchase. So while the first pathway does what it says it will do—track changes in consumer awareness and perceptions—it is almost impossible to relate those attitudinal measures to what customers actually do in the marketplace. The solution to this problem is often found in the measures and models used in Pathway 2, which focuses primarily on behavioral measures such as purchases, repurchases, and stocking up—in other words, measures of incremental product sales and income flows that are related to the marketing and communication activities used by the firm.

PATHWAY 2: SHORT-TERM INCREMENTAL BRAND SALES

Measurements in Pathway 2 are primarily dedicated to helping the organization identify the short-term incremental financial value, generally in the form of increased sales volume, premium pricing, customer retention, and the like, that has come as a result of the firm's marketing and communication activities. As a result, this pathway is heavily focused on the economic and financial aspects of customer-brand relationships rather than the attitudinal measures found in Pathway 1.

Two basic methodologies are used in Pathway 2. Both attempt to determine the impact and effect of the firm's marketing and communication activities on customer demand. The methods differ quite markedly, however, in the time frame being measured and the level of customer specificity in the analysis.

1. Marketing mix modeling is used to determine the aggregate historical returns obtained by the firm from various marketing and communication programs. The goal is to determine if short-term sales increases occurred and what specific marketing or communication activities were responsible for those increases.
2. Predictive modeling involves forecasting potential future returns from the use of specific marketing and communication activities among specific groups of customers or prospects.

In regard to the time frame of these two methodologies, marketing mix modeling typically is based on the previous two to five years of expenditures and sales results. Alternatively, predictive modeling estimates the possible sales results that might occur during the upcoming twelve to eighteen months. The other major difference is the level of customer or prospect granularity; in other words, the specific factors that can be attributed to either customer groups or individual customers themselves involved in the analysis. Marketing mix modeling typically looks at the aggregated results of the firm's marketing and communication activities across

Exhibit 8.3 **Parsing Out Incremental Returns From Base Sales**

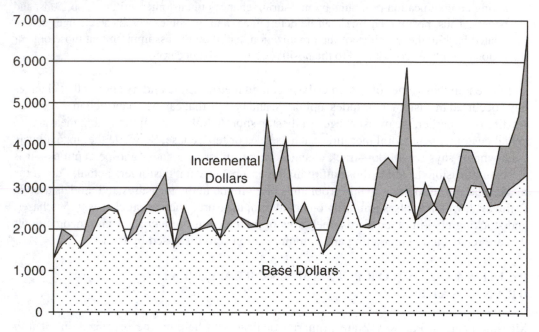

all customers. Predictive modeling attempts to forecast which or what specific individuals or groups of consumers and prospects are likely to respond to the various programs being contemplated and their level of response. Thus, the level of customer or prospect detail is a critical variable in both the approaches and provides the base for the development of customer-brand relationships. A brief description of each of the two approaches will illustrate these differences and the value they provide the marketing organization.

Marketing Mix Modeling: Understanding the Past

Marketing mix modeling is essentially a statistical technique that enables the firm to determine the incremental financial returns generated as a result of investments made by the firm in various types of marketing and communication programs in the past. The analysis period typically uses data from the past two to five years, ideally gathered on a monthly or even weekly basis. Since the methodology is complex, we limit our discussion here to a managerial understanding of the purpose of this approach, the outputs generally obtained, and the value the manager might derive from the use of this level of analysis.

The general purpose of marketing mix modeling is to separate out the base brand sales—that is, sales that would probably have occurred during the specific time period being analyzed had no marketing or communication program been implemented—from the actual sales results observed. In other words, what level of additional sales did the marketing program generate? This calculation is done through a combination of correlation and regression analysis, correlating observed sales with marketing and communication investments and then using various forms of regression analysis to parse out which specific marketing activity was probably responsible for the increase. An example of the output from a marketing mix analysis is presented in Exhibit 8.3.

As shown, approximately fifty-two months of sales data by dollar volume have been plotted on the chart. Using this data, the analyst has created what is called a baseline, which is the estimated dollar sales that would have occurred had the marketing communication program not been implemented. That is shown in the chart as "base dollars," the shaded area across the bottom of the chart. The top line is the actual dollar sales recorded. The difference between the base dollars and the actual sales dollars are the "incremental dollars" or the value that the marketing communication program is believed to have provided. Using this amount, the analyst can then compare the timing of the various marketing communication programs to the observed increase peaks and determine the value of the marketing program.

Another analysis is generally added to this baseline approach. That is a calculation that identifies which marketing activity probably generated the increase. By using regression analysis and inputting the level of expenditure on each of the various activities during the specific time period, the analyst can estimate which marketing activity was responsible for the increase. Thus, even when multiple marketing and communication activities, such as advertising and sales promotion and events, are used at the same time, it is possible through sophisticated statistical analysis to separate out the effect and impact of specific marketing and communication programs. This information is of substantial managerial value when trying to understand the importance of the various marketing and communication programs in order to build stronger customer-brand relationships in the future.

The primary weakness of the marketing mix modeling approach is that it is based on aggregated data—that is, on the response of all customers served by the marketing organization. Thus, it is generally related only to total sales. The marketing manager, therefore, does not know which customers or customer groups were affected and which were not; that is, it is not possible to tell if the increased sales came from existing or new customers. So, while it is possible to understand which marketing and communication tools seemed to work in the past, the marketer does not know whether the increases helped strengthen the customer-brand relationships with existing customers or whether new customers were acquired. To develop that estimate, predictive modeling is required.

Predictive Modeling of Future Returns

The goal of predictive models is to identify those customers or customer groups who might be most receptive to marketing and communication messages from the organization and then develop specific messages and offers for them. Predictive models start by identifying the customers or prospects most likely to respond to the marketing activities of the firm—that is, those people with whom a customer-brand relationship might either be initiated or continued. Estimates are then made of what the response might be if the marketing programs were effective; what response level might be expected or anticipated. The final step in the approach is to measure the actual response of the individual or groups targeted to see if their behaviors changed in the desirable way. Thus, the cost-benefit ratio can be calculated and a determination made whether the specific programs were financially successful.

The key elements in developing predictive models are (1) the selection of the appropriate customer or prospect, (2) the ability to deliver the intended marketing and communication messages and incentives to the selected groups, and (3) the ability to measure the response of those groups within fairly short time periods. In most cases, the future estimates are generally made for no longer than twelve to eighteen months, the argument being that the marketplace is so dynamic that longer forecasts will not be very accurate.

Being able to estimate in advance the value that the marketing and communication programs might achieve is a major step in determining how much the marketing firm could or should invest in upcoming marketing communication programs. We will deal with this issue in Chapter 9 in much more detail. For the moment, we will assume that if a relevant forecast of future customer behaviors can be estimated in advance, that would provide a major step forward in establishing future investments in both marketing and communication programs. It would go a long way in helping the firm understand how it might build and maintain ongoing customer brand relationships.

Summary of Pathway 2

The two approaches just described, marketing mix modeling and predictive forecasting, are fairly well established in the marketplace. While new approaches are being developed on a regular basis, they are, for the most part, variations or adaptations of the basic principles just discussed.

The results of either of the two approaches can be very beneficial to the marketing manager in planning and implementing customer-brand relationship programs. There are, however, some difficulties in developing these initiatives. For example, obtaining the data for the analyses is often difficult and time-consuming. Although most of the information needed is located somewhere within the firm, too often marketing and communication people either do not have access to it or do not even know where to start in locating it. The second major issue is that the marketplace is dynamic. Thus, what happened three or four years ago may be relevant only to that time period and not projectable into the future. Finally, these tools and approaches are dependent on both managerial judgment and statistical techniques, both of which can be quite subjective. The manager should always keep in mind that the result of any of these methodologies is at best an estimate of what happened in the past or what might happen in the future. Thus, the results must be couched as some level of probability associated with the estimate.

The primary problem with all the approaches in Pathway 2 is that they are short-term in nature. That is, they estimate the results of specific periods of time using the various marketing and communication programs and techniques employed. So while these measurements have substantial value in explaining what happened or what might happen in the near future, they have limitations when it comes to estimating the long-term results of building or maintaining a customer-brand relationship. To understand these relationships, it is necessary to employ some of the techniques and methodologies found in Pathway 3.

PATHWAY 3: BRANDED BUSINESS VALUE

In the previous two pathways, the goal was to measure the impact of specific, identifiable, quantifiable investments made by the firm in marketing and communication activities and then to relate them to specific marketplace results achieved in the short term, either at the aggregate or individual level. The goal of Pathway 3, however, is quite different and much more closely related to the way in which long-term customer-brand relationships are created and maintained.

We argued in Chapters 1 and 2 that the brand, rather than the product, service, company, or marketing and communication activities, is the primary factor with which customers have ongoing relationships. It is therefore the long-term, residual brand value that is important to understanding customer-brand relationships. Indeed, Tim Ambler of the London Business School has likened the brand to a long-term reservoir of uncollected future income for the firm, meaning that, over time, the relationship the brand has with customers will likely produce some level of ongoing future income.[8] It is this future income that is being estimated in Pathway 3.

Thus, if the marketing manager can estimate the future value of the brand, making the assumption that future income flows and value will come from customers and prospects, then it should be possible to determine how much the firm should invest in brand-building activities and to estimate the future returns it expects to receive. To develop a useful analysis, however, certain tenets of brand development and management must be accepted, and individual brand relationships, where they exist, must be aggregated.

Brand Valuations as the Basis for Customer-Brand Relationships

The basis for determining the type of marketing and communication programs to be developed and the amount to be invested in those programs is an accounting practice called brand valuation. Brand valuation has existed for many years, although only recently has it become a major factor in marketing and communication accountability.

Originally, valuation was conducted primarily to determine the estimated value of the intangible assets the firm owned, including the brand or brands the firm controlled. This valuation was particularly useful when brands were being either bought or sold. As intangible assets increasingly have come to make up the bulk of the value of an organization, the valuation of the brand has grown in importance. It is now a regular part of merger and acquisition negotiations. And it is equally helpful for the marketing relationship manager. Thus, as brands have grown in importance to the overall value of the organization, the need for brand valuation has changed.

Today, increasing the value of the brand or brands is considered one of the prime ways an organization can create future shareholder value. If the value of the brand increases for customers and prospects, they become brand loyal. That means they are likely to continue purchasing the brand into the future, may be willing to pay premium prices, may become advocates and help sell the brand to others, and so on. This future value is important to the firm and its shareholders for it signifies a long-term gain or appreciation as a result of current period investments. Those gains may come in the form of long-term income flows from sales or from increased brand value among investors should the brand be sold.

To justify current period investments in the brand, however, it is necessary to estimate future returns in some way. That is typically done in brand valuation calculations and measures, which are described next.

A GENERAL MODEL FOR BRAND VALUATION

The following sections describe one of the basic methods of brand valuation. The approach is the one used by Brand Finance PLC, a London-based brand consultancy. Most other brand valuations follow similar approaches.

Exhibit 8.4   **A General Model for Brand Valuation**

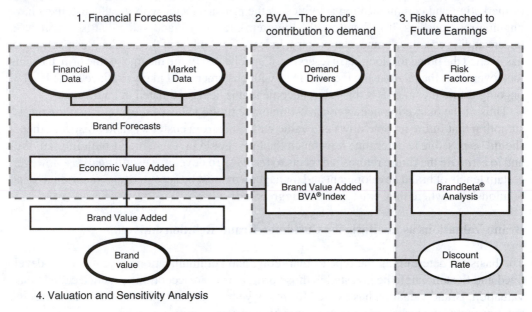

Source: Used with permission of Brand Finance plc.

The basic idea of brand valuation is that the financial value of the brand is a function of the level of profitable earnings it will generate over some future time period above and beyond the profits that can be attributed to just the physical product or service delivery. Thus, the process is based on determining the portion of future earnings that might be attributed to the brand above the generic value of the product or service, and the likelihood that those earnings will continue for some time into the future. Since brand earnings are derived from purchases by customers, there is a direct correlation between investments and returns that enables the firm to relate expenditures on the brand to future income flows. Since these future brand sales are generally estimated by the firm, the primary questions in brand valuation are (1) what portion of sales can be attributed to the brand, (2) what risks exist that the estimated sales will be achieved, and (3) what discount rate should be used to account for the current value of these future incomes. All these estimates are based on fairly straightforward accounting procedures.

The Brand Finance approach consists of four steps, which are illustrated in Exhibit 8.4. By understanding the four steps, the manager should have a fairly good understanding of the overall process.

Step 1: Financial Forecasts

The first step is to review the brand's historical financial performance, typically for the previous three to five years. That is then factored against the firm's forecasts of the brand's future volume, revenue, costs, and profitability, generally also three to five years into the future. In addition, relevant market data are considered to determine overall category trends, the brand's strength relative to competitors, various levels of customer awareness, preference, purchases, and loyalty, and so on. In most cases, these analyses are conducted at the customer segment level since the brand typically has greater strength with some customer groups than others.

Step 2: Brand Value Added or the Brand's Contribution to Demand

Here the relationship between the brand, the customer, and the future income flows becomes very relevant. The key element is to understand what portion of estimated future earnings can be attributed to the brand based on the customer's involvement with it. Thus, the second step is to separate out the contribution of the brand from the overall value of the product sales. For example, a marketing organization manufactures women's lipsticks at a cost of $1 per unit. If those lipsticks are branded with the corporate name, say, Acme, they might sell for $5 per unit. If, however, they are branded with the Coco Chanel name, they might sell for $25 each. This $20 retail differential between the generic value of the lipstick and the value of the lipstick branded Chanel is what Brand Finance calls the Brand Value Added or BVA®.

There are any number of elements that contribute to this added brand value, such as distribution, advertising and promotion, customer advocacy, and customer service, all of which, when bundled, create the brand. Brand Finance uses a proprietary method to make this estimation, as do other brand valuation organizations. By analyzing these contributing factors, Brand Finance is able to determine the estimated value that the brand brings to the base product or service. These values can range from 1 percent or so for a commoditized industrial product to 50 to 70 percent or more for some luxury goods.

Step 3: BrandBeta® Analysis

The third step is to determine the likelihood that the brand earnings will continue at the estimated rate into the future. That means calculating the risk factors involved. That risk could be the incursion of new competitors, the cost of capital, the life cycle of the product or service, and so on. This risk is then related to the assumed net present value of those earnings based on the time frame used.

To assess this earnings risk, Brand Finance uses another proprietary methodology called BrandBeta® Analysis. By identifying a number of factors that could influence the brand's future performance, then assessing and scoring the brand in relationship to its competitive set, using such factors as distribution, yield, and market share, among other drivers of demand, a level of risk is determined. Once these factors have been scored, they are applied against the forecasted sales to provide the appropriate discount rate to be used in the balance of the analysis.

Step 4: Application of Discount Rate and Estimation of Brand Value

The final step is to develop a long-term estimate of projected brand earnings using a net present value calculation, as shown in the simplified durable product example in Exhibit 8.5. The methodology used is called the economic value calculation of the brand. This estimate is what the brand is expected to earn during the period of time used in the calculation. In other words,

Exhibit 8.5

Brand Valuation: Consumer Durable Product (Simplified) (in millions of dollars)

	Year 0	Year 1	Year 2	Year 3	Year 4	Year 5
Net sales	500	520	550	580	650	650
Operating earnings	75.0	78.0	82.5	87.0	93.0	97.5
Tangible capital employed	250	260	275	290	310	325
Charge for capital at 5 percent	12.5	13.0	13.8	14.5	15.5	16.3
Intangible earnings	62.5	65.0	68.8	72.5	77.5	81.3
Brand earnings at 25 percent	15.6	16.3	17.2	18.1	19.4	20.3
Tax rate (in percent)	33	33	33	33	33	33
Tax	5.2	5.4	5.7	6.0	6.4	6.7
Post-tax brand earnings	10.5	10.9	11.5	12.1	13.0	13.6
Discount rate (in percent)	15					
Discount factor	1.00	1.15	1.32	1.52	1.75	2.01
Discounted cash flow	10.5	9.5	8.7	8.0	7.4	6.8
Value to year 5	50.8					
Annuity	45.1					
Brand value	95.9					

Source: Used with permission of Brand Finance plc.

this is the shareholder value that the brand is expected to create during that time period. It assumes the additional value that current and previous brand investments have created among customers that will be later returned to the firm.

As can be seen in Exhibit 8.5, future estimated sales and earnings make up the base of the model. The brand is estimated to generate $75 million in earnings in the base year, growing to $97.5 million in year 5—that is, it is growing at a compounded rate of 4 per cent per year.

The firm has $250 million employed in tangible capital to develop and manufacture the brand. A charge for this capital is made by the firm against the earnings of the brand at the rate of 5 percent per year, deducted annually.

The resulting intangible earnings of $62.5 million provide the base for the balance of the analysis. In this example, the BVA® analysis determines that 25 percent of the brand's intangible earnings could be attributed specifically to the brand, separate from any other elements of the offering. As shown, that amounts to $15.6 million in the base year, growing to $20.3 million in year 5; that is at the rate of 4.5 percent annually.

Next taxes must be taken into consideration. Those are estimated at 33 percent per year and are deducted from the estimated brand earnings. Thus, post-tax earnings are calculated to be $10.5 million in the base year, growing to $13.6 million in year 5.

The discount factor is the final calculation in this estimate of brand value. From the BrandBeta® analysis, the discount factor is determined to be 15 percent. Thus, the discount factor of 1.15 is shown in year 1, growing to 2.01 in year 5. That is deducted from the earning stream. The figures then show a discounted cash flow from the brand of $9.5 million in year 1, declining to $6.8 million in year 5.

The final calculation is to summarize the discounted cash flow for each of the five years. When this is done, the total is $50.8 million. Since the estimate has been done for only the next five years, some consideration must be given to the value of the brand beyond that time frame. The accounting profession has developed a generalized estimate of future earnings into perpetuity and published them in a table. By referencing that table, the annuity factor for the five-year discounted earnings is found to be $45.1 million. Adding the five-year estimate of discounted earnings ($50.8 million) to the annuity figure ($45.1 million), the total brand value of the durable product is $95.9 million at this point in time.

As before, while knowledge of the brand value is interesting, putting the value of the brand into perspective for management use is particularly helpful if the brand were being sold. The key element for ongoing brand management is the understanding that past, present, and future investments in the brand have created and will likely continue to create some level of value. Some of this is the residual value—that is, the value left over in the customer-brand relationship that will be drawn on in the future—while other value is being created for the firm going forward. If we assume the brand value created in the past and that which will accrue in the future are combined, then the value of the brand as a percentage of the sales is approximately 25 percent (the brand earnings from the fourth line in Exhibit 8.5). As long as all things hold in the estimates and the firm invests less than the 25 percent in brand earnings to keep the brand viable, the return from investment in this brand will be positive. In other words, the customer-brand value is increasing. Thus, the customer-brand relationship manager, through marketing and communication activities, might be said to be contributing to the ongoing relationship and enhancing the financial value of the brand.

SUMMING UP

With this brief discussion of how long- and short-term investments of marketing and communication might be measured, we have completed our review of the three pathways. The next question is how marketers can use this information on accountability and estimated returns on marketing and communication to develop more relevant and useful methods of determining how much to invest in ongoing marketing and communication. That discussion follows in Chapter 9.

NOTES

1. S. Dutka and R. Colley, *DAGMAR: Defining Advertising Goals for Measured Advertising Results* (New York: Association of National Advertisers, 1995).

2. I.P. Pavlov, *Conditioned Reflexes: An Investigation of the Physiological Activity of the Cerebral Cortex*, trans. G.V. Anrep (London: Oxford University Press, 1927); F.S. Keller and W.N. Schoenfeld, *Principles of Psychology* (Cambridge, MA: B.F. Skinner Foundation, 1995).

3. J.Z. Sissors and L. Bumba, *Advertising Media Planning* (Lincolnwood, IL: NTC Business Books, 1995).

4. W.M. Weilbacher, "How Advertising Affects Consumers," *Journal of Advertising Research*, June 2003.

5. J.P. Jones, *When Ads Work* (New York: Lexington Books, 1995).

6. Portions of this section have been adapted from D.E. Schultz and H. Schultz, "Measuring Brand Value," in *Kellogg on Branding*, ed. A. Tybout and T. Calkins (Hoboken, NJ: John Wiley, 2005).

7. D. Aaker, *Managing Brand Equity* (New York: Free Press, 1991); K.L. Keller, *Strategic Brand Management: Building, Measuring and Managing Brand Equity* (Upper Saddle River, NJ: Prentice Hall, 1998), p. 60.

8. T. Ambler, *Marketing and the Bottom Line* (London: Financial Times/Prentice Hall, 2000).

CHAPTER 9

Investing in Customers, Not Marketing Communication

For most marketing and communication organizations, four critical questions regarding budgeting for customer-brand relationship programs commonly arise:

1. How much should the firm invest in marketing and communication programs?
2. What types of programs should the firm invest in and why?
3. What rate of return will the firm achieve on those marketing and communication investments?
4. Over what period of time will those returns occur?

Unfortunately, these are questions that marketing and communication managers often have difficulty answering. Yet the answers are vital to the success of the organization, today and into the future.

These questions are difficult because traditionally marketing and communication managers have not focused on them. More importantly, in some cases, these issues have not even fallen within the purview of the marketing or communication manager. For example, the first question, how much to invest or spend, has often been predetermined by the CEO or CFO. While the marketing and communication people may make budget requests, they commonly do not have the final authority. That is because most organizations perceive marketing and communication as nothing more than cost centers. From an accounting standpoint, marketing and communication expenditures must typically be expensed (i.e., deducted from revenue) during the accounting period in which they occur. Therefore, they are under the watchful eye and tight cost control of the financial manager and other senior management whose job it is to balance income and expense in order to make sure the firm is profitable. As an expense item, therefore, expenditures on marketing and communication programs have generally been determined based on the capabilities, needs, and objectives of the organization, not on the potential demand that could be generated among customers and prospects.

In many cases, one of the primary challenges is the lack of agreement among managers and department heads about how the success of the marketing and communication programs should be measured. Disagreements continuously arise based on what should be measured (e.g., attitude change or actual sales), whether results should be reviewed in the long term or short term, and so on.

As a result, the tendency of many marketing and communication managers has been to

174

focus on the second of the four questions: What types of programs should the firm invest in and why? Thus, most marketing and communication managers assume that they will be allocated a certain budget and that their primary task is to properly allocate the available funds among the myriad alternatives that could be used to develop a customer-brand relationship program. Many, if not most, marketing and communication planning models and methodologies therefore focus on the allocation of available funds and not on the determination of what the appropriate investment level should be.

ABOVE- AND BELOW-THE-LINE COMPLICATIONS

The other issue in determining how much to invest revolves around the arbitrary internal allocation rule based on "above-the line" and "below-the-line" expenditures. These expressions date back to a time of limited communication alternatives and simple client-agency relationships. The "line" referred to was an imaginary one, drawn within the marketing budget to distinguish between commissionable and noncommissionable activities carried out by the agency. "Above the line" referred to commissionable media that the agency would place on behalf of the marketer. The agency would withhold a portion of the billing for media expenditures as its commission and remit the balance of payment to the TV station or publication. Communication efforts that were not commissionable to the agency were said to be "below the line." Initially this referred to such activities as public relations, sales promotion, direct response, and other activities for which the marketer would pay a fee to the agency for the services rendered.[1] While the financial arrangements between clients, agencies, and media have changed dramatically over the years, the expressions "above the line" and "below the line" have come to refer to communication activities that are believed to provide long-term versus short-term returns.

Thus, most (but not all) traditional media advertising is generally considered to offer long-term or residual value and is therefore still often referred to as "above the line," while time-sensitive, short-term promotions and incentives such as coupons, price-offs, discounts, circulars, mailers, and the like are referred to as "below the line." That is, they are assumed to have little or no long-term value to the organization beyond the immediate results they produce. While this issue is declining in significance as the broad range of promotional possibilities has exploded in the last few years, there is still the hangover that some expenditures are assumed to have greater long-term value than others.

Some companies have argued that advertising offers benefits to the organization well beyond the immediate period in which the commercial or print ad runs and that therefore some portion of the expenditures should be capitalized and amortized over time. It is true that some great advertising can provide value to an organization for many, many years (for example, the ad campaigns featuring the famous lines "Only her hairdresser knows for sure," "Mikey, he likes it!" and "Got milk?"). However, since it is extremely difficult to predict the success of any one campaign, and because so many intervening variables and issues can come into play, for tax and financial reporting purposes the accounting profession has resisted the idea of allowing capitalization of investments in communication programs. The primary exception is the cost of product catalogs and direct mail brochures, which do not necessarily need to be entirely expensed at the time they are printed. Certain printing costs may be deferred until such time as the materials are actually mailed to customers and prospects if a direct relationship between a sale and the specific communication piece can be clearly demonstrated.[2]

The argument against capitalization of advertising and other communication activities rests largely on their unpredictable nature. In a very high profile case, AOL was forced by the Securities and Exchange Commission (SEC) to cease capitalizing its costs of promoting to new customers. Additionally, the company was forced to pay a civil penalty of $3.5 million. In that case, the SEC found that AOL did not meet the essential requirements for capitalizing its marketing expenditures and that its unstable business environment precluded reliable forecasts of future net revenue. Moreover, the SEC found that AOL did not properly assess the recoverability of its capitalized costs either.[3]

Another issue that has gained substantial attention in recent years concerns how sales promotion costs are treated from an accounting standpoint. Some companies historically chose to treat items such as discounts, coupons, slotting fees, trade allowances, and other similar incentives as part of their marketing costs. Other companies, however, have treated them as a reduction in gross revenue, making it difficult to compare two companies with differing treatments of their sales promotion expenditures. In 2001, a revenue ruling from the Financial Accounting Standard Board (FASB 01–9) established a requirement that from that point forward, all such expenditures were to be treated as a reduction in revenue. While this ruling makes no difference in the bottom-line profitability of the company, it represents a dramatic change in how companies report their top-line revenues. Among consumer packaged goods companies, where it is not unusual for manufacturers to have trade promotion budgets of 15 to 20 percent of their gross sales, the ruling was particularly controversial.[4]

Accounting issues aside, however, the marketing and communication manager still needs to address the four questions with which we opened this chapter. In Chapter 8, we provided methodologies by which managers could determine how to measure or evaluate the results of marketing and communication programs—in other words, methods of dealing with questions 3 and 4. The following chapters in this book will provide new and improved methods of allocating resources to various marketing and communication programs in order to generate measurable returns on customer-brand relationship programs. These methods constitute tools to answer question 2: What type of marketing and communication programs should the firm invest in and why? Therefore, in this chapter, our primary focus will be on question 1: How much should the firm invest in marketing and communication programs in order to develop and maintain immediate and ongoing customer-brand relationships?

We start with why the firm should invest funds in any type of marketing and communication program—in other words, the importance of focusing on outcomes rather than outputs. That explanation is followed by a discussion of how marketing and communication budgets have traditionally been developed. The final part of this chapter is devoted to a process that will allow the marketing and communication manager to determine what level of expenditure should be made and how that level can be connected to the measurement sections discussed in Chapter 8.

WHY SHOULD THE FIRM INVEST IN MARKETING AND COMMUNICATION PROGRAMS?

One of the basic questions all senior managers ask is "Why should we invest in marketing and communication programs? Our products are superior. Our sales are increasing. What can marketing contribute?" It is this increasingly difficult question that this section will address.

Fundamentals of Investing in Marketing and Communication Activities

Investing is clearly different from spending. Yet the marketing and communication field has been beset by this difference for ages. Investing is based on the assumption that some return will accrue to the organization as a result of obtaining an asset that will have a greater value in the future than it does today. In other words, the investment will generate some level of return on the funds used to acquire it and will provide some type of increased shareholder value. Spending, in contrast, is buying something that has current or short-term value with little or no regard for the future. Of course, buying or acquiring something is assumed to have some type of future value, but that value is not generally critical to the immediate decision to buy or acquire. Thus, investments must have expected returns sometime in the future, while funds that are spent have no such requirement or even any expectation for the long term.

Unfortunately, this question of investing or buying has long plagued marketing and communication managers. They buy advertising media or pay for the distribution of coupons or pay the postal service to deliver their mailings. In these cases, managers are paying some amount of money to purchase a service or acquire a product. They are buying outputs or distribution systems or methodologies to deliver their messages and incentives to customers and prospects. Alternatively, as was discussed in Chapter 8, in the customer-brand relationship approach, the firm is focused on investing in customers and in the relationship the firm has, or can develop, with those customers. While the firm may be purchasing advertising or sales promotion or direct marketing or other activities in making that investment, the assumption is that the return will come from the customer, not from the activity itself. That is the primary change in the view of investments and spending and between outputs and outcomes. In other words, marketers are trying to influence the outcomes or returns to the organization, and those generally come from customers.

It is this focus on outputs versus outcomes that really differentiates customer-brand relationship development from traditional exchange-based marketing and communication programs. In an exchange-based system, the focus is on the short-term returns to the firm. In the customer-brand relationship approach, the focus is on short-term returns but also on the development of ongoing, long-term customer relationships that can be estimated or calculated in advance. So the basic challenge for customer-brand relationship managers is reorienting their focus from outputs, or what is being done, to outcomes, or what the returns will likely be. With this idea of generating some type of ongoing income flows to the organization, we now look at what type of investment strategies might be employed.

The Four Goals of Investing

One way of making this change internally is to start with what investments in marketing and communication, especially customer-brand relationships, are designed to do. Since we are basing our approach on building customer-brand relationships, we, of course, start with customers, not with marketing or communication activities.

In Chapter 1, we discussed the primary reasons organizations invest in marketing and communication activities. It is appropriate to recap that discussion here since it allows marketers to determine how much the firm should be willing to invest in its marketing and communication programs.

Organizations invest finite resources in customers for only four reasons:

1. *To acquire new customers.* These are generally customers who are new to the firm, either first-time users who are new to the product or service category or current users in the category who have been purchasing from another supplier. In either case, acquisition of these customers means new income flows to the marketing organization.

2. *To maintain present customers.* Companies often invest substantial funds in existing customers simply to maintain their business. These customers are currently providing some level of income flow to the firm. Thus, the goal of the customer-brand relationship program is to maintain that income flow today and into the future at a cost less than the revenue being generated. These customers may not grow in value over time, but their business relationship with the marketing firm is typically the base of the organization's success.

3. *To grow the current value of present customers.* These customers are similar to those in the maintenance area in number 2 above. However, they have the potential (a) to increase their use of the marketer's products or services by purchasing other products and services marketed by the firm or (b) to increase their present usage or requirements of the products and services currently being purchased or (c) to pay higher prices for the existing products or services in the belief that greater value is being received. Whatever the reason, these customers have greater and, as yet, unrealized potential future value than that demonstrated through their past behaviors. Thus, these customers can grow in value over time. As a result, the organization is willing to invest some of its finite resources in an attempt to increase these future income flows.

4. *To migrate the customer through some type of product or service portfolio.* In this case, the marketing organization recognizes that its product and service offerings may not be appropriate for current customers in the future. Changing lifestyles, aging, evolving social systems, and a host of other personal and marketplace situations may encourage customers to change or replace their current product or service requirements from the organization. Anticipating those changes, the marketing organization attempts to have available alternative products or services that might fit those changing customer needs. Thus, the customer can "migrate" from one product or service to another without leaving the organization's customer base. There may be no increase in value of the customer in these situations, but the income flow is maintained by the firm through alternative offerings.

With these four basic reasons for making investments in customers, we can now turn to the continuing issue of short-term versus long-term returns.

When Will Those Returns Occur?

As discussed earlier and in some detail in Chapter 8, using the three pathways model, one of the most important issues in determining how much to invest is deciding when the returns can be expected. This time frame is important for two reasons, (1) to manage the finite assets of the organization and maintain an orderly cash flow, and (2) to have some understanding of when and in what way the returns will occur. This is critical in developing an effective strategic plan for the firm. Thus, these issues are as important to the management of the organization as they are to the development and maintenance of ongoing relationships with the customers involved.

Generally, in the customer-brand relationship approach, we have used returns in the current fiscal year to define short-term returns and periods longer than the current fiscal year to define the long-term value. While these are convenient methods of managing the two types of investments and returns, they are not absolute rules. In Chapter 8, for example, in developing predictive models of customer investments and returns, we used the base of the next twelve to eighteen months to estimate future returns. So while we will use these basic definitions of short-term and long-term returns, there are instances where they may have to be adapted or adjusted.

There is one additional element that must be brought into the estimate of returns. That is a financial term called the firm's internal rate of return (IRR). IRR is a corporate financial tool used in most large or publicly held companies. It is the rate of return on its investments that the organization tries to achieve. It is the yardstick against which all corporate expenditures are judged. In other words, the financial management of the company determines what the organization has to pay in order to obtain and use additional external capital, including the interest rate for borrowing the expected capital needs of the organization and the like. Using that figure, the firm then determines the rate of return needed to cover this cost of capital acquisition. Thus, the IRR is determined for the organization. The IRR is then used as an evaluation tool by senior management, which allows them to compare various investments or uses of the company's resources. For most consumer product organizations, the IRR is in the general range of 8 to 16 percent. For high-tech companies, it may range up to 30 or 40 percent, and other firms may have even higher rates.

Why is the IRR important to the marketing and communication manager? For one simple reason: it is the basis on which most marketing and communication investments will be judged. Thus, if the IRR of the organization has been set at 14 percent, a marketing return of 3 or 4 percent will not be favorably evaluated by senior management, for it does not represent an optimum use of the firm's finite resources. This does not mean that every marketing or communication activity must meet or beat the organization's IRR, but it can be a key performance indicator for the marketing and communication manager to determine the attractiveness of the customer-brand communication investment being developed or recommended.

With this view of customer-brand relationship investment basics, we can now turn to how budgets for marketing and communication have traditionally been set by marketing firms. As we will explain, they reflect a different view of marketing and communication than the approach we are recommending for customer-brand relationship programs.

TRADITIONAL METHODS OF MARKETING AND COMMUNICATION BUDGETING

Historically, marketing and communication budgets have been modeled on those used for advertising programs. Since advertising is often the largest promotional expenditure for many marketing organizations, that is where most of the knowledge and understanding has developed. The approaches have simply been adapted or transferred to the marketing and communication budgeting process.

As suggested before, most advertising (marketing and communication) budgets are established by senior management as control mechanisms for the management of corporate resources. By allocating a certain amount to the purchase and management of advertising, marketing, and communications, the financial managers of the organization believe they gain a certain level of control of the expenditures of the firm.

While the budgets are generally set by senior management, there usually is some level of input by the advertising, marketing, or communication managers. They recommend or propose certain levels of expenditure for the coming periods. Thus, the budgeting for most forms of promotion becomes an internal negotiation between the advertising, marketing, and communication people and the financial managers. Over the years, the tradition has developed that marketing people ask for more than they believe they need, assuming that the financial managers will reduce their requests. The financial people, aware of this tactic, commonly enter the negotiations with the goal of reducing the requests of the marketing people. Therefore, the final budget is not necessarily what is needed or required for the marketing and communication job to be done but, rather, an agreed-upon sum that finance always believes is too large and marketing always believes is too small. Unfortunately, since the measurement of advertising, marketing, and communication returns is still in the developmental stage for many firms, neither the marketing and communication nor the financial people can demonstrate that they are either right or wrong. In short, budgeting is essentially a sufficing system within most organizations with much more work still to be done.

In spite of these difficulties, allocations or expenditures must be determined for some future period, generally one year to coincide with the annual financial considerations of the firm. Thus, a number of alternative budgeting procedures have developed over time. All have difficulties and, as will be seen, none of them really focuses on building customer-brand relationships. They are essentially methodologies used to gain some internal consensus on the amount to be allocated for the purchase of various marketing, advertising, and communication programs.

Since there are a number of traditional budgeting methodologies, an easy way to consider them is to group them along two dimensions, as illustrated in Exhibit 9.1.[5] The x-axis in the exhibit is based on "Easy to Difficult" and the y-axis shows whether the methodology is "Conceptual or Mechanical." "Conceptual" methods essentially rest upon some underlying theory such as the hierarchy of effects model discussed in Chapter 8; "mechanical" simply means that some type of agreed-upon formula is applied. While there are a number of elements to each of the methodologies shown in the exhibit, a brief description will provide a view of the general approach and elements.

The upper right-hand quadrant shows the Mechanical and Easy methodologies.

1. *Advertising/Sales Ratio.* This is a fairly simple calculation in which the marketer estimates or is given an estimated sales revenue projection for the coming period. Then, some type of ratio is applied to that sales forecast to set the marketing and communication expenditures. Since the ratio is a fixed number or percentage, if sales go up, the marketing budget goes up; if sales go down, the marketing programs are reduced. Thus, marketing investments have nothing to do with generating sales; they are simply a reflection of the success the firm is having in the marketplace at that time.

2. *Share of Voice.* This is a pure advertising budgeting approach. The assumption is that for advertising to break through the clutter of other advertisers, the firm must invest in advertising at the same level as its competitors. Commonly, this level is equated to a share of market figure. In other words, the assumption is made that share of market and share of advertising expenditures are directly related. Thus, to gain share of market, the organization must invest disproportionately more than its current share of sales or market. For example, if $1 million is being spent in the category by all marketers and if the subject firm has a 25 percent share of that market, then the marketer should invest at that level (i.e., $250,000) to maintain that

Exhibit 9.1   **The Field of Advertising Budgeting Methods**

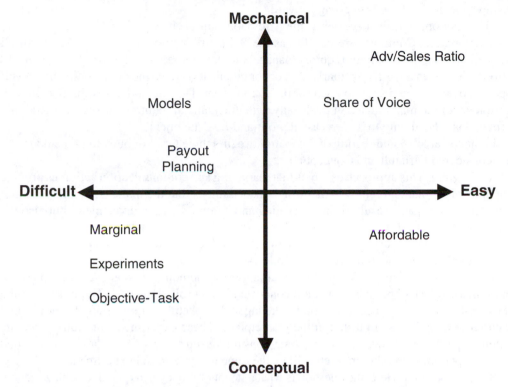

Source: Edward F. McQuarrie, Santa Clara University.

share. If the goal is to gain sales or share, then disproportionately greater spending is suggested. Clearly, if competitors are overspending in marketing and promotion, the subject company will overspend; alternatively, it will underspend if that is what competitors are doing. Thus, the advertising and marketing budget is driven by competitive spending, not by any rational investment policy.

In the top left quadrant, two Difficult, Mechanical methods are listed.

3. *Payout Planning.* This approach requires the manager to estimate, in advance, the impact and effect of the advertising, marketing, or communication program along with the costs that will be incurred. The methodology then aligns the estimated costs with the estimated returns using time as the key variable. In other words, the manager estimates how long it will take for the proposed program to break even and when profits will start to accrue to the firm. This is, essentially, an incremental return model such as was discussed in Chapter 8: the manager forecasts the impact of the promotional program and how long it will take the marketing firm to recoup its promotional investment.

4. *Models.* Models are simply simulations of expected outputs that are then compared to estimated returns. These are commonly based on some previous experience of the firm or other firms in the category. The marketing mix modeling approach described in Chapter 8 is an example of this type of approach. By knowing the results of previous marketing, advertis-

ing, or communication programs, the manager can estimate how much would be required to achieve the goals of the firm going forward.

In the bottom right-hand corner is the Affordable approach.

5. *Affordable.* Commonly referred to as the "leftover" method, this is the simplest of all budgeting systems. It simply requires managers to determine what the firm believes it can afford to invest in advertising, marketing, or communication once the organization has developed its overall organization budget for the coming year. This method has nothing to do with customers or the marketplace. It deals only with the financial requirements of the marketing firm and is related only to its forecasted profit-and-loss statement.

In the lower left-hand section of the matrix, we find three types of budgeting methods. All are considered Difficult and Conceptual.

6. *Marginal.* This approach assumes that marketing and communication activities provide some level of financial return to the firm. It also assumes that the manager can forecast not only future sales as a result of the marketing and communication investment, but also the costs of obtaining those future sales. This is very close to the methodology employed in the development of customer-brand relationship budgets, so we will postpone discussion of this method until Section III, which follows.

7. *Experiments.* This is essentially a trial-and-error method. The manager sets up one or more marketplace experiments that are conducted in controlled markets. Hypotheses of the relationship between expenditures on marketing and marketplace returns are developed and then these hypotheses are tested in the marketplace. These experiments are fairly accurate when properly conducted, but they are time-consuming and expensive. It is also assumed that future experiences in other markets will be the same as those initial experiments.

8. *Objective-Task.* Here, the question is what amount of money is required to achieve certain advertising, marketing, or communication objectives in the marketplace. The marketing manager estimates in advance what level of marketing or communication activity is required to achieve certain marketplace goals. Then, those marketplace activities are converted into the funding required to purchase or acquire those levels of marketing and communication activities in the marketplace. For example, if the marketing manager estimates that 150 gross rating points (GRPs) of television advertising will be required each week for the next ten weeks in order to achieve a certain level of awareness in the market, the cost of those 1,500 GRPs will then be established as the budget.

As can be seen, all these traditional approaches have their strengths and weaknesses. Unfortunately, none really gets to the issue of making investments in customers and prospects. They are primarily focused on what it will cost to purchase various types of marketing, advertising, and promotion—for example, gross rating points in broadcast, exposures in print, showings in outdoor, coupons dropped or delivered, and so on. They are all, as discussed in Chapter 8 and in this chapter as well, internally focused approaches to marketing, advertising, and communication, relying in most instances on some basic acknowledgement and acceptance of a stimulus-response model founded on behaviorist psychological tenets.

In the customer-brand relationship approach proposed in this text, however, the purpose of marketing and communication is not merely to send out messages and incentives, but to invest in customers and thus generate some type of return income flow. In the following sections, we outline a customer-brand relationship approach to determining how much should or could be invested in customers. In the following chapters, we provide guidelines on what those investments should entail and what specific programs could be employed.

BASING BUDGETS ON THE VALUE OF CUSTOMER-BRAND RELATIONSHIPS

As has been stressed in the previous chapters, the primary difference between the traditional approach and the customer-brand relationship approach to marketing and communication is the focus on outcomes, or what the organization will receive in return for its marketing activities and investments. Historically, the emphasis has been on outputs, or what the organization will develop and deliver to customers and prospects, as shown by the budgeting methodologies discussed in the previous section. Clearly, how the organization manages its message and incentive delivery systems and the content contained in its communication activities has much to do with the returns it receives. But the far more critical issue is the audience to whom those messages and incentives will be delivered. The best distribution plan and the most creative messages and incentives imaginable will not be effective if they do not go to the right audience for the firm's products and/or services.

The key word is, of course, the *right* audience—the customers or prospects who need, want, can use, or would like to acquire the product or service the firm is offering. For the most part, determination of the rightness of customers and prospects is based on their current or previous behaviors. If they have either purchased or signified their intention to purchase the product or service in the past, that is much more relevant than simply estimating their potential value based on their attitudes, opinions, or feelings. These people have already voted for the product or service with their wallets. So the right audience is the audience who has the potential to purchase or repurchase or expand purchase or migrate to another product or service in the marketer's line (according to the discussion above on the four reasons organizations spend money on marketing and communication).

Spending (Investing) Based on Estimated Returns

If the plan is to invest in customers and prospects who are likely to respond, that gives the firm a unique way to develop customer-brand relationship investment strategies and thus marketing and communication budgets. Quite simply, if the organization knows the financial value of a customer and can estimate the type or level of response that might be generated by making investments in that customer, the firm can develop a closed-loop marketing system. In that system, customer value is known. Therefore, returns on investments in those customers can be estimated in advance.

The marketing and communication investment to be made is a managerial decision determined by these two elements, (1) current and expected customer value, and (2) some type of managerial investment decision on the value that might be created in the future. This allocation and investment decision is determined and constrained by the contribution margin of the product or service. This too is a radical departure in advertising, marketing, and communication budgeting. The focus is on the contribution margin, not gross sales. By contribution margin, we are referring to gross revenue less all the fixed and variable product costs, as well nonmarketing administrative expenditures. In the traditional methodologies used in budgeting, for the most part, the focus has been on gross sales, the top-line value to be generated. In customer-brand relationship marketing, the focus is on the contribution margin, or what the firm will receive that can then be reinvested in customers and customer-brand relationships in the future, something not possible with a focus only on top-line sales returns.

Exhibit 9.2   **Closed-Loop Model**

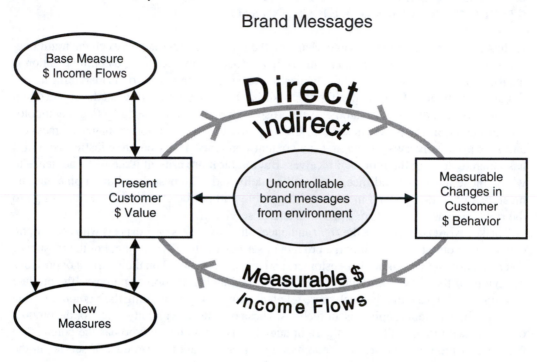

We already have in place most of the elements needed for this new type of budgeting system. In Chapter 7, we presented the customer-brand value (CBV) formula:

$$CBV = P \times BR \times SOP \times CM$$

where

$$P = penetration$$
$$BR = buying\ rate$$
$$SOP = share\ of\ purchases$$
$$CM = contribution\ margin$$

The Closed-Loop Model

The primary item needed to develop a rational, supportable budgeting approach is the addition of a "closed-loop" investment system. As Exhibit 9.2 shows, the marketing manager first determines the current value of a customer or prospect at the contribution margin level. Then, a managerial estimate is made of what the likely future value of that customer might be. This estimate determines how much could or might be invested in marketing and communication to influence the future behavior of that customer or prospect. The amount to be invested, of course, is moderated by the internal rate of return (IRR) that the organization believes it must achieve on any investment, particularly marketing. An example will illustrate the concept.

Let us say the organization has a customer who is purchasing the product or service at a rate so that a contribution margin of $1,000 was generated last year (100 units sold at $90 each, less $80 in product costs, leaving a contribution margin of $10 each). The marketing or communication manager estimates that the customer has the potential to purchase an additional 25 units during the period for which the budget is being determined. With a contribution margin of $10 generated for each new unit purchased, the available funds for marketing and communication to obtain those future sales would be $250 (25 units at $10 per unit). Thus, the manager would conclude that the firm could invest $250 in marketing and communication to generate that expected return.

The major problem with this scenario, however, is that if the manager invests the entire $250 in various marketing and communication programs, the best result would be simply a breakeven, not an attractive return on the use of finite corporate resources. In other words, if the manager invested all the estimated future incremental income in generating the contribution margin of $250, nothing would be left for profit. That is where the internal rate of return comes in.

Factoring in the Required Internal Rate of Return for the Firm

If the firm requires a 12 percent rate of return on its investments, the marketing/communications manager really has only $220 available to invest in the customer through marketing and communication programs. That is, to generate the return ($250) estimated contribution margin from increased sales less 12 percent required IRR return to the organization ($30), the calculation would be $250 − $30 = $220. Thus, to make the required return to the firm, the manager has to recalculate the investment in marketing and communication in the customer in line with the organization's IRR. Of course, if the goal is to generate more returns than the IRR, then a lower amount would be available.

To develop a budget for the coming year, the manager estimates the value of the customer, determines the amount of that growth in customer value at the contribution margin line, and then deducts the required IRR. That provides the available funds that can be invested and thus the budget for the program. To do that for the entire product or service line, the manager develops that calculation for each of the customers in whom a marketing and communication investment is to be made.

At this point, the reader is probably saying, "That is a tremendous amount of work simply to set an estimated budget for investing in a customer-brand relationship program. Wouldn't it be easier to set an estimated amount and use that?" Unfortunately, that is what has too often been done in the past. Amounts have been spent on marketing and communication that have no relationship to what could or might be returned to the firm. Remember, the customer-brand relationship approach is based on customers, their current and future value. Thus, only by estimating what might be returned can the manager have any idea of what should or might be invested.

While the approach described above sounds complicated when based on an individual customer, the approach can be simplified by aggregating like-behaving or like-value customers, as was discussed in Chapter 7. Thus, those customers who generate certain income returns to the firm can be aggregated for budgeting purposes. For example, assume there are 1 million individual customers who are purchasing an average of 100 units per year at an average contribution margin rate of $10 per unit. If the manager estimates that an average 25 percent increase is possible for the coming period, that would generate a total available investment pool of $2,500,000 (1,000,000 × .25 × $10). If the same 12 percent IRR is required, then the maximum available marketing and communication budget for the coming period would be $2,200,000 ($2,500,000 × .88). The mathematics is the same; only the scale of investments and returns changes.

An Illustration of the Customer-Brand Relationship Budgeting Approach

An actual budgeting case will illustrate how the basic concept described above can be employed. At the end of the case, a worksheet is provided that can be used as an aid in developing, implementing, and justifying the budgeting process.

Company Background

The company, Carioca Cartridges, for which the budget is being developed, sells printer cartridges to small and medium-sized businesses within a region of the southeastern United States. It sells both direct to cartridge users through an online ordering system and through retail outlets such as office supply stores, computer retailers, and mass merchandisers. The Carioca brand is in the midrange category with reliable products and a reputation for excellent customer service. It competes against a few premium cartridge suppliers, a number of direct competitors, the traditional low-price entries, and even some private labels, developed primarily by retailers.

Carioca senior management has established an internal rate of return of 15 percent on all investments the company makes.

Customer Value Calculations

Over the course of the past few years, the firm has developed a database of about 100,000 printer ink cartridge users within the regions it serves. Of this group, 40,000 purchase the Carioca brand. According to our customer valuation methodology from Chapter 7 (and above), Carioca has a 40 percent penetration (P) of the market. That is, 40 percent of the customers in the database buy from Carioca. The company regularly sends marketing communication to this customer base and also captures name and address information on customers who buy at retail through various retail customer loyalty programs.

From previous research, the Carioca marketing manager has determined that the individuals in the company's database own, on average, two printers and purchase approximately two cartridges per printer per month. In other words, the average buying rate (BR) of these customers and prospects per printer is 24 units per year.

Carioca's present customer base of 40,000 purchases approximately 65 percent of its cartridges from the company. Thus, Carioca has a share of purchases (SOP) of 65 percent among its customers. The other 35 percent of the cartridges are purchased from competitive manufacturers or from retailers where the firm has no distribution.

The contribution margin for an individual printer cartridge is $6.50 per unit (CM = $6.50). For purposes of illustrating this case, we will assume that all competitors have essentially similar cost structures and hence the same contribution margin.

Thus, if we populate the customer-brand value formula for Carioca's customer base, it would look like this:

$$CBV = P \times BR \times SOP \times CM$$
$$CBV = 24 \times 65\% \times \$6.50 = \$101.40$$

Using that data, we can say the average Carioca customer is worth $101.40 per year (24 cartridges per year × 0.65 share of purchases × $6.50 per unit). Alternatively, the average value of all customers in the database is $156, which is split between all suppliers from which they purchase (24 cartridges per year × 100% of purchases × $6.50 per unit).

Based on this information, the customer-brand relationship manager at Carioca would appear to have substantial opportunity to invest in customers and prospects and generate substantial returns.

Alternatives Facing Carioca

Given these simple facts, Carioca's marketing manager has three broad alternatives:

1. *Increase Carioca's penetration of the category.* There are 60,000 prospects that do not currently buy Carioca brand cartridges. Thus, there would appear to be significant untapped potential if some of these prospects can be converted to the Carioca brand for some portion of their cartridge usage.
2. *Increase the share of purchase of present customers.* Current Carioca customers are purchasing 35 percent of their cartridge needs from competitive suppliers. If Caricoa can capture a larger share of its own customers' purchases, it can positively impact its sales volume and profitability.
3. *Dig deeper to aggregate customers according to their value, and market to them accordingly.* Presently, Carioca markets on the basis of an "average customer." However, actual customer demand varies widely from only one or two cartridges per year up to several dozen. Additionally, not all customers have the same level of brand loyalty or purchasing behavior.

The major questions, of course, are which alternative offers the greatest potential return and how much the manager would be willing to invest in those customers to generate those returns consistent with the company's 15 percent IRR threshold. That will determine the budget to be requested and also justified to senior management.

Additional Research

The Carioca manager uses a combination of database analysis and market research to develop a more detailed view of the customer universe. This research shows that while the average cartridge demand is 24 per customer per year, there are actually three levels of purchasing and usage.

1. Heavy users, those using 34 or more cartridges per year (average of 42.4), account for 20 percent of the 100,000 customers in the Carioca database.
2. Medium users consume 14 to 33 units per year (average 24) and constitute 60 percent of the customer universe.

Exhibit 9.3 **Overview of Printer Cartridge Customer Universe**

	Heavy 20%	Medium 60%	Light 20%	Total
Loyal 15%	3,000	9,000	3,000	15,000
Switchers 50%	10,000	30,000	10,000	50,000
Price Buyers 35%	7,000	21,000	7,000	35,000
Total	20,000	60,000	20,000	100,000

3. Light users, those using 13 or fewer cartridges per year (average of 7.6), make up the remaining 20 percent of the customer base.

In addition, Carioca has also identified three types of buyers in this particular printer cartridge market: loyals, switchers, and price buyers.

1. Loyals give all or virtually all of their purchases to a single favored supplier. Some 15 percent of the 100,000 (15,000) total buyers are classified as loyals.
2. Switchers account for 50 percent, or 50,000 buyers. They split their purchases between two to three preferred brands.
3. Price buyers represent the balance of the customer base, 35 percent or 35,000 purchasers. They tend to buy only when there is a sale or a price reduction on printer cartridges. Then, they stock up.

The manager compiles all this information about Carioca customers and prospects into a chart like that in Exhibit 9.3. Because buyers have differing motivations, purchasing patterns, and potential profitability to the organization, a truly customer-focused approach starts by taking these differences into account. Thus, each box within the matrix potentially calls for a different marketing strategy. We will briefly discuss three potential approaches that could be developed based on this data.

Heavy Users/Loyals. As shown in Exhibit 9.4, if the Carioca manager decides to pursue the heavy user/loyal group, consisting of approximately 3,000 customers, the potential revenue would be roughly $273 per customer. Since these customers buy all their cartridges from a single supplier, any new loyal customers acquired will be extremely profitable to the firm. They bring high volume, consistent buying patterns, and lack of price sensitivity. Assuming Carioca already has about 50 percent of this group as its customers, that would mean an additional 1,500 are still prospects. The key challenge for Carioca is to maintain the loyal customers it already has while attracting similar loyal heavy users. In this segment, the 1,500 prospects account for a total demand of 42 units, 100 percent of which are purchased from a single supplier, at a $6.50 margin per unit, which equates to an additional potential contribution margin of $409,500 (42 × 100% × 6.50 × 1,500). However, going after another company's loyal customers is not without substantial risk, since they are loyal to their present supplier. The likelihood that Carioca could attract all—or even a majority—of the heavy users/loyals

Exhibit 9.4   **Strategy Formulation: Heavy Users/Loyals**

Each customer represents
42 × $6.50 = $273 in value to preferred suppliers
Goal: Acquire and retain

	Heavy 20%	Medium 60%	Light 20%	Total
Loyal 15%	3,000	9,000	3,000	15,000
Switchers 50%	10,000	30,000	1,0000	50,000
Price Buyers 35%	7,000	21,000	7,000	35,000
Total	20,000	60,000	20,000	100,000

Exhibit 9.5   **Strategy Formulation: Medium Users/Switchers**

	Heavy 20%	Medium 60%	Light 20%	Total
Loyal 15%	3,000	9,000	3,000	15,000
Switchers 50%	10,000	30,000	1,0000	50,000
Price Buyers 35%	7,000	21,000	7,000	35,000
Total	20,000	60,000	20,000	100,000

Each customer represents
24 × 65% × $6.50 = $156 on value split among 2–3 suppliers
Goal: Increase share of purchase

is not great. However, given the company's strong product offering and its reputation for solid customer service, the Carioca manager believes it would be possible to capture about 30 percent of the 1,500 heavy user/loyal group who are not already Carioca customers. Thus, the 1,500 potential customers are now reduced to a realistic objective of 450 new customers to be acquired. Using the same $6.50 per cartridge times the estimated 42 units would yield $122,850 in contribution margin ($450 \times 100\% \times \$6.50 \times 42 = \$122,850$). Allowing for the required 15 percent IRR, the Carioca manager would be willing to invest up to $104,423 to acquire those customers and still make the required return on investment ($\$122,850 \times .85 = \$104,423$).

Exhibit 9.6 **Strategy Formulation: Light Users/Price Buyers**

	Heavy 20%	Medium 60%	Light 20%	Total
Loyal 15%	3,000	9,000	3,000	15,000
Switchers 50%	10,000	30,000	1,0000	50,000
Price Buyers 35%	7,000	21,000	7,000	35,000
Total	20,000	60,000	20,000	100,000

Each customer represents
7.5 × $4.50 = $33.75 in value (at best), split among all suppliers
Goal: Retain as cost effectively as possible

Of course, the heavy user/loyal segment—profitable though it may be—is a relatively narrow segment. While individual users consume at an above average rate, the size of the group means they could not generate a high volume in the aggregate. In order to broaden the base of the business and support manufacturing economies of scale, the company must also consider cultivating other segments within the universe. Exhibit 9.5 illustrates a strategy focused on the much larger segment of medium users who switch between a given consideration set of suppliers.

Medium Users/Switchers. This group consists of approximately 30,000 purchasers who use, on average, 24 cartridges per period, purchasing them from 2 or 3 preferred suppliers. Carioca presently sells to about 40 percent of these customers, meaning there are approximately 18,000 potential new buyers available to Carioca (30,000 medium switchers × 60 percent available). Given the information from the matrix, the medium users/switchers represent a total value of $1,950,000 spread across their purchases from all suppliers. (Remember, we are assuming all suppliers have the same contribution margin.) Again, however, the Carioca manager is not likely to capture all those medium users/switchers. Nor will the company capture a 100 percent share of purchases from these customers, since switching behavior is a defining characteristic of the group. However, it can seek to gain a larger average share of purchases than the 65 percent it currently enjoys. The marketing manager hopes to acquire 25 percent of the available prospects (i.e., 4,500 new customers) and hopes to achieve an average 75 percent of their share of purchases. Thus, the potential for the prospects to be acquired in this group is 24 units x 75 percent share of purchases x $6.50 margin x 4,500 customers = $526,500. However, the manager must be sure to cover the 15 percent IRR requirement, leaving only $447,525 in available funds ($526,500 × 0.85 = $447,525).

Yet another alternative for the Carioca manager is to attempt to acquire some of the price buyers. At first glance, that alternative does not appear to be very attractive, given their value as shown in Exhibit 9.6. However, it is an approach Carioca might consider in order to build unit volume or capture a greater share of market, if either of these is a corporate goal.

Light Users/Price Buyers. The group consists of 7,000 price-sensitive buyers who use only 7.5 cartridges per year versus the 24 units used by the average customer. Because they are price buyers, their contribution margin is lower, $4.50, compared to the average buyer contribution margin of $6.50. This assumes that whatever discount, promotion, or other incentive is given essentially reduces the net contribution margin by $2.00. At this point, Carioca estimates it has very few of these light users/price buyers, only about 5 percent of the customers in this segment. Thus, there would be approximately 6,650 prospects that the company could go after. On average, those prospects generate $4.50 per unit at the contribution margin line times the 7.5 units they would purchase, or approximately $33.75 in value, which is split over the various suppliers who offer cartridges on discount or promotion. Since Carioca offers a high-quality product line and does not compete on price alone, the company is unlikely to capture many of these price-sensitive buyers. In fact, the manager estimates that only 10 percent of the potential customers in the segment could be converted and that Carioca would only achieve a 40 percent share of purchases among those customers. That would translate to an additional net contribution margin of $8,977 (6,650 × 0.10% × 7.5 × 40% × $4.50= $8,977). Factoring in the IRR requirement leaves only $7,630.87 available for communication activities ($8,977 × 0.85 = $7,630.87). Given the other, seemingly more lucrative alternatives, the Carioca manager must now determine if this return is sufficient to cover the time commitment required to develop effective marketing and communication programs.

Of course, additional scenarios could be developed for each block within the matrix. However, as can be seen from the three we have discussed, focusing on investments and returns, rather than on the cost of marketing programs, gives the manager a highly relevant and useful view of customer-brand relationship budgeting. If the manager determines that all three segments just discussed should be pursued and all available resources should be invested in the three customer groups, the proposed budget for new customer acquisition for the coming period would be set at $410,412 ($104,432 for heavy users/loyals + $447,525 for medium users/switchers + $7,630 for light users/price buyers). Assuming the programs are successful, the manager could assure management that the required internal rate of return could be achieved and new customers brought into the firm.

A Planning Tool

To assist the manager in planning these types of customer-brand investment strategies, a planning tool has been developed in Exhibit 9.7. It is simply a recap of the methodology used in the examples above.

Clearly, this approach focuses on customers and their value and directly relates investments to potential returns. This methodology, however, is useful only for short-term budgeting—that is, the next year or the next period—since, given most accounting procedures and conventions, only the next future period is considered for most marketing and communication investments. Earlier, we said that customer-brand relationships also should consider the long-term value of the customer. In the next section, we discuss a concept that is useful for the manager in developing longer-term strategies.

Exhibit 9.7 **Customer-Brand Value Planning Tool**

Penetration (P)

1. Total customers in market _____
2. Number of your customers _____
3. Your penetration (Line 2 / Line 1) _____

Buying Rate (BR)

4. Total market demand (in $) _____
5. Demand per customer (Line 4 / Line 1) _____

Share of Purchases (SOP)

6. Annual demand for your brand _____
7. Your share of purchases (Line 6 / Line 4) _____

Margin Contribution to Brand (M)

8. Gross margin for brand per unit sold _____

Value of a Customer (P x BR x SOP x M)

9. Line 3 x Line 5 x Line 7 x Line 8 _____

LIFETIME CUSTOMER VALUE AND CUSTOMER-BRAND RELATIONSHIPS

While it is true that the real value of a customer is based on a long-term relationship, current management approaches and accounting procedures make it quite difficult to plan or execute marketing communication programs for more than the short term, usually the coming year or so. Thus, the customer-brand value-planning tool we just detailed is essentially used in developing budgets for the short term, usually a single year. In this section, however, we provide a brief overview of how the long-term value of a customer might be determined with the understanding that only a few data-rich, progressive organizations can, at this time, implement these longer-term investment strategies. For example, airlines, hotels and hospitality units, catalog marketers, magazine publishers, financial institutions, and others that have direct, ongoing contact with customers are able to consider long-term marketing and communication investment approaches. Airline frequent flyer programs, retail customer loyalty programs, and the like are current examples of the long-term view. Yet no matter how sophisticated the marketing and communication programs become, they are still hamstrung by the financial requirement that all investments and returns must be accounted for on an annual basis. In spite of this limitation, however, it is useful to discuss the concept of lifetime customer value.

Lifetime value (LTV) is a very simple concept that can become quite complicated quite quickly. A simple description, related to the goal of customer-brand relationships, will suffice at this point to illustrate the concept.

As defined by Roland Rust, Valerie A. Zeithhaml, and Katherine N. Lemon, the LTV of a customer is "the total, across all future periods, of the customer's contribution to profit in each of those periods. Future periods are discounted to reflect the fact that future income is worth less than current income."[6] Typically, the information required to develop an estimate of lifetime customer value includes the following:

- the cost of acquiring a new customer;
- the company's discount rate (cost of capital);
- the customer's frequency of repurchase;
- the average contribution from the purchase of this brand;
- the probability that the customer will make a repeat purchase; and
- the number of years being considered (usually three to five years, but longer in some instances).

Some marketers may factor in additional issues, such as the likelihood that the customer may make cross purchases of a related brand or service.

Thus, a customer might be estimated to be worth $1,000 per year at the contribution margin line and expected to stay with the firm for the next seven years. Using an 8 percent discount factor, the estimated lifetime value of the customer would be $606.36

But this simple calculation is not quite accurate. During the next seven years, the customer's purchases are not likely to be static; customers may increase their purchases, providing more lifetime value, or, alternatively, decrease their purchases. In addition, not all the value of a customer is captured in the contribution margin. Some customers may become advocates for the firm and its products and services, thus bringing in new customers. Other customers may continue to purchase but be very unhappy with the relationship and make negative remarks about the company, thus either driving prospective new customers away or reducing the purchasing level of current customers.

There are also accounting issues involved in estimating lifetime customer value. In this text, we have used a contribution margin calculation. But other marketing and accounting models may use different margins, such as fully allocated profit from a customer, the marginal financial contribution of the customer, or even the amount of free cash flow the customer creates for the firm. Clearly, lifetime customer value is a complicated subject, but knowing that there are an increasing number of ways to estimate or calculate these values further enhance the importance of the customer-brand relationship approach. It is certainly much more relevant to today's organizations than the traditional exchange-based marketing approach that looks at each customer and each transaction as a separate activity with no consideration for ongoing purchases or any long-term relationships.

SUMMING UP

With this brief discussion of long-term marketing and communication investments in mind and the tools and techniques presented in this chapter for developing short-term marketing and communication budgets, we can now move to the next steps in the customer-brand relationship methodology; that is, the delivery systems to be used and the content to be delivered. We start Part III with delivery systems, for we believe that the task of reaching, touching, and influencing customers and prospects is probably the most challenging job facing marketers today. If marketers cannot reach the customer or prospect with their messages and incentives, the content of those messages—what the marketers say and how they say it—will make no difference.

NOTES

1. S. Broadbent, *Spending Advertising Money* (London: Business Books, 1970), p. 38.

2. U.S. Securities and Exchange Commission, Division of Corporation Finance, Frequently Requested Accounting and Financial Reporting Interpretations and Guidance, Sec. IB, "Accounting for Advertising Costs," www.sec.gov/divisions/corpfin/guidance/cfactfaq.htm.

3. Ibid.

4. B. Houk, "FASB Ruling 01–9: Bigger Than It Looked," Trade Promotion Management Associates, www.tradepromo.org/legal/FASB.aspx.

5. Harvard Business School, "Lifetime Customer Value Calculator," http://hbswk.hbs.edu/archive/docs/lifetimevalue.xls.

6. R.T. Rust, V. Zeithaml, and K.N. Lemon, *Driving Customer Equity: How Customer Lifetime Value Is Reshaping Corporate Strategy* (New York: Free Press, 2000), p. 39.

PART III

COMMUNICATING WITH CUSTOMERS IN A FRAGMENTED MARKETPLACE

Exhibit PIII.1 **Integrated Brand Communication Model**

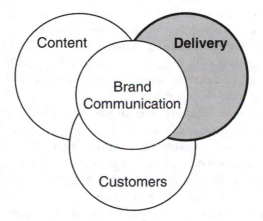

We turn our focus now to the "delivery" circle of the four-circle integrated brand communication model. Through the next several chapters we discuss the rapidly changing delivery systems available to marketers for dissemination of brand communications content.

To be clear, when we speak of "delivery systems," we are talking about media. *Media*, the plural form of the word *medium*, from the Latin *medius*, meaning "middle," is of course a perfectly good word as is. In the context of marketing communications, it is generally used to refer to a means of delivering communications between a sender and a receiver. However, throughout the age of modern marketing communications, the term *media* has come to mean "advertising media," the standard, traditional, advertiser-supported media forms like television, newspapers, magazines, radio, and out-of-home. That is the problem. While that usage was once perfectly fine, it no longer seems accurate. We need to broaden the perspective.

That is why, for this book, we have chosen to use the term *delivery systems* interchangeably with *media*. This broader term more effectively captures the broad spectrum of today's communication media without any preconceived notions or other limitations. The term *delivery systems* allows us to consider the full range of standard, traditional forms of "advertising media" as well as a full array of developing integrated communications media and emerging new media forms: on-line banners, social media, search engines, and the like.

We are not alone in this choice. Practitioners in the many fields of marketing communications are developing a whole new vocabulary to address what widely is considered the limited scope of the word *media*. For example, many advertising agencies today promote a "media neutral" or "media agnostic" approach to media planning. These agencies promise that they will not provide the client with a media plan comprised only of standard, traditional outbound-only advertising forms. Instead, they will use the entire media delivery system.

Another example of this new vocabulary can be found in department names and job titles at certain advertising agencies, such as Crispin, Porter + Bogusky. Like many other agencies, CP+B is a full-service advertising agency with a fully staffed media department whose employees analyze, plan, execute, and evaluate advertising media activities for its clients. However, while most other agencies still use the job title "Media Director," the person(s) who heads the media department at CP+B goes by the title "Director of Creative Content Distribution." Further, the staff members at CP+B go to great lengths to avoid using the word *media*. They feel the word itself limits their ability to think beyond the traditional, and in fact they work to convince their clients to reach beyond the safety of the traditional media forms.

So, from here on, it should be understood that when we speak of delivery systems, we are referring to media, and when we talk about planning for the delivery of brand communications we are talking about media planning—all in the broadest possible sense. More than just a simple nuance of language or game of semantics, this shift allows us to explore and use the communication media in a whole new way.

We will use these next several chapters to set up this different way of thinking about delivery systems. One of the first things the reader should notice here is that we are discussing delivery systems in this book before we get to communication content. This also is no simple matter of nuance. We have consciously developed a process in which message delivery is planned before message content is developed. This is a key point in the development of the model and process we propose throughout this book for building effective customer-brand relationships. The fundamental idea is that in today's vastly fragmented media marketplace, the marketer's media selection can and generally should drive development of the marketer's message. This is just the reverse of the traditional brand communications planning methodologies.

We start this section with a discussion of what has changed in today's media marketplace. We consider the fragmentation of traditional media and the development of new media delivery forms. We discuss the direct result of this fragmentation: a splintering of media audiences and a radically different world of media, where customers actually have more control than ever over their media environment. We go into the details of new consumer media usage behaviors and discuss how these changes lead directly to a new consumer-first media consumption model for planning in this radically different media environment.

Finally, near the end of this busy section, we lay the groundwork for a new way of thinking about media delivery systems by looking at delivery as either outbound or interactive, based on the consumer's media usage behavior. Here we begin to explain how marketers use outbound media forms to "push" marketing messages through the media to consumers. We also highlight the newer phenomenon today, as marketers use messages to "pull" or draw consumers into an interaction with the brand. This discussion shows that certain media forms lend themselves more effectively to either an outbound push or interactive pull application.

In Chapter 12 we move on to a discussion of media research, both proprietary and syndicated. We cover traditional research techniques as they relate to both traditional and nontraditional media delivery systems. We also consider new developments in media research and discuss the need for further improvement in this area.

In Chapters 13 and 14 we explore in detail the distinction between outbound, push forms of delivery and interactive, pull forms of delivery. This distinction too is rather a new concept in marketing communications planning. For one thing, practitioners in this field, while recognizing the interactive possibilities of certain media delivery systems, have never really classified media forms in this manner. Our approach here is unique also in the sense that our range of media forms is more extensive than usual. In considering outbound forms of delivery in Chapter 13 we discuss the strengths and weaknesses of most of the traditional delivery systems aimed toward a specified audience, including advertising and sales promotion media as well as direct and public relations media. In Chapter 14 we consider a full array of interactive media delivery systems ranging from personal selling to events and sponsorships and newer forms like Web sites, blogs, and social networking sites. Here we will suggest how both outbound and interactive media forms can be combined for maximum marketing effect.

Part III thus provides a full explanation of the broad scope of communications delivery systems as opposed to just "media" and how media selection can drive message development in building effective customer-brand relationships. At that point, we will discuss the final step in our integrated brand communication model, the methodologies for message and incentive development, the content circle of the model.

CHAPTER 10

Touching Customers With Communication

Clearly, audiences or customers or consumers or whatever you want to call the people who buy and use the products and services marketers offer are the key elements in any type of customer-brand relationship. They are the ones who see, hear, or come in contact with the brand and its messages and incentives. They are the ones who dig down in their wallets or whip out their credit or debit cards so they can purchase and use the products and services being offered. They are the ones who create the income flows discussed in Chapters 8 and 9. And they are the ones who build and maintain the marketplace success of the brand.

So, if marketers know their audience, how do they connect with it? Answering that question is the purpose of the next five chapters. Only a few years ago, this topic was called media planning, and it still is in some marketing and agency organizations. But the term *media* has a much broader meaning today, as we discuss in Chapter 11. We have thus chosen to use the term *delivery systems* to cover this broad range of message and incentive alternatives.

The reason: that is what marketers are trying to do, deliver or make available to consumers and prospects useful, valuable messages and incentives about their brands. But this idea of "delivery" or "sending out" is not quite correct either. In many cases, the marketing organization does not send out all the messages and incentives that customers and prospects see, hear, or experience. Many of those come from sources other than the marketer, as we will see in Chapters 11 and 12. That is, there is a multitude of brand messages in a multitude of forms to which customers and prospects are exposed every day. All of these must be considered, whether the marketing organization controls them or not. In fact, in many instances, these uncontrolled or uncontrollable messages are the ones that really determine the product or service's marketplace success.

It is this concept of control that is critical in the push and pull marketplace of the twenty-first century. Historically, marketers have controlled, or at least managed, the products and services they have developed and distributed. That is the entire basis of the 4Ps of marketing: they are all controlled by the marketer. That is what makes them so seemingly important and valuable. In that era, the marketer controlled the consumer's brand experience simply because most of what people heard about the brand was what the marketer said. The "golden ages" of radio and television almost guaranteed that the entire population was exposed to and accepted the messages that major advertisers such as Procter & Gamble, Unilever, Nestlé, Ford, Chevrolet, Philip Morris, and the like sent out. Almost everyone in the United States grew up knowing that Ivory soap "floats" and that "Mikey" likes LIFE cereal and that Betty Crocker's cookbook is a staple of the American kitchen and that customers were not supposed to "Squeeze the Charmin." During that time, there were limited media distribution systems and eager listening and watching audiences. But the use of technology to increase media distribution and fragment the audiences has transformed brand and marketing communication today.

In the next four chapters, we provide great detail about how these changes have occurred and the impact they have had on marketing organizations trying to develop customer-brand relationships. To make this transition from the historical view of audiences and advertising and commercial distribution to customers and delivery systems, some basic concepts and tools are needed. These are covered in this transition chapter.

In the following sections we discuss four major tools that will help readers move from thinking about advertising and promotion to thinking about audiences and delivery systems. These are (1) the concepts of monochronicity and polychronicity, which enable consumers to simultaneously process multiple media forms at the same time, sometimes called media multitasking, (2) the issues of brand communication relevance and receptivity, rather than how many messages were sent out, and (3) the broad topic of brand contacts and how they might be identified and measured. As a corollary, we also will discuss (4) the increasingly important concept of engagement or how the marketer can encourage consumers to pay attention and respond positively to the firm's marketing communication activities. This chapter thus serves as the foundation for delivery systems that allow the marketer to use various communication forms to build ongoing customer-brand relationships.

MEDIA MULTITASKING

One of the major marketing communication changes has been the increasing number of people who are simultaneously multitasking with various media forms. Most of us have had the experience of being online with the television blaring in the corner while we carry on a conversation with a friend across town on a cell phone. That is multitasking, the use of multiple media forms at the same time.

It is this "same time" issue that creates problems for marketers. Traditionally, media were consumed or used one at a time, or at least marketers thought they were. The family gathered around the radio in the 1940s to hear network radio stars such as Jack Benny, Fred Allen, and Milton Berle or follow the adventures of Sam Spade or the Thin Man. In the television era, the family gathered on Sunday night to see the unique acts Ed Sullivan had booked or follow the ongoing adventures of Beaver Cleaver or Andy Taylor in Mayberry. While marketers knew that audiences were doing other activities, such as eating, reading the newspaper, or talking with other family members while watching the television program, the importance of the primary medium was such that it was assumed that each media form was being consumed singly and individually. Little thought was given to the interactions of the media audience or to activities in which they might otherwise be engaged. Thus, traditional media measurement systems were developed to measure individual media forms, such as newspaper reading, television viewing, or radio listening, separately and individually.

This single medium measurement was important because marketers were primarily interested in the audience makeup of the media form being used. They had already made their decision to advertise on television; the question was, which program? The same was true of other media forms—for example, once magazines had been selected as the media form, the question became, which title? These methods of media measurement or evaluation were important in the era of "dominant media," but those days no longer exist.

Today, as new media forms emerge, people do not give up one form for another; they simply add the new one to their media inventory. Television did not kill radio and the Internet will not kill television. People simply begin to "mix and match," using several media at the same time, more often and in different ways, often simultaneously. They do that because they can; and they do that because today it is necessary to use several media forms simply to keep up with what is going on around them. People have always been able to multitask. Mothers have been able to cook dinner, change the baby's diaper, and talk on the telephone with a friend, all at the same time. Drivers have always been able to steer a car, sip coffee, and fiddle with the radio setting. What has changed is the multitude of media or message delivery forms available and the fact that many people have been trained to use them simultaneously simply because of availability and exposure. What is challenged is our lack of understanding of how people have changed their media capabilities.

In Chapter 4 we explored how people take in, process, and use information, but we made no distinction on how that multitasking capability was achieved. So to be able to discuss delivery systems, we must dig a bit deeper into consumer information processing.

Researchers have developed a name, polychronicity for multitasking that will help marketers understand how they might deliver customer-brand relationship messages. That name is based on how we believe consumers take in and process information. For example, some people process and use incoming information sequentially, that is called monochronic, one bit of information at a time. Once a bit of data is processed, they move on to the next and then the next. That is how children are trained in learning to read. They read one word after another, one page after another, one chapter after another, in an ongoing sequence of events and actions. The same process occurred in radio and television programs that tell a story, one action after another, all in sequential order. People who process and use information in this way are monochromic or sequential information processors.

Alternatively, there are people who process information in parallel; that is, they process multiple bits of information all at the same time or at least rapidly enough so that it seems they are, in effect, simultaneously processing information, performing multiple activities all going on at the same time. But there is more to multitasking than just consuming media. Think about your own experience. Can you recall a time when you were working online with the television in the background? You were focused on your online work, but at the same time you were partially processing the information from the TV. Suddenly, a breaking event in the world was reported on the television. You did not see the event on the TV screen; you simply heard it announced. You immediately shifted your focus from the Internet to the television. Clearly, you had been processing the information from the TV while you had been on line. This was not what we could call "active information processing," but clearly you were monitoring the television at the same time you were working online. If you are able to do this type of media multitasking, we say you are a polychromic information processor; that is, you can process multiple media forms at the same time or in parallel. This is what creates the phenomenon of simultaneous media exposure.

The problem for marketers is that they measure each media form separately and independently. But if consumers are online, monitoring the television, and talking on a cell phone, all at the same time, what media audience are they in? Only one or maybe two or perhaps all three? We discuss these issues of simultaneous media usage and media multitasking in the chapters that follow. Understanding media multitasking and simultaneous media exposure can help marketers understand the impact these changes in consumers, customers, and audiences have on how message delivery is developed, implemented, and measured.

RELEVANCE AND RECEPTIVITY

Two other relatively new concepts are needed to properly evaluate delivery systems in the customer-brand relationship arena: relevance and receptivity.

The concept of relevance refers to what is important to the customers; and that means in their terms, not those of the marketing organization. Referring again to Chapter 4, we know that there are two ways to get people to process incoming information. One is through volume; that is, increasing the level of information delivery. Marketers can do that through increasing the number of messages they send out, the volume of their commercials, the colors and design of their messages, and the like. This volume approach, which marketers have used for years, is often called "frequency" in media planning. In today's marketplace, which is truly a cacophony of sights, sounds, and experiences, simply turning up the volume often does not work, even though it is the basis for almost all traditional media planning.

The alternative to sending more messages is being more relevant; that is, finding methods and messages that are important and useful to customers and prospects at the time they want to receive or acquire them. Thus, in our new delivery system approach, relevance plays a critical role. It is far more important than sheer volume or the number of messages the marketer distributes. Relevance refers to the point when the customer or prospect wants to see or hear the marketer's messages, not when the marketer wants to send them out or talk. That simply means being in tune with the customers; understanding their wants, needs, and requirements; and developing marketing programs in an appropriate manner.

Relevance goes hand-in-hand with receptivity; that is, when and how and in what form the customer or prospect would like to receive or acquire information about the marketer's products and services. This means not when the marketer wants to deliver it, but when the customer wants to acquire it or access it. And that is a major difference in the customer-brand relationship approach to marketing. Chapters 1 and 2 discussed traditional outbound or push marketing and communication as compared to the new forms of inbound or pull marketing and communication, where the customer or prospect directs the communication process. Receptivity is simply understanding customers or prospects well enough so that the marketer's brand communication messages are available whether they would like to acquire them through traditional outbound or push media forms or through such alternatives as the Internet, Web sites, or a blogs

These two concepts, relevance and receptivity, are key in the rapidly developing push-pull systems that are so prevalent today. To frame this concept, we offer a relevance-receptivity model in Exhibit 10.1. In this model, we have developed another new delivery term, *customer touchpoints*. This term allows marketers to focus on all the ways their organization touches the customer or prospect, whether through outbound marketing communication or any other of a myriad points of interaction. This idea of touchpoints is truly the differentiating factor

Exhibit 10.1   **Touchpoint Model of Message and Incentive Delivery**

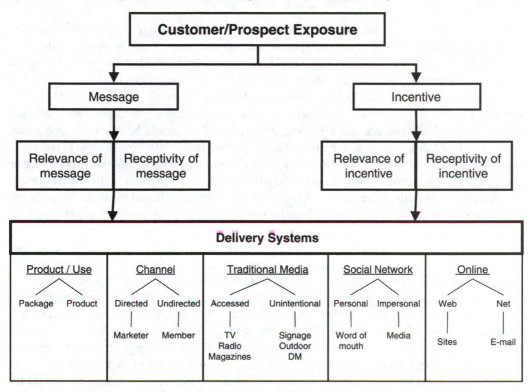

between customer-brand relationship and traditional marketing for it starts with the customer, not the delivery system.

As shown in Exhibit 10.1, planning starts with two basic concepts: messages and incentives. We define messages as those things we want people to remember about the brand and store away in their long-term memory. These are things that would, should, or could influence their purchase decisions or their agreement to provide word of mouth or advocacy about the brand in future periods. Alternatively, incentives are activities designed to encourage the customer or consumer to act or react to the brand in the short term. Thus, the marketer starts with a basic decision of whether the delivery goal is a message, that is a particular benefit that the product offers in use, or an incentive such as a money-off coupon or price discount—short term or long term, idea or added value. With that decision, the marketer then starts to think about when the message or incentive would be most relevant to customers or prospects and when they might be most receptive to it. That consideration then opens up the whole range of media or communication delivery options that are now available or could be available in the future. This truly does provide a method of considering all forms of delivery alternatives, enabling the planner to be media neutral or media agnostic, as we discuss in the following chapter.

With this touchpoint model in mind, we can now move to the third element necessary to develop an effective customer-brand relationship program. That is the idea of brand contacts—how customers and prospects come in contact with the brand, no matter what the circumstances.

UNDERSTANDING BRAND CONTACTS

Following from the touchpoint approach, it is clear that some methodology or approach is needed to formally consider how customers and prospects come in contact with a brand or an organization and how marketers might use that information to plan better delivery methods. Lisa Fortini-Campbell has written extensively about such a methodology, which she refers to as a brand contact audit.[1]

According to Fortini-Campbell, a brand contact audit is a formalized method for identifying and valuing all the ways a customer or prospect might come in contact with the brand during a period of time, and for assessing the priority that should be given to each touch point. It is quite different from a media plan, which tries to identify how the marketer might efficiently distribute messages or incentives in an attempt to reach or contact a customer or prospect through various types of outbound media. The brand contact audit is just the opposite and substantially broader in scope and intent. It starts with the information gathered from the touchpoint methodology and then identifies all the ways or methods or places where a customer or prospect might come in contact with the brand. Obviously, some of those are areas and activities the marketer develops specifically to attempt to influence the customer or prospect, but many others are factors or actions or activities that might be developed by the brand organization that are not normally considered persuasive controlled messages; for example, customer service representatives, billing statements, the physical condition of the company's trucks and equipment on the highways, the actions and activities of channel partners, and simply other people talking about or referencing the brand and its value. All those carry strong messages to customers and prospects, often stronger than the messages and incentives that the organization purposely develops and sends out. Because these are all important contacts with the brand that contribute to the brand experience, it is important for the manager to at least be aware of these brand contacts and try to manage them as much as possible so that they deliver useful and supportive customer-based messages.

Exhibit 10.2 illustrates the basic brand contact audit form, which allows the brand manager to identify, consider, and manage all the brand contacts that customers or prospects have no matter how or when they occur. The goal of the audit is to ensure that all contacts are positive, support the brand value proposition, and provide a positive brand experience. All are critical in the development of successful customer-brand relationship programs. The brand contact audit helps the manager work through the insight process:

- Where do customers and prospects come in contact with the brand?
- Do those contacts add to or subtract from their brand understanding or their brand relationships?
- Which brand contacts does the marketer control?
- Which brand contacts does the marketer not control? These are ones the marketer should simply try to manage.
- Which brand contacts are most important to the customer and therefore to the brand's future?
- Are resources being invested in the most influential or important points of contact?

As Exhibit 10.2 shows, the marketer starts with the basic contact points between the customer or prospect and the brand. Then the marketer considers the customer's expectation

Exhibit 10.2 **Brand Contact Audit Form**

Target Segment: _____

Contact points	Expectation at each	Experience at each	Message sent	Positive or negative	Importance of contact	Target for improvement

when that brand contact occurs: Does the customer expect a positive or negative or neutral experience? Then, what is the customer's actual experience at that brand contact? Does the brand contact match the customer's expectation? Meeting customers' expectations is critical in a push-pull marketplace because the customer has so many other alternatives. The next set of questions is as follows: What is the message sent through that brand contact? Is the brand contact positive or negative? Does the brand contact reinforce the customer-brand relationship or does it challenge or destroy the good relationship that existed? Next, the marketer asks: How important is that particular brand contact in building or maintaining the proper brand experience and brand relationship? Given the finite resources of the firm, is this a brand contact that the marketer should address directly and, if so, with what emphasis? The final set of questions involves the marketer's target for improvement: If the brand contact is deficient, how does the marketer improve it? If it is good, how does the marketer retain and reinforce it? By using this type of brand contact audit, managers can quickly determine where their focus should lie and when, where, and how they should try to improve, enhance, or sustain the messages and incentives customers and prospects are receiving about the brand and the impact those have on the customer-brand relationship program that the firm is trying to develop.

Exhibit 10.3 illustrates a small portion of a completed brand contact audit for the printer cartridge company discussed in Chapter 9. (We show only three brand contacts out of the dozens that were identified for the brand.) By reviewing the case and then reflecting on how these brand contacts developed and what occurred, the brand manager can see what impact brand contacts have on the ongoing success of the firm in trying to build long-term customer-brand relationships.

Exhibit 10.3 **Brand Contact Audit Form for Printer Cartridges**

Target Segment: Printer Owners

Point of brand contact	Expectation at contact	Experience at contact	Brand message	Positive or negative?	Importance of contact to brand judgment	Target to reinforce or improve?
Saw an ad in a magazine	Positive portrayal of new features in the line	Became interested in the brand	These ink cartridges will help me be more productive	Positive	High	Reinforce
Went to the store	Expected to find on the shelf	Salesperson tried to sell me another brand	Store staff not convinced of brand's value	Negative	High	Improve
Called customer service	Expect to have my problem solved promptly	Put on hold	Company does not think I am important	Negative	High	Improve

With these basic concepts in mind, we are now ready to consider the final element in the planning process that precedes the formal development of an integrated system; that is, the customer-brand value delivery system. That involves the increasingly important area of engagement.

ENGAGEMENT

Over the past few years, a new term, or rather an old term with new meaning, has emerged in communication planning development and delivery. The term is *engagement*. Engagement is how involved or attentive the customer or prospect is to the marketer's message or incentive. Clearly, the marketer wants to create engaging messages and incentives. If the customer or prospect becomes engaged with the product or service, the message or incentive, or even the media form itself in which the message or incentive appears, there is a greater possibility that a positive reaction to the communication will occur. This consumer preference can take many forms, from product preference to advocacy to actual purchase. So the first step in any marketing communication program is to be engaging: that means the product or service, the actual communication, the brand, or the medium through which the message or incentive is delivered. In today's marketplace, if it is not engaging, it is likely to be ignored.

From the marketer's view, there are several types of engagement. One is simply the engaging nature of the product or service itself. Some products or services are more engaging than others. For example, an iPhone is more engaging than the bearings in an automobile wheel. Second, the creative message or incentive the marketer creates can be engaging. Dull, drab, boring marketing communication forms and formats have little chance of success in today's overcommunicated, cluttered media marketplace. Third, and this is the one most relevant to this discussion, is the engagement power of the media form itself.

Based on earlier research, some media have been found to be or are thought to be more engaging than others. For example, television, thanks to its use of sight, sound, and motion, is often considered more engaging than radio, which appeals to only one of the senses. Television viewers are assumed to be paying more attention to the programming than a person who is simply listening to radio. Specialized subject magazines are thought to be more engaging than broadly based daily newspapers because of the greater detail about specific areas of the subject matter.

Engagement has become a major concern of marketers and advertisers over the past few years as the traditional audiences have been splintered and fragmented as a result of the influx of new media forms. As we have mentioned earlier, many media audiences use continuous partial attention when engaged with the media. That is, they are multitasking and using various media forms simultaneously, thus decreasing the amount of attention given to any specific medium or message. Sitting in front of a television set does not necessarily mean the viewer is engaged, nor does subscribing to a newspaper or passing an outdoor sign signify engagement. Engagement generally means "mentally engaged" and that is a most difficult activity to identify and measure. The challenge for both marketers and their media partners is how to engage these audiences and gain their attention and involvement with not only editorial content but with advertising and promotion as well. As a result, the media themselves and various marketing and other associations have produced a dramatic increase in research on the topic of engagement and specifically media engagement. Here, we point out only two of the major streams of thought and research.

Media Engagement

Engagement, as the concept has been developed in the United States and other Western countries, has generally been focused on the engagement of the consumer or audience with the media form or delivery system. Since many marketers still focus their communication efforts through outbound marketing communication activities such as advertising, sales promotion, direct marketing, and public relations, this makes a great deal of sense. Thus, much engagement research focuses on how involving or engaging the media form is or can be, based on the assumption that marketers will primarily develop and deliver their marketing communication through various forms of outbound media, such as television, magazines, newspapers, and radio. They will select those media forms that they believe are most engaging and that will enhance their own messages and incentives. As a result, most of the research on engagement has tried to measure the level of engagement the audience has with the media form. For example, is television more engaging than newspapers or is radio more engaging than a magazine? The more involving the media form, it is assumed, the more opportunity the marketer will have to persuade the customer or prospect to consider the brand. A number of studies about media engagement have been developed under the supervision of the Advertising Research Foundation (ARF) in the United States. ARF has defined engagement as "turning on a prospect to a brand idea enhanced by the surrounding content."[2] In other words, the ARF question is: Can or will a media vehicle improve advertising results? And, if so, how can those results be measured?

While a number of research studies have investigated this issue, some of the most relevant have come from Malthouse and Calder at Northwestern University.[3] In their studies they have sought to determine if the media form used by the advertiser increases or enhances the response to the advertisements in those media forms. To do that, they connected two basic concepts:

experience, or the determination of why the consumer uses the particular medium in which the advertising appears, and involvement, or the level of engagement the reader, viewer, or listener has with the medium. Their premise, therefore, is that the medium has specific value for the reader, viewer, or listener. Thus, if there is inherent interest in the media form, there must be greater potential for engagement with the advertising.

Over the course of several studies, Malthouse and Calder have tested the engagement power of newspapers, magazines, and Web sites to determine this enhancement value of the media form. They found five common media experiences:

- *Utilitarian*: the media form provides rational benefits from its use; for example, a certain medium makes people believe it improves them or gets them to try new things
- *Intrinsic*: this is the inherent value of the media form itself; for example, magazines are often thought of as a break from everyday life and thus a form of relaxation
- *Positive emotional*: this is the attitude or feeling that the medium engenders in the user; for example, people would be disappointed or feel a void in their lives if the medium were no longer available
- *Social*: this is how the medium is viewed by other people; for example, certain media make the user believe they themselves are more interesting people (are more interesting to other people to be around or interact with to others)
- *Source*: this is how credible and valuable the medium is as a source of information; for example, the *New York Times* is likely to be viewed as a more credible source than a poster on the same subject plastered on a wall

In addition, the researchers found that there are one or two other experiences that are unique to each particular media form. Thus, while all media have some relationship to the five primary values, each medium has its own specific value as well.

In summary, Malthouse and Calder found through their research that different media have specific values for various audiences and thus they hypothesize that these values also impact the advertising and promotion contained in those media as well. As might be suspected, not all media have the same enhancement of engagement power; not all media enhance advertising equally nor in the same way. Thus, identification of the various values becomes an important issue for the media planner. The most important finding is that there is some value to the advertiser and the messages based on the medium used and that this enhancement can be measured and evaluated.

Engagement With the Brand

An alternative to this idea of media involvement, which is essentially a surrogate for involvement with the brand, has developed in Japan. The Hakuhodo advertising agency has developed the concept of Relationship Rings. This is an attempt to determine the engagement consumers have with the brand. This, we would argue, is a much more important and powerful concept than simple engagement with the media form.

The development of brand engagement has been long studied in the Japanese advertising and marketing community. But the Japanese approach to consumer behavior and information gathering has not been well understood or explained in the West, the assumption being that it was unique to Japanese culture.

Starting in the 1980s, the Hakuhodo agency began to explore the concept of *sei-katsu-sha*, a very different view of consumer behavior. Instead of viewing the person in the marketplace as simply one who consumes or uses up various products and services offered and thus is to be manipulated by the marketer, sei-katsu-sha views the customer and the marketer as forming a bond or attachment to each other. They work together to create value for each other. This is essentially the Japanese version of the customer-brand relationship. This idea of sei-katsu-sha, which forms the base for Hakuhodo's new view of the brand's customers, is much more involving and relevant in today's customer-controlled marketplace.

The idea of sei-katsu-sha suggests that the customer and the brand unite in creating value for each other or, as the Japanese say, "creating happiness in the marketplace." The brand creates value for the customer and the customer creates value for the brand. The two must work together for this mutually beneficial relationship to occur and continue. The basis for this holistic approach to communication planning is simple. *Engagement*, translated into Japanese, means "promise" or "agreement" or "betrothal," terms that signify a unique relationship between the customer and the brand, who share a joint goal of creating a better life for the customer through the brand.

The multitude of new media forms clearly changes the relationship between the marketer and the sei-katsu-sha. No longer can the marketer talk and expect the sei-katsu-sha to simply listen, accept, and purchase. The sei-katsu-sha can reject the brand's messages, turning instead to many other voices and many other alternatives in the marketplace. Thus, traditional, outbound, linear communication systems simply do not work in today's marketplace.

Hakuhodo sums up this new relationship by suggesting that marketers need to move their communication programs from "To C" (to consumers) to "With C" (with consumers). That shift forms the basis for the new approach that truly connects the customer with the brand. The result is brand engagement, not just media engagement.

The Hakuhodo planning system is based on what are called "Engagement Rings." The model is illustrated in Exhibit 10.4. The key element in the Engagement Rings approach is the creation of "feeling and emotion" in the sei-katsu-sha who is at the center of the planning process. That comes about through the use of an "Engagement theme" that sets the tone for the entire communication process. Thus, the primary goal of the marketer is to create an emotional bond with the customer that will lock both of them into an ongoing relationship. In the illustration, this relationship is identified as "feel curiosity about the brand, learn more about it, generate ongoing interest, feel that the brand is relevant to their lives, and feel moved to do something to build the brand relationship."

The surrounding rings, as shown above, encourage the sei-katsu-sha to choose, share, and commit to the relationship with the brand. The Choose ring focuses on encouraging the sie-katsu-sha to gather more information about the brand; that is, to become better informed about the value and meaning of the brand, experience the brand in the store or other purchase locations where it might be obtained, try the product or service, and finally purchase and use the brand.

The Share ring is focused on sharing information about the brand with other people through direct or indirect contact, sharing the customer's own experience of the brand with others, passing on opinions about the brand to the relevant social networks, and, finally, recommending the brand to others—in other words, using very persuasive word of mouth to bring others into the sharing ring.

Exhibit 10.4 **Hakuhodo "Engagement Rings"**

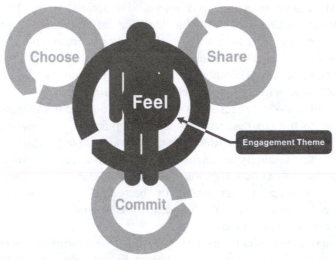

Source: Hakuhodo, Inc.

The third ring, Commit, has a very personal meaning for it suggests that the sei-katsu-sha buy the brand often and keep buying it over time—the single most important behavior the sei-katsu-sha can perform. This ring assumes that the shared value of the brand has been created and can be demonstrated through purchase and use over time. This ring encourages the customer to communicate with the company and the brand, creating an ongoing dialogue in which ideas and values can be shared. In addition, it signifies the company's goal of getting the sei-katsu-sha involved and participating in brand activities, signifying support for the company and the brand. That comes from co-creating additional value between the brand and the sei-katsu-sha, a reciprocal arrangement where both parties benefit.

As can be seen, the concept of engagement in Japan is considerably more complex and involving than simply trying to understand the customer or prospect's involvement with the media form. Brand engagement is a much higher level of engagement than most of the concepts developed in the West.

SUMMING UP AND MOVING ON

With the descriptions and discussions of the four concepts of media multitasking, relevance and receptivity, brand contacts, and engagement, we are ready to tackle the subjects of delivery systems and delivery planning, which are covered in the next four chapters. Clearly, these four factors play a key role in how marketers use the four elements of the customer-brand relationship methodology to create effective and long-lasting involvements with customers and prospects. They also will have a major impact on how the marketer arranges and uses the four elements of product or brand, audiences, delivery systems, and content. With this in mind, we move on to the next chapter, which explains why delivery systems may be the most important part of building customer-brand relationships in the push-pull marketplace of the twenty-first century.

NOTES

1. L. Fortini-Campbell, "Communication Strategy: Managing Communication for the Changing Marketplace" (paper presented at Northwestern University, Evanston, IL, October 19, 1999).

2. E. Burns, "Marketers Mulling ARF's 'Engagement' Definition," April 4, 2006, www.thearf.org/about/news/2006–04–04clickz.html.

3. E. Malthouse and B.J. Calder, "Measuring Involvement With Editorial Content: Conceptualization, Scale Development and the Effects on Advertising" (paper presented at Worldwide Multi Media Measurement conference, ESOMAR World Research, June 3–6, 2007).

CHAPTER 11

Delivering Customer Communication Connections

The media marketplace of the twenty-first century is a vastly different space from what it was just a few short years ago. Indeed, the media marketplace today is a vastly different space from what it was just six months ago! The changes have been dramatic, and the pace of change has been truly remarkable. Unfortunately for all of us, the changes are coming so fast that it is hard to keep up.

One good example is this book. We sit here today, writing material for a book that will not be published until some time next year. By the time you read this material, the media world will almost certainly have changed again. The challenge for us, as authors, is significant. We know how things used to be, and we know the things that have changed. We spend our time watching for the newest developments and studying the most current research, all in an effort to understand what is happening today so we can effectively project what might work for marketers in the future.

Another good example can be seen in what is happening today in the marketing business. Until very recently, practitioners in this field, professionals who deliver branded communications to consumers, have been using many of the same old methods and techniques, despite the rapid changes in marketing communications. Reports as recent as 2004 show major advertisers and agencies still planning communications on the basis of concepts and models that were developed more than fifty years ago.[1] Even the media themselves and the major research companies that support the industry have lagged significantly behind the changes.[2] As a case in point, advertisers and agencies today, after years of calling for changes, are finally hopeful that they will have "commercial audience ratings" for television advertising for the first time some time this year.[3]

While it is true that the industry has been slow to adapt, the new realities of this business are coming. So let us take a look at some of the biggest changes impacting the twenty-first–century media marketplace.

CHANGES IN THE TWENTY-FIRST–CENTURY MEDIA MARKETPLACE

We see new developments in the twenty-first–century media marketplace as attributable to two primary change agents. The first is the media itself and the technology behind media

212

delivery systems. The second locus of change lies in the media consumer and how audiences have changed the way they consume the communications media. In order to understand what is happening and what will happen in years to come, we need to consider both.

History of Communication Media

Everyone with even just a passing knowledge of the field of media and communication delivery systems should, at a minimum, understand that change is a constant and that the key driver of change in this field has been and is still technology. In the mid-1400s, Gutenberg developed the technology for movable type, which led to the development of print media. In the late 1800s, advancements in printing technology created the four-color rotary press. That led to the development of new media like magazines and comic books. In the 1830s, telegraphy was developed in the United States and England. Then came the telephone in the 1870s. Around the turn of the century, advancements in telegraph technology gave birth to radio as the first broadcast media. In the mid-1920s, teenager Philo Farnsworth invented the first complete electronic television system. In the 1960s, the United States launched communications satellites. In the early 1980s, the U.S. National Science Foundation launched the first TCP/IP wide-area network of what we today know as the Internet.[4]

Clearly, every media form today is a direct result of some technological advancement. This will still be the case in the future; technology drives change in the communications media. The biggest factor is the accelerating pace of technological change and its effect on communications media. In the history of communications summarized above, it took hundreds of years to get from printing Bibles with movable type to printing magazines and comic books using a rotary press and color ink. It took only about one century to advance from telegraphy to broadcast radio. It took less than half a century to move from radio broadcasting of sound only to television broadcasting of images and sounds. And it has taken only about a quarter of a century for Internet technology to advance to a wireless, on-all-the-time communications delivery system available to almost everyone.

This accelerating pace of technological change has had two major impacts on the landscape for media practitioners and marketers today—first, rampant fragmentation of traditional mass media delivery systems like newspapers, magazines, radio, and television, and second, explosion in the development of new, alternative media through such personal media devices as cell phones, iPods/MP3 players, video game systems, and now the "all-in-one" iPhone.

Media Fragmentation

The fragmentation of traditional media is common knowledge and evident in almost every form of media. In 1950 the average television household in the United States received broadcast signals from three television channels. By 2000 the number of television channels receivable in the average U.S. television household had climbed to just over seventy.[5] Today that number is approaching 100 channels, and the heaviest television systems today deliver an average of more than 150 channels per household.[6] In terms of print media, the Magazine Publishers association (MPA) reports a total of more than 18,000 magazine titles in publication for the year 2005.[7] Among the traditional media, radio is one of the few showing any kind of consolidation, with fewer than 11,000 licensed commercial radio stations in 2006 compared

Exhibit 11.1   **Navigating the Chaos of Digital Media**
Internet technology has evolved into an extensive and ever-expanding
array of digital media.

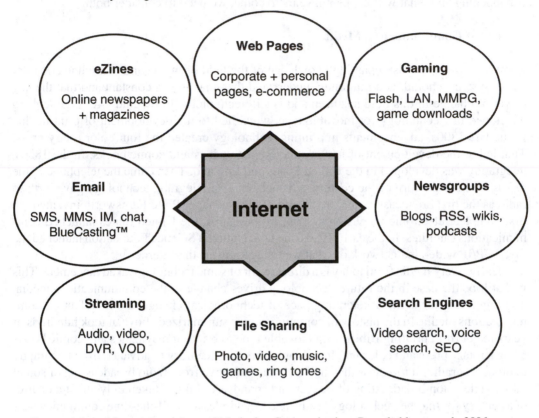

Source: Adapted from Advertising and Marketing Communications Roundtable research, 2006.

to almost 14,000 in 2000.[8] Even with the decline in radio stations, that is still a lot of media channels vying for the limited time and attention of the average U.S. media user.

Emerging New Media Forms

Beyond the traditional media, we have the other major factor—a veritable explosion of new, alternative media delivery systems. According to a recent report on digital media by the Advertising and Marketing Communications Roundtable, the average media consumer today enjoys an extensive selection of digital media content accessible across a broad array of media platforms, including television, personal computers, and portable, personal devices like mobile phones; personal digital assistants (PDAs); satellite radio, audio, and video players; and gaming consoles.[9] Exhibit 11.1 presents a graphic depiction of how the Internet has led to this ever-expanding array of digital media. Nondigital media forms include in-store media and promotional devices, media-delivered news articles about products, newspaper-delivered promotional inserts, direct marketing media, and in-programming product placements.[10]

Media audiences today have a vast selection of traditional and new information and entertainment delivery systems and platforms from which to choose.[11] This fragmentation of available and easily accessible communication channels has led to a splintering of the previously "mass media" audience into a seemingly infinite number of smaller, addressable, media audiences. This brings us to our second major locus of change in the media marketplace—changes in consumer media usage.

Changes in Consumer Media Usage

The technological advances that fragmented media choices and splintered media audiences have been matched by a companion trend in the development of consumer-side technology leading to major changes in the ways consumers use the media and process the information they glean from the media.

One big change on the consumer side has been the increased use of time-shifting and commercial-avoidance technology. Time-shifting technology includes such devices as video-cassette recorders (VCRs) from as far back as the 1970s and today's digital video recorders (DVRs) like TiVo. VCRs reached peak penetration with over 90 percent of all U.S. households somewhere around 2003, which was about the time that DVR sales began to take off. According to the Television Bureau of Advertising, U.S. DVR sales in 2005 were almost double the sales of 2004, and sales almost doubled again in 2006.[12] Although the household penetration of the DVR is still low, most professionals in the media and marketing business project continued adoption as manufacturers expand the services that are available to DVR owners. For example, TiVo announced in 2005 that future TiVo owners would have the ability to record television programs on the DVR and download the programming to a video iPod.[13]

This is an issue for marketers because consumers are using these devices to record and then watch programming without commercials. Forrester Research, a research consultancy that specializes in technology, estimates that 70 percent of consumers use their DVRs to skip television commercials.[14] As a direct result, marketers are aggressively seeking new ways to integrate branded communications into editorial and programming content.

Another big change in consumers today is multitasking and what researchers call "polychronic media consumption."[15] The consumer's ability to undertake two or more tasks simultaneously has recently been recognized by researchers studying consumers' media usage behavior. In 2002, researchers Don Schultz and Joseph Pilotta piloted a study in conjunction with Ohio-based research company BIGresearch that has evolved into a biannual study of simultaneous media usage known as SIMM.

Early in this study, Schultz and Pilotta found evidence that consumers do in fact engage in simultaneous consumption of media forms: for example, watching television while surfing the Internet. In their report to the Advertising Research Foundation, the authors discuss the mental processing developmental differences between today's generations of media consumers raised on television and Internet media as compared to previous generations raised on newspaper and print media.[16] As suggested by Marshall McLuhan in 1967,[17] a consumer raised on print media would develop a mind that works linearly, engaging in one activity at a time, while a consumer raised on television would engage in activities in a more nonlinear, multitasking way.

Marketers face two significant issues as a result of consumers' multitasking media usage behavior. The first is a question of attention when the consumer is engaged simultaneously with multiple media forms. By necessity, one medium must be the dominant or foreground medium while the other serves as background.[18] Of course this foreground-background distinction can change for any given consumer at any given moment. The other major issue, related to the first, is a question of measurement. We will deal with this and other measurement issues in Chapter 12, but the basic issue is how marketers can measure the synergy effects of multimedia consumption when current media measurement systems are all designed to track one specific medium at a time. This brings us to the unique challenges of media planning in an environment of simultaneous media usage.

THE TRADITIONAL MEDIA-PLANNING MODEL

As media delivery systems and consumers' usage of media have changed, so too we would expect to see changes, even major changes, in how professionals plan for distribution of branded communications via the media—yet we have not. Instead, we see that many marketers and their agencies still plan for media delivery according to the same basic model that has been in use for almost fifty years.[19]

Jim Stengel, Procter & Gamble's chief marketing officer, pointed this out in his address to the American Association of Advertising Agencies (AAAA) at its annual media conference in February 2004. He said, "I believe today's marketing model is broken. We're applying antiquated thinking and work systems to a new world of possibilities." Looking toward the future, he called for "holistic marketing" and "permission marketing," elements of a consumer-first approach leading to a more expansive use of multiple and new media forms, beyond the traditional.[20] Stengel reiterated this position three years later at the 2007 AAAA's Media Conference where he called for a "mindset shift from 'telling and selling' to building relationships." Stengel noted that in today's environment, where consumers are in control, marketers need to "commit to building honest, authentic relationships with the people [they] serve."[21]

Stengel's point was well taken and convincingly made. A key concept behind this thinking is the notion of "push versus pull" in the delivery of marketing messages to consumers. In the traditional push approach, marketers believe that if they push out enough messages, consumers will eventually get the marketing message. The pull approach, a newer way of thinking about message delivery along the lines of Stengel's argument, is about engagement; marketers assume that the consumer wants to get information about products and will actually seek out marketing messages to learn more. In order to understand this shift clearly, let us consider first the traditional media-planning model. This will then lead us to a discussion of Stengel's "new world of possibilities," highlighting the need for a new media-planning model.

The traditional model used to plan for delivery of branded communication to consumers is derived from stimulus-response behavioral psychology theory. The basic idea is that consumers exposed to branded communications will become aware of the brand and eventually experience an attitudinal effect that will (hopefully) positively impact their purchase behaviors. The stimulus in this model is the exposure to branded communications messages, while the response is at first awareness and eventually attitudinal effect. As we mentioned earlier, this is the push approach to media planning and message delivery; marketers push out message exposures expecting that consumers will get the message. The implications of this model for media planning purposes are pretty straightforward. First, the marketer needs to *reach* consumers in order to expose them to the message. Then, the marketer needs to achieve enough *frequency* of exposure to move the consumers from awareness to attitudinal change.

Reach and frequency are the foundational concepts of the traditional media-planning model. As long as marketers know they are targeting the right consumer audience, the successful media plan is the one that delivers enough reach and frequency, within the marketing budget, to achieve the objectives of the communication plan. Since reach and frequency are such basic concepts in media delivery, their definitions follow:

- Reach: The number of individuals or households within a specific target audience that are exposed to a particular marketing message at least one time within a specific time period. Reach can be expressed as a number or a percentage of the target audience. When using a percentage, marketers typically refer to unduplicated reach, which means that they are counting each person exposed only one time, no matter how many times the person may be exposed to the message. As such, expressed as a percentage, reach will never exceed 100.
- Frequency: The number of times that individuals or households are exposed to a particular marketing message within a specific time period. Frequency is always a count of exposures and often expressed as average frequency, which represents the mathematical average of the number of exposures delivered to all consumers who were reached with the message.[22]

Obviously, reach and frequency are companion statistics. The combination of reach and frequency gives a measure of message tonnage, how many messages are delivered by a plan and to how many people. Media planners use the combination of these two numbers to judge the quality of different media plans. Likewise, they use these two numbers to convince their client marketers that the one recommended plan would most effectively deliver the marketer's branded communication.

Together, reach and frequency represent one of the central trade-offs in the traditional media-planning model. The balance of reach and frequency is a trade-off because the marketer's budget is usually constrained. Working within a fixed budget, the media planner has basically three choices when it comes time to select the media delivery systems for the plan: (1) optimize reach, (2) optimize frequency, or (3) balance the two. The media planner makes this choice based mainly on the objectives of the communication plan.

Matching Media and Communication Goals

In the traditional model, communication objectives are generally set according to a hierarchy-of-effects view of how the communication process works. The illustration in Exhibit 11.2 shows the hierarchy-of-effects model adapted from the 1960s hypotheses of Lavidge and Steiner. One of the earliest, simplest, and most memorable versions of the hierarchy-of-effects theory[23] is known as AIDA, which stands for Attention-Interest-Desire-Action. As discussed in Chapter 1, while there are some problems today with the stimulus-response model,[24] it is nonetheless still a useful tool in setting objectives for media planning.

For now, we will use a simplified version of the AIDA model to illustrate how media planners make the choice in the traditional media-planning model of whether to optimize

Exhibit 11.2　**The Hierarchy of Effects Model**

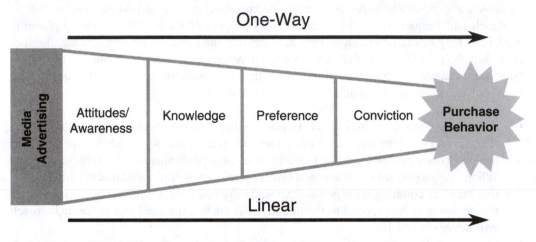

One-Way

| Media Advertising | Attitudes/ Awareness | Knowledge | Preference | Conviction | Purchase Behavior |

Linear

"Influencing and Persuading Consumers"

Source: Adapted from R. Lavidge and G. Steiner, "A Model of Predictive Measurements of Advertising Effectiveness," *Journal of Marketing* 25 (October 1961).

reach, optimize frequency, or balance the two. Our simplified hierarchy has only three steps: (1) awareness/attention, (2) interest, and (3) attitude/desire. Exhibit 11.3 shows how media planners can connect the goals of the media plan with a corresponding goal for the communications effort. If the goal of the communications effort is to build awareness of the brand or product, then the media planner will work to optimize reach so that the optimum number of people in the target audience will have the opportunity to be exposed to the message and thereby become aware. If the goal of the plan is to accomplish an attitudinal change, then the media planner will optimize frequency because conventional wisdom suggests that it takes repetition to convince consumers to change their minds. In the middle of the continuum between awareness and attitude, there is interest. In this case, the conventional wisdom holds that interest is easier to accomplish than attitude change, but harder to achieve than awareness. Therefore, the media planner has some flexibility to plan for some balance between reach and frequency.

From the preceding discussion, it is clear that the traditional media-planning model is focused on message tonnage with an emphasis on efficient distribution within the constraints of the marketer's budget. Whether the plan delivers the message more times to fewer people or fewer times to more people, efficiency within the budget becomes the common media-planning goal.

Although the model seems pretty simple, the actual work of media planning is quite challenging. Even when using the traditional media-planning model described here, the media planner has to know the media in general and, more specifically, understand how each individual medium works in terms of audience delivery. Given the fragmentation of the media and the splintering of media audiences, trends to which we referred earlier, the media planner's job today is more challenging than ever.

Exhibit 11.3 **Matching Media and Communication Goals**

Emphasis Reach	Balanced Reach Frequency	Emphasis Frequency
Awareness/ Attention	**Interest**	**Attitude/ Desire**

What Is Wrong With the Traditional Media-Planning Model

The traditional media-planning model served this industry well throughout most of the latter part of the twentieth century. As long as the media delivery systems were fairly stable and as long as media audiences behaved in a fairly predictable manner, even if we were not entirely right about our underlying assumptions, we could see that we were having some positive effect. Planners and researchers learned how to measure discrete media audiences based on existing models like the hierarchy-of-effects model and developed new models to help planners prove that there was a positive correlation between delivery of branded communications and increased product sales. Then, as we approached the turn of the twenty-first century, we began to see the future of a fragmented media,[25] the splintering of media audience groups, and the all but disappearance of certain key audience segments; like young adult men.[26] At the same time, we saw dramatic growth in costs and communications spending by major marketers.[27] In time, marketers like Jim Stengel, agencies, researchers, and even industry observers all came to realize that this industry was going to need a new media-planning model, fast.[28]

Then there was the growing realization that today's consumers multitask with media just as they multitask in their other daily activities.[29] According to the early and subsequent findings of the simultaneous media (SIMM) studies as summarized in Exhibit 11.4, a preponderance of consumers, approximately 80 percent, report that they engage in some form of simultaneous media usage either regularly or occasionally.[30]

This presents marketers simultaneously (no pun intended) with both a problem and an opportunity. The problem is significant because most current media audience measurement techniques are based on individual media forms. There are services that measure television, and different companies that measure radio, newspapers, magazines, and the Internet. For each media research company, the measurement techniques and primary measures reported are unique to the media form.[31] The current research system is not designed to measure combinations of media forms, much less measure media audiences attuned to more than one medium at a time.

The opportunity presented by simultaneous media usage is equally significant. Marketers for years have imagined that variations of the same brand message, delivered to consumers

Exhibit 11.4

Simultaneous Media Usage (in percent; $n = 14{,}847$)

	Online	Newspaper	Magazines	Radio	TV	Mail
Radio[a]						
R	21.0	14.3	13.1		3.8	12.9
O	38.4	31.6	34.9		14.2	49.9
TV						
R	37.7	23.6	18.9	8.2		21.3
O	29.4	38.3	43.0	22.2		49.9
Magazines						
R	6.8			8.8	9.6	
O	23.9			35.4	14.6	
Newspaper						
R	9.3			12.4	16.9	
O	19.1			36.9	46.8	
Mail						
R	19.9			11.2	14.6	
O	28.3			40.6	49.6	
Online						
R		8.3	6.7	19.4	28.6	11.1
O		17.2	20.7	35.8	34.6	30.8
Engaged in other activities						
R	24.4	8.9	7.9	24.5	18.3	9.1
O	46.3	32.1	32.7	39.4	49.9	40.2

Source: Adapted from BIGresearch SIMM VI, May 2005.
[a]R = Regularly, O = Occasionally.

through multiple media forms at the same time, would probably have some kind of multiplicative or synergistic effect. The thinking is that the message delivered in one medium reinforces or supports the message delivered in the other medium.[32] Marketers also believe they can use cross-platform, multimedia communications to realize cost efficiencies and ultimately save money. While many marketers hope to take advantage of such synergies, thus far only the biggest marketing companies, like Procter & Gamble and Unilever, have been successful, and even these companies have no effective way to measure the returns on their multimedia efforts.[33]

That is to say, at least not yet. Prasad Naik and Kalyan Raman are two academic researchers who have made progress in developing a new methodology to estimate the synergistic effects between and among multiple media forms.[34] Their early findings suggest that it is possible to measure this kind of synergy. We will come back to this point later in this chapter and in Chapter 12.

Finally, we need to consider the likelihood (indeed, probability) that, since all traditional media measures are calculated for individual media forms, the very fact of consumers' simultaneous media usage renders many traditional media planning concepts irrelevant.[35] We earlier defined the key media terms *reach* and *frequency*. The whole idea of planning and measuring message exposures approaches the process of communication from an outbound-only and output-oriented perspective. The idea of the traditional model is that marketers push communications out into the mediasphere where consumers can be exposed, and so they will be. But the model fails to account for the fact that consumers are in control of their own media exposure. And there is certainly no accommodation in the traditional model for the foreground/background media attention issues that arise when consumers engage in multitasking media usage behavior.

From this discussion, it should be quite clear that there are important defects in the traditional media-planning model. What we need for the future is a new model that takes into account the major changes in the twenty-first–century media marketplace. We need a model that recognizes the way that today's media consumers actually consume the media forms.

THE MEDIA CONSUMPTION PLANNING MODEL

As we have discussed, the marketing industry needs a new media-planning model. With the fragmented twenty-first–century media marketplace and consumers' multitasking media consumption, what is needed in particular is a media consumption-planning model. What we mean by that is a model that starts with consumers and how they consume and interact with the media today.

Unlike the traditional media-planning model, which approaches planning from the perspective of advertiser message dissemination, a media consumption planning model would guide the media-planning process with a true focus on today's consumer. Working from a media consumption perspective, literally any touchpoint can be considered a potential delivery point for a brand-specific marketing communication. In Chapter 10, we defined touchpoints as any point of contact between the customer or prospect and the brand or marketing organization.

One idea for a media consumption model is presented visually in Exhibit 11.5. This model illustrates a process that begins with the media consumer, who is here engaged with multiple media. This is consistent with what we have learned from the SIMM research studies discussed earlier in the chapter.

With the media consumer as the starting point, the marketer first determines with which media the consumer most regularly interacts, thus identifying which media are actually providing the communications exposure. This means that marketers need to study and understand their consumers. Specifically, marketers need to learn which media the consumers favor and how they prefer to interact with each medium throughout the day. This information is available to marketers through the data collected for the ongoing SIMM research studies, the work of research firm BIGresearch and Joseph Pilotta in collaboration with authors Don Schultz and Martin Block.[36]

Also available from the same research is the information that marketers need to know next: at any particular point in time, which medium is the foreground medium and which becomes the background medium, and how much time is allocated to each media form? This is critically important information for this model because in a multitasking media usage context the consumer will move back and forth among the media. As the consumer's attention shifts, so too the media will shift between foreground and background status.

That shifting of media status can work either for or against marketers depending on whether they observe a synergy effect or a message fragmentation effect, as shown in the model. A synergy effect can occur when the consumer is exposed to the same message in various media forms simultaneously. If the consumer experiences a shift in attention that is smooth, purposeful, and meaningful (to the consumer), the experience would be positive and synergy should

Exhibit 11.5 **The Media Consumption Model**

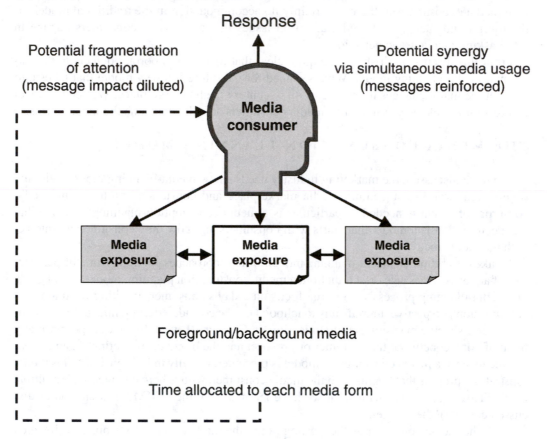

result. Alternatively, if the consumer experiences the shift in attention as a fragmentation or distraction, then the effect of the message is likely to be diluted.

The big idea in this model is that it starts with the consumer first and recognizes that media are just one part of the consumer's busy life. The media consumption planning model works because it considers when and how and in what form the customer or prospect would like to receive or acquire information about the marketer's products and services. The emphasis is on relevance and receptivity, as discussed in Chapter 10.

Too often, marketers get caught up in their own world and forget that consumers, no matter how strongly they may feel about a product, do not wake up in the morning and go to bed at night thinking about the product. The media consumption model forces marketers to stay focused on the consumer. In order to use this kind of model effectively, they need to know more about the consumer. The expectation is that if marketers can gain a clear understanding of the consumer's life and the role of media in it, they can find ways to make product information available on the consumer's terms.

This particular model is still a prototype. Only recently, in 2005 and 2006, has BIGresearch marshaled the data needed to populate this model.[37] These data are rich, including information on time spent with media forms, simultaneous media usage, and finally the influence of various media forms on purchase interest across common product categories. And these data are currently being captured in places around the world, including the United States, China, and Mexico, with other countries scheduled to come online within a couple of years. While the preliminary findings are compelling, the data are not yet widely available. If the data and the applications of the model prove as we expect, this could become the media-planning model of the future because it is the one model specifically designed to recognize and measure the multitasking by media consumers we know exist in the media marketplace today. However, more time is needed to know whether the media consumption model will prove itself or not.

OTHER CONSUMER-FIRST MEDIA-PLANNING MODELS

In the meantime, other media researchers and planning professionals, understanding that the media marketplace is changing and understanding that the traditional media-planning model is no longer as viable as it once was, have worked to develop and employ a couple of different, consumer-first media-planning models. One such model that we will consider here is the "day-in-the-life" model and the other is a model based on brand contacts or touchpoints.

The "Day-in-the-Life" Model

The "day-in-the-life" media-planning model has been in use for several years. This is a media encounter model that starts with an analysis of the targeted consumer's average day in order to identify the key points at which the consumer will encounter various information and entertainment media.[38] This particular model was originally used in business-to-business marketing where the base of targeted "consumers" was generally a specific group of known business customers. Agencies today use this model successfully in many other situations, especially with small segments of consumers and in localized media planning. The key to this model is knowledge of the targeted consumers so that the marketer can forecast their average day and expected encounters with media delivery systems.

Application of this approach for a product with a consumer audience begins with a thorough review of all research available about the consumer segment. Having been briefed on the research, the media planning team then brainstorms its expectations of the consumer's average day, from waking up in the morning until retiring at night. The team creates a timeline of the day, inserting what the team members imagine are the events and activities of the average consumer's typical day. The next step is to overlay the points during the typical day when the average consumer will encounter a media delivery system.

At this point in the brainstorming, it is critical that every member of the media planning team keeps an open mind about what might serve as a media delivery system. This approach to media planning is meant to guide the identification of media beyond the traditional, but this only works if the media planning team can be as open-minded about media as is the targeted consumer. For this approach to work, the media planners have to train themselves to envision branded communications delivered in places where messages may have never been previously imagined. This takes a special kind of media creativity, vision, and imagination.

We saw an excellent example of this "day-in-the-life" approach and how it leads to new media ideas with the Rheingold Brewing Company and its 2004 campaign in New York City (Exhibit

Exhibit 11.6   "Day-in-the-Life" Media Placement

Source: Used with permission of JustinK, www.justinK.info.

11.6). Rheingold, a small local brewer, was looking for ways to gain a marketing foothold in a key New York City neighborhood, the Lower East Side. Based on its analysis of the young, unorthodox residents of that neighborhood, Rheingold's agency determined that the nighttime was the right time for delivery of the Rheingold message. The problem, though, was that most of these young consumers were out and about at night where traditional media like television and radio would not be effective, so the agency needed to find a new way. With some further analysis, it came to see that the nighttime roll-up window shades in the neighborhood stores could serve as a medium.

What the agency did at that point broke ground in many ways. It commissioned graffiti artists to create images of Rheingold beer and then negotiated with individual shop owners to paint the graffiti images on the stores' roll-up shades.[39] Then, at night, as the shops closed and the shades were pulled down, the Rheingold messages were everywhere; they owned the night.

The Brand Contacts Model

Another model for consumer-first media planning uses a product's brand touchpoints with its consumer. We discussed brand touchpoints, the points at which the consumer and the brand come into contact with each other, earlier in this chapter and in Chapter 10. Early in the development of the integrated marketing communications (IMC) concept, author Don Schultz identified brand contacts as an important messaging point for marketers.[40] Shortly thereafter, agencies began to promote a brand contact approach. Leo Burnett, for example, was cited in 1994 as planning media with a "brand contact audit" that "tallies each time a consumer comes into contact with a brand name," according to Burnett director of media research Jayne Spittler.[41]

As a media-planning model, the idea is still in use today. The concept is that any brand contact or touchpoint can (and should) be leveraged as a communications medium. The media-planning team identifies a list of brand contact points and then brainstorms ways to deliver the brand's message. As with the "day-in-the-life" model, it takes a very open-minded media planner to make this model work the way it should. In this particular case, the planner must be able to think through a thorough list of brand contacts and imagine a media messaging capability where it may never have existed previously.

We have already talked about the kind of creativity and vision needed to "see" new media opportunities. Coming up with a good, complete list of brand contacts can be equally challenging. Take a moment to consider this: think about a brand, any brand that you feel you understand well, and then try to list that brand's contact points with its consumers. How many can you come up with? The answer, of course, will be very different depending on the brand you chose for this exercise. Some of the most obvious points are media advertising, product packaging, sales representatives, sales brochures, customer service representatives, and sponsorships. Other touchpoints may not be so obvious: for example, company employees, including managers (not just the employees who regularly interact with consumers), retail store employees, the brand's production and distribution facilities (plant locations and vehicle fleet), recommendations from current consumers, and brand uses in entertainment. In order to use brand contacts as a media-planning model, marketers must start the process with a comprehensive list of the brand contact points.

Once the marketer has the list of all contacts, the next step is to identify a short list of the most influential brand contact points, the most important points to leverage for communications purposes. Researchers are working in this area to help marketers and agencies effectively identify the right brand touchpoints. For example, in an article in the *Journal of Advertising Research*, Amitava Chattopadhyay and Jean-Lois Laborie present the market contact audit as a method of identifying the most efficacious brand contact points.[42] Their method uses a combination of qualitative and quantitative research to identify and measure key factors that can then be used to guide a marketer's decision making. They start with qualitative research, first interviewing the brand marketer and/or planner to identify as many brand contact points as possible and then conduct a focus group with consumers, identifying any additional contact points. The result of this step is a comprehensive list of brand contact points that is then narrowed to a final list of thirty-five discrete touchpoints—what the researchers refer to as the "brand experience." The next step is quantitative research, with a sample of at least 500 respondents asked to rank each brand contact according to four proprietary criteria.

As they describe the process, Chattopadhyay and Laborie use the research responses to calculate a couple of key statistics that planners then use as a guide to identifying the most effective brand contact touchpoints. For example, one statistic, the contact clout factor, is a measure of the "strength" of a brand contact touchpoint as perceived by the consumer.[43] The strength of a contact point is measured according to the consumer's perspective on how effectively it conveys information, its attractiveness, and its influence. The higher the contact clout factor, the more effective is that brand contact point from the consumer's point of view.

Like the media consumption model discussed earlier, the market contact audit, though it still needs time and testing to prove its effectiveness, appears to have some promise for the future. Each of these models, and the simpler "day-in-the-life" model as well, takes an important consumer-first approach to media planning, an approach that we think is critical to the future of the media planning business. Further, each of these models requires a broad-minded perspective, a creative imagination and vision to see a media delivery vehicle where none previously existed. These are the kinds of solutions that we see as needed to address the major changes that are transforming the twenty-first–century media marketplace.

The one change we have not addressed yet is the change in the media themselves and how that too will require a new perspective for the future.

CHANGING THE VIEW OF MEDIA

Thus far we have talked about the changes affecting the business of delivering branded communications and how professionals in the business have, by necessity, responded and adapted. Let us take a moment now to consider a general perspective on media and how that perspective must change in order to keep up with what will be the future of the marketplace.

We will start with the historic view of media systems and then consider the new view that arises from the technological changes of today. This will lead us to a more detailed discussion of the media synergy issues to which we referred earlier in the chapter.

The Outbound View of Media Delivery Systems

The historic view of media delivery systems is an outbound-oriented view. In the common marketing view of the communication process, the sender sends a message and the receiver receives the message; that is, marketing as outbound communications.

Most of the traditional media still operate today according to this outbound orientation. From the earliest days of printing and print media, through the development of telegraphy and broadcast media such as radio and television, and even in today's emerging world of satellite and telephony media, the media owners and operators, together with marketers, send out information, entertainment, and marketing messages to consumers, who then receive what is sent. At least marketers like to believe the consumer receives the messages they send. A vast infrastructure of agencies, researchers, marketers, and media companies has been designed and assembled to work in this outbound way.

That huge infrastructure is proving hard to maneuver as the times and the media are changing all around the world. As we pointed out earlier, some people in this business think this infrastructure is too large, too heavy, and too slow to turn in the face of these new developments. While we would agree that the system needs more maneuverability, we are not quite ready to give up. Those of us who do see a promising future, like Jim Stengel's "new world of possibilities," recognize that the revolution of technological change has brought us to a place where media delivery systems are becoming increasingly personal and interactive.

The truth is that the traditional media will not go away. Throughout time, as new media emerge and take hold, the previously existing media forms persist. This is not a zero-sum game. Just because a new media form comes along does not mean an old media form has to die off. Newspapers, one of the earliest forms of modern media, and magazines have persisted for generations. Radio has persisted, despite dire predictions of its demise, in the face of expanding television service and even today in the face of commercial-free satellite subscription radio. And we fully expect that broadcast television as we know it today will also persist as a viable, advertiser-supported media form.

Interactive Media Delivery Systems

While these and other traditional outbound media forms will persist, we also see a future literally teeming with new, personal, and interactive media forms. Arthur Tauder talked about such a future in an article in the *Journal of Advertising Research* as an era of "advanced television" resulting from the "convergence of broadcast and digital technologies."[44] Tauder, a consultant and visiting scholar at the Massachusetts Institute of Technology Media Lab, sees this new media form characterized by four new features. The first is *time-shifting*, which refers to the consumer's ability to control (for example, with DVR devices) when media content will be consumed. The second new feature is *addressability*, which represents the increasing personalization of digital media forms; marketers can direct specific messages to specific audiences and the audience can select the communications it will receive. Tauder's designated third feature is *interactivity*; the audience will have the power to bypass or respond to messages, a form of responsiveness or interaction that will be a benefit to marketers everywhere. The fourth feature of Tauder's "advanced television" is *interoperability*, the ability of audiences in the future to receive and interact with content and communications across a broad array of media devices.

The first-week sellout of the new Apple iPhone in the summer of 2007 was just one example of this phenomenon. With wireless access to Apple's iTunes Internet entertainment store, iPhone users can download on demand any music, movies, TV shows or games they may desire.

Looking forward we expect to see continued expansion of personal media devices and interactive delivery systems. We see this trend as a good thing for the marketers who can maneuver and adapt to these changes. In his 2004 AAAA address, Procter & Gamble's chief marketing officer Jim Stengel noted that as technology has become more interactive and personal, marketers need to work harder to develop communications that will be "invited into consumers' lives and homes."[45] The key, from a media perspective, is to recognize and embrace the values of and differences between the traditional outbound-oriented media and the new personal, interactive media.

The Importance of Synergy

In this exciting new future, marketers will employ traditional and new media in various combinations to create a mutually beneficial exchange of communications between brands and consumers. This is the central point of this book: the customer-brand relationship is characterized and in fact defined by this mutually beneficial exchange, where the customer has the ability and desire to access branded content and information as much as the marketer has the ability and desire to provide content and information that way. The customer will be engaged in multitasking media consumption just as marketers will make their messages available in multiple media forms.

We have tried to make it clear how important the ability to combine multiple media forms will be in the future. It will also be important to be able to measure the effect of various combinations of media. We believe that synergy is what will ultimately make any new media-planning model work in the future. Marketers who are already following this model today, and those who will in the future try to combine different media forms, will need a model and a measurement system to estimate the synergistic value of combined media applications, especially given the fact of foreground and background media status in a time of multitasking media consumption.

As we mentioned briefly earlier in this chapter, authors Schultz and Pilotta argue convincingly for the promise they see in the work of researchers Naik and Raman, who have developed a

Exhibit 11.7   **Summary of Key Points From the World Federation of Advertisers "Blueprint for Consumer-Centric Holistic Measurement"**

Understanding the consumer beyond demographics
Get information in a timely manner
Understand multimedia behavior
Respect for privacy
Reach target consumer at receptive moments
Deliver relevant content
Content that serves consumer interest

statistical method for calculating the synergistic effects of multimedia situations by building on a commonly used advertising model and adding some of their own adaptations.[46] The work of these researchers shows it is possible to effectively measure the synergy that can occur between multiple media forms applied in simultaneous consumption situations. We will come back to this idea in greater detail in the next chapter when we discuss audience and media research.

MOVING FORWARD TO A NEW MODEL

Regardless of any measure of synergy, pressure is mounting worldwide for a new marketing and media-planning model. To emphasize the need for a new model, the World Federation of Advertisers (WFA) issued, in September 2005, what it called the "Blueprint for Consumer-Centric Holistic Measurement."

Exhibit 11.7 highlights the key points of the WFA Blueprint, which calls for development of a robust model that the world's leading marketers hope will solve the many problems and challenges we have discussed here. In essence, the WFA Blueprint calls for a consumer-first (consumer centric) model, populated with single-source data (product and media usage data from just one research source), and based on a single measurement metric applicable to all media forms, traditional and nontraditional.[47]

In this chapter we have considered four media-planning models that are to some extent in use today. The traditional media-planning model will not fulfill the mandate of the WFA blueprint. As we have already said, the whole infrastructure of the traditional model is aligned too closely to each individual media form. Likewise, the "day-in-the-life" model will never satisfy the WFA charge. Although it is importantly a consumer-first approach, it simply does not bring with it the single-source data and measurement metrics required. The brand contacts model we discussed here, the market contact audit, comes a little closer to the WFA Blueprint in that it is consumer-first and it develops a key measurement metric, the Contact Clout Factor, which is then applicable to any media form.

Of the four models we considered, the media consumption model seems to come closest to the WFA Blueprint at this time. The media consumption model is both consumer-first and populated with single-source data, and it presents measurement metrics applicable across a range of thirty-one unique media forms, including the traditional and nontraditional.[48] Additionally, the media consumption model is seemingly the one best positioned to measure the synergy that may (or may not) accrue from simultaneous media contacts with today's multitasking media consumers.

SUMMING UP

We have covered a lot of ground in this chapter. We discussed the major factors driving significant changes in the twenty-first–century world of media delivery systems and the media audiences using those delivery systems. We considered the fragmentation of traditional media forms and the splintering of media audiences. We reviewed the details of new consumer media usage behaviors and we talked through several consumer-first approaches to media planning. We laid the groundwork for a new way of thinking about media delivery systems by looking at delivery as either outbound or interactive, based on the consumer's media usage behavior. We have tried to establish that a new model is needed and that such a model indeed seems to be on the way.

NOTES

1. T. Elkin, "Malcontent Is King at Agency Media Fest," *Media Post's Media Daily News*, February 13, 2004.

2. J. Gertner, "Our Ratings, Ourselves: The Mis-Measurement of TV," *New York Times Magazine*, April 10, 2005.

3. C. Atkinson, "TV Market Primed for Pay-by-Pod," *Advertising Age*, July 10, 2006.

4. Wikipedia, "Mass Media History," http://en.wikipedia.org/wiki/mass_media#history.

5. *TV Dimensions 2002* (New York: Media Dynamics, 2002).

6. Media Trends Track, "TV Basics: Preface to the Cyber Edition," Television Bureau of Advertising Research Central, March 2008, www.tvb.org/rcentral/mediatrendstrack/tvbasics/index.asp.

7. Magazine Publishers of America, *The Magazine Handbook: A Comprehensive Guide 2006/07* (New York: Magazine Publishers of America, 2006), www.magazine.org/content/Files/MPAHandbook06.pdf.

8. Radio Advertising Bureau, *Radio Marketing Guide and Factbook* (Irving, TX: Radio Advertising Bureau, 2006), www.rab.com.

9. Corporate Executive Board, Advertising and Marketing Communications Roundtable, "Boosting Returns on Digital Investments" (May 2006).

10. D.E. Schultz, J.J. Pilotta, and M.P. Block, "Media Consumption and Consumer Purchasing" (paper presented at Fifth Annual Worldwide Multi Media Measurement Conference, Shanghai, ESOMAR, June 5–7, 2006).

11. D. Peskin, "Make Way for the Mobiles," in *Synapse,* Media Center, American Press Institute, Washington, DC, March 10, 2004.

12. Media Trends Track, "TV Basics."

13. J. Peters and W. Donald, "Industry Surveys—Advertising," *Standard & Poor's*, December 29, 2005.

14. Ibid.

15. T. Daugherty, H. Gangadharbatia, and K. Kim, "Polychronic Media Consumption: Exploring Attitudes Toward Simultaneous Media Usage," American Academy of Advertising Conference Proceedings (2005).

16. J.J. Pilotta and D.E. Schultz, "Simultaneous Media Experience and Synesthesia," *Journal of Advertising Research* 45, no. 1 (March 2005).

17. M. McLuhan, *The Medium Is the Message* (New York: Random House, 1967).

18. Pilotta and Schultz, "Simultaneous Media Experience and Synesthesia."

19. D.E. Schultz and J. Pilotta, "Developing the Foundation for a New Approach to Understanding How Media Advertising Works" (paper presented at Third Annual World Audience Measurement Conference, Geneva, June 13–18, 2004).

20. J. Stengel, "The Future of Marketing" (AAAA Media Conference, Orlando, FL, February 12, 2004).

21. J. Stengel, "The New Future of Marketing: Building Consumer Relationships" (AAAA Media Conference and Tradeshow, Las Vegas, February 28–March 2, 2007, www.aaaa.org.

22. Peters and Donald, "Industry Surveys—Advertising."

23. R. Lavidge and G. Steiner, "A Model of Predictive Measurements of Advertising Effectiveness," *Journal of Marketing* 25 (October 1961); R. Colley, *Defining Advertising Goals*, 7th ed. (New York: Association of National Advertisers, 1973).

24. W. Weilbacher, "Point of View: Does Advertising Cause a 'Hierarchy of Effects'?" *Journal of Advertising Research* (November–December 2001).

25. R. Grover, "Must-See TV for Left-Handed Men under 30," *Business Week*, December 14, 1998.

26. J. McDowell and K. Novack, "Those Missing Young Men: A Network Mystery," *Time*, November 24, 2003.

27. R. Coen, "Presentation on Advertising Expenditures," *Insider's Report, Universal McCann*, June 2003.

28. B. Johnson, "Cracks in the Foundation," *Advertising Age*, December 8, 2003; B. Garfield, "The Chaos Scenario," *Advertising Age*, April 4, 2005.

29. D.E. Schultz, J.J. Pilotta, G. Drenik, and P. Rist, "Simultaneous Media Usage: A Critical Consumer Orientation to Media Planning," *Journal of Consumer Behaviour* 3, no. 3 (March 2004).

30. Pilotta and Schultz, "Simultaneous Media Experience and Synesthesia."

31. J. Sissors and R. Baron, *Advertising Media Planning*, 6th ed. (New York: McGraw-Hill, 2002), pp. 57–61.

32. Schultz and Pilotta, "Developing the Foundation."

33. M. Azzaro, D. Binder, R. Clawson, C. Lloyd, M.A. Shaver, and O. Werder, *Strategic Media Decisions* (Chicago: Copy Workshop, 2004), pp. 447–452.

34. P. Naik and K. Raman, "Understanding the Impact of Synergy in Multimedia Communications," *Journal of Marketing Research* 40, no. 4 (November 2003).

35. Schultz and Pilotta, "Developing the Foundation."

36. Schultz, Pilotta, and Block, "Media Consumption and Consumer Purchasing."

37. Ibid.

38. Azzaro et al., *Strategic Media Decisions*, pp. 329–331.

39. J. Barron, "Welcoming Graffiti as a Partner in Promotion," *New York Times*, November 14, 2004.

40. D.E. Schultz, "Maybe We Should Start All Over with an IMC Organization," *Marketing News*, October 25, 1993.

41. J. Liesse, "Buying by the Numbers? Hardly," *Advertising Age*, July 25, 1994.

42. A. Chattopadhyay and J.-L. Laborie, "Managing Brand Experience: The Market Contact Audit," *Journal of Advertising Research* 45, no. 1 (March 2005).

43. Ibid.

44. A. Tauder, "Getting Ready for the Next Generation of Marketing Communications," *Journal of Advertising Research*, 45, no. 1 (March 2005).

45. Stengel, "The Future of Marketing."

46. Schultz and Pilotta, "Developing the Foundation"; Naik and Raman, "Understanding the Impact of Synergy."

47. World Federation of Advertisers, "Blueprint for Consumer-centric Holistic Measurement" (Brussels: World Federation of Advertisers, September 2005), www.wfanet.org/pdf/med_documents/BlueprintFor-Consumer-CentricHolisticMeasurement_EN.pdf.

48. Schultz, Pilotta, and Block, "Media Consumption and Consumer Purchasing."

CHAPTER 12

Customer Consumption of Communication

In this chapter we will look at media and audience research in its many and evolving forms. In the previous chapter we discussed how dramatically the world of media has changed. Those major changes, across all media delivery systems and media audiences as well, have spawned significant changes in media research technique and practice.

In the following pages we will consider the existing media and audience research techniques, from proprietary and syndicated services, for both traditional and nontraditional communications delivery vehicles. We will look at current measurement practices for each major media form and discuss the strengths and weaknesses of the current methodology. We will also look at some of the new developments in each area and discuss the changes we anticipate for the future.

Also in this chapter we will consider some of the omnibus issues across the field of media and audience research and review their implications. Many of these issues form the basis of the World Federation of Advertisers' "Blueprint for Consumer-Centric Holistic Measurement" that we mentioned at the end of the previous chapter. The implications of these overarching issues will apply to all media in the future, traditional and nontraditional as well as new media not yet imagined.

THE CULTURE AND EVOLUTION OF MEDIA RESEARCH

Before analyzing the methods and techniques, we will first discuss the culture of media and audience measurement. A familiarity with the roots of current business practices allows marketers to grasp the research concepts and evaluate the strengths and weaknesses of each. Ultimately, the developmental opportunities that marketers need to address in the future will make more sense if they first have this kind of understanding.

The culture of the media research field evolved as the media and the business of media evolved over time. In the last chapter we provided a very brief history of the evolution of media. We will now discuss this evolution in more detail and consider the business model that drives the media business as it exists today.

Development of Media Silos

From the very brief history presented in Chapter 11, it should be clear that the media delivery systems of past centuries developed individually as unique technological advances were realized. In 1455 Gutenberg's invention of the printing press with movable type led to the printing of newspapers in Europe beginning in 1609, almost 300 years later the 1892 invention of the four-color rotary press led to the printing of advertiser-supported magazines, at the same time in the late 1800s advances in telegraphy led to the first radio broadcasts early in the twentieth century, further improvements in technology led to Farnsworth's invention of television in 1927, and so on.[1]

Because the early pace of development was slow, each media form had time to develop as its own business. One by one, each new media form gathered its own audience. And marketers, drawn to each medium, sought to communicate with that audience. The result is what we see today as the development of each form of media as a "silo"—an individual structure standing alone in a field. The media business evolved one media form at a time and never really had the chance to become a larger, interconnected, multi-media infrastructure.[2]

On a local level, one newspaper competes with another for the newspaper-reading audience and marketers who want to address that audience. The same holds for local radio stations. On a national level, one television network competes with another for the marketers who want to communicate with the television audience, and the same holds for magazine publishers. Magazine publishers considered themselves to be in the magazine business, not the media business. Likewise for each of the other media forms: television stations were in the television business, newspapers were in the newspaper business, and radio stations were in the radio business. Only recently have media owners begun thinking about their work as being in the broader media business.

Only recently, since 1995, has one media form competed against another media form for a greater share of total marketing dollars.[3] This phenomenon came as a result of two factors affecting media owners. The first is acquisitions among media companies. As media owners began to see their businesses as media and not just one medium, the biggest media companies began to acquire other media assets. The second major factor is increasing financial pressure to succeed in the face of splintering and sometimes disappearing media audiences. In the pursuit of funding to acquire more media assets, many previously privately owned media companies have become publicly traded companies, responsible to shareholders for producing financial results. Largely because of these two factors, extended competitiveness becomes possible and necessary, and the major media companies aggressively compete for share of marketing dollars.

In the marketer-supported media business model in most of the world's developed nations, the media audience is the valued commodity. Marketers have to pay the media for the right to access these media audiences. If the media audience is diminishing, marketers are not willing to pay as much. Media researchers, as third party evaluators, are often caught in the middle of this intricate relationship.

The Research Relationship Between Media and Marketers

For as long as marketers have used the media to deliver branded communications messages, there has been a marketer-driven need to measure the audience value of any one medium as compared to any other. And for as long as the media owners have worked under the current marketer-supported business model, there has been a media-driven need to measure the audience attracted to one medium over another. In this kind of business model, it is the responsibility of the media to attract an audience that marketers will want to communicate with. And it has become the responsibility of the media research companies to serve both media and marketers with measurement metrics. The very essence, the basic culture, of this field is defined by this tenuous business model and the relationship with the researcher squarely in the middle.

Researchers thus had to develop measurement techniques with the objectives of both parties in mind. While it is true that both media owners and marketers want accuracy in measurements of a media audience, there are opposing pressures also at work. Media owners want research to prove a large media audience. This makes it possible for the media to command a higher price for media time (broadcast) or space (print). Marketers want the opposite so that lower prices can be negotiated.

In the days of media silos, up through and including the Internet, as each media developed its audience, researchers developed methods for measuring the specific media audience. Researchers worked with both marketers and media owners to develop measurement techniques and metrics that would serve the relationship between the two. However, the resulting research technique was almost always unique to the media form.

Research companies emerged for each media form as researchers succeeded in developing techniques and measurement metrics that effectively served media owners. Thus, research companies provided a research source that was developed for one particular media form. For example, the yesterday-reading technique was used to measure newspaper audiences, and the recent-reading technique and frequency-of-reading technique were used to measure magazine readership. In broadcast media, listener diaries were used to measure radio audiences, and a combination of personal diaries and electronic meters was used to measure television audiences. Each of these techniques was developed by specific research companies to support an individual media form.[4] The media owners were the primary customers of such media research companies.

Later, research companies expanded their data collection and improved their techniques to develop measurements that were comparable across media forms. These services came to be known as syndicated research services because they served the broader business community, not just one media form. Marketing agencies in particular were interested in syndicated research services because these made it possible to evaluate and compare media forms.

We have talked so far about media owners and marketing agencies as customers of media research, but what about the marketers? Marketers are also customers of the general forms of media research, but all along they have understood that their media research needs are different. While marketers have access to, use of, and even influence over the general forms of media research, they also have a need for independent validation of the effectiveness of their brand communication activities. To this end, some of the world's largest marketers have contracted with researchers, agencies, and the media to develop their own proprietary, individual company media research services.

Today we see both kinds of media research: proprietary, individual company services and syndicated research services. Each serves a particular purpose in the marketing process so it is important to understand each kind of research service. It is also important to understand how the current media environment is affecting media research in general and both proprietary and syndicated research services in particular.

Proprietary Research Services

Proprietary, individual company research services are, for the most part, those services developed specifically to collect and analyze data for one particular marketing company. Proprietary research services have been developed by some of the world's largest marketers seeking new ways to measure audiences for both traditional and new media forms as well as better ways to measure the effects of the marketers' media activities.

For many years, the primary focus of proprietary media research has been developing ways to measure the audiences and marketing impact of marketing activities such as sales promotions and direct marketing. Marketers have invested heavily in trying to learn how these activities work and how they return value to the organization. Through these efforts, marketers and marketing agencies have developed new ways to gauge the effectiveness of marketing efforts ranging from coupon and newsletter distribution to event sponsorship and word-of-mouth (viral or buzz) campaigns.

Procter & Gamble, for example, has been particularly active in developing new models for tracking and evaluating all forms of media. The company has used proprietary research across all media forms as a way to understand its customers and their preferences in accessing and receiving news and information about P&G products. Findings from this kind of research, in fact, led to a major realignment of product assignments among the Procter & Gamble media agencies in 2003 and 2004.

Major marketers like Procter & Gamble, General Motors, Kraft, Unilever, and Colgate-Palmolive have spent years working to encourage media owners and media research companies to develop new techniques for evaluating both traditional and new media forms. After years of nominal success, several of these major marketers have initiated their own efforts. Working in partnerships with media research companies and sometimes including the marketers' major agencies, these companies are breaking new ground in media research. The findings from this kind of research are generally proprietary to the sponsoring marketer and not usually available for application to other businesses.

One exception, however, is a recent joint effort sponsored by Procter & Gamble and one of its major marketing agencies, Euro RSCG. Working with Procter & Gamble and key retailers, Dallas-based Euro RSCG Retail developed a proprietary system to measure consumer interaction with different media forms. According to Frank Nichols, senior vice president of media services for Euro RSCG Retail, the Retail Area Media Planning (RAMP) process links retail transactional (sales) data with media research to calculate brand-weighted values for local-area media choices.[5] This particular example is unique in that we can know some of the details of the work because the terms of the partnership allow Euro RSCG Retail to market the RAMP system to its retail clients. This is one known example of the kind of research developed by and for major marketers, but more often than not, this kind of proprietary work is not generally publicized.

Syndicated Research Services

Syndicated is the term used to describe research companies that sell a research product to multiple customers across multiple consumer markets. In this sense, the research product is the data source, and selling the research product means making the data source available to any and all marketers, marketing agencies, and media services willing to pay for subscription to the service. There are many such research companies supporting the marketing and media businesses today. There are syndicated marketing data sources that marketers and agencies use to understand product consumers, syndicated media data sources used by agencies and media owners to help them understand media audiences, and syndicated marketing and media data sources primarily used by agencies to understand media usage by product consumers.

Marketing Data Sources

Two major research companies—A.C. Nielsen Company and Information Resources Inc.—provide marketing data primarily used by marketers and marketing agencies.

A.C. Nielsen Company was founded by Arthur Nielsen in the early 1920s. Nielsen started the company as a retail measurement service to give marketers "reliable, objective information about competitive performance and the impact of their marketing and sales programs."[6] Today Nielsen monitors products sold in grocery stores, drug stores, and mass merchandiser outlets, including warehouse clubs, via a weekly national sample of stores. Using the data provided by Nielsen, marketers can monitor a product's weekly share-of-market relative to average pricing, retailer support, and media advertising activities. As a matter of practice, Nielsen sells its data only to marketers, who then generally pass along certain Nielsen data to their agencies.

Like A.C. Nielsen, Information Resources Inc. (IRI) is a research service that offers marketers a source for tracking product sales through food, drug, and mass merchandiser retail outlets. Whereas Nielsen data are projected from a sample of retail stores, IRI data are gathered as a census of scanned product sales using Universal Product Code (UPC) scanners. IRI reports the same kind of data that Nielsen provides on the same weekly basis.

Media Data Sources

Many research companies provide syndicated reports of data on media audiences. As mentioned earlier, most of these provide data specific to each media form. The primary customer market for media data sources is media owners. Marketing agencies are also subscribers to multiple media data sources, but the media owners are usually the major source of revenue for research companies in this area. To illustrate the differences between different kinds of media data sources, we discuss here the developmental background of two of the most commonly used services—the television research company Nielsen Media Research (not the same company as A.C. Nielsen) and the major radio research company Arbitron. Later in the chapter we will discuss sources and specific measurements of each media form in more detail.

The Nielsen Media Research company was founded originally to measure radio audiences. The company founder, Arthur Nielsen, already ran the A.C. Nielsen Company, specializing in retail sales research, when he acquired a research device called an "audimeter" from professors at the Massachusetts Institute of Technology. In 1942 Nielsen introduced the Nielsen Radio Index as a commercial network radio measurement service based on audimeter readings in sample homes. In the 1950s Nielsen expanded his media research business into television measurement using the same audimeter technology. In 1962 Nielsen Media Research discontinued its radio measurement practice in order to focus exclusively on developing better television research methods.[7] Today Nielsen Media Research is the primary source for television audience measurements. Using a sample of U.S. homes wired with electronic measurement devices called "people meters," Nielsen reports television audience data for all national television forms (broadcast networks, cable networks, and syndicated national programming). Nielsen uses these same meters together with television viewer diaries to also measure and report local television viewing behavior.

The Arbitron Company is the dominant radio measurement service in the United States. It started as a television research company in the early 1950s. Just as television was gaining in popularity, the American Research Bureau (ARB) created a new television research product called Arbitron that measured television audiences using a viewing diary. Arbitron used the same technique to gather and report data on radio audiences based on personal listening diaries. After almost forty years of head-to-head competition with Nielsen, the Arbitron Company discontinued its television measurement service in 1993 in order to focus on its radio research service.[8]

Marketing and Media Data Sources

Just as there are marketing data sources to support marketers and media data sources for media owners, there are research companies that provide regular reports that combine marketing and media audience data to serve the marketing agencies in this business. There are two major research providers in this area, Mediamark Research Inc. (MRI) and Simmons Market Research Bureau (SMRB).

Both services use a major survey of U.S. consumers to report data on the products consumers use along with the demographics, lifestyles, attitudes, and media preferences of product users.[9] Both SMRB and MRI survey a panel of about 25,000 consumers in periodic research waves throughout the year. Each company sells subscriptions to its data reports such that marketing agencies can match media usage habits with product usage behavior for a long list of marketer products included in the survey instrument. This particular combination of product usage data together with information about usage of multiple media forms all in one place is what the industry has come to think of as "single-source" data.

The Goal of Single-Source Data

Services like MRI and SMRB represent a step forward to what the industry hopes will someday be single-source data services, but neither is truly a single-source data service. While services like MRI and SMRB do provide consumer information for both media and product usage, the problem is that this is, for both services, self-reported usage, not independently measured behavior.

The idealistic goal of single-source data is one source reporting independently measured media and product purchase behavior that all of the industry's constituents—marketers, marketing agencies, and media owners—can use. One of the leading researchers in this area has been John Philip Jones and his work developing the measure he calls Short-Term Advertising Strength" (STAS). Through the late 1980s and early 1990s, Jones worked with Nielsen data to analyze consumer exposure to television advertising as well as product purchase behavior for specific brands in twelve heavily advertised product categories.[10] His research broke ground in several ways, and he is considered one of the first to argue convincingly for single-source data as the best way to understand the impact and effect of advertising.

Over the past ten years, both Nielsen and Arbitron have continued testing ideas that might make single-source data a reality. However, despite substantial effort, attempts have foundered for many reasons, including the high cost of starting a new system and the obvious demands of creating a system to serve multiple and sometimes conflicting purposes.

Since 2005 Arbitron and Nielsen, now sister companies under the VNU Media company umbrella, have combined efforts in a system referred to as Project Apollo. Project Apollo was a collaborative effort to collect multimedia exposure and product purchase information from a common sample of consumers. The idea was to combine data using Arbitron's Portable People Meter (PPM) media measurement technology together with Nielsen's HomeScan product purchase technology to create the holistic single-source data service that marketers wanted.[11] Arbitron's PPM is an electronic device, about the size of a cell phone or pager, that reads signals from electronic media sources to passively record a consumer's exposure to the media. Nielsen's HomeScan technology gathers product purchase information direct from consumers who used a special device in their own homes to scan the UPC codes of products they purchased. A panel of consumers using both the PPM and the HomeScan scanning wand provided both media and product usage gathered in a single-source.

The pilot effort of Project Apollo ran with a panel of 11,000 people in 5,000 U.S. households. Reports from the early data from the pilot study showed that single-source measurements could improve media planning and buying efforts with a better focus on brand targets and a better understanding of the media usage behaviors of brand buyers. An average 20 percent improvement was measured across fourteen different product category case studies in the pilot.[12]

There are, of course, problems that Project Apollo still needed to overcome. One problem is that the Arbitron PPM technology was designed to measure consumers' use of electronic media passively by reading signals embedded in the media. One of the first hurdles was convincing the media to embed the signals required to make the PPM work.[13] Another issue was that PPMs are designed mainly for electronic media; Project Apollo was supposed to use an online survey to supplement the PPM with a measure of exposure to nonelectronic media. Similarly, the Nielsen HomeScan technology was initially designed by A.C. Nielsen to measure purchases of products that carry UPC scanner codes; Apollo used supplemental surveys to include a wider array of products and services. And, finally, all the industry constituents, with competing and often conflicting needs, had to agree that the findings from this new service were realistic and reliable.

Although all the industry constituents insist that they want and need a single-source data service, these issues proved to be insurmountable. This kind of agreement will come about only through selfless collaboration by all parties, which is unlikely in the face of increasing pressures for financial success. In fact, after millions of dollars and years of effort, Arbitron and Nielsen announced the end of the Apollo project in early 2008. Despite the failure of Project Apollo, marketers are sure to remain focused on single-source data as a solution to the demands of marketing in the future; this much is clear from the World Federation of Advertisers' "Blueprint for Consumer-Centric Holistic Measurement."[14] The marketers of the world consider the idea of single-source data something akin to a Holy Grail.

This section has given the big picture of media audience measurement and the availability and role of media research in the marketing process. In the next section, specific methods and practices that are often unique to individual media forms are discussed.

MEASURING THE AUDIENCE AND EFFECT OF ADVERTISING MEDIA

As mentioned earlier in the chapter, many of the media research techniques in use today were developed to serve the measurement interests of each individual media form. Here we consider each media system separately, looking at the research companies supporting the business, and the most common measurement metrics in use for each area. Most of the material on current measurement practices in this section is paraphrased from two prominent books on media planning: *Strategic Media Decisions* by Marian Azzaro and her colleagues and *Advertising Media Planning* by Jack Sissors and Roger Baron.[15] As things are changing so quickly and dramatically in this field, we will conclude our discussion of each media form with an eye toward the future and what changes might be expected.

We emphasize that we are talking here about media audience measurements; we are not talking about measures of communication effectiveness. Communication measures, like brand recall, awareness, and brand liking, were discussed in Chapter 8.

Broadcast Media

The term *broadcast media* is generally used to refer to radio and television because these media originated from telegraphy technology, where first audio and then both audio and visual signals were broadcast from a sender to a receiver.

Broadcast media are generally measured via a combination of measurement devices and techniques including electronic meters and self-reported personal viewing or listening diaries. The most common measurement metric for broadcast media is called a rating point. Simply put, one rating point is 1 percent of all available viewers or listeners. While the metric is the same, the process and techniques used to measure television and radio are different.

National and Local Television

Audiences for national television forms, including broadcast networks (like ABC, CBS, NBC, and FOX), cable networks (like CNN, Nickelodeon, Lifetime, and ESPN), and nationally syndicated television programming (like the game show *Jeopardy*), are measured by Nielsen Media Research using an electronic device called a people meter. Throughout the United States, Nielsen maintains a sample panel of 5,000 homes in which people meters are wired to the television sets and each family member has an assigned code number. The meter automatically records the channel being viewed on any television set and prompts viewers via on-screen messages to identify themselves using a special push-button remote control.

Nielsen also measures local television station-by-station viewing audiences in 210 unique, local television markets throughout the United States. In 53 major (large) markets, Nielsen uses a combination of household meters supplemented with personal viewing diaries of television watching. The remaining 157 small and mid-size markets are measured by personal diary only.

For both national and local television, Nielsen uses its sample panel of meter and diary homes to project ratings, audience size, and audience characteristics for all television programs. Sampling is the generally accepted practice in media research, and not unique to Nielsen Media Research. Although a sample of 5,000 may seem small compared to a universe of more than 100 million U.S. households, Nielsen maintains that its sample is statistically balanced and projectable and therefore reliable. Its reliability has become something of an issue in the industry over the last several years as Nielsen has tinkered with the sample in an effort to better reflect certain demographic constituencies. Every minor change can and does have a major impact on the ratings results.

It is true that sampling and the sample techniques used are an important issue for Nielsen; however, the bigger issue is the question of what, exactly, Nielsen is measuring. As we mentioned earlier, Nielsen meters and diaries are designed to measure audiences for television programming. As media usage behaviors have changed, marketers have become much more interested in measuring audiences for television commercials, rather than programming.

With the advent of remote control devices for changing channels, VCRs, and now recording devices like TiVo, marketers no longer accept that the audience that tunes in to a television show will stay tuned into the commercials that run during the breaks inserted in the show. In fact, for several years marketers and agencies have sought television ratings based on commercial minutes instead of programming. It is a generally accepted belief that many television viewers tune out (chat, go to the bathroom, get a sandwich, etc.) during commercial breaks. From our discussion in Chapter 11, we might also expect that commercial breaks represent an opportunity for a shift of consumer attention between foreground and background media forms in multitasking media situations. Yet despite this conventional wisdom, the primary metric used for television audience estimates has continued to be program ratings.

We expect that this situation will change in the future. Late in 2006, Nielsen Media Research began its efforts to measure "average commercial ratings per program,"[16] allowing marketers to get closer to their goal. However, "average commercial ratings per program" is an average ratings estimate for all commercial minutes contained within a television program. Therefore, it is still not a rating for any one particular commercial.

Nielsen and its media owner clients feel it is important to look at an average of commercials so that the media are not penalized for what might be poor-performing commercials. This is a good example of the tenuous relationship between media owners, marketers, and media researchers to which we referred earlier in this chapter. If a commercial does not get a large viewing audience, then the marketer would not be willing to pay much for the media time. If it is the commercial's audience that is being estimated, the media could argue that the low audience rating was a result of a boring commercial—the marketer's fault, not the fault of the media. Nielsen, the media researcher in the middle, hopes to avoid this issue by providing only an average rating of all commercials run during a program.

Radio

For the time being at least, radio ratings are projected based on a sample panel of consumers who report radio listening in a daily diary. A sample group of consumers in a total of 270 radio markets across the United States keep a daily radio listening diary for a one-week period during a couple of different times during the year. The Arbitron Company is the primary radio researcher projecting ratings and average quarter-hour audience sizes for all commercial radio stations in the United States. Arbitron has been using this diary measurement technique for more than fifty years. Although there are acknowledged problems with the self-reported diary technique, it has long proven the most cost-effective way to collect this kind of broad-scale data needed to measure the many thousands of radio stations broadcasting across hundreds of U.S. media markets, large and small.

For the future, Arbitron has worked with Nielsen experimenting with a portable people meter that would measure all electronic media usage automatically based on signals produced by broadcasters, both radio and television. As we mentioned before, a key to this new technique is convincing broadcasters to embed the signals needed to automatically record the media usage. At this point, the Apollo project has been abandoned.

Another big issue for the future of radio is the as yet unknown audience effect of sub-scription-based, noncommercial, satellite radio systems like Sirius and XM. More and more car manufacturers are offering satellite radio systems in cars. This will become an issue for marketers and marketer-supported commercial radio because so much radio listenership takes place in cars. More than 80 percent of the radio audience reports listening while in the car; of the average twenty hours per week that consumers spend listening to the radio, as much as one-third of that time is spent in the car.[17] Marketers using radio to deliver their branded communications may seek other ways to get their brand messages out.

Print Media

Print media audiences are measured by circulation and readership. Circulation is a count of how many printed copies of a publication are distributed at a point in time—a fairly simple measure. Both major print media forms, newspapers and magazines, use circulation as one measure of audience delivery. In each case, circulation is reported by the publisher and audited for consistency and accuracy by a third-party auditor. For newspapers and consumer magazines, the third-party auditor is the Audit Bureau of Circulation (ABC). For business publications in the United States and around the world, the primary third-party auditor is BPA Worldwide.

Readership is a more complex measure determined via different measurement techniques for different print media forms.

Newspapers

Newspaper readership is measured according to the yesterday-reading technique. This is a simple interview technique in which participants are asked to identify which newspaper they read yesterday. Scarborough Research is the major research provider in this area. Scarborough measures daily and Sunday newspaper readership as well as readership by newspaper section.

Although this research technique involves an interview, it is typically brief because most consumers in the United States read only one daily newspaper. And most U.S. cities have only one or two daily newspaper options. However, several newspaper alternatives besides local papers compete for the consumer's limited reading time—for example, *USA Today* and the *Wall Street Journal*. One of the big issues for the future of the newspaper industry is the consumer's limited reading time. According to a recent study, the average adult in the United States spends about thirty minutes a day reading a newspaper.[18]

Another issue, or opportunity, depending on perspective, for the future involves the newspaper Web site traffic. Virtually every major newspaper today has a companion Web site, as do even small-market free papers like Colorado's Steamboat Springs *Steamboat Pilot & Today*.

Some professionals are concerned that newspaper Web sites will eventually replace printed publications. So far, however, this has not been the case; in fact, the newspaper Web sites seem to be adding audience. Scarborough Research released its "Integrated Newspaper Audience" findings in 2005 indicating that newspaper Web sites contribute a significant number of readers, particularly young adult readers, who do not usually read the printed newspaper on a daily basis.

Magazines

Mediamark Research Inc. (MRI) is the primary magazine audience researcher in the United States. MRI measures magazine readership using the recent-reading research technique. The recent-reading technique involves a personal interview with a sample group of subjects who are shown different magazine logotypes one by one and asked if they have read or looked at the magazine in the last month or week, depending on the magazine's standard publication period. Respondents are counted as readers if they indicate they are "sure they have" read or looked at the magazine in that time period.

Another common audience measure for magazine readers uses the frequency-of-reading research technique to account for the fact that not everyone reads every single issue of a magazine. This particular technique is also conducted via interview. Research subjects are shown a list of magazine logotypes and asked to record the number of issues read out of the last four published—for example zero out of four, one out of four, and so on. Magazine researchers feel that this technique offers a more accurate reflection of a magazine's audience when compared to the recent-reading technique.

There are, of course, problems with both measures. The recent-reading interview can be costly, and respondents may be confused by similar magazine titles—for example, *Ski Magazine* and *Skiing Magazine*. With the frequency-of-reading measure, some question the validity as respondents may have trouble remembering how many issues they have read.

Like newspapers, all magazines now publish Web sites in addition to the printed version of the publication. The value of the Web site audience with free access to the magazine's content as compared to the printed magazine's paid subscriptions is as yet undetermined. Marketers and their agencies, using the print media to deliver branded communications in the future, will have to find ways to assess the value and effect of each.

Another problem for the future of print media audience research is the self-reported nature of the techniques currently in use. Each of the three techniques discussed here, yesterday-reading, recent-reading, and frequency-of-reading, uses interviews to estimate and project publication readership. Interview research has always been subject to the possibility of interviewer bias and respondent confusion. The broadcast media are moving toward passive, electronic capture of audience data via embedded broadcast signals. The print media have not yet found an automatic, passive way to estimate audiences. Even Project Apollo proposed to use a supplemental survey to record print media audiences. Until this issue is resolved, there will always be questions about whether audience measurement metrics are comparable across all media forms.

Other Media

Many marketers classify out-of-home media as a form of print media and the Internet as a form of broadcast media. Here we discuss Internet and out-of-home under a separate "other media" heading simply because the audience measurement practices are different from those for print and broadcast media. While some may consider the term "other media" demeaning in some way, this is not in any way our intent. In fact, if anything, we see both out-of-home and Internet media as communication delivery systems with explosive growth potential for the future and therefore worthy of separate discussion.

Out-of-Home (Outdoor)

As a group, out-of-home media include traditional media like outdoor billboards and bus and train transit signage as well as newer, emerging media like messaging on sidewalks, in restrooms, at venues such as airports and stadiums, at movie theaters, and even previously unimagined media like the Rheingold roll-up window shades we discussed in Chapter 11. While each medium is unique, they are all similar in terms of measuring audience potential.

One key measure for each out-of-home media form is daily circulation. This is not the same thing as newspaper or magazine circulation. Daily circulation is rather a traffic or flow measure of out-of-home audiences, literally a count of the number of people who "flow" past a particular media location. One major research service in this area is the Traffic Audit Bureau for Media Measurement (TAB). TAB audits the count of people who have the opportunity to see a particular out-of-home media location, using Department of Transportation figures and proprietary research to create the standardized metric called Daily Effective Circulation (DEC) across most major U.S. markets.[19] TAB reports its DEC metric for U.S. billboard locations as well as major train station and bus shelter sign locations.

Other services use their own techniques to provide a similar daily circulation estimate and other measures for other out-of-home sign locations. A big research company may provide an independent, third-party evaluation; for example, the Arbitron Company monitors and reports on movie theater audiences. Other estimates are projected by the media owner, so the data may be self-serving. The marketer should cautiously consider the source of the audience estimate before deciding to use a particular media form.

The future of out-of-home media services is bright because this is the area from which many new media forms have emerged. The challenge for today and the future is finding an acceptable way to quantify and evaluate audience estimates for these new media forms. Most marketers will want to have some estimate of the audience for their communications, even if the media idea is new and exciting. For a campaign like the Rheingold Beer roll-up window shades on Manhattan's Lower East Side, the marketer could start with TAB figures, particularly if there are any prominent billboards or bus shelter locations in the same neighborhood. The Department of Transportation can provide estimates of vehicle traffic on the major streets where the marketer's signs will be located. The U.S. Census Bureau can provide neighborhood population figures. And, finally, the marketer could hire a team of counters, each with a clicker in hand, to stand on the street corners and count pedestrians for some period of time.

Besides finding creditable, reliable ways to estimate such audiences in the first place, another key challenge for users of out-of-home media is to assess the value of a new media audience as compared to other media audiences. For new media forms and for existing, established out-of-home media like billboards, the issue of comparability with other media is crucial. As we said before, daily circulation is a simple count of the people who have the opportunity to be exposed to a particular billboard location, not a true measure of the audience that actually views the branded message at that location. The question of passive measurement versus self-reported media audience measurements also remains an issue in this media category.

Internet

The key audience measure for the Internet is site visitors. As with daily circulation for out-of-home media site visitors is a count of Web site traffic, or the flow of people who visit a particular Web site. As with out-of-home media forms, this is a measure of the people who have the opportunity to be exposed to a branded message at a particular Web site location. It is not a true measure of the audience who actually views the branded message in the context of the location.

On the plus side, though, the data on Internet site visits are collected in a passive and automated way. The major research service for audience measurement of the Internet is Nielsen/NetRatings, a Nielsen Media Research sister company. Nielsen/NetRatings gathers data on Internet audiences via a large sample of Internet users. With the users' permission, Nielsen/NetRatings loads special software onto the user's computer. The software monitors and reports data for every Web site visited from the host computer. The software records the length of time spent at each Web site, the depth (how many pages into the Web site) of each visit, and the number of times a computer returns to the same Web site.

There are still problems with Internet audience estimates. As mentioned before, site visitors are a potential audience, not an actual audience for the marketer's branded message. Another issue has to do with the anonymity of the Internet. The Nielsen/NetRatings software monitors the computer, not the person or people using the computer. Where there are multiple people living in one household, there is often more than one person using the household computer. It may therefore be difficult to get reliable demographic details about the audience for particular Web sites.

One of the compelling media measurement issues for the future is audience responsiveness to marketing messages. In this area, the Internet is at the forefront. Since its beginning as a marketing medium, Internet site operators have been able to track "click-through" as a measure of audience response to branded communications. "Click-through" rates represent a measure of the number of site visitors who click on a marketer's message, expressed as a percentage of the total number of site visitors. This is the kind of responsiveness measurement that other media forms are still hoping to accomplish.

MEASURING THE AUDIENCE AND EFFECT OF OTHER DELIVERY SYSTEMS

To this point we have discussed all the traditional forms of media delivery systems and some of the newer media forms as well. In this burgeoning world of marketing communication, we feel it is also important to address the issues of media audience measurement for the other important media forms related to other marketing communications activities such as direct marketing brochure mailings, promotional coupon newspaper inserts, or public relations press mentions. Until recently, these systems were not widely considered "media" because the industry was inclined to think of media as "advertising media" only. As more and more marketers are thinking of all branded communications under one domain, it becomes increasingly important to consider all communication media delivery systems within the same context.

This section will be relatively brief. While each particular field has developed its own measurement practices, the media audience measurement research in most of these areas is not yet as well developed as it is for the traditional advertising media. On the next pages we will discuss some of the current industry practices in terms of measurement metrics and techniques. We will come back to each of these media forms in greater detail in Chapters 13 and 14.

The other communication delivery media will be an increasingly important developmental area for the future of marketing communications as an industry. As we have said, any touchpoint of contact between a brand and its consumers could serve the marketer as a media delivery system. As the industry moves forward to the consumer-centric, holistic model outlined in the WFA Blueprint, it will become critical for marketers to measure and compare the effectiveness of message delivery across the broadest possible spectrum of marketing communication systems.[20] Across all these other media delivery forms, where marketers most need research help for the future is in finding ways to compare and eventually combine the effects of these media with the traditional advertising media discussed above.

We will begin with a discussion of the media forms used to deliver branded communications in the fields of direct marketing, sales promotion and public relations.

Direct Media

For our purposes here we will define direct media as those communication delivery systems used to present marketing messages directly to targeted consumers, individually or in small groups, along with a direct consumer response device of some sort (reply card, Web site, phone line, etc.). Of the many media systems that meet this definition, we will focus on the ones used most often: direct mail, telemarketing, email, and broadcast infomercials (direct response television or DRTV).

Mail is the most frequently used medium of direct marketing. There are many types of direct mail media, from simple postcards to catalogs and from flat mail pieces to what are called "dimensional mail" pieces (larger format or die-cut mailings). In terms of direct marketing activities (not spending) by major companies in twenty-one different product and service industries, the Direct Marketing Association (DMA) reports that telephone or telemarketing is the next most frequently used medium, followed by email and DRTV infomercials.

Regardless of the medium, circulation is the most common audience measure for direct marketing efforts. In the case of mail, telemarketing, and email, marketers know their planned audience circulation in advance of their media activity based on the number or count of names included on the mailing list, calling list, or listserv being used. In the case of DRTV infomercials, the audience is estimated based on television research projections for the time period when the infomercial will be broadcast.

The other important measurement metric for direct marketing media is response rate. In service to its membership, the DMA annually publishes a report detailing average response rates by media form for all direct marketing media. According to its most recent report, despite the U.S. government's implementation of the "do-not-call" registry, the telephone is still the medium with the highest average response rate at 8.6 percent.[21] Second on the list for 2005 was DRTV at 8.1 percent and then mail and email, with response rates ranging from 2.2 percent for postcards to 2.5 percent for email to 3.7 percent for catalogs and dimensional mail campaigns.

Promotional Media

In very general terms, promotional marketing is defined as marketers' use of incentives (of any kind) together with branded communications to spur an increase in product sales. Such incentives include price discounts and cents-off coupons, sampling and value-added premiums, and postpurchase rebate offers. Regardless of the kind of incentive offered, there are certain, specialty delivery systems that serve as the media of promotional marketing. In this section we will look briefly at newspaper-delivered promotional media and store-delivered promotional media.

Several different media companies deliver promotional marketing messages specifically through newspapers. Two of the biggest companies in this field are Valassis and the News America Corporation. One of the most frequently used services (especially among consumer packaged goods companies) offered by Valassis is the freestanding cooperative insert distributed through Sunday newspapers nationwide in the United States. The cooperative freestanding insert by Valassis is a multipage, preprinted collection of branded messages and incentive offers from multiple marketers. Store-delivered promotional media include checkout or cash register coupons and on-shelf coupon dispensers, among other services, offered by companies like Catalina Marketing.

As we have seen with many media already, circulation is one of the key audience measurement metrics for promotional media as well. However, once again, circulation is only a measure of potential, not actual, audience for any message. In promotional marketing, because the branded message carries with it an incentive of some sort, response rates are another key metric that marketers use to compare media alternatives.

Marketers track consumer response to promotional marketing activities by measuring redemption of the incentives offered. Whether the incentive is a simple cents-off coupon or something more complicated like a mail-in rebate or some branded premium item, the marketer has to cover the cost associated with the incentive. Marketers have therefore established effective systems for counting redemptions. Often marketers will even imprint the incentive form (for example, the coupon) with special codes unique to each medium employed in delivering the offer.

Public Relations Media

The primary media for traditional public relations activities, like press releases and publicity events, could be any of the current or future news media systems. The basic goal of public relations is to secure mentions in the press, so it makes sense that press mentions are a measure of public relations success. Of course, a press mention by the *Cedar Rapids Gazette* (Iowa), with 64,000 in circulation and about 250,000 in adult readership, should not be counted the same as a press mention in the *Cleveland Plain Dealer* (Ohio), with its circulation of 360,000 and 884,000 adult readers.

If the objective of a public relations effort is to extend the marketer's message, then it would be important to count the total potential audience either by circulation/audience or by readership/listenership/viewership. Good public relations firms will collect press clippings in a neat book and match audience numbers with the press clippings to project what are called total impressions. Across all media forms, the total impressions figure represents the total, gross sum of all audiences reached with a message. Impressions are a kind of gross audience number that can be totaled across media forms using either the unduplicated circulation/audience estimates or readership/listenership/viewership projections for each medium, so long as the method is applied consistently for each medium.

New developments in public relations are changing the traditional perspective on public relations measurement metrics. For example, one new area in public relations is blogging. The term *blogging* comes from the Internet term *Web log*, a kind of online, real-time journal. Companies and public relations firms have found that they can in effect manufacture their own favorable press mentions by posting news and information with a company slant regularly on Web logs. Many public relations firms today are helping corporate clients develop and maintain topic-specific Web logs as a public relations tactic.

Blogs exist on the Internet almost exactly like any other Internet site. They are easy to create, can be built with syndication features to automatically "broadcast" new postings to interested readers, and can be designed to capture typical Internet audience counts in the form of site visitors. More importantly, topic-specific blogs can become very important to people who care about the same topic. When that happens, readers can become regular readers who might actually link to the blog site. In the Internet domain, links are like audience gold, and companies with the most relevant topic blog sites can become the chief Internet source for information. We will talk in more detail about blogs and other Internet-based new media forms in Chapter 14.

Events and Sponsorships

Marketer branded special events, named sponsorships, and branded product placements are nothing new to marketers. These tactics may seem new because of all the recent coverage in the trade press about high-profile brand name integration activities, but marketers have been using these tactics for many, many years. Back in the 1950s and 1960s, major marketers like Procter & Gamble owned television programming; Procter & Gamble still owns daytime soap opera programming today. And other marketers were major television sponsors; remember the Geritol sponsorship of the now infamous television game show *21*? If not, you might want to take a moment and have some fun with this; rent the 1994 movie *Quiz Show* to see just how involved some television sponsors were. Product placements were usually a big part of such sponsorships back then. So why all the big press these days?

After many years of withdrawal and retreat from tactics that were widely considered over-commercialized and inappropriate (even unethical at times), marketers in the last several years have rushed back headlong to embrace these tactics once again. One of the primary reasons for the change in sentiment has been the sea change in consumer media usage behavior. We discussed this at length in the previous chapter, but it bears repeating. Consumers today are time-shifting and multitasking their media consumption, and marketers fear that this divided attention renders moot the customary delivery of brand communications.

Another factor in this equation has been a growing sense of dissatisfaction among marketers with the declining audiences of traditional communications media and a lack of consistency in, and applicability of, audience measurement techniques. Marketers have turned away from the traditional communications media to other tactics like events because they can see firsthand consumers' attendance and involvement with the event and by extension the sponsoring brand. The result of this recent rush to these new/old tactics, coupled with today's steady emphasis on company financial performance, has been an increase in demand for consistent audience and performance measurement techniques.

In the area of sponsorships and event marketing, regardless of the specific tactic in use, the primary measurement metric is audience impressions. As we mentioned earlier, impressions are a gross audience figure, a gross sum of all people potentially exposed to a sponsor's message or signage, counted for each potential exposure. Gross audience measures for events and sponsorships can be very small or very large depending on the marketer's tactic. In addition to the gross audience measure, marketers also need some way of assessing the quality of the audience contact associated with the event or sponsorship.

For example, with special events run by the marketer, the audience impressions figure is generally small compared to larger media activities, but highly focused on a specific target audience. Marketers that use events as a key marketing tactic do so not for the chance to reach a large audience, but for the quality contact time accomplished with a smaller, selective target audience as was the case when the Procter & Gamble laundry detergent brand Tide hosted its first pajama party event at the Plaza Hotel in New York City in 2004.

Sponsorships, on the other hand, can generally accomplish very large counts of audience impressions, but the quality of message delivery may be nominal. For example, if a marketer has purchased a sign placement in a stadium and that sign can be seen on televised broadcasts of sporting events in the stadium, then the cumulative audience impressions figure for that sign would count the stadium attendance for each sporting event and the television audience for each broadcast for every time that the sign appeared during the broadcast. This can add up to a very large audience count, but the message exposure may be very limited—merely the marketer's name, maybe a Web site address or phone number.

Big sponsor marketers spend a lot of money for this kind of simple name recognition. Chase bank invests $75 million to $80 million every year sponsoring sports teams and events just for the name recognition. For example, the marketer's name is publicized every time its Chase Field, where the Arizona Diamondbacks play baseball, is mentioned in newspapers and magazines, on television and radio. While Chase bank probably paid a lot more, it has been estimated that stadium naming rights throughout the United States cost an average of $2.9 million.[22]

Most of the time marketers rely on marketing agencies using a combination of sources to estimate the audience potential and resulting value of a sponsorship deal. Certain agencies specialize in developing sponsorships and events for major clients, while other major marketing agencies have special divisions dedicated to event and sponsorship marketing. The idea is to centralize the particular expertise needed to create and evaluate this kind of marketing activity. With so much marketing money now going in this direction, marketers have a growing need for systems to measure audiences accurately and consistently. In July 2004, for example, Nielsen Sports, a division of Nielsen Media Research, launched the Sponsorship Scorecard service, which measures marketer signage appearing on television broadcasts of sports events.[23]

Product Placements

Product placement is the marketing practice of integrating branded products or brand name mentions into entertainment content. This includes branded product placements in movies, television shows, music videos, cartoons and comics, and video games. It also includes brand name mentions in music lyrics and written works of fiction like short stories and novels. We are also now seeing branded product placements in the virtual world with brand avatars on Second Life Island and brand character profiles on social networking Web sites. For example, MySpace.com members can join the "friends" network for Miss Helga (Volkswagen) or the Roaming Gnome (Travelocity), among others.

The idea, of course, is to integrate the brand into an entertainment environment rather than interrupting the entertainment to pause for a marketer's message. When a marketer's message interrupts the entertainment, the consumer may time-shift, skip, or otherwise avoid it, but when the brand is displayed in the context of the entertainment there is no interruption to avoid.

Product placement can be accomplished in many different ways, and the costs and value of the exposure can vary significantly depending on the extent of the integration. On the simplest level, the branded product might be visible in the background of a scene. The next level shows the branded product in use, something like James Bond driving his BMW. Then there is character interplay with the brand, providing an endorsement of sorts, as when Tony Soprano (in the 2004 season of the HBO series *The Sopranos*) said, "This is a Motorola, the best f...... phone there is." Finally, the highest level of product placement is integration into the plot, like FedEx in the movie *Castaway* and the Mini Cooper automobile in the movie *The Italian Job*.

As with sponsorships and events, measuring product placements requires both an estimate of the audience reached and an assessment of the quality of the brand name exposure based on the level of integration. Some marketers and agencies use their own means to determine the value of product placement opportunities. Others like General Motors, Kraft, Unilever, and Ford are working with outside researchers and third-party evaluators.

Nielsen Media Research is one of the many companies developing measurement techniques in this area. Nielsen started tracking product placements on prime-time network television programming in September 2003.[24] Marketers and agencies that subscribe to Nielsen can get a report on the number of minutes and seconds of brand exposure along with the rating for the program where the brand was placed. Another major researcher in this area is the product placement firm iTVX, which has developed a metric it calls a Q-ratio to measure whether a product placement is effective or not.[25] The iTVX Q-ratio uses a matrix of variables to assign a value for any given product placement based on such factors as foreground versus background or audio versus visual placement of the brand.

So far, we have discussed the current techniques and practices of media audience research across a broad spectrum of advertising and integrated marketing communications (IMC) media delivery systems. We have also touched briefly on some of the changes we expect to see in the near future. Our focus has been fairly specific to each particular media form, because, as we have said, the field of media audience research developed in support of each individual media form. In the final section of this chapter, we will shift our focus to the future across all media forms and address some of the biggest media research issues facing this industry.

OMNIBUS ISSUES IN MEDIA AND AUDIENCE MEASUREMENT

By this point in the chapter we have identified some of the major problems that marketers face today in this field of media audience measurement. The entire industry infrastructure is based on using audience measurement techniques that are unique to specific media forms. The one and only common denominator, the only measure that can effectively be compared across all media and IMC activities, is total audience impressions, a gross measure of total potential audience exposures. And even that is measured differently for different media; sometimes it is a passive, automated measure and sometimes a self-reported measure.

As marketers push forward to delivering integrated branded communications across multiple media systems, the media research industry is faced with several far-reaching omnibus issues. In this section we will discuss the five big issues that span all the major media forms we considered in this chapter. All of these omnibus issues were either identified explicitly or implied in the WFA "Blueprint for Consumer-Centric Holistic Measurement," to which we have referred several times.[26]

Audience Measurements Should Be Comparable Across All Media Forms

The first problem faced by marketers is that audience measurement metrics and techniques today are not applicable or comparable across multiple media forms. If marketers are to effectively integrate communications across multiple media forms, they have to be able to measure audiences and combine and compare audience measures across all forms of media. This is virtually impossible to do today on any meaningful level.

Research services currently measure broadcast audiences one way, print audiences a different way, and interactive media audiences in a couple of different ways. Marketing agencies have the ability to combine media audiences across multiple media forms only at a gross, aggregate level. There are circumstances, often at the request of the client, where agencies will prepare such aggregate calculations; they do so by aggregating audience measures at a gross level first and then discounting the gross measure down to a more meaningful, net audience effect. In these circumstances, most media planning and research professionals will caution clients about some of the underlying issues that make combined media measures somewhat suspect.

One of the biggest underlying issues we have already discussed is the question of passive or automated audience measurement techniques as compared to self-reported interview and survey measurement techniques. Interactive audience measurement techniques are for the most part already passive, and there is hope for a future of passive measurement of broadcast media audiences; however, no such techniques exist yet for print media. The WFA Blueprint explicitly calls for passive measurement techniques across all media forms, seeing this as the most accurate accounting of an audience, not subject to confusion, forgetfulness, misrepresentation, or other bias.

Product and Media Usage Information Should Be Derived
From a Single Source

Single-source data is important to marketers and marketing agencies as they work to match current and prospective product users to their media preferences. The most common media audience research services today provide their audience estimates, at best, in terms of basic demographic subsets like gender and age. Today's marketers have already learned to think of targeted audiences in terms that go well beyond simple demographics. Unfortunately, though, because of the way the media audience measures are reported, marketers have to simplify target audience definitions into basic demographics to be able to compare media forms.

Many marketers wonder whether demographics will have any meaning at all for targeting purposes under a consumer-first planning model in the future. The WFA Blueprint explicitly addresses this point, calling for consistent sources of information to "better understand the relationship between shopping and media usage" as well as better linkage between target audience analysis and media audience measurement techniques used by marketing agencies.

We mentioned earlier in this chapter that services like MRI and SMRB are making some progress toward this goal, but these services are used only by marketers and agencies. MRI and SMRB audience measures are not considered acceptable by media owners. This issue cannot be resolved until all the industry's constituents can agree on a consistent set of measurement metrics.

Techniques Should Be Consumer-Centric and Measure Multitasking
Media Consumption

In the previous chapter we discussed at some length the issues of media fragmentation, audience splintering, and multitasking media consumption behavior by today's consumer. Almost everyone in the industry seems to understand that the answer is to approach the media planning problem from a consumer-first perspective so marketers can deliver branded messages at the times and in the places where the right consumers will be available and receptive to the marketing communications.

The media owners and marketing agencies also need to recognize that multitasking media consumption behavior exists and will continue into the foreseeable future. In the WFA Blueprint, the world's major marketers call for measurement sources that will provide insight into the consumer's multitasking media behavior.

What will be particularly important in this area of development will be the ability to effectively measure synergy between the media in those multimedia situations. As we discussed in Chapter 11, Prasad Naik and Kalyan Raman have done promising work in this area. In their 2003 paper "Understanding the Impact of Synergy in Multimedia Communications," Naik and Raman propose a new measurement methodology to estimate and calculate the interactions and synergistic effects that occur in a multimedia communication situation. In his most recent work, Naik advances this methodology further to an even more robust measure of multimedia synergy and carryover.[27] This is the kind of work that will be needed in the future to allow marketers to effectively measure the synergies that they have long expected would accrue from integrated communications activities.

Research Should Measure Outcomes of Marketing, Not Merely Outputs

So many of the current measurement metrics we discussed throughout this chapter are focused on potential audience exposures. This is looking at outputs, a fundamental feature of the outbound-only communication model that the industry has used for years. Measuring opportunities to be exposed is the best marketers can get when they as communicators focus on sending out messages to which receivers may or may not attend.

Marketers should instead be looking at and measuring actual audience contacts and the results of the marketing communication efforts. Marketers have for years been pleading for industry measures of returns or results. Today, as the media have become more interactive and as media consumers become more comfortable interacting with the media, the time is right for media research that measures the outcome, the results of marketing communication.

Measurements Should Quantify the Effects of Foreground and Background Messaging

Last but certainly not least, a research system or process for identifying and measuring the differential effects of foreground and background messaging will be needed in the future. This kind of sensitivity is needed primarily to ascertain foreground and background media status and understand consumers' attention shifting in multimedia situations. As discussed in Chapter 11 with the media consumption planning model, the communication effect of attention shifting can be either synergistic, adding impact to messaging, or distracting, diminishing the impact of the message. Marketers will need a special kind of research to help them understand and quantify these opposite effects.

This kind of measurement and sensitivity could also be useful in understanding how alternative IMC activities, like product placements, may work for different marketers. Of the different product placement levels described above, the minimal level, where the branded product is merely visible in a scene, is basically a background kind of placement. The highest level, where the product is integral to the plot of the show, is a foreground placement. For marketers with a high enough preexisting profile, this type of measurement might be able to show that background messaging alone is enough to positively impact the business. Many marketing dollars could be saved and increased financial returns might be gained if marketers could know this about their brands.

SUMMING UP

In this chapter we have talked about current methods and techniques used in measuring media audiences. We discussed the nature of this business model, with the researcher in the middle between the sometimes-conflicting interests of media owners, marketers, and marketing agencies. We considered the measurement metrics and methods used most often for each of the individual media forms, for traditional media as well as for media delivery systems and other touchpoint marketing activities that have become increasingly attractive to marketers.

Finally, we briefly reviewed some of the bigger issues that the media research industry will face in the future. Despite these issues, maybe even because of these issues, we see a challenging and exciting future ahead for media research.

NOTES

1. Wikipedia, "Mass Media History," http://en.wikipedia.org/wiki/mass_media#history.

2. I. Darby, "'Silos' Preclude Digital Process, IAB Asserts," *Campaign,* April 12, 2002.

3. A. Baldo, "Media: The Enemy Within," *Financial World,* April 16, 1997.

4. J. Sissors and R. Baron, *Advertising Media Planning,* 6th ed. (New York: McGraw-Hill, 2002), pp. 57–61.

5. F. Nichols, "ROI Begins at the Cash Register: Transactional Data Paired With Ad Spending Yields Accountability," *Mediaweek,* March 21, 2005.

6. AC Nielsen, "Our History," http://acnielsen.com/company/history.shtml.

7. Nielsen Media Research, "Nielsen & TV: A Shared History," www.nielsenmedia.com/nc/portal/site/Public/menuitem.138fa1f1af8ff0919a69c71047a062a0/?vgnextoid=fb5579a21afc5010VgnVCM100000880a260aRCRD.

8. Museum of Broadcast Communication, "Arbitron: U.S. Ratings Service," www.museum.tv/archives/etv/A/htmlA/arbitron/arbitron.htm.

9. MediaMark Research Inc., www.mediamark.com; Simmons Market Research Bureau, www.smrb.com.

10. J.P. Jones, "Single Source Research Begins to Fulfill Its Promise," *Journal of Advertising Research* 35, no. 3 (May/June 1995).

11. J. Mandese, "Hitting the Mother Lode," *Broadcasting & Cable,* November 8, 2004.

12. M. Hess, "Finding the Missing Link," *Mediaweek,* June 11, 2007, www.mediaweek.com/mw/departments/columns/article_display.jsp?vnu_content_id=1003596683.

13. S. McClellan, "Ratings Companies Turn to Nets to Fund ROI Tool," *Adweek,* October 3, 2005.

14. World Federation of Advertisers, "Blueprint for Consumer-Centric Holistic Measurement" (September 2005), www.wfanet.org/pdf/med_documents/BlueprintForConsumer-CentricHolisticMeasurement_EN.pdf.

15. M. Azzaro, D. Binder, R. Clawson, C. Lloyd, M.A. Shaver, and O. Werder, *Strategic Media Decisions: Understanding the Business End of the Advertising Business* (Chicago: Copy Workshop, 2004), 134–138; Sissors and Baron, *Advertising Media Planning,* pp. 58–61.

16. C. Atkinson, "TV Market Primed for Pay-by-Pod," *Advertising Age,* July 10, 2006.

17. Radio Advertising Bureau, *Radio Marketing Guide and Factbook* (Irving, TX: Radio Advertising Bureau, 2006), www.rab.com.

18. Television Bureau of Advertising and Nielsen Media Research Custom Survey 2006, "Adults Spend More Time With Television Each Day Than They Do With Any Other Medium: Time Spent Yesterday (in Minutes)," Presentation: Media Comparisons 2006, slide 3, www.tvb.org/ppt/events/Conference-2006-Med-Comp.ppt.

19. Traffic Audit Bureau for Media Measurement, "What TAB Measures," www.tabonline.com/what-tabmeasures.aspx.

20. World Federation of Advertisers, "Blueprint for Consumer-Centric Holistic Measurement."

21. Direct Marketing Association, *2005 Response Rate Report,* www.the-dma.org/cgi/disppressrelease?article=712.

22. J. Barker, "Show Time," *Sales & Marketing Management,* June 2005.

23. R. Thomaselli, "Nielsen to Measure Sports Sponsorship," *Advertising Age,* May 3, 2004.

24. T. Wasserman, "How Much Is This Shot Worth?" *Brandweek,* January 17, 2005.

25. T. Wasserman, "Coming Soon: Placement Measurement for Movies," *Brandweek,* August 1, 2005.

26. World Federation of Advertisers, "Blueprint for Consumer-Centric Holistic Measurement."

27. P. Naik and K. Raman, "Understanding the Impact of Synergy in Multimedia Communications," *Journal of Marketing Research* 4, no. 3 (November 2003); P. Naik, D.E. Schultz, and S. Srinivasan, "Perils of Using OLS to Estimate Multimedia Communication Effects," *Journal of Advertising Research* 3, no. 3 (September 2007).

CHAPTER 13

Outbound or Push
Communication Delivery Systems

In this chapter we consider the many forms of outbound communication delivery systems in use among marketers today. As defined earlier, *outbound* is used in the sense that the sender sends a message and the receiver receives it. Many of the traditional media and even the new, emerging forms were designed for delivering outbound messages—from marketers to consumers.

We discuss a wide range of media in this context, from those forms used to deliver advertising and promotional messages to direct marketing and public relations. Our classification of outbound media forms by discipline will generally be consistent with conventional marketing communications wisdom; for example, radio is almost universally considered an advertising medium available for marketers to use on either a national or local level. Some classifications in this chapter, however, may not seem quite so conventional. For example, sponsorships, usually seen as a promotional or public relations medium, are classified here as an advertising tactic under the heading of out-of-home media. Our reasons for certain classifications will become clearer in Chapter 14, where, for example, we address sponsorships as an interactive media form.

Each section is written to provide a basic understanding of the characteristics and marketing uses of each communication channel, followed by a discussion of the strengths and weaknesses, or advantages and disadvantages, of each. The detail provided will be sufficient for an effective understanding of each media form. The reader should be aware, however, that entire books have been written on most individual media forms. Readers interested in a more thorough discussion of any specific medium should consult a library or bookstore for a listing of pertinent materials.

ADVERTISING MEDIA

The already extensive list of media forms used to deliver advertising communications has expanded significantly in the last twenty years. As discussed in Chapter 11, the rapidly accelerating pace of technological change has led simultaneously to the creation of new media forms as well as the development of more advanced advertising avoidance systems. These technological changes have led marketers and agencies to develop new uses of traditional advertising media and to seek out new ways to deliver advertising messages.

It might be useful to first agree on a basic definition of what we mean by advertising. Convention generally considers a communication to be advertising when it is (1) paid for, (2) mediated (delivered via some medium), and (3) attributable to an identifiable sponsor. Using this definition, advertising could include anything from a simple brand name sign in a stadium to a sixty-second branded commercial message on the radio to a long-form branded infomercial on television. So, within the marketing and media services industry, filters have been applied as a way of differentiating marketing communication tactics.

- If a paid-for, mediated, and branded message also contains a promotional offer or incentive of some kind, it is generally considered to be sales promotion, not advertising.
- If a paid-for, mediated, and branded message is delivered addressed to a specific individual consumer or a small group segment of precisely targeted consumers, it is generally considered to be direct marketing, not advertising.
- If a mediated, branded message is delivered, usually unpaid, via some third party like the press, it is generally considered to be public relations, not advertising.

Even with this filtering scheme, our working definition of advertising is still quite extensive. Virtually any communication delivery system could serve marketers as an advertising medium, including the brand contacts discussed in Chapters 10 and 11 and the very new media forms just entering the market, such as iPods, cell phones, and personal digital assistants (PDAs).

For our purposes, we will limit our discussion to the traditional advertising media and some of the new advertising media and activities. We will revisit some media and consider others in the context of our later discussions on sales promotion, direct marketing, and public relations media forms. We begin with the traditional advertising media, including television, radio, magazines, newspapers, and out-of-home formats. We then move on to the newer advertising media, including the Internet and mobile devices. Throughout, where appropriate, we have incorporated discussions of some of the new advertising activities like product placements and sponsorships.

Television

Television is a wonderfully versatile advertising medium. Consumers and marketers alike initially flocked to television because, unlike other media, it delivered communications, news and information, and entertainment. Before the advent of streaming Internet content and cinema advertising, television was the only medium that allowed a marketer to leverage sight, sound, and motion for communicating with its consumers. Personal selling was the only sales communication technique considered better than television, but that was very expensive.

Of course, television was also very expensive as an advertising medium. The television audiences were so large, however, that marketers could average the advertising cost over a large audience base. Media owners and marketing agencies call this calculation the efficiency of a medium—the cost of an advertisement in a medium divided by the total audience delivered by that medium. The most common efficiency measure is called cost-per-thousand (CPM), which means literally the cost of the advertisement per every thousand audience members delivered.

These are the compelling reasons why television, as a medium, has commanded a major

Exhibit 13.1 **U.S. Television Spending as Percent of Total Advertising Spending**

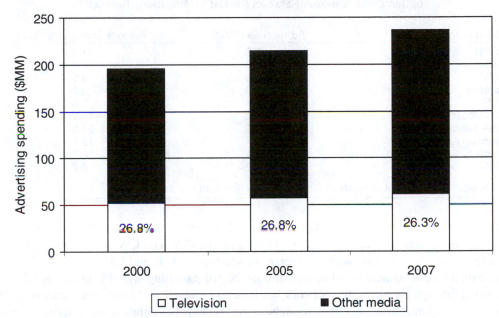

Source: J. Peters and W. Donald, "Industry Surveys: Advertising," *Standard & Poor's Industry Surveys,* December 29, 2005; "100 Leading National Advertisers," *Advertising Age,* June 2003, 2008.

share of all advertising spending in the United States for many years. The multisensory impact, together with the overall efficiency of the medium, made television a powerful advertising form. Even in the last ten years, as advertising costs have escalated and audiences have diminished, television has still attracted more advertising dollars than any other single medium in the United States. According to a recent report by the top-ten media services agency ZenithOptimedia, the television share of all measured advertising expenditures in 2005 (excluding direct mail spending) was 26.8 percent, almost exactly the same as it was in 2000. Exhibit 13.1 shows the consistent percentage of spending on television over this period. Trade industry magazine *Advertising Age* reported that total U.S. television advertising spending for the year 2007 was more than $65 billion.[1] ZenithOptimedia projects that the television share will begin to decline but only slightly.

Part of the continuing attraction of the television medium is that marketers can choose to use television as either a nationally or locally distributed medium.

National Television

There are three commonly recognized ways to deliver marketing messages using television as a national media delivery system: through broadcast television networks, cable television networks, and syndicated program distributors. Each form is named essentially for the way in which its programming content (news and entertainment) is disseminated. Regardless of how the content is disseminated, in each case the advertisers' messages are distributed embedded as commercial breaks in the content.

Exhibit 13.2 **2005 Advertising Spending by Cable Network**
Top Ten Cable Television Networks Ranked by Advertising Revenue

Cable network	Ad revenue ($MM)	Percent Change vs. 2004
ESPN	1,295	11.3
TNT	914	25.2
MTV	865	3.5
Lifetime	856	3.0
TBS	774	2.8
Nickelodeon	712	−15.7
USA Network	708	24.9
Discovery Channel	464	12.4
Comedy Central	451	16.0
CNN	442	4.2

Source: Advertising Age FactPack 2006, Crain Communications, Inc.

Broadcast Television Networks. There are currently five major broadcast television networks in the United States: ABC, CBS, NBC, FOX, and The CW. The CW is the newest, having started in the fall of 2006 with the merger of the former WB and UPN networks.[2] These are called broadcast networks because of how the programming signal is broadcast; that is, beamed through the air from a network headquarters transmitter to receiver locations at affiliate television stations in cities throughout the country. Local television stations become network affiliates when the station owner or manager signs an exclusive affiliation agreement with a broadcast network.

Cable Television Networks. There are at present about 500 cable television networks available to consumers and marketers throughout the country. Cable networks are different from broadcast networks in the way the programming signal is distributed. Cable networks also send signals from a network headquarters transmitter, but cable programming signals are beamed to satellites and bounced to cable system operators equipped with satellite receivers who then forward the signals to subscribing homes where the home owner has paid a fee to receive the cable network programming from the cable system operator.

In the 1970s and 1980s, when cable television became popular, programming was delivered to cable system operators by satellite and then distributed to consumer homes by special underground or overhead wiring. Satellite receiver (i.e., satellite dish) technology became affordable and accessible to consumers on a wide scale in the late 1990s. Consumers today receive cable network programming in their homes either through cable wiring or through satellite dish receivers. Either way, the technology is still referred to as "cable" because of the original delivery system.

Cable network television is a large and growing part of the national television business. Advertiser spending on cable network television increased to almost $20 billion in 2007, an increase of almost 7 percent in a year when total advertiser spending declined slightly. The largest of the individual cable networks draw a lot of advertising revenue as shown in Exhibit 13.2.

Syndicated Program Distributors. Syndicated program distributors take popular television shows and market them directly to local stations. Stations pay syndicators for the rights to air a show and marketers pay the syndicators to embed commercials in the show. When a syndicator puts together enough stations, the effect is almost as good as network television in terms of national coverage area. And if the show is popular enough, as are game shows, talk shows, and primetime reruns like *ER* and *Friends*, then the audience can be almost as good as network television, too.

Media owners have a vested interest in syndicating programming to realize the added revenue potential both from local stations that want and need programming to fill time slots and from marketers that may use syndicated programming to achieve national advertising effects at a lower cost. Many of the companies that own the major broadcast networks in the United States also maintain a syndicated programming division. For example, CBS, which owns the CBS television network, also owns Showtime King World Productions, which is a major distributor of syndicated programs.[3]

Local Television

Advertisers can also utilize television as a local market medium. National advertisers sometimes use local television to add marketing emphasis in stronghold or developmental cities. Also, local advertisers such as restaurants and auto dealers use local television advertising to support their business. Whether the marketer is a national or a local brand, there are two different ways to leverage television in a local geography.

The first is to work through a local television station. Many local television stations in cities throughout the country draw much of their television programming from a national programming source like a broadcast network or a national program syndicator. Even so, these same local stations also create original programming of their own, such as local news programs. Whether the programming originates nationally or locally, the local station has a certain amount of commercial time to sell locally. National and local advertisers and agencies alike negotiate with the stations to run local advertisements the same way they do on the national side.

The second way is to work through a local cable system operator, the local media company that takes the cable network signal and forwards it to subscriber homes. Cable system operators do not usually have as much available time to sell, but they do have some. What often happens is that local advertisers' commercials are dropped in to replace other commercials embedded in the cable program. Sometimes, when the locally purchased commercials are cut-in over national commercials, the national commercial runs for a second or two, then stops and switches to the local commercial.

Television as a Marketing Medium

Television offers many strengths that marketers can use to their advantage, even in the face of escalating costs and diminishing audiences. It also, however, has some disadvantages.

One advantage already mentioned briefly is impact. Television allows marketers to deliver multisensory branded communications with sight, sound, and motion as well as bright, vivid colors and graphics. This kind of multidimensional communication makes television powerful; consumers can relate to the stories they see on television, even the short, thirty-second advertising stories.

Second, television is very flexible as a marketing medium. Marketers can use a variety of common commercial lengths, from a brief mention of a brand name to a sixty-second unit. Marketers use this flexibility to address their particular marketing needs. If brand-name awareness is what matters, then a short commercial can get the brand name out in a cost-effective way. If the marketer's message is more complex, then a longer commercial may be needed to tell the marketer's story.

Also, marketers can choose to run television commercials at different times of the day, called dayparts. For advertising and programming purposes, the typical television schedule is presented in six dayparts: early morning, daytime, fringe (the brief block of time just before primetime programming begins), primetime, late night, and overnight. For marketing purposes, we know that consumers and their motivations can be different at different times of the day and this can be an important advantage of television.

A third feature of television as an advertising medium is its intrusiveness, which can be a bad thing for consumers and both a strength and a weakness for marketers. Television advertising interrupts the program. While commercial disruption of the television story can draw attention to the advertising message, it may also be an irritation to the consumer, who can either watch the commercial or do something else. With the technology available today—Video-on-Demand (VoD), digital video recorders (DVRs), and even remote controls—consumers are likely to avoid the commercial interruption. In a recent survey of 400 DVR owners, 87 percent reported they frequently use the "skip" function to bypass commercials.[4] However, marketers and agencies feel that if the advertisement itself is worthy, informative, and entertaining, then consumers will stay tuned and pay attention.

Another major problem for marketers is the increasing cost associated with television advertising; cost-efficiency is no longer an offsetting advantage. Marketers using television as an advertising medium have to be prepared for the escalating costs of buying the advertising time from the television station or network. A major consulting firm, McKinsey & Co., reported in 2006 that advertising spending, in real dollars (adjusted for inflation), on primetime broadcast network television commercials had increased about 40 percent over the previous ten years.[5] Over the same ten-year period, the audience for primetime broadcast network television declined by almost 50 percent. That represents a major hit to the cost-efficiency of television as a marketing medium.

Changes Affecting Television

We have already discussed some of the many changes and technological advancements affecting television as an advertising medium. For example, one factor is the growing popularity of product placements in the United States. As we mentioned in Chapter 12, product placements are those occasions when a marketer pays a fee to have a brand name product integrated into program content. Product placements are happening in all forms of entertainment programming, including movies, music videos, and video games, but the biggest area has been television programming.

Marketers are increasingly using product placements in television as a way to circumvent consumers' current time shifting and commercial avoidance behaviors. The general idea is to integrate the branded product into the content of the television program so that the consumer will see the brand name and perhaps even interpret the stars' use of the brand as an endorsement of some sort. This strategy, of course, will not work for every brand.

Exhibit 13.3 **Radio Advertising Revenue Trends**

1996

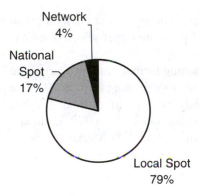

Network
4%

National
Spot
17%

Local Spot
79%

2005

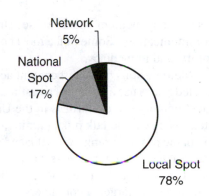

Network
5%

National
Spot
17%

Local Spot
78%

Source: Radio Advertising Bureau, *Radio Marketing Guide and Factbook* (Irving, TX: Radio Advertising Bureau, 2006), www.rab.com.

Product placement deals are usually negotiated by the marketer's agency directly with the production company creating the television program. Deals are negotiated differently depending on the degree of product integration into the program. It generally costs less to simply show a branded product in a show and considerably more to have the stars say something about the product while they interact with it. Most television producers understand that brand name product use in their show may be seen as an endorsement, so they set their prices accordingly.

Radio

Radio is a predominantly local medium. According to the 2006 *Radio Marketing Guide and Factbook*, there are about 10,700 licensed commercial radio stations in cities throughout the United States.[6] Most of these operate in one of the 270 cities where radio audiences are measured by the Arbitron media research service. The *Radio Marketing Guide* reports that radio advertising revenues have grown more than 60 percent over the last ten years to $20 billion, 95 percent of that invested at the local station level as shown in Exhibit 13.3.

There are also radio networks and radio syndicators so national marketers can utilize radio as a national medium. While network radio spending by national advertisers has doubled in the last ten years, total spending in this area was only $1 billion, about 5 percent of all radio spending in 2007.

Radio remains a successful media form because of its predominantly local nature. Radio stations get out there with their listeners. Many stations conduct live remote broadcasts from locations in their home market. Others broadcast phone calls from listeners who want to speak on some matter. These tactics have helped consumers know and identify with their favorite local stations. Except for the occasional syndicated radio star, consumers primarily know the local station personalities, the on-air talent. All of this makes radio a very personal kind of medium, and the personal nature of the medium is what makes it attractive to marketers.

Radio as a Marketing Medium

As with any medium, marketers see strengths and weaknesses in using radio to deliver brand communications. Some of the most compelling strengths of radio are target selectivity, flexibility, and immediacy.

Radio stations broadcast content according to a programming format. Stations across the United States use a variety of an estimated thirty-two different programming formats. The five most popular station formats in the United States are country music, with more than 2,000 stations; news and talk programming, with 1,300 stations; oldies music, with 770; Latin and Hispanic programming, with 700; and adult contemporary music, with 680. Marketers understand that consumers' mind-set and motivations can be very different depending on whether they listen to country music or news and talk radio. Marketers can use station formats to focus selectively on targeted consumers.

As a medium, radio offers marketers great flexibility. For example, marketers can use radio for different purposes at different times of the day or on different days of the week. Fast-food marketer McDonald's advertises a full menu of breakfast items on radio during the morning hours, when many people are in their cars driving to work. McDonald's then uses different commercials later in the day to advertise lunch and dinner menu items. For McDonald's competitor Wendy's, whose key brand promise is that it stays open late, late-night radio advertising is an effective way to reach consumers who may have missed dinner or stayed out late partying.

Marketers also create different radio commercials to match different station programming formats. Producing radio commercials is relatively inexpensive compared to television, so marketers can make multiple versions of the same commercial message. This kind of creative flexibility makes it possible for the marketer's message to come across as relevant in the context of the media environment.

Finally, radio stations broadcast commercial messages in a flexible range of styles. The most common radio commercial is a sixty-second prerecorded advertisement, but marketers can also create longer or shorter advertisements. Marketers can also prerecord part of a message and have the local radio station staff read locally specific information. Or marketers can provide the radio station with a script and have the local station personalities read the script live.

A third major advantage of radio is immediacy. Radio is live and on all the time. Marketers can run or change radio messages on very short notice. If a marketer one morning wants or needs to put out a message to consumers, that message can be on the air on radio stations locally or nationwide within a couple of hours. This immediacy can be very important to some advertisers. A local retailer who wants to announce a special sale merely needs to write the script for the message and contact the station to buy the time for a live-announcer read.

As personal, adaptable, and flexible as radio is, it also has some serious limitations as a marketing medium. The high level of advertising clutter and the background nature of the medium together present marketers with the challenge of having to break through so that consumers will notice their communications.

When any advertising medium carries too many advertising messages, we call the result clutter. In broadcast, clutter is measured by the ratio of commercial minutes per every hour of programming. While television clutter has increased significantly over the last several years, studies show that radio clutter has always been high. Because it is a less expensive advertising medium and attractive to both local and national advertisers, radio stations run advertising for about 20 percent of each programming hour. Some of the largest U.S. radio owners, such as Clear Channel Communications and Infinity Broadcasting, have taken steps lately to declutter the radio airwaves, but clutter is still a problem for both marketers and consumers.[7]

Another major problem for radio is that most people, most of the time, are doing something else while they are listening. We talked about this phenomenon generally in our Chapter 11 discussion of simultaneous media consumption. With radio in particular, this has been going on for many, many years. People listen to radio while driving in the car, reading a book or magazine, or falling asleep at night, and radio is frequently used as a form of pleasant background noise in the workplace or at the grocery store. As reported in a recent SIMM (Simultaneous Media Usage Studies) study, almost 60 percent of the survey respondents indicated they regularly or occasionally listen to radio while they are online.[8]

Changes Affecting Radio

Radio is one media form in which some consolidation is occurring as a result of new technology. In 2002 there were almost 14,000 licensed commercial radio stations in the United States. That number dropped to fewer than 11,000 stations in just three years. One recent development that may be behind this trend is the emergence of subscription-based satellite radio services like XM and Sirius. XM and Sirius earn their revenue from consumer subscriptions and they do not sell advertising. The result, for consumers, is a blissfully commercial-free listening experience. Consumer subscriptions to satellite radio have increased significantly in recent years, especially as car manufacturers have started making satellite radio a part of their options packages in popular makes.[9]

The problem for marketers is also significant. We earlier reported that advertising spending on radio has increased dramatically. This has happened while the number of radio stations nationwide has declined. The implication is even more advertising clutter in an already cluttered media environment. Since there is a limit to how much advertising clutter a consumer will tolerate, this could lead to long-term troubles for radio as a marketing medium.

Magazines

Magazines are useful as a marketing medium in many ways. Marketers utilize magazines, especially in published, hard-copy form, to deliver all manner of branded communication messages, including simple advertising pages; pages with free product samples, coupons, or reader response cards; and multipage pullout inserts. Simple advertising pages are by far the most common marketing application, but this is changing as more marketers aggressively seek new ways to make their advertising messages stand out.

As a part of the total media picture, ZenithOptimedia projected magazine advertising revenues for 2005 would reach more than $24 billion, about 11 percent of all marketers' media spending. While business has been good and revenue growth is projected to continue, the projected rate of growth of advertising spending for magazines is expected to be slower than that for most of the other major media forms: 1.8 percent growth per year (2000 through 2008) for magazines compared to 2.8 percent per year for all media spending.

Marketers advertise in magazines to reach specific audiences, which are measured by circulation. Unfortunately, circulation trends are not entirely healthy in the magazine business. Consumer subscriptions account for 87 percent of all U.S. magazine circulation, according to the Audit Bureau of Circulation, while 13 percent of circulation comes from single-copy magazine sales. Over the last five years, subscription-based circulation has declined by an average of 0.3 percent per year. At the same time, single-copy sales have declined an average of 4.3 percent per year.[10]

One of the contributing factors in declining circulation is probably change in consumers' reading behavior. General indicators today suggest that consumers in the United States have become scanners rather than readers. Magazine publishers insist that consumers still read magazines, but, while they have research to prove their point, it might be more accurate to say that consumers still look at or quickly flip through their favorite magazines. Annual multimedia comparison studies from several sources show that consumers in 2005 spent about 16 minutes per day (on average) reading magazines, as compared to 265 minutes watching television and 85 minutes on the Internet.

Another contributing factor in declining circulation is the decline in the number of consumer magazine titles available in the United States. A full one-third of consumer-only magazines have folded since a publishing high point of 9,300 titles in 1999. Even so, according to the 2008 National Directory of Magazines, there are still more than 6,800 consumer magazines published in the United States and another 12,000 business-to-business magazines. Magazines are still a very important part of the U.S. media mix for both national and local advertisers.

Marketers use advertising in national, regional, and local magazines to deliver brand messages to consumers. The list of national magazines includes such well-known titles as *Newsweek*, *Sports Illustrated*, and *Better Homes & Gardens*. These magazines are written from a national perspective, covering the title subject matter in a way that is relevant to all of the United States and not just one particular area. Regional and local magazines, like *Sunset* (Pacific coast) and *Chicago Parent*, respectively, provide information and entertainment specific to a narrower coverage area.

Magazines as a Marketing Medium

The Magazine Publisher's Association (MPA) cites a list of ten reasons why marketers should use magazines as a marketing medium. That is its job, to support the members of the association. Here we consider two important strengths of magazines: target selectivity and advertising staying power.

Marketers can use magazine titles to zero in on narrow target audiences for selectivity and focus of brand communications. Of course, there are large circulation, general market magazine titles like *TV Guide*, *Reader's Digest*, *People Weekly*, and *Time*, but there are far more subject-specific magazines than there are general market publications. The range is very broad, from magazines like *Architectural Digest*, well suited for marketers like Anderson Windows and Kohler Faucets, to extremely focused magazines like *Cat Fancy*, which is perfect for brands like Meow Mix and Tidy Cat.

Another important advantage of magazines is staying power. Most consumers keep magazines around for some length of time. That means the advertisements in the magazine stay around as well. Most people do not read a magazine in one sitting; they tend to read a little and then put the magazine aside for another day. Every time a person picks up a magazine represents another advertising opportunity, another possible exposure to the brand messages within. This can be particularly important for marketers with a lot to say in their advertising. If the advertisement has to be lengthy or complex, consumers can refer back to the message as needed.

On the downside, magazines are often cluttered with advertisements. According to the MPA, magazines today run an average of 53 percent editorial content with 47 percent advertising pages. That ratio is considerably higher than in television or radio. It should be noted that despite the high-clutter environment, most consumers do not mind advertising in magazines, mainly because magazine advertisements do not intrude or interrupt in the same manner as broadcast commercials. Consumers flipping through a magazine can choose to stop and read an advertisement or simply flip past it.

Another marketing disadvantage is long lead times for advertising. Because of the publishing process, many magazines require advertising materials well in advance of the actual publication date. For a magazine published monthly, the lead time can be two to three months in advance. That could be a deal breaker for marketers with time-sensitive messaging needs.

Changes Affecting Magazines

Two big factors are impacting the ways that marketers use magazines. One is magazine Web sites, as more and more magazines are publishing content and selling advertising space on the Internet. Magazine publishers use Web sites as a way to extend circulation. This is especially true for magazines that were created for a young target audience. For example, the magazine *Teen People*, launched as an immediate success in 1998, added a Web site shortly thereafter to build interest and circulation among its targeted audience, teens. In July 2006 the publisher, Time Warner, announced it would no longer produce a print edition.[11] The Web site will continue because it is popular among teens and the advertisers who want to reach them.

The other factor for the future of magazines is custom publishing. In an effort to escape from the cluttered environment of magazines and in order to more directly control the editorial content surrounding their advertisements, marketers have started publishing their own magazines. One example is Kraft's *Food & Family* magazine. This is both a magazine and a Web site sponsored exclusively by Kraft brands. Consumers can sign up for the magazine by visiting the kraftfoods.com Web site. It has one of the largest circulations in the United States because it is free. Another marketer example is Chrysler, with its Chrysler, Jeep, and Dodge magazines published for and mailed to consumers who own these vehicles. Publishing for custom magazines is handled by major magazine publishing groups like Meredith, Time Inc., Hachette, and Hearst.[12] In addition to traditional magazines and magazine Web sites, these publishers have found custom publishing a lucrative new source of marketing revenue, and marketers have found it an extremely effective way to communicate with the small group of consumers representing the largest percentage of the product's volume.

Exhibit 13.4 **Declining Readership of Daily and Sunday Newspapers**

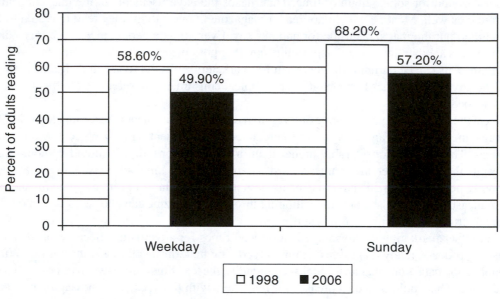

Source: Newspaper Association of America, 2006 Scarborough Research Report.

Newspapers

Like radio, newspapers are a predominantly local advertising medium. Most newspapers deliver in-depth news and information that is immediately relevant at a local level. Newspapers deliver local or national news, business information, sports scores, and feature articles, usually on a daily basis and often at your front door. Newspapers are a rich, dynamic communications medium with something to appeal to almost everyone.

Consumers really use their newspapers and, importantly, they use the advertising in the newspapers. Studies have found that as many as 60 percent of consumers say they look forward to advertising in newspapers. The typical daily newspaper contains advertisements for movies showing at the local cinema, advertising promoting a sale at the local department store or auto dealership, advertisements for local sporting events, and weekly circulars for grocery and electronics stores; of course consumers consider these advertisements to be relevant.

Several newspapers are considered national, with a national perspective on the news and a geographically national audience base. For example, *USA Today* is a truly national newspaper. Another example is the *Wall Street Journal*, which is national in its coverage of business and financial news. The *New York Times* is another paper that many consider national because so many people throughout the country subscribe to it, especially the Sunday edition.

In 2006 there were about 1,460 newspapers published daily in the United States and another 6,700 newspapers published weekly.[13] Just over half of the adults in the United States report that they read the weekday newspaper, while just under 60 percent say they read the Sunday newspaper. Although newspaper readership has declined over the last several years (see Exhibit 13.4), the remaining audience is still large, an upscale group with higher than average educational background and likely to work in a professional or managerial capacity.

The average newspaper reader today is also likely to be older, as young adults have turned to other sources like the Internet for their daily news.

Newspapers as a Marketing Medium

Newspapers are utilized as a marketing medium by local and national advertisers for many reasons. We have already mentioned some of the strong points of newspapers, but two others are prestige and immediacy.

Many people today still think of newspapers as "the press," a third-party, independent observer of the world not influenced by commercialism. Whether or not this view is accurate, people believe what they read in newspapers. Newspapers also have some measure of influence in the community; for example, when they make political endorsements at election time. These factors together lend a certain credibility and prestige to the medium. Many marketers, rightly or wrongly, believe that aura of credibility extends to those businesses that advertise in newspapers.

Immediacy is another benefit of newspapers as a communications and marketing medium. They are published new each day and, in some large U.S. cities, even several times throughout the day. Though newspapers are not as immediate as radio, a marketer can deliver a new advertising message to consumers in tomorrow's morning newspaper.

Aside from declining readership, newspapers as a marketing medium face two other problems today. One is the potentially adverse editorial coverage of a topic. Newspapers are still the press and the editorial and reporting staff will report the news as they need to. Depending on the advertiser and its situation, this can sometimes be bad news for the marketer. For example, airlines tend to be frequent newspaper advertisers, but there are few good news stories about airlines in the paper. Instead, newspapers print news stories about airport security issues, flight cancellations due to bad weather, and, worse still, airplane disasters. Most airline marketers make it a standard part of the contract that advertising should be pulled in the event of a disaster; however, the marketer cannot control the news.

Another issue with newspapers is advertising clutter. In 2007, newspapers took in a total of about $42 billion in advertising revenues. About half of that revenue comes from local retail advertising and 15 percent from national advertisers. The remainder comes from local classified advertising (help wanted, garage sales, personals, etc.). The broad-based marketing appeal of newspapers contributes to an average 50:50 ratio of advertising to editorial content. Although about one-third of the advertising in newspapers is classified advertising, all the advertising adds up to a cluttered environment where marketers have to work hard to stand out.

Changes Affecting Newspapers

Many newspapers throughout the country are trying different methods to draw young adult readers back into the newspaper audience. In a high-profile effort in Chicago, both major newspapers introduced competing dailies written in an irreverent, sound-bite kind of style thought to be appealing to a young adult audience. The *Chicago Sun-Times* introduced *Red-Streak* and the *Chicago Tribune* introduced the *RedEye*. Neither paper succeeded as hoped. The *RedStreak* folded altogether and the Tribune's *RedEye* is offered as a free paper in locations accessible to Chicago commuters.

What has taken hold among newspapers is the Internet. Most newspapers, large and small, now offer Web sites where anyone can access the local news at any time. As with the printed newspaper, consumers tend to consider the newspaper Web sites highly relevant, especially on a local level. Research by the Newspaper Association of America shows that when looking for local news online, 62 percent of all Internet users go to the local newspaper Web site, which is more than the number of users who go to any other online source, including Web sites for the local television stations (39 percent).

Out-of-Home

Place-based, out-of-home media include the traditional outdoor medium—billboards—as well as many newer, nontraditional signage opportunities such as stadiums, convention centers, bus shelters, bus benches, shopping malls, and airports. Other place-based locations that have not yet been monitored and tracked by marketing industry researchers include bar and restaurant restrooms, sidewalk café umbrellas, on-sidewalk signage, wall murals, and graffiti displays (like the one for Rheingold Beer in Manhattan). Out-of-home advertising is also becoming increasingly mobile, including signage on buses and in subway and commuter rail cars. Other mobile out-of-home applications that have not yet been monitored and tracked within the industry include taxi-top signage, bus or train vehicle wraps, sides of truck, and airborne and airplane-towed signage. Personal vehicles are also now being used as mobile signage. Almost anything is fair game in this area.

Out-of-home advertising is one of the growth areas of marketing communication. More and more marketers, searching for new ways to connect with consumers, are realizing how much time consumers spend away from their homes and potentially exposed to out-of-home media. Marketing spending on out-of-home media has grown steadily over the last several years to an estimated $7.2 billion in 2007. And this growth is expected to continue at least over the next several years.

Out-of-home is a very local medium. Many out-of-home advertising locations are in fact "place-based," which means posted in one place. This makes out-of-home an ideal medium for local area merchants who want to effectively point to their store or facility.

According to the Outdoor Advertising Association of America (OAAA), the major industry association that tracks such things, as of 2005 there were almost one million place-based locations and mobile out-of-home applications throughout the United States.[14] Given the recent growth in this area and the many locations that were not consistently reported in 2005, it would be reasonable to expect that these figures have continued to grow.

Another important out-of-home location that also was not widely reported in 2005 is cinema advertising. This includes advertising posters and signage in theater lobbies as well as sponsored slides and full-production video commercials presented in the auditorium. Cinema advertising, common for decades in other parts of the world, has only recently become popular among marketers in the United States. The Arbitron Company, which together with its sister company Scarborough Research conducts audience assessment for several specific out-of-home advertising applications, including cinema, released its first study of audience attitudes toward cinema advertising in 2003.[15] The cinema advertising council (CAC) reported that 2007 advertising industry revenues among CAC members had reached an all time high of $540 million, an increase of almost 20 percent compared to 2006.

Although it is a very local medium, there are plenty of national marketers utilizing out-of-home. National advertisers use out-of-home as an effective way to build emphasis for key brands in stronghold or opportunistic cities, depending on the needs of the brand. National advertisers also frequently use out-of-home as a place-based medium to direct local shoppers to local store facilities in a given area. For example, the OAAA reports that McDonald's was one of the top spending outdoor brands in 2007; this is completely understandable given the many thousands of McDonald's store locations throughout the United States.

Out-of-Home as a Marketing Medium

Out-of-home advertising offers national and local marketers alike certain advantages that cannot be realized with other media. Two of the most important advantages are the place-based nature of the medium and its visual impact. There are also disadvantages to using out-of-home media, including a lack of audience selectivity and the inherent limits of often fleeting exposure time.

On the plus side, as already suggested, out-of-home is largely a place-based medium: advertisements are displayed in fixed locations. This can be an extremely useful advantage for marketers that use the medium properly. Local advertisers, such as car dealerships, restaurants, and shopping centers, can seek out the out-of-home locations that might effectively guide consumers to the advertiser's facility. National advertisers, particularly national retailers like telecom companies or national store brands, can also choose advertising sites to guide consumers to nearby locations.

Another advantage of out-of-home is visual impact. Out-of-home is a powerfully visual medium usually presented in larger than life form. Marketers usually take full advantage of size to get the message across. The most common billboard size in the United States is the standard bulletin, which is fourteen feet high by forty-eight feet wide. Movie theater screens and the long side of a semi truck also present large images with high impact. There are also about a thousand "spectacular" outdoor sites, such as New York City's Times Square, where advertisers can utilize the whole side of a building (or two or three sides of buildings) for a truly spectacular messaging opportunity. Even for the smaller out-of-home placements like signs in buses and subway or rail cars, visual impact can attract and retain attention from a captive audience.

On the negative side, the lack of audience selectivity can be a disadvantage. The audience is anyone and everyone who passes within viewing range of the location. Marketers may work with creative teams to make the message more relevant to the right target audience, but even so the media owners sell advertising based on the total audience of a site. This means marketers wind up paying for all eyes on the site, not just the right eyes. Therefore, out-of-home is not necessarily a very cost-efficient advertising medium.

Another downside to out-of-home is the often-fleeting exposure time available for delivering the message. In most of the static out-of-home locations, the consumer has only a few seconds to see and read the marketers' messages. In developing creative material for out-of-home, there is no time at all for any kind of complex message. In its guide for designing effective outdoor advertising, the OAAA recommends a limit of seven words and three visual elements to enhance clarity. That extreme brevity can be a hard thing to accomplish, especially for marketers who want to boast about the benefits of their brand.

Internet

The Internet is virtually exploding as an advertising medium. ZenithOptimedia projects an accelerating pace of growth in marketer spending. For the five-year period from 2000 to 2005, the average annual growth in advertising spending on Internet media was 9.6 percent per year. *Advertising Age* reported that Internet advertising spending for 2007 was up 16 percent over 2006. ZenithOptimedia, echoing the sentiment of many forecasters in this area, is projecting a growth rate in Internet advertising spending averaging 13 percent per year over the next several years. The only thing limiting the growth of the Internet as an advertising medium is capacity. According to advertising researchers specializing in Internet, "There wouldn't be room today if everybody wanted to shift online [to Internet advertising]."[16]

Part of the attraction among marketers is that the Internet is a truly global medium; it is, after all, called the World Wide Web for a reason. Worldwide, there are about 1.2 billion Internet users. About 85 percent of the total worldwide usage is split between North America (United States and Canada), Europe, and Asia. In the year 2007 there were 188 million Internet users in the United States (persons over the age of three).[17] That figure, increasing by about 3 percent per year, represents about 65 percent of the total U.S. population.

There are many different ways to use the Internet as a marketing medium. Almost every marketer maintains some kind of Web site presence as a home base on the Internet. In addition to a Web site presence, marketers also use email messaging, Web logs (blogs), consumer-triggered messaging, and general display advertising. While most Internet advertising has some kind of interactive element, in this section we will focus on the more outbound-intended Internet advertising forms, including email messaging, search messaging, and general display advertising. We will come back to the Internet and blogs in particular in the next chapter, where we address interactive tactics in detail.

Email messaging and email distribution of newsletters are two of the ways that marketers today use the Internet to deliver outbound branded communications. Emails and newsletters are usually sent to consumers on a permission or opt-in basis. Most consumers get email notices and newsletters from marketers as a result of the consumer's registration via the marketer's Web site. Marketers use Web registration forms as a way to qualify consumer visitors to their Web sites by collecting important consumer information, including email addresses. And most registration-based online sites offer consumers a check box listing on the registration form as a way to either opt in or opt out of topic-specific emailings.

The email-messaging tactic includes everything delivered by email, from the highly promoted services like "Ding" from Southwest Airlines to simple email notices from a Web service like carepages.com. Southwest Airlines uses television advertising to encourage consumers to sign up for its "Ding" service alerting consumers to special low-price air travel opportunities. Carepages.com, a Web service that allows families and friends to communicate about the care of seriously ill patients, sends a simple email alert to notify consumers when something new has been posted about the patient. Email delivery of newsletters is another example of this kind of messaging. Most of these messages today use some combination of text and graphics known as rich media.

Consumer-triggered messaging is another common form of outbound Internet marketing. Triggered messages usually look like a simple search listing, a short heading with a brief blurb of explanation. As a category, triggered messaging includes such tactics as search engine optimization (SEO) as well as contextual and behavioral messaging. SEO is sought by marketers who purchase rights to certain key words that consumers may use to search for information in particular areas. Search engines like Yahoo! and Google sell key words to marketers who want their Web site to rise to the top of a listing of search results.

The other kind of triggered messaging is the category that includes contextual and behavioral messaging. Contextual messages are advertisements specifically about a subject of interest to the consumer doing a search; these advertisements are presented to consumers based on the consumer's search subject, usually above or to the side of the other search results. Such contextual messages are most likely to be delivered through search engine services. Behavioral messages are advertisements based on a consumer's past behavior on a Web site. Behavioral messages are the triggered advertisements commonly seen on broad-spectrum shopping sites like amazon.com and eBay, the messages that remind consumers of other items they may have looked at during their last visit to the site.

The most common form of general display advertising on the Internet is banner advertising, the rectangular or square advertising spaces seen today on so many different Web sites. As with emails and newsletters, many Internet display advertisers now use a rich media combination of text and graphics as well as animation to draw consumer attention to their advertisements. In 2006, about 30 percent of all online advertisements were delivered in a rich media format. Industry researcher JupiterResearch projects that by 2011 about half of all online advertisements will be done in rich media format.[18]

The Internet as a Marketing Medium

The advantages of the Internet as a marketing medium are probably obvious to most people. Of the many advantages available to marketers, we will discuss four of the most important: target coverage, target selectivity, global reach, and measurability.

As mass media audiences have splintered and all but disappeared from the old mass media forms like television, marketers have found new ways to achieve target coverage by reconnecting with important audience segments through the Internet. Young adults and especially young men are more likely today to be found surfing the Internet than watching primetime television.

Marketers can use specific Web sites to target messages to specific audiences with a high degree of certainty. A financial services marketer can use Web sites like MSN Money, Yahoo Finance, or Forbes online to deliver a message to consumers looking for information on financial services. Likewise, a movie marketer could use Web sites like IMDB.com, Yahoo Movies, or Moviefone online. Precision targeting can be fairly easy to accomplish with a medium like the Internet where the marketer can focus on specific consumer interests.

The Internet can be an effective marketing medium for any kind of marketer, from the multinational manufacturer selling products worldwide to the guy down the block selling an old computer. As we mentioned above, the total global reach of the Internet is about 1.2 billion people. That makes it an incredibly powerful communications tool no matter how large or small the marketer may be.

Internet measurement metrics are still evolving, but one thing that has always been true is that marketers can effectively measure advertising exposures on the Internet better than for any other media form. Any device a consumer uses as a way to access the Internet has a signature, either an Internet protocol (IP) signature or a wireless application protocol (WAP) signature. Internet measurement services can trace Internet activity to a specific IP or WAP address that is usually (but not always) unique to a specific computer or device. This is a design feature unique to the Internet that makes it possible for marketers to learn more about the consumers who visit a Web site or click on an advertiser message.

There are two disadvantages to the Internet worth mentioning: depth and anonymity. Studies have shown that many consumers will not explore an Internet location much deeper than the first page presented. This is a problem especially for search engines and marketers that use search engine advertising. Marketers compete, sometimes at high cost, for positioning on the first page of any listing so that consumers will see their message.

Anonymity is another problem for marketers using the Internet. As mentioned above, consumers' IP and WAP addresses are usually but not always unique to the Internet access device. Some companies and organizations with a large number of computers will use a series of IP addresses randomly assigned and rotated around licensed computers in an effort to minimize email and spam messages. Also, the person using the device may be anonymous. The IP or WAP address is specific to a device, but almost anyone could be using that device. Marketers today increasingly use registration forms to collect email addresses together with IP addresses to be able to connect effectively with specific consumers. Even so, the person (or people) behind the email address still has a certain degree of anonymity.

Mobile

Mobile is arguably the newest development in marketing. With an on-the-go worldwide consumer population, marketers are increasingly turning to mobile communication devices for new ways to deliver brand messages to prospective consumers. Mobile advertising messages can be delivered to consumers through any wireless phone, computer, or gaming device via WAP.

According to eMarketer research, worldwide mobile advertising spending in 2006 was $1.5 billion, while mobile ad spending in the United States was less than one-third of that (about $400 million).[19] This discrepancy is largely because mobile marketing worldwide is both a push (outbound) and pull (interactive) medium, while in the United States mobile marketing is primarily pull. We will deal with mobile in greater detail in the next chapter on interactive media channels; however, here we will briefly describe an outbound mobile application currently popular in Japan.

Retailers in Japan use GPS technology and digital coupons to send promotional messages to the phones of consumers who are near their stores.[20] Once they get the message on their phone, consumers can go to the store and print a copy of the digital coupon by waving the phone in front of a printer located in the store.

NTT DoCoMo is the largest mobile phone operator in Japan and a worldwide leader in expanding mobile phone applications to include such features as e-wallet and e-credit card services for use with all-in-one handsets. DoCoMo pioneered the i-Mode rich-content service that makes this kind of outbound messaging possible.

OTHER MEDIA DELIVERY SYSTEMS

Thus far we have focused our discussion on the advertising media and some of the specific outbound communication applications of advertising. To round out this chapter, we now turn to outbound messaging applications for the other media forms, including sales promotion, direct marketing, and public relations. While we covered measurement techniques and metrics for these forms briefly in Chapter 12, we will revisit each here for a somewhat more complete picture of the media applications unique to each practice.

As we explained above, it is not customary in this industry to consider these marketing activities in media terms. We do so here because we are thinking about media in the broadest sense of the word. We are talking here about message delivery systems, which we believe should encompass all forms of marketing communication.

Sales Promotion Media

Sales promotion messages are different from brand advertising in that they incorporate some form of incentive specifically intended to spur an increase in product sales. Some of the most common promotional tactics use prices, premiums, samples, or prizes as incentives. When selecting message delivery systems, marketers choose to use the media forms that make it easy for the consumer to take advantage of the incentive.

In outbound messaging, promotional incentives are frequently delivered to consumers either at home or in the store where the product is sold. Whether home- or store-delivered, promotional media forms provide consumers with some tangible evidence of the marketer's incentive offer, usually something the consumer can subsequently redeem. It may be a coupon, a rebate form, a prize card, or even a free product sample.

Most of the promotional media exist in some kind of print form, such as freestanding newspaper inserts, retailer circulars, coupons available from machines located on store shelves and from checkout registers. Marketers will also sometimes piggyback promotional offers along with advertising communications in printed forms: for example, in magazines. However, there are other ways to deliver a promotional incentive so that consumers can redeem the offer.

More and more marketers have started using the Internet to deliver and redeem promotional incentives. This can be accomplished in two fairly easy ways. One way is to provide the consumer with a page that can be printed on the consumer's printer and then taken to the store for redemption. Another, increasingly popular way is to provide consumers with a code number that they can enter either at the time of purchase, when purchasing via an online system, or at a store kiosk that can then print the offer.

Kiosks, one of the new forms of promotional media, are usually small, freestanding computer booths. The computer in a kiosk is usually a remote station linked to a larger computer system. Kiosk computers use touch-screen monitors that are easy for consumers to use. Some kiosks are also equipped with printers or scanners. For example, printer-equipped kiosks in airports allow consumers to enter their flight information for speedy check-in and even upgrade their tickets for better seats at a special at-the-airport price. Scanner-equipped kiosks in grocery store self-checkout lanes allow customers to scan their shopping cards and coupons in addition to their purchases.

Direct Marketing Media

Direct marketing messages are addressed directly to specific people either by name or according to their identifiable membership in some small, distinct group of addressable consumers. It is this addressability that makes a communication direct marketing. Such messages can be advertising, promotional, or simply informational. Regardless of the intent of the message, the three most important considerations in planning a direct marketing effort are selecting the right mailing or distribution list, communicating the right offer message, and choosing the right media. Here we will discuss the media forms of direct marketing.

Direct marketing allows the marketer to connect with the consumer on a personal, one-to-one basis. The media of direct marketing are generally personal media: the mailbox, the telephone, and the personal computer. Consumers therefore feel that direct marketing is more intrusive than any other kind of marketing activity. However, the intrusiveness and personal connection are also what makes direct marketing a highly successful marketing tactic. In Chapter 12 we noted that success in direct marketing is measured by consumer response rates, and telephone marketing (or telemarketing), a most personal form of communication, is consistently the media form that generates the highest response rates.

Telephone

Telemarketing is big business in the United States. Even after the creation of the national "do-not-call" registry in 2003, the telemarketing industry is thriving. The traditional outbound form of telemarketing, where marketers initiate contact with consumers or prospects, suffered only a brief period of adjustment after the "do-not-call" legislation. Marketers quickly realized that the people they could contact, after excluding those on the "do-not-call" list, were just as likely if not more so to respond to their messages. Outbound telemarketing has remained and will continue a strong part of the marketing business.

The newer telemarketing activities are now on the inbound side, where consumers initiate the contact. We will discuss them in detail in the next chapter.

Mailbox

Mail has long been one of the major media of direct marketing. In fact, the direct "marketing" business was originally called the direct "mail" business. The national advertising tracking services today routinely monitor marketing spending on direct mail. *Advertising Age* reported Robert J. Coen's finding that marketer spending on direct mail reached $60 billion in 2007, up almost 3 percent compared to 2006.[21] ZenithOptimedia forecasts continuing growth in direct mail spending over the next several years.[22]

National and local advertisers alike use direct mail in many different forms to deliver personal or almost personal messages to individuals or small groups of individuals throughout the United States. Marketers target direct mail to individual people and small audience segments using names and addresses from lists that marketers buy or rent from major list providers. The goal for the marketer is to craft a message specific enough to an audience that the message seems like a personal communication.

One of the big issues in direct mail marketing is the problem of junk mail and growing concern about consumers' disposal of unwanted pieces of mail. For many consumers, unwanted mail is a nuisance, and whether they throw it away or recycle it, they worry that all this extra trash is taking up landfill space and using up natural resources. Fraud is another big problem with unwanted mail. Consumers, in order to safeguard their personal information, are encouraged to shred their unwanted mail before disposing of it, but many do not, and the result is more and more instances of consumer fraud.

Computer

Email is a relatively new marketing medium. Technological advances have made it possible now to incorporate text and graphics as rich media into the body of an email message, making this an increasingly attractive way to deliver communications to consumers. Technology consultant Forrester Research reports marketing spending on email distribution was about $1.5 billion in 2006 and expected to grow at a modest rate of just over 2 percent per year through the year 2010.[23]

National and local advertisers use email as a marketing medium to deliver promotional messages and offers to retain current consumers. Marketers and organizations alike utilize email distribution of newsletters to recruit new consumers or donors. In total, JupiterResearch estimates that the average U.S. email consumer received almost 6,000 email marketing messages in 2005. Slightly less than half were legitimate marketing communications, while 55 percent were spam email.[24]

Spam is the biggest problem right now with email marketing. However, the forecast is hopeful as Internet service providers (ISPs) have gotten better at filtering spam emails to protect their users. The average number of spam emails in the United States is expected to decline significantly, by as much as half, by the year 2010.

Public Relations Media

Public relations marketing communications are customarily unpaid and delivered to consumers via some third-party communications medium, often the press and sometimes consumer-to-consumer word of mouth. The general focus of public relations messaging is building image and goodwill rather than explicitly selling product. Of course, it is generally accepted that companies with a strong brand image and corporate goodwill do effectively sell more product, so although the goals of public relations may seem different, they are still directly related to the goal of generating product sales for the brand.

The media of public relations include the news media in their many forms, broadcast, print, Internet, and even consumer-to-consumer. Marketers who hope for mentions or coverage by the broadcast press need to pitch stories and provide materials suitable for the broadcast medium, including video footage for television; a basic written news release will not usually be enough. Sometimes, depending on the situation, marketers may even create video interview segments where an executive of the company is taped responding to particular questions. This is not common, but used as a tactic in cases where the news is potentially important and the executive is not normally available for interviews.

The Internet is becoming a very popular media form for public relations activities. Marketers have for many years utilized their Web site presence on the Internet as a place to archive company press releases. More recently, though, marketers have started using Internet-based syndication services called really simple syndication (RSS) as a way to "broadcast" public relations messages to consumers and the news media alike. RSS "broadcasts" alert subscribers when new messages are posted at a Web site of particular interest to them. Consumers who use the news groups function provided by their ISP (like My Yahoo) are already receiving RSS "broadcasts," some of which may be public relations messages from companies depending on what sites the consumer ranked as "of interest." Web logs, another new and popular Internet-based media form for public relations, will be covered in our next chapter on interactive marketing communications.

SUMMING UP

The focus of this chapter has been a review of the many media forms that marketers use in disseminating outbound marketing messages to consumers. Outbound messages are those in the traditional model of communications, messages sent from a sender to a receiver. We discussed the basic characteristics, strengths, and weaknesses of each marketing medium.

We spent a lot of time in this chapter discussing advertising media forms, both traditional and nontraditional, which for the most part evolved from the outbound-only model of how communications work. We also considered the media of other marketing communications activities, like promotions, direct marketing, and public relations. We alluded here to the promising interactive future of many media forms. This will be the subject of our next chapter.

NOTES

1. J. Peters and W. Donald, "Industry Surveys: Advertising," *Standard & Poor's Industry Surveys,* December 29, 2005; *Advertising Age,* "100 Leading National Advertisers," June 23, 2008, p. S15 ("Ad Spending Totals by Medium").

2. Christopher Lisotta, "Forming One Network from the Assets of the WB, UPN," *Television Week*, May 15, 2006.

3. *Advertising Age*, "Major Divisions, Properties of the Nation's Leading Media Companies," *Interactive Marketing and Media Fact Pack*, April 17, 2006, p. 27.

4. R. Grover and J. Fine, "The Sound of Many Hands Zapping," *Business Week*, May 22, 2006.

5. A. Klaasen, "Major Turnoff: McKinsey Slams TV's Selling Power," *Advertising Age*, August 7, 2006.

6. Radio Advertising Bureau, *Radio Marketing Guide and Factbook* (Irving, TX: Radio Advertising Bureau, 2006), www.rab.com.

7. S. McClellan, "Radio Takes the Lead in Cleaning Up the Clutter," *Adweek*, February 7, 2005.

8. D.E. Schultz and J. Pilotta, "Simultaneous Media Experience and Synesthesia," *Journal of Advertising Research* 45, no. 1 (March 2005).

9. A. Gilroy, "VW, Audi Sign Exclusive Sirius Deal Through '12," *Twice*, March 17, 2006.

10. Magazine Publishers of America, *The Magazine Handbook: A Comprehensive Guide 2006/07*, www.magazine.org/content/Files/MPAHandbook06.pdf.

11. N. Ives, "Teen Mags? So Five Years Ago," *Advertising Age*, July 31, 2006.

12. J. Myers, "Marketers Ramping Up Custom Publishing Initiatives," Custom Publishing Council, July 30, 2003, www.custompublishingcouncil.com/why-custom-Marketers-Ramping-Up.asp.

13. Newspaper Association of America, "Total paid circulation," www.naa.org.

14. Outdoor Advertising Association of America, "Number of Outdoor Displays/Vehicles," www.oaaa.org/outdoor/facts/number.asp.

15. Arbitron Custom Research, *The Arbitron Cinema Advertising Study: Appointment Viewing by Young, Affluent, Captive Audiences*, 2003, www.arbitron.com/study_cr/cinema_study_2007.asp.

16. Klaasen, "Major Turnoff."

17. *Advertising Age*, "Internet Users in the US," *Digital Marketing and Media Fact Pack*, pp. 30–31.

18. E. Benderoff, "Soaking Up Web Exposure," *Chicago Tribune,* August 14, 2006.

19. *Advertising Age*, "Mobile Phone Advertising, Revenue and Penetration," *Digital Marketing and Media Fact Pack*, p. 43.

20. N. Madden, "Cellphones Spawn New 'Fast' Promos in Japan," *Advertising Age*, November 7, 2005, p. 14.

21. *Advertising Age*, "100 Leading National Advertisers," p. S15.

22. Peters and Donald, "Industry Surveys: Advertising."

23. *Advertising Age*, "US Email Marketing Spending," *Digital Marketing and Media Fact Pack*, p. 44.

24. *Advertising Age*, "E-mail Volume Forecast," *Interactive Marketing and Media Fact Pack*, p. 44.

CHAPTER 14

Interactive or Pull Communication Delivery Systems

This chapter deals specifically with interactive communications delivery systems and the new marketing tactics that utilize interactive channels. So far in our delivery discussion, we have emphasized how these recent changes have impacted the way marketers reach out to communicate with their customers. Even in our last chapter, where we considered the traditional outbound communications delivery systems, we also discussed many new uses of those traditional marketing media. It is time to look to the future of marketing communications, what we expect to be an exciting future in an experiential and interactive world.

EXPERIENTIAL MARKETING

Let us start with that word *experiential*. A 1998 article published in the *Harvard Business Review* gave a name to the emerging fourth stage of the U.S. economy. Authors B. Joseph Pine II and James H. Gilmore, analyzing U.S. manufacturers' tendency to mass customization and commoditization of goods, named this fourth stage "the experience economy." Pine and Gilmore explained it this way:

> How do economies change? The entire history of economic progress can be recapitulated in the four-stage evolution of the birthday cake. As a vestige of the agrarian economy, mothers made birthday cakes from scratch, mixing farm commodities (flour, sugar, butter, and eggs) that together cost mere dimes. As the goods-based industrial economy advanced, moms paid a dollar or two to Betty Crocker for premixed ingredients. Later when the service economy took hold, busy parents ordered cakes from the bakery or grocery store, which at $10 or $15 cost ten times as much as the packaged ingredients. Now, in the time-starved 1990s, parents neither make the birthday cake nor even throw the party. Instead, they spend $100 or more to "outsource" the entire event to Chuck E. Cheese's, the Discovery Zone, the Mining Company, or some other business that stages a memorable event for the kids—and often throws in the cake for free. Welcome to the experience economy.[1]

Pine and Gilmore developed the premise that the United States had begun the shift to an experience economy in which companies build brands and profits by staging memorable customer experiences. They pointed to the entertainment industry and the Walt Disney Company in particular as an example of this new economy. Their key point, however, was that marketers in any industry can and should stage brand experiences as a way to effectively differentiate overly similar or commoditized product offerings. Marketers embraced the concept of an experience economy, and marketing communications agencies rushed in to create the communications interpretation, "experiential marketing."

"Experiential marketing" is generally defined as any kind of live event marketing experience where consumers have the opportunity to interact with a product or brand face to face. Jack Morton Worldwide, an experiential brand communications agency, has taken the lead in researching the consumer's point of view on experiential marketing. In the June 2004 issue of *Promo Magazine*, the agency published the results of its first experiential marketing survey, reporting consumer perspectives on this kind of marketing activity.[2] In its third annual survey in 2006, Jack Morton reported that experiential marketing was an effective way to generate brand understanding and purchase and even inspire brand advocacy or positive word-of-mouth communications among consumers.[3] We see experiential marketing as an important concept for the future. We will consider experiential marketing tactics in this chapter.

INTERACTIVE COMMUNICATIONS

Now let us take a moment to consider that other word, *interactive*. Many people in the marketing communications industry today think of *interactive* in reference to technology—in particular, digital or Internet technology. For example, the advertising industry trade publication *Advertising Age* has for several years published a regular column about interactive media forms as marketing tools. In April 2007, the magazine published only the second edition of its *Digital Marketing and Media Fact Pack*. This publication is loaded with useful information about online and mobile marketing, including Web sites, email, cell phones, games, and real simple syndication (RSS)—an Internet-based news distribution mechanism. As useful as that material is, we feel a more complete definition of *interactive* is needed. It is true that the Internet and interactive technology have changed the marketing business; however, there are many other interactive tools and tactics available beyond the technological and digital.

In terms of the basic communications model, the word *interactive* means communication between people. There is nothing in that definition that says interactive communication has to be digital. The operative word in that definition is *between*, meaning two-way communication, not just one-way. In the world of marketing, we are talking about communication between marketers and consumers—not simply marketers to consumers, but back and forth between both parties. This kind of interactive communication can be person-to-person (experiential) or digitally facilitated.

In this chapter we cover a range of interactive marketing activities based on this broader, communications definition of the word. We will discuss both digital and nondigital interactive marketing activities. We will start with nondigital, person-to-person marketing and then move to interactive marketing enhanced by today's digital technology. In each section we discuss the specific tactics and then briefly review some important considerations. At the end of this chapter we present an approach for combining outbound and interactive media forms for maximum marketing effect.

PERSON-TO-PERSON INTERACTIVE MARKETING

Person-to-person marketing is not a new concept. Marketers have long understood that the most effective way to market a product, any kind of product, is face-to-face with the customer. Many business-to-business marketers hire, train, and maintain a skilled sales force explicitly for the purpose of calling on key customers. Two newer developments have contributed to what we see today as increasing utilization of person-to-person marketing.

First, the direct marketing industry popularized the concept of person-to-person marketing for consumer product marketers. Direct marketers took advantage of printing and database technologies to develop ways to cost-effectively communicate in a personal way with specific consumers. The idea really caught on after the 1993 publication of the book *The One-to-One Future: Building Relationships One Customer at a Time*, written by former advertising executives Don Peppers and Martha Rogers.[4]

Experiential marketing was the second major new development in the area of person-to-person marketing. Marketers realized they could sponsor or even create events at which consumers could connect with or experience an important aspect of the brand. And not just any consumer: marketers learned how to create and share live, branded experiences for their most important, influential, and/or highest-volume consumers.

Today we see this particular kind of interactive marketing in several different forms, from the traditional approach of personal selling to the recently popular practice of brand sponsorship. In this section we will discuss three specific person-to-person interactive marketing techniques: personal selling, event marketing, and sponsorship marketing.

All three are related activities in the general sense that they are marketer-customer interactive communications tactics. They are so closely related, in fact, that it can sometimes be hard to categorize specific marketing activities one way or the other. We are going to use a fairly simple definition in each area, although people in the industry sometimes classify these marketing activities differently.

Personal Selling

We will start with personal selling, the marketing practice of direct-to-customer sales generally in the customer's own space. In a business-to-business (BtoB) situation, this usually involves a marketer's sales representative making face-to-face personal contact at the customer's place of work or office. In a business-to-consumer (BtoC) situation, personal selling occurs when the marketer's sales representative makes face-to-face contact with a consumer or consumers, often in a consumer's home.

To be clear, we are talking here about personal selling by sales representatives working explicitly for a marketer. This is not the same thing as sales associates working for a marketing channel intermediary, like a retailer. Sales associates employed by retailers are generally expected to sell the retailer's selection of product offerings, sometimes from several different marketers' brands in a category. There are, of course, exceptions, where marketers' sales representatives work and make contact with consumers in a retail setting; we will return to this in a moment.

Personal selling is a tactic used in both BtoB and BtoC marketing situations. Well-known companies like Avon, Mary Kay Cosmetics, and Tupperware pioneered the modern practice of BtoC personal selling. These companies understood the selling power of personal communication. Today there are many companies using many different ways to implement this tactic. Personal selling, also known as direct selling, was reportedly a $30 billion industry in 2005.

One of the most popular approaches in BtoC personal selling today is called party selling. In party selling, a company sales representative joins with a consumer to host a small party of the consumer's friends who may be interested in a particular product category. Party-based selling accounts for about 30 percent of the total $30 billion direct sales industry.[5] These are not your grandmother's Tupperware parties. Party sellers today include such companies as the Pampered Chef, selling cookware and kitchen utensils; Pure Romance, selling sex toys and other personal items; Tomboy Tools, which sells a complete line of tools designed for women; ProShopatHome, selling men's golf equipment; and, of course, Tupperware. Traditional retailers like the Body Shop and catalog sellers like Lillian Vernon are also in the party-selling business now. And even major marketers like Procter & Gamble, which hosted a Tide brand pajama party for 1,200 women in New York City in September 2004, are joining in the fun.

A newer BtoC form of personal selling can be seen in retail stores where a marketer's sales representatives function like one of the store's sales associates except that they sell the marketer's brand. This occurs especially in electronics retail stores like Best Buy. Brand manufacturers of complex electronic products, like computers, and the retailers who sell such products work together on these sales. They have found that sales improve when they can train designated brand-product specialists and place them on the floor to handle the consumer's questions directly.

Personal selling on the BtoB side usually involves a direct sales force employed by the marketer. It is not as sexy as party selling, but the marketer's direct sales force is a critically important part of marketing communications today. The sales staff for any kind of business is often a first point of customer contact. According to a recent editorial in *CMO Magazine*, "marketing and sales should be helping each other to fuel the growth of the company," although often this is not the case.[6] In many businesses today, salespeople are expected to sell products while the marketing staff is building brands. While these two business goals do not have to be mutually exclusive, it is a matter of alignment that some companies have not yet addressed.

Whether BtoB or BtoC, the primary advantage of personal selling is the direct interaction with the consumer and the ability to answer the customer's questions on the spot. This is obviously important for complicated products about which the customer is likely to have a variety of questions. However, this advantage can also be important for simpler products like cookware or highly personal products like those sold by Pure Romance. The key, of course, is to recruit and train sales representatives who work well with customers to answer all their questions and put them at ease.

Although it can be a very effective marketing tactic, personal selling is also very expensive. In fact, it is probably the most expensive of all marketing tactics. First, the marketer has to consider the costs of recruiting, training, and employing a skilled team of sales representatives, then add the costs of travel and expenses as those salespeople go out on calls. Most party-selling BtoC marketers build such costs into the sales price for each product sold. This higher price then covers compensation, incentives, and other costs for the sales representatives. Although the price of the product in a party-sales situation may be higher than the same product sold through a store, consumers are generally willing to pay higher prices as part of the whole party and personal service experience (after all, we are in the experience economy).

Event Marketing

The Promotion Marketing Association defines event marketing as "any strategic-based face-to-face contact designed to impact a brand's perception among its constituents."[7] The professional association for meeting and event planners, Meeting Professionals International (MPI), agrees that event marketing is any circumstance where companies can interact with a targeted audience, such as exhibitions at association trade shows and conferences, participation in special themed consumer events, and production of individual company or brand special events. It is estimated that marketers in 2005 spent about $170 billion on brand-sponsored or brand-specific events in the United States.

Trade Show Events

Trade shows and conferences represent an important part of BtoB marketing today. These events, usually organized and produced by the major associations supporting particular industries, can be an effective way to deliver brand messages to key customers. Marketers rent and decorate an exhibit space where the companies' sales representatives can meet with interested customers to make sales presentations, answer questions, and ideally even demonstrate the product's potential. There is an association and a trade show or conference event in almost every industry. Restaurant product marketers participate at the annual trade show for the National Restaurant Association. Food product suppliers and distribution companies exhibit their products and services at the Food Marketing Institute show. Consumer electronics companies display products at the Consumer Electronics Show. Even television production companies have an annual trade show produced by the National Association of Television Program Executives where they market programming to the country's local television stations every year.

Themed Consumer Events

Specially themed consumer events include state fairs and community festivals. Every state in the United States hosts a state fair at some point during the summer; nationally, state fairs attract hundreds of thousands of attendees each year. Many marketers, large and small, look at state fairs as a grassroots opportunity to meet face-to-face with consumers. Community festivals operate the same way, and though they may sound smaller, that is not necessarily the case. There is a late-summer Renaissance Festival every year in almost every state, together drawing about 6 million visitors. Then there are local city festivals like the Taste of Chicago food festival, the Summerfest music festival in Milwaukee, the annual Jazz Festival in New Orleans, and the Gilroy Garlic Festival, drawing an average attendance of 120,000 per year over its twenty-eight-year history in Gilroy, California.

The World's Fair for Kids is another specially themed consumer event. This is a family themed event scheduled to coincide with spring-break season in the kids' mecca of the United States, Orlando, Florida. The 2006 event was the kick-off for what is planned to be a ten-year run in Orlando. It took place at the Orange County Convention Center, where sponsoring marketers like Amtrak, *Family Fun Magazine*, Kellogg's Fruit Loops, and Lego paid for signage rights and sponsored family activities at one of the eighteen pavilions reflecting the theme of a kid's life: sporting kids, travel kids, kids in the kitchen, and so on.[8]

Corporate Events

Corporate events—events developed and produced by individual companies—are a tactic gaining some momentum in event marketing. Marketers who previously supported trade shows or community events have come to realize that they can do more and do better when they own the show.[9] Recent examples include touring programs like the Old Spice RedZone Deodorant mobile display at high school football games nationwide as well as special invited events like the Daimler-Chrysler Camp Jeep program. Part of the attraction of corporate events is that the event is custom-made to fit the brand and communicate its message to customers.

A different kind of corporate-owned event uses viral marketing as a key tactic. Viral marketing is a particular kind of marketing tactic that uses consumer-to-consumer communications (via word-of-mouth or online social networking) to spread the marketer's message. For this kind of effort, companies may, for example, recruit a temporary staff of selling "ambassadors" and send them out into the market to publicize the brand. Tobacco companies have been known to use this tactic, sending ambassadors out to locations where people who smoke are likely to gather. The ambassador is armed with a supply of the company's cigarettes and trained to approach smokers and offer them a cigarette to try. Liquor companies also use this tactic, with the brand ambassador approaching consumers and offering to buy them a drink. The Chicago Museum of Science and Industry used this tactic to launch its genetics exhibit. The museum recruited and trained a small group of ambassadors to go out into Chicago area neighborhoods wearing shirts with provocative sayings like "Ask me why my eyes are blue." The idea behind such viral marketing is that the ambassador delivers the brand message via conversation with the consumer, so the brand message comes through as if it is word of mouth.

Corporate-owned and -staged word-of-mouth activities such as these are becoming more common, so much so that a growing number of marketing services agencies now specialize in design and execution of word-of-mouth programs. Jim Stengel, in his 2007 address to the American Association of Advertising Agencies (AAAA) Media Conference and Trade Show, spoke of the work and activities Procter & Gamble has done with its word-of-mouth agency, Tremor. Stengel made special note of the fact that in order to effectively engage consumers in this process of spreading brand messages, marketers need to build meaningful relationships with consumers, communicating marketing messages and brand information that adds value to the consumers' social relationships. In using word of mouth as a media channel, marketers need to understand that consumers will only relay information they think is meaningful to their friends; they will not simply reiterate a marketer's brand claim. Stengel reminded his audience that this strategy is not easy and that marketers need to rise to the challenge of leveraging such corporate events as a media channel.

Event marketing can be a very effective way to deliver branded communications and spread word of mouth, but just being there is not enough. The brand message must also fit the context of the event. This is generally easier to accomplish with corporate events, but

Exhibit 14.1 **Projected 2007 North American Sponsorship Spending by Property Type**

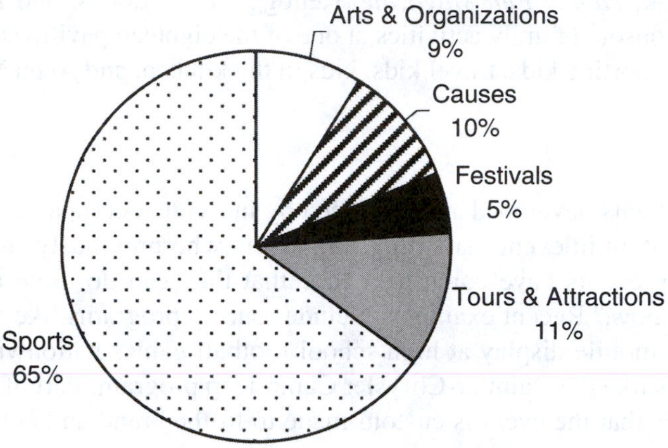

Arts & Organizations
9%

Causes
10%

Festivals
5%

Tours & Attractions
11%

Sports
65%

Source: IEG Sponsorship Report, December 2007.

it is possible in any event format. For a themed consumer event like a fair or festival, it is important to match the marketer with the theme: for example, *Family Fun Magazine* and the World's Fair for Kids. Even working within the structure of a major trade show, marketers can design and execute exhibit programming to effectively deliver the branded message. As is the case with personal selling, events are an effective selling tool because the marketer can interact directly with customers. It is not necessarily one-to-one communication, but it is face-to-face with groups of like-minded customers or prospects.

Sponsorship Marketing

One of the major sponsorship industry organizations, IEG Inc., defines sponsorship as "a cash and/or in-kind fee paid to a property (typically sports, entertainment, non-profit event or organization) in return for access to the exploitable commercial potential associated with that property."[10] This is a big and growing business around the world. According to the *IEG Sponsorship Report*, marketer spending for sponsorships in North America (United States and Canada) leads all world regions with $14.9 billion, about 40 percent of total sponsorship spending worldwide. Europe and then Asia and the Pacific are the next largest regions, with $11 billion and $8 billion respectively. Spending on sponsorship marketing activities has been growing for the last several years.

Marketers engage in a variety of different sponsorship activities across a wide range of properties. In North America, the leading property type by far is sports properties.[11] Exhibit 14.1 shows the breakdown of property types for sponsorship spending for 2007. After sport properties, with 65 percent of all North American spending, the next largest category, with only an 11 percent share, is entertainment tours and attractions.

Sponsorship marketing or sponsorship-linked marketing has been defined as "the orchestration and implementation of marketing activities for the purpose of building and communicating an association to a sponsorship."[12] For our purposes in this chapter, we will focus on sponsorship-linked marketing tactics developed around a marketer's sponsorship of a property. We already discussed sponsorship signage activities in a more general sense as an outbound form of communication delivery in Chapter 13.

The key difference between simple sponsor signage and sponsorship marketing is collateral communication—specifically, the use of other marketing communications activities to promote or publicize the brand's involvement with a sponsored property. Some professionals in this business call this "leverage," as in leveraging the equity of the brand-property relationship to advance the image of the brand.[13]

In its sixth annual survey of sponsorship decision makers, IEG reports that 62 percent of sponsorship spending in 2006 was invested in collateral communications to "activate" a sponsorship. The remaining 38 percent went to cover sponsor rights fees; that is, the marketing cost of buying the rights to sponsor a property.[14] About three-quarters of the marketers surveyed for the IEG report said they use public relations, employee communications, and/or traditional advertising tools to leverage sponsorships. About 60 percent reported they use some other marketing communications activity like Internet promotions, direct marketing, or on-site promotions like product sampling or coupon distribution.

Empirical research exploring the marketplace effects (outcomes) of collateral communications leveraging sponsorships is limited. What is available so far suggests leverage is important both in terms of the weight and the nature of added communications activities. In terms of weight, marketer use of leveraging communication activities can improve perceptions of differentiation between like brands.[15] *Nature* here refers to the role of collateral communications in improving the fit of the brand-property relationship. The stronger the fit, the stronger the outcome for the brand, and added communications activities can be used to strengthen the consumer perception of fit.[16]

Marketers participate in and leverage sponsorships to accomplish a wide variety of business objectives. The most common reasons include building brand loyalty, increasing brand awareness, and strengthening brand image. Strengthening the brand image was one of the primary objectives of 7-Eleven Inc. during its sponsorship of the 2007 summer movie hit *The Simpsons Movie*. The goal was to make 7-Eleven stand out as a fun, relevant brand for the young adult target market and sponsorship of the Fox Studios and Gracie Films release was a great fit. The partners in this effort pulled out all the stops to leverage the sponsorship by converting twelve 7-Eleven stores into Kwik-E-Marts, the fictional convenience store from *The Simpsons*. The store signage was changed, the store buildings were painted, store employees wore Kwik-E-Mart uniforms, and the stores sold "Squishee's" instead of "Slurpee's."

Another aspect of the sponsorship involved the introduction of "Sprinklicious" donuts that were sold in 7-Eleven stores nationwide as the store was trying to increase sales of fresh (bakery) items. The donut product, created in the image of Homer Simpson's favorite pastry, was reported as the most successful new product introduction of 7-Eleven's recent history. 7-Eleven management reported a 15 percent increase in bakery sales for the sponsorship period of 2007 as compared to 2006.

No matter what the reason, sponsorships and sponsorship marketing have become a key part of the marketing mix for many major marketing companies. Marketers use sponsorships the same way they use personal selling and event marketing, as an effective way to interact person-to-person with customers in a selling context. This kind of interaction directly and positively influences product sales, which is, after all, one of the most important goals for any kind of business.

DIGITAL INTERACTIVE MARKETING

Digital interactive marketing is a fairly new thing in marketing communications. The Internet as a medium reached a critical mass audience of 50 million by the mid-1990s. Since that time, and with new advances in digital technology, marketers have scrambled to find new ways to communicate digitally with consumers. Most marketers by now have created a Web site presence, and many are using some form of digital marketing in addition to the Web presence. Many new companies today actually launch with a Web presence and use digital marketing as a key part of their start-up plan.

The attraction of digital marketing is easy to see. Marketers can use digital technology to create a marketing environment that is logical, responsive, and comprehensive, a place where marketers can interact with consumers without having to pay for a building and a sales force.[17] Digital marketing uses databases to track consumer preferences, allowing marketers to serve and even anticipate the needs of customers. In a digital environment, marketers can quickly and effectively communicate with customers around the world regardless of time zones and datelines.

Spending on the booming field of digital interactive marketing hit $16.4 billion in 2006.[18] Marketers have rushed in despite indications that consumers do not fully understand the media. A 2006 report from technology consultant JupiterResearch found that only 22 percent of adults in the United States read blogs, and a separate study by WorkPlace Print Media reports that 88 percent of U.S. adults do not know what RSS is.[19] Whether consumers realize it or not, marketers seem to believe that digital marketing will be important in the future, and we agree.

In this section we discuss specific digital media channels and how marketers today are using each channel to deliver branded communications. We will look first at Internet-based interactive marketing, then mobile interactive marketing, and finally interactive television systems.

Internet-Based Interactive Media

As an interactive media channel, the Internet itself changes every day, and just as frequently marketers change the way they use the Internet to deliver brand messages. Some of the most common interactive Internet channels in use today are Web site applications, Web search applications, and Web logs. We talked about Web media as outbound marketing channels in Chapter 13. Here we will focus on interactive applications involving these same communications systems. We are not talking here about static ad spaces on the Web or even clicking through to advertiser Web sites; we are talking about specially designed and created interactive environments where marketers and consumers share experiences related to brands.

Web Sites

Most marketers today have a web presence of some sort, often a corporate homepage with an underlying structure of brand-specific pages. For example, consumers can go to www.goodhumor.com to learn everything they want to know about the novelty ice cream brands marketed by Good Humor, including Popsicle, Klondike, Breyers, and, of course,

Good Humor. In today's marketing world, such a Web site is basic stuff, marketing 101, even though the Internet became popular as a marketing medium only since the turn of the twenty-first century.

The really exciting applications of interactive Internet marketing started to appear in 2003/2004 as marketers began in earnest to evolve their basic Web presence into truly interactive environments. These include such activities as incorporating advergames, creating new Web-based environments called microsites, and participating online in social networking and virtual reality Web sites.

Advergames. Advergames are online games or activities designed around brand-name products. They are still a relatively small part of overall marketing activity but quickly gaining popularity. Marketing spending in this area was reportedly $164 million in 2006, more than double the spending of 2003 and projected to double again by 2009 as more and more marketers pay for development of original game concepts to include on their Web sites.

Many advergame Web sites are designed for kids. At popsicle.com, kids play games with Popsicle superhero Man of Popsicle; at poptarts.com, kids play Fruit Dodgeball; and at the Kellogg's Fun K Town arcade, kids play Celebrity Squares tic-tac-toe with Kellogg's spokes-characters like Tony the Tiger and Toucan Sam. There are also advergames for adults, like the Pepsi Mixed Signals game, mimicking baseball coaches' hand signals, at the Pepsi World FunZone Web site at www.pepsi.com.

Marketers use advergames as a creative way to engage consumers and communicate key points about the brand. For example, the Pop Tarts Fruit Dodgeball game shows off the variety of fruit flavors available as players move the Pop Tart to avoid being hit by a piece of fruit. Pepsi uses its advergames to promote its major sponsorships, like major league baseball (MLB) with the Pepsi Mixed Signals game and the Pedal to the Metal Pepsi/NASCAR racing game.

Microsites. A microsite is an individual Web page or group of pages designed as a supplement to some other primary Web site. As a marketing medium, microsites are special brand-content Web sites created by marketers as a key element of an integrated marketing communications (IMC) campaign. One of the first companies to do this effectively was automaker BMW, which debuted its BMW film series on its Web site in 2001. For the last several years BMW has hired popular and aspiring film directors to create minifilms featuring its new line of automobiles or new characteristics of BMW autos. This has been a very successful marketing tactic for BMW, encouraging consumers to visit the site and view and comment on the films.

Another highly publicized brand-content microsite was created by the Georgia-Pacific Corporation for its Brawny brand paper towels. For several years Brawny advertising featured the Brawny Man character, a strong, sensitive man who cares enough to clean up around the house. In 2006, Georgia-Pacific used its traditional advertising (television and print) to introduce the Brawny Academy, a microsite Web site and reality-based video series available for consumer viewing at the Web site.

The Brawny microsite offered consumers a wide variety of interactive communications opportunities. The Brawny Academy video series was a schedule of eight Web episodes of a reality show featuring men, nominated by their wives, who needed to learn to be more helpful around the house. The series brought to life the strong but sensitive Brawny Man as the host of the show.[20] Consumers could also explore biographies of the "campers" participating in the show, play a trivia game based on the show, download the Brawny Field Guide academy curriculum, and visit the souvenir shop for desktop wallpaper or screensavers, photos, and even a Brawny Man face mask. Consumers could also vote for campers, enter a sweepstakes, forward the site to a friend, or sign up to receive automatic updates at a browser home page or by email.

Those automatic updates are a key part of what made this microsite feel personal and interactive. Most marketers utilize a kind of syndication service called RSS to send updates to consumers. Although consumers may not know what RSS is or how it works, they may be using RSS reader services to keep content current on their browser homepage.

Microsites, advergames, and other Web-based interactive marketing efforts are becoming increasingly popular as marketers seek out new ways to engage consumers and break through today's cluttered media environment. The goal is to draw the consumer's attention to the brand in a format that the consumer can pass along to other consumers. Marketers believe that brands that succeed in such efforts can achieve a kind of word-of-mouth consumer endorsement that will ultimately build brand value. At least it can help develop that customer-brand relationship that we have been talking about in this book.

Social Networking and Virtual Reality. Social networking and virtual reality Web sites are Internet spaces that marketers today are developing as interactive media channels. Social networking sites, like MySpace and Facebook, exist as Web places where people can establish a personal profile and Web presence, where new friends can connect and old friends can check in, chat, or swap pictures or videos. Virtual reality sites, like Linden Lab's Second Life and MTV's Virtual Laguna Beach, are social networking sites with a three-dimensional twist. Virtual reality sites exist as virtual worlds where members "live" as three-dimensional avatars. In addition to the usual connecting and chatting and swapping pictures with other members, avatars in the virtual world can build and create things and buy or sell what they create with other avatars.

Marketers in the real world have found new ways to tap into these sites as interactive media channels. In Chapter 12 we noted that Volkswagen and Travelocity created brand characters with a profile and presence on MySpace.com. Volkswagen's Miss Helga and Travelocity's Roaming Gnome have their own friends' network. These brand characters keep their pages up-to-date with pictures, videos, and postings designed to amuse and entertain visitors while subtly communicating a brand message and building a brand relationship with prospective consumers.

Virtual reality sites allow marketers (those who are willing to pay and play) to interact with prospective consumers and build relationships in several different ways. Linden Lab, a California software developer, created and launched the virtual world space SecondLife.com. In the summer of 2007, the member population of the Second Life virtual world was about 8.5 million. Second Life does not sell advertising space, but marketers can buy virtual property and create buildings, islands, parks, and other places where residents of the virtual world can visit and shop or otherwise interact with the company.

For example, Toyota was the first car manufacturer to enter the Second Life world.[21] Toyota started by giving away Scion cars to Second Life avatars who wanted virtual wheels. Toyota created its virtual Scion to demonstrate its ability to handle corners and the sounds it makes when shifting gears so that avatar drivers could experience the brand.

In May 2007 Kraft Foods created Phil's Supermarket for Second Life. Kraft created the property initially to introduce some seventy new products at the food industry's Food Marketing Institute show.[22] As part of its deal, Second Life members can visit the store, link to Kraft's Web site and other sites for nutrition information, and even chat with Kraft Kitchen experts. Kraft plans to maintain the store as a regular feature on Second Life.

There are, of course, some problems associated with marketing products in the Second Life virtual world.[23] Some companies that were once active in Second Life have cut back or left altogether. One issue is the actual size of the online community. Second Life claimed a 2007 population of 8.5 million, but only 30,000 to 40,000 users are actively logged on even at peak times. Another problem is that the residents of Second Life seem to be more interested in virtual vices (gambling, brothels, and strip clubs) than they are in virtual products. Probably the biggest issue is the fact that virtual reality for now is a fantasyland where avatars do not need the trappings of the real world.

Despite these drawbacks, marketers can and do use their presence in the virtual world to build relationships with consumers. The tricky part is to play along with the fantasyland so that the residents will invite the marketer's presence; sometimes just being there can be costly. Reebok's shoe store presence in Second Life was attacked by a group of avatars calling themselves the Second Life Liberation Army (SLLA). The attacks are of course virtual, with virtual nuclear bombs, not real; however, the marketer has to incur the real costs of cleaning up the site and restoring its property.

Web Search

Search is by far the leading category of Internet-based advertising spending in the United States. According to Forrester Research, search marketing spending in 2006 reached more than $7 billion, a total that was expected to grow at an average rate of 13 percent per year over the next four years.[24]

Marketers understand that consumers use Internet search engines to help them locate the news or information they seek. Marketers also know that most consumers look only at the first page or two of search results. For this reason, marketers work hard to see their Web presence "pop" on the first page of any search results.

Marketers can accomplish such first-page returns in a couple of different ways. Marketers can use keywords in the text and tags of their Web site presence. They can bid for a better position in search returns (higher dollars for higher position) or pay-per-click based on keyword searches. And, finally, marketers can pay for contextual advertising listings.

The cheapest way is to use keywords when designing a Web site. Marketers can insert keywords in the text and in the short descriptive passage about the Web site (called a metatag). Then when a consumer types a relevant keyword into a search engine, the search engine will find the words and return the marketer's Web site, and if the keywords are unique and relevant enough the marketer may get on the first page of returns. One word of caution, though: marketers need to be sure to use content-appropriate and relevant keywords in the metatag. Some marketers in the past, hoping to appear higher up in search results, have been caught loading their sites with keywords that do not relate to the content of the site, but that works against the consumers' interest in search. Search engine managers consider themselves responsible to the consumer and when they discover marketers scamming the search process, the punishment can be severe. Search engines recently have completely delisted marketer Web sites as punishment for this kind of abuse.

Another way to get a higher listing is to pay for it. One way is to "pay for position," which is usually a bidding process where marketers bid against each other, paying more to get a higher position in the search returns. Another way to do this is to pay-per-click, where marketers pay a negotiated amount for every time an Internet user clicks through a search listing to the marketer's page.

Finally, marketers can pay for a contextual advertising listing that is separate from the search returns. Google is the leader in Internet search, with a share of almost 50 percent in the United States. The Google contextual search ads are listed to the right of the search returns and usually identified as advertisements. In addition to the search returns, Google will present the contextual ads for consumers based on the keywords or phrases that the consumers used in their search.

In the beginning of search marketing, the marketer's goal was to receive a large quantity of clicks. The thinking was that more clicks meant more chances for consumer engagement. However, as the Internet and search marketing have evolved, the goal today is qualified clicks. Like qualified leads in sales jargon, a qualified click is when a consumer clicks to view a Web site in which he has real and not just passing interest. The result will be a higher-quality experience for Internet users and higher-quality leads for marketers.[25]

Web Logs

Web logs, also known as blogs, are a particular kind of web-based journal or diary in which entries or postings are displayed in reverse chronological order (newest entries first, oldest entries last). Blogs exist as uniquely addressed Web locations where authors periodically post comments or observations about subjects of particular interest to them.

A particularly useful article about the background and development of blogs is available on Wikipedia, the free encyclopedia.[26] We will focus here on the evolution of blogs as an interactive marketing medium. Any marketer considering the use of a blog as a marketing medium needs to be aware of three important issues: finding the right topic, the timing and objectivity of postings, and the reader comment policy.

Choosing the Topic. Since blogs are generally topic-specific, they tend to attract as an audience of people who share an interest or concern about the same topic. There are blogs about fashion, politics, parenting, sports, pets, music, theater, movies, finance, businesses, industries, and many other topics. In just the last couple of years marketers have begun to realize that blogs can be used to build small communities of like-minded people—specifically, like-minded consumers who might be interested in a particular brand.

Marketers today are creating corporate blogs where company employees write postings about a subject of particular interest to the brand and where consumers who read the postings can reply with comments about the subject. Marketers understand that it is very important to first find a subject area that is meaningful to consumers and relevant to the brand, fitting with the brand's character. For example, Starwood Hotels and Resorts publishes a corporate blog at www.thelobby.com. The subject of the Starwood blog is travel, a topic of interest to Starwood and prospective Starwood consumers. Another example is the media company Cox Communications and its blog "Digital Straight Talk: Your Inside Guide to Broadband Communications" at www.digitalstraighttalk.com. In each case, the marketer was able to find a common and not necessarily commercial subject area where the company can post its perspective and the consumer might actually want to read the posting.

Postings. Having found the right topic, marketers need to create and maintain a stream of postings with a certain quality of objectivity. Blog readers can easily detect and often resent overcommercialization of their favorite medium. For example, the McDonald's corporation publishes a blog on corporate social responsibility (CSR) called "Open for Business" at http://csr.blogs.mcdonalds.com. The McDonald's blog is edited by a McDonald's vice president for corporate citizenship and issues management, with contributions from other senior managers at the company. The editor and the other authors work very hard to avoid over-commercializing the McDonald's blog by keeping their postings about general subjects like environmental issues, but every once in a while they add a posting lauding McDonald's activities, which tends to diminish the non-partisan view that readers may have. General Motors has another way of handling the issue of objectivity. General Motors publishes two blogs. One, called "Fast Lane" (http://fastlane.gmblogs.com), is written by GM managers offering their take on products and new product developments. The other, called "FYI" (http://fyi.gmblogs.com), is written by GM employees and other interested parties offering a different perspective.

Timing in the sense of frequency of postings by the authors is another factor in blogging. Marketers who want to build and be part of a community have to be willing to be active themselves. In blogging, that means posting thoughts and exchanging ideas with consumers frequently and regularly. The right frequency can sometimes be hard to figure out, but marketers should expect to write postings more frequently rather than less. How frequently to post is a matter that each marketer has to figure out; McDonald's managers have settled into a pace of about twice a month for its CSR postings. GM managers post to the Fast Lane blog every couple of days or so. Starwood's blog, "the Lobby," offers five different blogs on one page with a new posting from one or more blogs every single day. The blog's readers ultimately will let the marketer know how frequently they expect to see new postings.

Comment Policy. Finally, marketers need to keep in mind that a key component of any blog is its reader comment facility. Every blog offers readers an opportunity to make comments, which are posted for anyone to read. This feature is critical to blogging because it makes blogging an interactive tool and turns a blog Web site into a community of like-minded people. This is what marketers want and what makes blogging a potentially powerful marketing tactic. Marketers who get this feature right can cultivate a community of active consumers with a common interest pertinent to a brand, ideally reflective of the brand's meaning or key point of difference.

Marketers can provide for reader comments in several ways. Like a newspaper editor deciding which letters to the editor should be published, every blog manager maintains some level of control over reader comments. Some blog spaces are very open about reader postings; they allow almost all reader postings while electronically scanning for and eliminating only the inappropriate or offensive comments. Other blogs are very strict about postings; they require that readers submit the posting so it can be read first and then the editor decides which comments will be posted. The comments policy is an important part of building a community around a blog; too strict a policy will discourage reader involvement and engagement, but a policy that is too loose may reflect negatively on the marketer. Either way, it is customary to state the reader comment policy prominently on the Web site so readers will know what to expect.

Mobile Media

In interactive marketing, any personal and portable electronic device capable of interfacing with the Internet or other devices can be considered a mobile messaging medium. This category includes cell phones, personal digital assistants (PDAs), portable digital music or video players like iPods or MP3 players, and portable game systems like the Playstation Portable (PSP) or Nintendo DS. Cell phones can carry marketing messages in a couple of different ways, via messaging, either short message service (SMS) or multimedia message service, or by the Internet via wireless application protocol (WAP). Other personal devices receive marketing messages through connection to the Internet, either through cables or docking stations or by WAP interface.

Mobile marketing is not a new idea. Marketers have been interested in the concept since the turn of the twenty-first century, when cell phones exploded in popularity and wireless Internet technology became widely available. However, actual marketer use of mobile media is only just beginning in earnest. Estimated marketing spending on mobile efforts in the United States in 2005 was only about $45 million, but projections suggest more than $1 billion in spending by 2010.[27] Marketing spending on mobile media channels is much larger in other parts of the world. In Japan, for example, consumers can use a DoCoMo cell phone to send and receive emails; download music, videos, and movies; buy a can of Coke; print e-coupons from retailers; and even scan (using the camera feature) Quick Response codes that will direct the phone to a designated marketer's Web address (URL).[28]

On one level, marketers are waiting for consumers to show more interest in using their mobile devices. By the end of 2006, only about 40 percent of all U.S. mobile device subscribers indicated they had used their mobile device to send a text message. Only 10 percent of mobile subscribers had used their cell phone to retrieve news, buy a ringtone, or send a photo message to a friend. And an even smaller percent had ever used the cell phone to send or receive emails or download a mobile game.[29] However, these numbers are changing every day. As consumers learn to use these powerful communication tools, so too will marketers.

On another level, there are still some barriers to overcome before we see more widespread marketing use of mobile media. Many U.S. mobile marketing campaign applications right now are of a pull nature. The most common applications today use other marketing channels to invite mobile media users to opt in to a mobile element. This is probably because of issues like subscriber privacy, which is carefully guarded by the big U.S. mobile carriers like Verizon and Sprint/Nextel. Opt-in efforts, asking the consumer to send a message to the marketer, afford the marketer a little more leeway in sending a message back to the consumer.[30] For example, Procter and Gamble is one of the major marketers participating in mobile marketing. P&G coffee brand Folgers used mobile marketing as an element of its 2006 "Tolerate Mornings" campaign inviting consumers to register for mobile wake-up calls.[31] P&G toothpaste brand

Crest Whitening with Scope Extreme employed a mobile text messaging component in its 2006 nightclub-centered "Irresistibility IQ" campaign. The Crest campaign used several club media forms (bar napkins, restroom signage, etc.) to invite young adult consumers to take the Irresistibility IQ test by texting the words *IQ* or *Extreme* to C-R-E-S-T (27378).[32]

Podcasts are another form of mobile marketing that is gaining some popularity. Podcasts are broadcasts, either video or audio, delivered through the Internet to consumers' iPod digital player devices. They are called podcasts because the Apple iPod products hold a commanding 73 percent share of the market for portable digital players in the United States.[33] In order to receive a podcast, the consumer has to go online and download it. Again, marketers use a pull technique, employing other communications media to promote a podcast offering and enticing consumers to make the effort to download the program.

Whether using podcasts, wireless Internet, or text or multimedia messaging, mobile marketing is in the mix now and probably here to stay. Marketers across all industries are going mobile to tap into consumers on the go. The list in early 2006 included major automakers like Audi, Acura, Chrysler, and GM; packaged goods product manufacturers like P&G, Johnson & Johnson, Coca-Cola, and McDonald's; office equipment and solutions marketers like IBM and Hewlett-Packard; and even major retailers like Best Buy. As consumers get more comfortable with the technology, we expect to see more and more marketers as well.

Interactive Television

Even the television set sitting in the living room or hanging on the wall in the den or family room is becoming a tool for interactive marketing. Since its invention in the 1920s and widespread adoption in the 1950s, the television set has served marketers well as an outbound media channel, but now the technology exists to morph it into a powerful interactive marketing medium. Two technological advances in particular have made this possible. The first is the evolution of digital cable and video-on-demand (VoD) programming, and the second is the development of digital video recording devices (DVRs) like TiVo.

Household penetration of both technologies is still low in the United States, but growing rapidly. According to a Pulse research report for the Cable & Telecommunications Association for Marketing (CTAM), U.S. household penetration for digital cable systems reached 35 percent in 2007, up from 20 percent in 2005. The same report shows 2007 DVR penetration at 23 percent, three times its 2005 level of only 7 percent.[34] Industry experts are projecting further expansion through the year 2010, when digital cable with video-on-demand is expected to reach 66 million homes (about 60 percent) and DVRs will be in use in more than 30 million homes.[35]

Digital cable and VoD technology makes it possible for viewers to bypass commercial television programming and go directly to commercial-free movies and programs they can choose to watch at their convenience. We mentioned in Chapter 12 that more and more marketers are therefore using tactics like product placement to keep brands in front of consumers in a television environment. However, now the technology exists for marketers to create and offer their own form of branded entertainment content to consumers via VoD.

Most cable systems today provide some form of on-demand programming for their digital subscribers. One such provider, Comcast, also offers a commercial VoD channel it calls Searchlight. Marketers are working with television producers and cable systems to offer branded content via commercial VoD, which consumers can watch on their television set with just a click of the remote control button. For example, the National Geographic Channel is one of the television producers working with marketers to create branded VoD content. In 2005 National Geographic offered unique programming opportunities like special behind-the-scenes material, outtakes, and feature clips that marketers can use for special promotions or integrated branded content.[36]

DVRs offer another kind of interactive opportunity for marketers. TiVo, one of the leading DVR brands, offers marketers three different ways to interact with consumers via the television screen: TiVo Tags, TiVo Showcase, and TiVo Search. With TiVo Tags, marketers can insert special tags into regular television commercials displaying a brand icon or logo along with a call to action.[37] TiVo offers the tags in a large enough format that they can be seen by TiVo viewers in normal play or fast-forward mode. The viewer, if interested in the product, can then click a button on the remote control to view the brand's long-form message while the program remains in pause mode.[38] TiVo Showcase works like Comcast Searchlight as a place where consumers can directly access branded commercial content. From its vast database of information on viewer behaviors, TiVo reports that 10 to 15 percent of viewers on average use its interactive features like TiVo Showcase to watch commercial content, spending an average of two to four minutes per view.

In spring 2006, TiVo debuted another interactive feature for marketers it called TiVo Search. This new service applies the Internet search advertising model to video search for television programming.[39] TiVo viewers using keywords to search for video programs are presented with a selection of videos as well as a selection of marketer messages tied to the same keywords. This is the same as the Internet search contextual advertising model that consumers have seen on search engines like Google. Viewers then can choose to watch a program or may decide (as they do on the Internet) to click on a marketer's message if it seems relevant and interesting.

Interactive tools like these are remaking the living room television set into the "advanced television" we talked about in Chapter 11.[40] Marketers are just starting to use these new media; entertainment and media companies seem to be on the leading edge of such efforts. The 2006 annual CTAM awards featured cases from World Wrestling Entertainment, Universal, Time Warner, and Rainbow Media.[41] We expect that it will not be long before product marketers find their way into the mix.

THE HOLISTIC CONSUMER EXPERIENCE AND ACTIVATION

We have spent the better part of the last two chapters of this text discussing the extremely broad range of marketing communications delivery systems available today. We have talked about outbound and interactive media forms and the many variations of each. What most marketers need now is an effective way to combine multiple media forms to realize and capitalize on the full power of marketing communications in building not just brand value but durable customer-brand relationships.

Researcher Shu-pei Tsai in 2005 proposed a framework for "holistic consumer experience management (HCEM)" as a way of realizing the full potential of marketing communications by orchestrating both the mediated impressions of and direct encounters with marketers' brands.

In the context of this scholarly work, the phrase "mediated impressions of the brand" refers to strategic communications as the "blending of various communication devices into a unified and preferable brand image in the marketing campaign," while "direct encounters" with the brand refers to the brand management perspective of leveraging all marketing mix elements to engage consumers. The purpose of the HCEM framework is to realize "the essence of IMC as a comprehensive entirety in enhancing the consumer experience."[42]

We suggest that another way to look at the HCEM framework is from our viewpoint of media delivery systems as outbound and interactive. Throughout this book we have maintained a broad perspective and interpretation of what is or may be considered "media." We would suggest that the "mediated impressions" component of the HCEM framework comprises the many outbound media forms we discussed in Chapter 13, while the "direct encounters" component represents the new world of interactive media forms we have discussed here in Chapter 14. Putting the two together is what marketing is all about—that "comprehensive entirety in enhancing the consumer experience."

So how do marketers put it all together, the outbound and the interactive? The answer is activation, the process of developing and employing branded live consumer experiences to deliver and positively reinforce the essence of the brand. Activation as a concept grew out of the practice of sports sponsorships as marketers sought ways to improve the returns realized from money invested in sponsoring teams or sports organizations like NASCAR or major league baseball (MLB). Marketers pushed and marketing agencies responded by finding a brand meaning that might also be relevant to the sports property and then in turn developing a live event overlay to effectively leverage the brand's sports property sponsorship.

As a matter of practice today, what used to be considered activation of sports sponsorships has become a process for combining outbound and interactive media forms in order to implement marketing campaigns in such a way as to give life to the customer-brand relationship. One big difference, though, is that instead of seeking some linkage between the brand and the sports property, the marketer starts with the consumer and the customer-brand relationship and then identifies the combination of media forms that will provide experiences that build the relationship.

Shu-pei Tsai's HCEM framework leverages the five experiential components identified by Bernd Schmitt (sensing, feeling, thinking, acting, and relating)[43] to propose a model for implementing the holistic consumer experience:

- Gain original insight into the consumer's world.
- Develop an experiential strategy platform.
- Create a unique and vivid brand experience.
- Provide dynamic interactions at the consumer interface.
- Innovate continuously to improve consumers' lives.

Many major agencies today promise marketers this kind of "live marketing" activation. Advertising agencies, public relations agencies, promotional marketing agencies, direct marketing agencies—all marketing services agencies today recognize the importance of activating a brand's marketing messages.

Further recognition of the importance of activation came from the Promotional Marketing Association's annual REGGIE Awards for 2007. Across all categories, including big-budget and small-budget national brands, local and regional brands, and even international brands, the winners all employed a broad range of communications tactics and a wide variety of message delivery systems to drive outstanding sales results. The REGGIE (the name is derived from the term *cash register*) is all about sales results.[44]

The Gold REGGIE winner in the small-budget national consumer brand category in 2007 was Blue Moon Brewing for its "Artfully Crafted" campaign. This effort combined outbound media in the form of Internet banners, print and out-of-home advertising, and point-of-sale displays with interactive events, such as local artists painting wall murals and posters. The Gold REGGIE for local, regional promotion went to Ocean Spray for its "Bogs Across America" campaign for its packaged cranberries product. For this effort, the Ocean Spray agency used outbound television advertising together with a wide variety of interactive efforts, including "bog squad" product sampling teams, a web offer of free, bog-based photo greeting cards through Shutterfly, and an in-school educational program for fourth graders around the country.

The concept is simple: no matter what kind of agency a marketer uses, activation is the key that combines basic outbound media marketing communication activities and experiential, interactive media marketing activities to produce the holistic consumer experience that helps marketers build meaningful customer-brand relationships.

SUMMING UP

In this chapter we have considered the many interactive media forms available to marketers today. We have tried to be forward-looking in this discussion, but at best we can provide only a snapshot in time. The marketing communication delivery systems discussed here and in the previous chapter are constantly changing and evolving. Understanding the mechanics of the broad system of marketing communications media should help marketers embrace the changes we expect for the future of media. Now it is time to move on to the final part of this book, the development of marketing messages and incentives.

NOTES

1. B.J. Pine II and J.H. Gilmore, "Welcome to the Experience Economy," *Harvard Business Review* (July/August 1998).

2. L. Shuler, "Experiential Marketing Survey," *Promo Magazine*, June 2004.

3. J. Morton, "Global Experiential Marketing Study: 2006 Survey Reveals Insights, Benefits," Jack 360°, June 21, 2006, http://360.jackmorton.com/articles/article062106_2.php.

4. D. Peppers and M. Rogers, *The One-to-One Future: Building Relationships One Customer at a Time* (New York: Currency Doubleday, 1993).

5. A. Farnham, "The Party That Crashed Retailing," *Forbes*, November 1, 2004.

6. B. Stapp, "The Main Event," *CMO Magazine,* February 2005, www.cmomagazine.com/read/020105/main_event.html.

7. Promotion Marketing Association, "Councils: Event Marketing," www.pmalink.org/councils/default.asp?p=eventmktg.

8. D. Schlossberg, "Orlando World's Fair Targets Kids," ConsumerAffairs.com, March 5, 2006, www.consumeraffairs.com/news04/2006/03/travel_worldsfair.html.

9. C. Hosford, "Owning the Show," *Sales & Marketing Management*, January/February 2006.

10. *IEG Lexicon and Glossary*, "Sponsorship," www.sponsorship.com/resources.

11. *IEG Sponsorship Resource Center*, "2008 Sponsorship Spending," www.sponsorship.com/resources/.

12. T.B. Cornwell, C. Weeks, and D. Roy, "Sponsorship-Linked Marketing: Opening the Black Box," *Journal of Advertising* 34, no. 2 (Summer 2005).

13. Ibid.

14. *IEG Sponsorship Report*, "'06 Activation Spending to Match All-Time High," 25, no. 5 (March 13, 2006).

15. T.B. Cornwell, D. Roy, and E. Steinard II, "Exploring Managers' Perceptions of the Impact of Sponsorship on Brand Equity," *Journal of Advertising* 30, no. 2 (Summer 2001).

16. Cornwell, Weeks, and Roy, "Sponsorship-Linked Marketing."

17. M. Azzaro, D. Binder, R. Clawson, C. Lloyd, M.A. Shaver, and O. Werder, *Strategic Media Decisions: Understanding the Business End of the Advertising Business* (Chicago: Copy Workshop, 2004).

18. *Advertising Age*, "U.S. Online Ad Spending by Format," *Digital Marketing & Media Fact Pack*, April 23, 2007, p. 6.

19. A. Klaasen, "Reality Check," *Advertising Age*, August 21, 2006.

20. E. Benderoff, "Soaking Up Web Exposure," *Chicago Tribune,* August 14, 2006.

21. *Economist*, "Living a Second Life," September 28, 2006.

22. B. Spethmann, "Kraft Launches Second Life Supermarket," *Promo Xtra*, May 7, 2007, http://promomagazine.com/retail/news/kraft_launches_second_life_supermarket_050707/index.html.

23. A. Semuels, "Internet: Virtual Marketers Have Second Thoughts About Second Life," *Los Angeles Times,* July 14, 2007.

24. *Advertising Age*, "U.S. Search Marketing Spending to 2010," *Digital Marketing and Media Fact Pack*, April 23, 2007, p. 40.

25. *Marketing Week*, "Search Marketing: Searching for Answers," August 3, 2006, p. 31.

26. Wikipedia, "Blog," http://en.wikipedia.org/wiki/blog.

27. T. Wasserman, "Despite Some Hang-Ups P&G Big Believer in Mobile," *Brandweek*, June 12, 2006.

28. N. Madden, "Cellphones Spawn New 'Fast' Promos in Japan," *Advertising Age*, November 7, 2005, p. 14.

29. *Advertising Age*, "Mobile Device Use and Content Consumption," *Digital Marketing and Media Fact Pack*, April 23, 2007, p. 42.

30. D. Freedman, "The Future of Advertising Is Here," *Inc.*, August 2005.

31. A. McCains, K. Sampey, and A. Baar, "Nontraditional Isn't Untraditional Anymore," *Adweek*, August 7, 2006.

32. A. Cuneo, "P&G Tries Out Mobile-Marketing," *Advertising Age*, June 19, 2006.

33. *Advertising Age*, "Share of Portable Digital Player Sales," *Interactive Marketing and Media Fact Pack*, April 17, 2006.

34. Cable & Telecommunications Association for Marketing (CTAM), "As Digital Cable Penetration Surges, So Do DVRs," press release, July 17, 2006, www.ctam.com/news/releases/060717-pulse.htm.

35. A. Tauder, "Getting Ready for the Next Generation of Marketing Communications," *Journal of Advertising Research* 45, no. 1 (March 2005).

36. D. Whitney, "VOD in Marketing Mix," *Televisionweek*, October 31, 2005.

37. B. Morrissey, "TiVo's New Ad Strategy Tunes Into Viewer Choice," *Adweek,* July 25, 2005.

38. S. Curry, "Dump the :30 Spot and Embrace On-Demand," *Televisionweek*, July 25, 2005.

39. B. Morrissey, "TiVo Execs Bet Google Ad Model Will Work on TV," *Adweek*, December 5, 2005.

40. Tauder, "Getting Ready."

41. A. Waldman, "On-Demand's Battle Plans," *Televisionweek*, July 17, 2006.

42. S.-P. Tsai, "Integrated Marketing as Management of Holistic Consumer Experience," *Business Horizons* (September/October 2005).

43. B. Schmitt, *Experiential Marketing: How to Get Customers to Sense, Feel, Think, Act, and Relate to Your Company and Brands* (New York: Free Press, 1999).

44. Promotional Marketing Association, "REGGIE Award Winners 2007," www.pmalink.org/awards/default.asp?p=2007reggie_winners.

PART IV

THE RIGHT MESSAGE TO THE RIGHT AUDIENCE AT THE RIGHT TIME

Typically, the chapters that follow would have appeared much earlier in a traditional marketing communications text since they deal with the content or what has often been called the creative portion of a marketing communication program. Although we know that the messages and incentives to be delivered to customers and prospects are a critical part of any marketing communication program, we believe that, given the changes currently occurring in the delivery systems, finding effective, efficient, and involving ways of reaching customers and prospects is the first task of the planner. Quite simply, if the message or incentive is not noticed, seen, or heard by the customer or prospect—what we call media consumption—it makes no difference how creative, involving, or persuasive the message might be. Unseen or unheard messages and incentives are a waste of the marketing firm's resources.

Therefore, we have held the content portion of this text until now. Additionally, Part IV differs substantially from what is normally found in a marketing communications book. The focus in the chapters that follow is the strategic use of content in the four-element planning process—product/brand, audience, delivery, content—on which this text is based. The challenge is to develop strategic approaches to messages and incentives, not ones that are here today and gone tomorrow in a flight of creative frenzy. That is why the emphasis in the next chapters is on developing value propositions, that is the offers being made through the brand promise or promises that the organization makes to customers and prospects in all their marketing communication activities, not on creating television commercials or print ads or slogans or icons or logos. The challenge today is to identify the most critical elements in the marketing communication program, those that are most relevant to customers and prospects, and then bring all those creative elements together to provide a coherent, complete, relevant set of messages and incentives for the intended audience. That process requires, first, a comprehensive understanding of customers and prospects—identifying their wants, needs, and requirements—and then developing solutions they will find interesting, involving, and relevant to them, not to some indefinable "target audience." It is not enough merely to create some type of attention-getting element that has little to do with the issues and challenges that customers and prospects are facing.

It is our belief that a solid value proposition can be executed in any number of ways through any number of delivery forms by the creative communication people. Most important, a solid value proposition, rather than being a straitjacket for creative development, is really a license to create. The boundaries that the value proposition provides are simply a framework in which all types of creative expression can occur.

Further, if the marketer knows which delivery forms are accessed by customers and prospects, the ability to develop creative executions within those media is expanded exponentially.

Finally, the development of messages and incentives, given the broad array of delivery systems available, is a critical ingredient in creating truly innovative, long-lasting customer-brand relationships. As we illustrate in Chapter 16, the range of delivery systems in a push-pull marketplace is almost unlimited. That is why it is important to understand initially which delivery systems are the most customer-appropriate and then, based on that knowledge, what type of content should be developed and delivered.

Interestingly, we provide few examples of advertisements or promotions or even creative elements or executions in the following pages. One reason is that most of them would be terribly dated by the time this text appears. Second, the days of seemingly unbridled creativity are far behind us. Today, the focus is on customers and brands and relationships, not on clever paeans to the creativity of the writers or artists who developed the messages or incentives. Marketing communication is simply too important for firms to consider messages and incentives as "art"; instead, they must be an inherent part of a scientific approach to developing better customer-brand relationships. And that is what a value proposition does: it focuses the development of messages and incentives so they solve customer problems and provide customer value, not just generate accolades from peer groups.

So here is the fourth area of *Building Customer-Brand Relationships*: content.

CHAPTER 15

Linking Customers and Marketers With Value Propositions

The value proposition is at the core of the customer-brand relationship. It is what the brand provides customers in exchange for their money, time, and effort. Simply put, it is the promise the brand makes and delivers to customers and what they gain when they buy and use the brand. But unless the value proposition is truly unique relative to competition, useful, and worthwhile to them individually, customers are not likely to enter into a relationship with the brand, let alone continue that relationship. An old maxim holds that nothing ruins a bad product faster than good advertising, since good advertising generates product trial, which quickly highlights the product's poor performance. In today's customer-driven marketplace, nothing will doom a product faster than a poorly conceived, internally focused value proposition. The value proposition has value precisely because it is seen as something that is unique to the brand and of true worth to the customer.

The value proposition must hold true and provide benefit to all of the brand's markets and stakeholders. While the methods and means of communicating the value proposition may vary for each market group, the value proposition itself must be the same for all markets, because today people truly live in a global marketplace. We will review how the value proposition is communicated in more detail in the next chapter. Here, we focus on a process of identifying the value proposition and then using it as the center of the distribution and communication strategy for the brand.

To start, reviewing the value proposition for several well-established brands should be helpful in understanding how to proceed. For example, Starbucks' value proposition is to be the premium provider of "the coffee experience." To ultimate consumers, this value proposition encompasses both the beverages and food products served in a Starbucks outlet and, even more importantly, the entire buying process and the environment within a Starbucks location. "The coffee experience" includes its own language (Tall, Grande, Frappucino, half-caf, etc.); the presence of the barista (the people who make and serve the beverages at Starbucks locations), a somewhat other-worldly character; an environment at once welcoming (through conversation areas, music, accessory products, etc.) and exclusionary (first-timers are easy to spot as they anxiously scan the product listings, trying to decipher which offering is best for them). All of these are elements of "the coffee experience" created by Starbucks. Competitors, no matter how hard they try, typically offer only inferior imitations.

How does this value proposition translate to other markets? There is great appeal for a coffee bean provider, dairy product producer, or bakery in being selected to supply a portion of "the Starbucks coffee experience." Surely that honor is something for the supplier to promote to its shareholders. The glow of "the coffee experience" even carries over to Starbucks' distribution partners; offering Starbucks coffee is generally promoted by hotels as a mark of excellence, and the brand extension of Starbucks ice cream appears in the superpremium area of grocery stores' freezer cases.

UPS provides another clear example. Its value proposition is implied by its slogan "What Can Brown Do for You?" The value proposition is a total solution for any shipping need. For ultimate customers, no matter the size of their company, the volume of their shipping, or their personal shipping needs, UPS has the optimal service that will best meet their requirements. "Best" here means reliability, speed, and price. The implied answer to the question "What Can Brown Do for You?" is "Everything you need when it comes to shipping." The slogan speaks powerfully to UPS employees as well as external audiences. It shows in their pride in wearing the uniform, in responding to problems, in meeting on-time delivery goals, and so on.

The value proposition for Tide Detergent is the solution for any laundry problem. Whatever laundry stains the ultimate customer must deal with, there is a Tide formulation to solve that problem. As we have discussed elsewhere, the quality assurance provided by the brand helps differentiate it from less expensive competitors, and the solution to problems Tide provides makes this value proposition resonate with the customer. The consistent quality of the range of Procter & Gamble's brands, including Tide, makes the company an attractive recommendation for the stockbroker influencer market. P&G may not be flashy, but it offers consistent value for risk-averse investors. Clearly, the functional value propositions offered by Tide and other P&G brands are a major contributor to that consistency.

DEVELOPING THE VALUE PROPOSITION

David Aaker defines the value proposition as "a statement of the functional, emotional, and self-expressive benefits delivered by the brand that provide value to the customer. An effective value proposition should lead to a brand-customer relationship and drive purchase decisions."[1] Functional benefits have to do with some tangible aspect of the brand or brand performance, such as those offered by UPS and Tide as described above. Kevin Lane Keller claims that functional benefits are often associated with basic needs, such as Maslow's core needs described in Chapter 3, and that value propositions based on functional benefits often deal with solving customer problems.[2] Unique functional benefits offered by the brand can differentiate it from other alternatives. However, the unique element must be something that customers both care about and place value upon. If the brand does have a truly unique aspect, this can be a powerful basis for a sustained positive relationship with customers. For example, the iPod's ability to provide high-quality music performance in a very small, transportable package is a compelling and unique functional value proposition.

Emotional benefits focus less on the physical attributes of the product and more on the feelings created through the experience of buying or using the product, such as in our Starbucks example. In Aaker's words, "Emotional benefits add richness and depth to the experience of owning and using the brand."[3] Emotional benefits often derive from the brand image or brand personality. This is psychological differentiation through establishing and maintaining a brand personality that customers see as unique and valuable. The emotional approach to the value proposition often creates a mystique around the product or service, something Starbucks has done very effectively.

Self-expressive benefits create a value proposition tied to the customers' view of themselves and the brand's ability to contribute to that view. The emphasis here is on the customers' lifestyle and how the brand can fit that lifestyle. Self-expressive benefits are also important to emotions and the building of relationships. Mazda's "Zoom-Zoom" campaign for its vehicles established a self-expressive value proposition by showing how customers can activate the free, racing driver spirit within them by driving a Mazda and embracing the "zoom-zoom" lifestyle. Many drivers of a certain age want to hold onto a sense of youthful rebellion even as they embrace a more sedate professional life. To them, the self-expressive benefit offered by Mazda is likely very appealing.

The value proposition developed for each brand must start with a focus on the needs of the brand's customer groups, not the marketer's needs, goals, or desires. As we discussed in Chapter 5, each customer group has different needs that come from its relationship, or potential relationship, with the marketer. Those needs must form the foundation for the value proposition and resulting strategy. A strategy that does not take customer needs into account will not result in a productive, long-lived relationship.

SIVA Revisited

The SIVA process introduced in Chapter 2—solutions, information, value, and access—is highly relevant to developing the value proposition for customers and customer groups.

- *Solutions*: A value proposition must provide a solution to a customer problem. An important step in developing the value proposition is to determine whether that problem can best be solved through functional benefits, emotional benefits, self-expressive benefits, or some combination. The particular focus of the value proposition must grow out of the marketer's understanding of the customer's problem. What do customers want or need from this brand, and what is it that the brand offers that will satisfy that want or need? Unless those very basic questions can be answered, and answered in a customer-focused way, there is very little point in proceeding with strategy development.
- *Information*: What information will customers need to evaluate the value proposition? What information or support is necessary to make the value proposition believable? Marketers may claim that a brand will solve a particular problem or meet a particular need, but it is far more challenging to provide the information that customers require to evaluate the believability of that claim both in absolute terms and in light of their own particular circumstances. The strategy growing out of the value proposition must address both what information is needed and how and where and when that information should be provided to the customers.
- *Value*: Value is, by definition, at the heart of the value proposition. What are the customers being asked or expected to provide in order to gain the solution promised by the value proposition? Is the benefit inherent in the value proposition worth the cost to the customers? How the value proposition is communicated, and the supporting information that accompanies it, will determine the customers' assessment of the overall value of the brand relative to their needs.

- *Access*: In order for the value proposition to be truly useful to customers and truly motivating, they must be able—and, perhaps more importantly, must believe they are able—to access the brand and its benefits easily and on their own terms. This is another important aspect of strategic decisions arising out of the value proposition. How can the benefit be best communicated and most easily acted upon?

The marketer's focus on SIVA requires attention to customers, forcing evaluation of possible value propositions from a customer's viewpoint. Without such an emphasis, the marketer runs the risk of developing an irrelevant offer that will not resonate with customers and will therefore fail to initiate or maintain the desired customer-brand relationship.

THE CUSTOMER-BRAND RELATIONSHIP STRATEGY DEVELOPMENT FORM

Our recommended framework for developing the customer-brand relationship strategy is shown in Exhibit 15.1. In the following discussion, we review each of the six aspects of customer-brand relationship strategy development: customers, brand, competition, message content, delivery systems, and long-term relationship building. That discussion is followed by two examples, one for an end-user consumer product and the other for a business-to-business technology product focused on the influencer customer group.

Who Is the Customer?

As we have argued throughout this text, all decisions must start with the customer, so that is where the strategy begins. The form begins with a summary of current behavior, information gleaned from the database or from secondary sources or the marketer's own primary research with current, competitive, or prospective customers. What brand or brands is this customer group currently using? How often do they purchase, from what sources, using what forms of payment, and for what uses?

The marketer then turns to an examination of this group as people in order to better understand the motivations underlying their behavior. What is the lifestyle of the people in this group? What types of activities do they enjoy? What are their attitudes on relevant issues? What do they think about the product or service category? Do they think about it much or at all? (This last question evokes levels of involvement.)

Thinking about the customer group's needs and requirements in the category should lead to the key customer insight. This is the primary component of the customer's brand network, the driving motivation that has the strongest influence on behavior. What does the customer want most from the category and from a specific brand within the category? And, given that insight, what is the critical element that can or should differentiate the marketer's brand from others in the category? What unsatisfied needs exist? Relationships are about satisfying needs: What need can the marketer seek to satisfy? The answers to these questions should help identify the brand's value proposition.

If the strategy successfully satisfies the customer's need, what does the marketer expect in return? That is, what behavior is expected from this customer and customer group—complete loyalty to the brand, or brand exclusivity? An increase in repurchase rates or volume bought?

Exhibit 15.1

The Customer-Brand Relationship Strategy Development Form

Customer group: _____
(ultimate customers, intermediaries, suppliers, referrals, influencers, or internal markets)

Customers: Who is the customer?

What do they buy now? How do they buy and use the product(s)?

What are their lifestyles, psychographics, and attitudes toward the category?

How do members of this group perceive the products or services in this category?

What is the key customer insight?

What is the key differentiation point for this customer group?

What do these customers want from the product category that they are not now getting?

What brand commitment do we expect from this customer group? (loyalty, repurchase rates, share of wallet, brand advocacy)

Brand: What is the reality of the brand?

What is our perceived quality? (zero defects, suitability to needs)

What is our brand identity/image? (values, attributes, traits, personalities)

What ongoing, enduring image do we want to sustain?

Does the product or service fit the customer group? Recommendation?

Competition: Who is the competition?

What is the brand network, the competitive frame? Why?

What is our competition's perceived quality?

What is our competition's brand identity/image?

Delivery Systems: How will we deliver information to the customer?

What means will we use to communicate with and build/maintain a relationship with this customer group?

What traditional media-based communication forms will be most effective with this customer group?

What other areas and opportunities will be most effective with this group? (in-store, Web sites, blogs, packaging, word-of-mouth, employees, customer service, channel partners, etc.)

How will we maintain consistency across communication forms?

(continued)

Exhibit 15.1 *(continued)*

Message Content: What message or incentive do we need to deliver?

Do we need to provide a message, an incentive, or both to this customer group?

If a message, what immediate benefit will we provide?

What ongoing benefits will we provide? (functional superiority; emotional/psychic benefits)

If an incentive, will it reduce price or add value?

What will be the ongoing communication elements with this group?

What should the personality of the brand, company, or product be? What unique personality will help further define the product or service and discretely differentiate it from the competitive frame?

Long-term relationship-building: What sustained relationship do we want?

What reputation do we want? (innovation, people management, use of corporate assets, social responsibility, quality of management, financial soundness, long-term investment, quality of products/service)

What value will we provide to this customer group?

A larger share of the customer's wallet? Will the customer perhaps become a brand advocate, actively promoting the brand to others thanks to this high level of satisfaction? A workable strategy must have a goal; this last customer question speaks to that issue.

Brand

Once the marketer has a sense of the customer firmly in mind, the next step is to look at the brand through the customer's eyes. Just what is the marketer offering in exchange for the desired customer behavior? What level of quality do customers in this group perceive the brand to have? What is the brand identity; that is, what values, attributes, and personality does the customer group associate with the brand?

Based on this understanding of the customer group and their perceptions of the brand, the next question looks to longer-term image. What image does the marketer want this brand to have? How should it be perceived by the customer group? Does the current product or service fit what the customer group wants and fit the image that the marketer wants to establish and maintain? If it does not, recommendations should be made to adapt the brand to better fit the marketer's goals.

Competition

Brands, of course, do not exist in a vacuum, and marketers cannot simply mold the market as they would like. Brand strategy must consider competition. Who are the chief competitors, based on customer perceptions? What brands does the customer group consider acceptable substitutes for the marketer's brand? How do they perceive the quality of those competitors: as good as the marketer's brand, better than the brand, worse but still acceptable? What image or identity do the chief competitors have? The answers to the questions in this section will aid the marketer in considering how the brand network for the product or service compares to that of competitors, and what perceptual barriers need to be overcome to result in the desired behavior from the customer group.

Delivery Systems

This section of the strategy addresses how information will be communicated to the customer. What types of traditional, media-based communication does the customer group use and respond to? What other types might be considered, either instead of traditional forms or as a supplement? If brand advocacy is the goal, might a blog or a podcast be the best way to spark word-of-mouth discussion? What role might employees play in delivering messages to other customer groups? Where can the marketer deliver the message with the greatest possible impact?

If more than one communication form is recommended, as is nearly always the case, the issue of message consistency must be addressed. What measures must be taken to ensure that the same core message is delivered across all communication forms? This question may involve personnel training, internal coordination of the work of multiple communication-provider agencies, and the like, but some focus on consistency is essential. In personal relationships, mixed messages create tension. The same is true with customer-brand relationships.

Message Content

The marketer must then determine what messages and/or incentives will need to be provided to effect the desired change in the customer's brand network and, ultimately, behavior. The first decision to be made is whether the emphasis should be on providing additional brand information through a message or whether the customer has all the necessary information and instead requires an incentive to spark the desired behavior. Of course, in many product categories, it is necessary to provide both messages and incentives to offset competitive activities.

Research from several perspectives suggests that messages are always a critical component of a successful promotional program. Many marketing case histories show that providing customers with new, useful information is the foundation for brand success.[4] Research on sales promotion has found that strategies combining an incentive with an informational message (consumer franchise-building approaches) result in much longer-term effects on sales than an incentive alone.[5] In short, unless customer research indicates that no further information needs to be communicated, the marketer should always start with a message focus and then decide whether an incentive is needed as well.

The message itself needs to provide a benefit to the customer by delivering the value proposition. What will they receive if they do in fact decide to buy and use the marketer's brand? This might be information as to how the brand is superior to competitive offerings due to functional benefits such as a unique feature or preferred offer terms. Or it could be a self-expressive benefit derived from the psychological effects of brand use. Whatever the foundation, the benefit must be something that truly has value to customers, something they will really care about, not a trumped-up feature the marketer wants to push.

If an incentive is to be used in combination with the message, the decision to be made is whether the incentive will itself add value to the brand or whether it will simply reduce the price of the brand. Added-value incentives, if tied in some way to the brand's personality, can have long-lasting effects on the relationship between the customer and the brand. Price-reduction incentives tend to have a shorter-term effect and are more vulnerable to competitive retaliation.

Once the decision has been made on messages and incentives, the next question is what communication elements will be used long-term to convey the message and/or incentive to the customer group. What forms of strategic communication are most appropriate given the customer group, the brand, and the competitive frame? Finally, what personality does the marketer want to convey through these communications, a personality that will set the brand apart from the rest of the category in a meaningful way?

Long-Term Relationship Building

The last section of the form considers how the immediate strategy will contribute to the long-term relationship that the marketer hopes to establish and maintain with the customer. What is the reputation the marketer wants to develop for the brand and for the company? What are the key elements of that reputation? If the company's reputation will rest largely on that of the brand, these questions will bring us back to a focus on brand quality. If the reputation is based more centrally, with the brand benefiting from the overall corporate reputation, what are the key elements of that corporate identity?

Finally, the form concludes with a statement of the value proposition. Taken altogether, what is the value this brand is providing or will provide to this customer group? Why should customers want to enter into a relationship with the brand or maintain an existing relationship? In short, what is in it for them?

As noted earlier, the Customer-Brand Relationship Strategy Development form offers a means of summarizing and organizing a great deal of information about the customer, the brand, and the competition into a coherent whole. Then, the planner can start to think about what needs to be done to effect the desired behavior from the customer group. What follows are two examples of the application of the strategy form, one for a consumer-focused marketer and the other for a business-to-business firm.

EXAMPLE ONE: TARGET AND ULTIMATE CUSTOMERS

In the example that follows, the proposed customer for whom the strategy is being developed is an existing Target store customer. Thus, the focus is on customer retention and growth.

Target is a discount retailer offering a wide range of products through 1,500 brick-and-mortar stores in forty-seven U.S. states and online at www.target.com. The company was founded in 1962.[6]

The Customer-Brand Relationship Strategy Development Form: Target

Customer group: Existing final consumers who shop at Target

Customers: Who Is the Customer?

What do they buy now? How do they buy and use the products?

The core Target final customer shops at Target often, visiting her local Target store or Target.com site three or more times every month. She buys a wide range of products when she shops: housewares, fashion, electronics, health and beauty products, pet items, even food. She views Target as her fill-in store for grocery shopping.

What are their lifestyles, psychographics, and attitudes toward the category?

The core Target ultimate customer is a busy woman. She works full-time, holding a professional or managerial position that requires a great deal of her time and attention. She is fun loving and active, always busy with errands, picking up the kids, and other family business even when she is away from work. She enjoys luxuries and pampering, but she is also practical and does not mind saving money. However, she is not willing to compromise quality (or convenience) for just the few pennies she thinks she will save at the competitive outlets.

How do members of this group perceive the products or services in this category?

The Target customer enjoys shopping and wants to feel that her business matters to the retailers where she shops. She does not like either of Target's primary competitors; she finds Wal-Mart overcrowded and too price-focused, and she questions the quality of the products at her local K-Mart. She likes the mix of merchandise at Target and especially the feel of the store: roomy aisles, with less clutter than at other discount department stores she has visited. Target feels classier, and that makes her feel classy, too.

What is the key customer insight?

Saving money is a good thing, but not at the expense of a positive shopping experience. Target gives her both.

What is the key differentiation point for this customer group?

Atmosphere. Target just feels like a better place than the competition, and that is important to the customer's self-image.

What do these customers want from the product category that they are not now getting?

Reassurance that the pricing in Target is low enough to reflect that she is a discriminating shopper, and reinforcement of what makes Target more appealing (upscale and young) than the competition.

What brand commitment do we expect from this customer group?

She's a loyal Target customer now, shopping there at least three times a month. We want to hold onto her business and keep her away from our competitors, who try to tempt her with price and promotional gimmicks.

Brand: What Is the Reality of the Brand?

What is our perceived quality?

Positive quality perceptions. Our brand mix is seen as higher-end than discount competition, while not as high-end (or high-priced) as traditional department stores. We are known for carrying a wide range of good-quality brands.

What is our brand identity or image?

We are seen as the fun brand in the category—irreverent, smart, knowing. We are the hip, fun younger sister who likes a good time but is smart enough not to get into trouble—on the edge, but definitely not over it.

What ongoing, enduring image do we want to sustain?

Similar to the existing image. We want to be perceived as offering really good products (better than the competition) for a really good price. We are not bargain basement, but we are smart, and we know it.

Does the product or service fit the customer group? Recommendation?

The product fits the ultimate customer group quite well. Constant updates, including new designers and new store designs, keep customers satisfied and coming back.

Competition: Who Is the Competition?

What is the brand network, the competitive frame? Why?

The primary competitive frame is large national discount retailers, particularly Wal-Mart. Wal-Mart most closely matches our range of brands (more so than traditional department stores, which do not carry the range of electronics, housewares, and food items found in most of our stores) and is aggressive in promoting its price deals.

What is our competition's perceived quality?

Wal-Mart is perceived as having lower prices, but also somewhat lower quality. The chief difference is in the in-store shopping experience. Wal-Mart's merchandising approach is much more cluttered than that of Target.

What is our competition's brand identity or image?

Low prices are the basis for Wal-Mart's business, and although it has experimented with higher quality and a broader selection, it is still the low-price store. Its focus is much more on price than on quality or attitude and, consequently, less on the customer herself.

Delivery Systems: How Will We Deliver Information to the Customer?

What means will we use to communicate with and build or maintain a relationship with this customer group?

Because this group is very time-pressed, they are much heavier users of the new media forms than traditional media. They prefer media options that adapt to their schedule. The core Target ultimate customer uses the Internet heavily and also tends to read magazines. She does not watch much television or listen to the radio a great deal. She does not mind direct mail if it is targeted to her interests.

What traditional media-based communication forms will be most effective with this customer group?

Print advertising (both magazines and newspapers, but especially magazines) and direct mail. In addition to fitting her lifestyle, magazine advertising has the added benefit of complementing the Target fashion-oriented image.

What other areas and opportunities will be most effective with this group?

In-store messages can be effective as long as they do not clutter the store. Displays need to be kept to a minimum. An attractive, easy-to-use Web site is a plus with this customer because of her comfort level with the online environment; a Web site also reinforces our up-to-date image. This busy customer does not want to wait in line at checkout and expects an open lane and a friendly, attentive, but not pushy cashier. The availability and ease of use of the Target REDcard and/or Target Visa card are also pluses for this customer, and something Wal-Mart does not offer.

How will we maintain consistency across communication forms?

Our logo (the target) and red-and-white color scheme are both instantly recognizable and must be maintained in all forms of communication. Our hip, modern brand personality must also be reflected in everything we do.

Message Content: What Message or Incentive Do We Need to Deliver?

Do we need to provide a message, an incentive, or both to this customer group?

Both. The message must constantly reinforce our brand personality, while incentives are necessary to keep this customer away from the price-focused Wal-Mart as much as possible.

If a message, what immediate benefit will we provide?

Superior quality. Our messages should feature our brands, both those designer brands exclusive to Target and the national brands we provide. The Target shopper expects, and should get, more from shopping at our stores than competitors can offer.

What ongoing benefits will we provide?

Our chief ongoing benefits are emotional and self-expressive. Shopping at Target makes our customer feel good about herself. She is getting good-quality merchandise, some of it exclusive to us, at a good price. And she is able to enjoy the shopping experience while she is in the store.

If an incentive, will it reduce price or add value?

Primarily price reduction. This is necessary to combat Wal-Mart's aggressive tactics, but it is also a way for us to show our customer how well we understand and appreciate her. We will use the information in our database, collected whenever she shops with her Target REDcard or Target Visa, to provide discount offers on both specific brands we know she buys and other targeted brands within product categories where we know she has an interest.

What will be the ongoing communication elements with this group?

Image-based advertising to reinforce our brand personality, a regularly updated Web site to provide convenience and reinforce brand image, and periodic, targeted coupon offers combined with brand information (TargetMail) to provide desired incentives.

What should the personality of the brand, company, or product be? What unique personality will further define the product or service and discretely differentiate from the competition?

We are much higher quality and more sophisticated than Wal-Mart, in a much more affordable (and fun) package than traditional department stores.

Long-Term Relationship Building: What Sustained Relationship Do We Want?

What reputation do we want?

Our primary reputation is one of quality, innovation, and fun. We provide consistent quality at a fair price in an appealing shopping environment.

What value will we provide to this customer group?

Good products at a fair price, in an environment that lets the customer enjoy the shopping experience and feel good about herself. (Target summarizes this value as "Expect More. Pay Less.")

Execution of Target's Strategy

Target uses many communication devices to maintain the relationship between its core customers and the brand. The Target card, whether the traditional store credit card or the Target

Exhibit 15.2 **Target Mail**

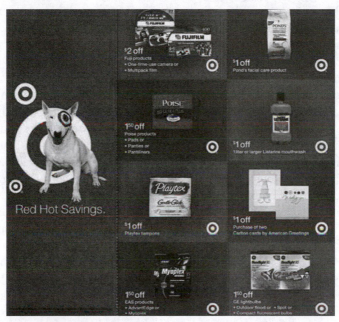

Visa, is the key to the relationship, because it provides Target with critical information on its customers' purchasing behavior. Target knows how often its cardholders shop using the card, what they buy, and how much they spend. It uses that information to provide: (1) general savings discounts when customers spend a certain amount using their card (for example, shoppers who spent $250 or more on their Target card over the winter holidays in 2007 got 10 percent off a store shopping trip and another 10 percent off a Web site visit); and (2) targeted coupons for specific brands. The latter are generally a mix of coupons for brands the customer purchases regularly and coupons for different brands in product categories the customer has shopped. These coupons come in the mail about every six weeks, in a red envelope with white text that heralds it as "Target Mail—Your news. Your store. Your savings. What's in store—great values & more." In addition to the coupons, the Target Mail package includes a four- to eight-page insert highlighting new or featured items, special savings, and the like. (See Exhibit 15.2 for an example of a Target Mail insert.)

Compared to Target's approach, Wal-Mart's communications tend to focus exclusively on price deals. Wal-Mart's core audience skews older and lower-income than Target's and tends to include more women who either do not work outside the home or work in jobs that are clerical in nature.[7] Wal-Mart is much less about the shopping experience than Target; the only emphasis is on saving money. Wal-Mart does offer a credit card, but whereas the Target card is promoted heavily on the homepage of the Target Web site, Wal-Mart's card is promoted much less aggressively.

While this example translates Target's value proposition for the final consumer group, that same value proposition works for Target's other customer groups, too. Because of the functional benefit of quality but with a continuing focus on the value proposition, Target's supplier brands gain some prestige from being carried by the retailer. Target's contracts with high-profile designers, including Michael Graves, Isaac Mizrahi, and Liz Lange, also contribute to supplier prestige. The quality proposition also gives Target some leverage with referral markets, important for a publicly traded company. The emotional and self-expressive benefits associated with the Target shopping experience speak to influencer customer groups such as family, friends, and associates as strongly as they do to the ultimate customer group.

Internally, Target's emphasis on quality translates to employee training programs, a comprehensive benefits package, and extensive support of community affairs at the local and national levels. Target donates 5 percent of its income to community programs related to education, the arts, and social services. The Target corporate Web site lists twenty-four national organizations Target supports, including America's Second Harvest, the Hispanic Scholarship Fund, the Salvation Army, the National Domestic Violence Hotline, and the Vietnam Veterans Memorial Fund.[8] This range of corporate philanthropy no doubt enhances the Target value proposition by adding yet another aspect to the emotional and self-expressive elements of the Target brand.

EXAMPLE TWO: CUSTOMER RELATIONSHIP MANAGEMENT PRODUCT

Visitar is a North Carolina–based company that offers a customer relationship management (CRM) product to help small businesses better manage their contacts with customers, with a focus on telephone-based activities. For example, the financial aid office at the University of Louisville uses 360° Care *via* Visitar to manage information collected from the roughly 100 calls about financial aid it gets each day from students and parents of students.[9] Founded in 2005, Visitar is a new company in the start-up phase of its operations. Unlike Target, whose primary goal is customer retention, Visitar's primary goal is to acquire new customers.

Product: Hosted customer relationship management via hosted telephony integration, offered by Visitar.

Customer group: Ultimate customers (small businesses with 5 to 250 employees)

Customers: Who Is the Customer?

What do they buy now? How do they buy and use the product(s)?

The targeted customer group currently addresses customer relationship management challenges using one of three approaches: pen and paper, spreadsheets and documents, or other hosted CRM products. For hosted CRM, clients purchase online directly from the supplier. The hosted CRM buyers are the smallest segment of this market, but also the fastest growing. Customers who already conduct most of their business by telephone are the group with the greatest need for, and interest in, this product.

What are their lifestyles, psychographics, and attitudes toward the category?

Since this is a new application, the attitudes for the category are just now emerging. They range from confusion and fear, due to horror stories of large company failures in implementation, to belief that CRM can provide the keys to rapid growth.

How do members of this group perceive the products or services in this category?

In general, both the products and the services are viewed as hard to use, hard to manage, and expensive—almost as a necessary evil. Many prospects wish that the problems would just go away.

What is the key customer insight?

Many of the decision-makers in the customer group are not fully familiar with the concept of customer relationship management systems and so have concerns and questions about the customer relationship management system process and capabilities. They are also fully aware that understanding and sharing detailed customer information is critical as their company grows. They are actively looking for a viable solution.

What is the key differentiation point for this customer group?

The ideal solution must be affordable without sacrificing key functionality, enhancing the customer's already heavy reliance on the telephone for the firm's sales and service.

What do these customers want from the product category that they are not now getting?

More affordable solutions that can feasibly be implemented within their firm.

What brand commitment do we expect from this customer group? (loyalty, repurchase rates, share of wallet, brand advocacy)

Loyalty that will drive ongoing subscription agreements (i.e., repurchase of the agreements Visitar has with customers) and brand advocacy to drive referral business.

Brand: What Is the Reality of the Brand?

What is our perceived quality? (zero defects, suitability to needs)

The brand itself is largely unknown, since Visitar is a start-up company. Early opinions center around innovation and partner friendliness. This brand is sold through channels, including distributors, value-added resellers with application integration experience, and standard resellers. Strong positive relationships within those channels are an important aspect of the brand's growing reputation as well as providing risk reduction for potential customers.

What is our brand identity or image? (values, attributes, traits, personalities)

The brand is seen as affordable and practical for small businesses. The service provides a telephony aspect to CRM; telephony is an accepted and understood technology. This makes the brand more accessible to potential customer groups than other CRM brands that are based on more complex technologies.

What ongoing, enduring image do we want to sustain?

We want people to think of Visitar as a partner-friendly company that provides innovative, affordable solutions to CRM challenges.

Does the product or service fit the customer group? Recommendation?

Yes. The telephony application is easily understood. To use the system, the customer only needs a telephone, a Web browser, and the 360° Care *via* Visitar service. Customers can "initiate interactions via the phone, email and other communication channels and manage those interactions with other customer information resources in a CRM system."[10] This ease of use and accessibility are critical elements for this customer group.

Competition: Who Is the Competition?

What is the brand network, the competitive frame? Why?

The greatest potential within this customer group lies with firms that are still relying on pen and paper or conventional electronic spreadsheets to manage their customer relationships. Direct competition in the hosted CRM subsegment comes from one major competitor, salesforce.com.

What is our competition's perceived quality?

Traditional solutions (pen and paper or spreadsheets) are seen as offering acceptable quality (subject to human error) but are unable to cope easily with the growing complexity that comes with company growth and increased customer demands. Salesforce.com offers acceptable quality, but with an aggressive direct selling focus that may be off-putting for some prospective customers within this group.

What is our competition's brand identity or image?

The direct competitor is fairly well known in this customer sector, but is perceived to be losing interest in small business and wanting to move upstream to larger organizations. There is also the perception that its à la carte service approach ultimately costs users more as they generally seek added functionality as their needs grow.

Delivery Systems: How Will We Deliver the Message and/or Incentive to the Customer?

What means will we use to communicate with and build and maintain a relationship with this customer group?

Local value-added reseller (VAR) channels including Cincinnati Bell Technology Solutions and Penn Telecom are the focal point for communication. This customer group has established relationships with these resellers and trusts them to help identify business solutions. Visitar's VAR partners include local telephone companies, business consulting firms, and other organizations that have established relationships with small businesses.

What traditional media-based communication forms will be most effective with this customer group?

Traditional media communication forms such as advertising and analyst reports are relatively ineffective with this group for this type of product, because prospects do not yet know enough about their requirements or the availability of solutions to seek out information. Visitar-originated communications are most effectively directed to VAR partners, who can in turn communicate that information to their clients.

What other areas and opportunities will be most effective with this group? (in-store, Web sites, blogs, packaging, word of mouth, employees, customer service, channel partners, etc.)

Word of mouth (active encouragement of referrals), channel partner recruitment, and education and ongoing public relations efforts through press releases and case histories are the important support elements.

How will we maintain consistency across communication forms?

With our emphasis on channel partners and word of mouth, consistent quality of service is the most important element in maintaining communication consistency.

Message Content: What Message or Incentive Do We Need to Deliver?

Do we need to provide a message, an incentive, or both to this customer group?

Both. A message is needed to inform and educate the customer group about our brand and our value proposition. Incentives are also needed to induce trial of what will be, for most members of the customer group, an untried solution to their problem.

If a message, what immediate benefit will we provide?

Affordable solutions to customer management that are usable and functional because we link the telephone (the key customer interaction device) with the software, enabling more information to be captured without extra work by employees. This ability increases the customer's own productivity and profitability.

What ongoing benefits will we provide? (functional superiority, emotional or psychic benefits)

Better business practices and probably more profitability through lower costs (to acquire customers and deploy and manage the salesforce) and improved manageability. Functional superiority for companies that rely on the telephone for customer interactions. Functional and emotional benefits of local support through the partner network.

If an incentive, will it reduce price or add value?

Price reduction offers are needed to drive trial and subsequently build customer advocacy.

What will be the ongoing communication elements with this group?

Local service, support, and interaction by regionally focused partners who already communicate regularly with this customer group. We will provide them with literature and Web access for the information needed by customers to make a trial decision.

What should the personality of the brand, company, or product be? What unique personality will further define the product or service and discretely differentiate it from the competition?

Helpful, small-business focus, a trusted ally, and improved business results communicated through affiliation with known partners that serve the customer group and are trusted regionally. We offer innovation without high cost.

Long-Term Relationship Building: What Sustained Relationship Do We Want?

What reputation do we want? (innovation, people management, use of corporate assets, social responsibility, quality of management, financial soundness, long-term investment, quality of products and service)

We want to be seen as offering affordable innovation to solve the problems of small, but growing, businesses.

What value will we provide to this customer group?

Our value proposition is quality CRM that improves the value of the firm's telephony investment while also enabling our customer group to gain more value from each of their own customers. This is both a functional benefit provided through service delivery and an emotional benefit of better, more effective business practices.

Execution of Visitar's Strategy

With its focus on partners, Visitar offers a specialized Partner Portal on its Web site with exclusive information for partners to use in selling Visitar's service. The company also produces a newsletter for partners, *The Voice of Visitar,* that includes company news, selling tips, case histories, and other information to help partners. Partners also receive collateral marketing materials prepared by Visitar that they can label with their company name for distribution to customers and prospects.

Visitar's public relations area generates frequent press releases highlighting new product developments, new partners, and new customers. Visitar has also received coverage in key trade journals, including *CRM Buyer* and *PC Magazine.*

To encourage word of mouth among ultimate customers, Visitar offers a referral program that rewards current customers who recommend the service to new prospects. The referring customer gets credits toward its service from Visitar once the referred business has been a Visitar customer for two months.

SUMMING UP

These two examples illustrate how the Customer-Brand Relationship Strategy Development Form can be applied to develop a framework for creating and maintaining the customer-brand relationship, with a focus on the value proposition. In the following chapter, we further develop the application of this framework in a discussion of value proposition communication through a variety of marketing communication techniques.

NOTES

1. D. Aaker, *Building Strong Brands* (New York: Free Press, 1996), p. 95.
2. K.L. Keller, "Conceptualizing, Measuring, and Managing Customer-Based Brand Equity," *Journal of Marketing* 57, no. 1 (1993): 1–22.

3. Aaker, *Building Strong Brands*, p. 97.

4. C.H. Patti and C.F. Frazer, *Advertising: A Decision-Making Approach* (Chicago: Dryden, 1988).

5. R.M. Prentice, "How to Split Your Marketing Funds between Advertising and Promotion Dollars," *Advertising Age,* January 10, 1977, pp. 41–44.

6. Target Corporation, "About Target," http://sites.target.com/site/en/corporate/page.jsp?contentId=PRD03–001085.

7. Consumer profile information for both Target and Wal-Mart from MRI-Plus Fall 2006 study, available by subscription from Mediamark Research.

8. Information on Target's community programs and employee programs may be found at http://sites.target.com/site/en/corporate/page.jsp?ref=nav%5Ffooter%5Fcompany&contentId=PRD03-000482.

9. *CRM Today*, "The University of Louisville Chooses Visitar to Enhance Service and Communications with Students," January 11, 2007, www.crm2day.com/news/crm/121052.php.

10. Since this case study was written, Visitar has ceased operation. The basic market approach described in this example was valid, but the company was not able to secure sufficient long-term funding to provide the time needed to establish the selling channel strategy the case describes. The authors chose to leave the case study in the present tense because it describes Visitar's approach during its operation.

CHAPTER 16

Communicating Brand
Value to Customers

As was seen in the customer-brand relationship strategy development form introduced in the previous chapter, once the customer has been defined, the brand reality evaluated, the competition identified, and the key delivery systems selected, the remaining decision to be made is the content of the communication. Put simply, what information needs to be delivered (a message) or inducement offered (an incentive) to build and/or maintain the desired relationship between the customer and the brand? The messages and incentives must contribute to establishing and maintaining the value proposition, creating or bolstering the perceived value of the brand to the customer.

In earlier chapters, we have discussed how customers take in and process information related to the brand, and the stages many customers move through in making purchasing decisions. What goes on in problem recognition, information search, alternative evaluation, purchase decision, and post-purchase processes, particularly the likelihood that any particular brand will be selected out of all those considered, has much to do with the customer's brand knowledge. Before looking specifically at how messages and incentives may be communicated to customers, we look first at the components of brand knowledge as a basis for message and/or incentive content.

BRAND KNOWLEDGE

The conceptualization of brand knowledge used most widely comes from the work of Kevin Lane Keller, a marketing professor at the Tuck School at Dartmouth College. Keller developed a framework for customer brand knowledge, shown in Exhibit 16.1.

As shown, brand knowledge has two primary components, brand awareness and brand image. Obviously, customers and prospective customers cannot be knowledgeable about a brand unless they are first aware of it. The two aspects of brand awareness, brand recall and brand recognition, identify two possible processes of knowing about a brand. Brand recall is the customer's ability to pull identifying brand information from memory, while brand recognition is retrieval of brand information when cued.[1] Whether recall or recognition is the better measure of awareness is the subject of ongoing debate. Those who argue in favor of recall cite the greater demands of being able to pull brand information from memory, while those in favor of recognition point out that many purchasing decisions are, in fact, recognition

Exhibit 16.1   Keller's "Dimensions of Brand Knowledge" Chart

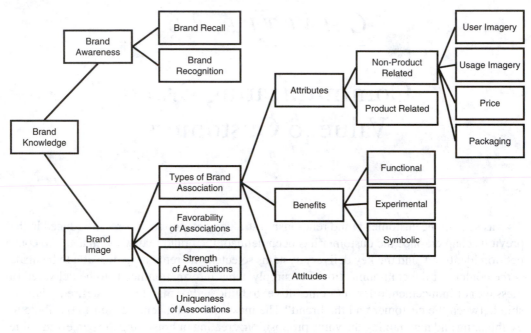

Source: K.L. Keller, "Conceptualizing, Measuring, and Managing Customer-Based Brand Equity," *Journal of Marketing* 57 (January 1993): 7.

situations in which the brand package in the store acts as the recognition cue. In either case, basic awareness of the brand is a necessary component of brand knowledge.

The second component of brand knowledge, brand image, is the far richer aspect. Keller defines brand image as "perceptions about a brand as reflected by the brand associations held in consumer memory. Brand associations are the other informational nodes linked to the brand node in memory and contain the meaning of the brand for consumers."[2] This terminology recalls our discussion of neuronal systems, consensus maps, and schemas from Chapter 4. Whatever term is used, understanding the customer's knowledge of the brand must involve examining the components of brand image; that is, the brand associations stored in memory.

Keller describes three types of associations: attributes, benefits, and attitudes. Attributes can be physical characteristics of the brand itself or things outside the brand, but still closely associated with it. Those include the brand's packaging, the price charged for the brand, and perceptions of who uses the brand (user imagery) and in what situations the brand is most appropriately used (usage imagery).[3] Identification of the most important brand attributes is part of the brand reality section of our customer-brand relationship strategy development form.

Benefits, the second type of brand association, are critical to developing the value proposition. Keller's terminology differs slightly from that of David Aaker introduced in the previous chapter, but the underlying principles are the same. Keller's conceptualization of benefits includes three dimensions: functional, experiential, and symbolic. Functional benefits are the tangible things customers receive from brand use, most often tied to attributes. Experiential benefits derive from the emotional satisfaction of using the brand. Symbolic benefits, similar to Aaker's self-expressive benefits, deal with what the customers' use of the brand communicates to the customers and to others about the customers themselves.[4]

The third type of brand association is attitudes, the "overall evaluations of a brand."[5] Attitudes can be positive, negative, or neutral. A negative or neutral attitude does not necessarily mean that the consumer will never choose the brand; situations can arise in which a brand that is evaluated negatively is the only choice. But it is much more likely that a positive attitude will spark brand acceptance, and certainly a positive attitude is an important component of a favorable, lasting relationship between the customer and the brand.

Having identified the types of brand associations, Keller notes the other aspects of brand image: how favorable or unfavorable those associations are, how strong or weak the associations are, and how unique the customer's associations with the particular brand are compared to other brands about which the customer is knowledgeable. Association favorability is most important for associations that strongly affect the customer's decision making. For example, if the customer does not particularly care for the color of the brand's packaging (a non-product-related attribute), but that packaging is disposable and so will be discarded after brand purchase, the unfavorable association with the packaging is not likely to be a major issue. The chief concern in evaluating favorability of associations, as an aspect of the customer's relationship with the brand, is the assessment of those associations most material to the customer's decision regarding purchase and repeated use of the brand.

Association strength is affected by the quantity and quality of the customer's information processing.[6] The more time and effort the customer puts into learning about the brand, paying attention to communications from the marketer and from other people about the brand, and the better the quality of the customer's learning process, the stronger and more enduring the associations will be. To foster stronger associations during the decision-making process, the customer should be given reasons to spend more time on the information search and alternative evaluation stages. One way of doing that is to provide information in a variety of forms and locations, such as by using a mix of delivery systems and communication techniques; that is, using both push and pull techniques implemented through those multiple systems.

We have noted the importance of brand differentiation in building successful customer-brand relationships throughout this text. Brand differentiation means that many or most of the associations customers have with a marketer's brand are unique to that brand. The problem faced by many brands today is that the attributes, benefits, and attitudes customers associate with them are not very dissimilar from those they associate with competitive brands. Establishing and reinforcing unique associations is a critical aspect of communicating a meaningful value proposition. Keller argues that brand success comes with "the creation of a familiar brand that has favorable, strong, and unique brand associations."[7] Attainment of that goal must drive the marketer's communications with customers.

PUSH VERSUS PULL COMMUNICATIONS

Now that we have established the goal for marketing communications, the question becomes how best to achieve the desired result. There are essentially two types of communications with customers, push communications and pull communications.

Push communications are the messages and incentives the marketer sends out, utilizing the delivery systems that have been identified as most appropriate for the particular customer group. Push communications are the traditional mass communication forms, including advertising, marketing public relations, and personal selling for long-term message communication and sales promotion and most forms of direct marketing for short-term incentive communication. All share the common characteristic that they are forms marketers use to push messages and incentives to customers at the time and place of the marketer's choosing, whether or not the customer is particularly interested in or receptive to that communication at that time or in that place.

Pull communications are communications that customers seek out and therefore have far greater control over. Pull communications include Internet-based communication, many types of event marketing, and new media forms such as social networks and blogs. Although the customer is in control in pull communications, the marketer must still make messages and incentives available in these venues so they will be there when the customer comes looking.

We turn now to closer examination of each of these communication forms to see how they may best be used in push and pull situations to enhance customers' brand knowledge and, ultimately, the customer-brand relationship.

PUSH COMMUNICATIONS FOR MESSAGES

Marketers typically communicate with customers through either messages or incentives or a combination of the two. Messages generally involve providing the customer with information about the brand, either as a reminder of material communicated previously or to deliver new information about attribute changes, additional benefits, and the like. Messages can be thought of as long-term types of communication, intended to build the brand's image over time by either strengthening or changing the value proposition. Three principal brand communication techniques are most often used for message communication: advertising, marketing public relations, and personal selling.

Advertising

From the customers' perspective, just about every communication that a marketer pushes toward them is seen as advertising. However, the term has a more precise definition for brand communication professionals. Advertising is buying media time or space in which to place informative and/or persuasive messages about the brand. Because marketers pay for the space or time, they can say what they want about the brand within that framework as long as they do not violate any regulations.

Advertising is most frequently used to reach relatively large audiences (as discussed earlier in this text, the size of the audience will depend on the particular media type chosen and then on the specific vehicle used within that media type) with a standardized message. Advertising can be used to deliver functional brand information through a combination of text and visuals (depending on the media type used). Advertising is also very useful for communicating emotional and self-expressive social benefits and is thus often a fundamental element in any campaign seeking to build brand image.

Anheuser-Busch buys multiple ad time slots in the National Football League's Super Bowl broadcast each year, at a cost per spot that is often near $3 million dollars. While the cost is high,

Exhibit 16.2   **TV Frame From Budweiser Commercial**

the large audience for the broadcast gives the variety of ads for Anheuser-Busch brands created by multiple advertising agencies an unparalleled platform to increase brand awareness and bolster brand image. The ads Anheuser-Busch runs during the game usually include a strong element of humor and are often among those rated as most liked by audiences evaluating the in-game ads. The ads traffic in emotional and self-expressive benefits, two things television advertising tends to communicate quite effectively. For example, one of the highest-ranking ads in the 2007 Super Bowl was a Budweiser ad showing a stray dog finding a way to get on the wagon pulled by the famous Clydesdales. The ad played on viewers' emotions by showing his sad wanderings, then ended humorously with the dog, disguised by mud spots that made the dog look like a Dalmatian, riding high on the wagon (see Exhibit 16.2 for a frame from the commercial).

One of the major challenges in creating effective advertising is to translate the value proposition into a "big idea," a creative execution that will both capture customers' attention and effectively communicate the message. As we have noted earlier, getting the customer's attention is increasingly difficult due to media fragmentation, simultaneous media use, and myriad other challenges. The humorous approach used by Anheuser-Busch is one way of doing it; the task facing advertisers is to come up with new ways of communicating messages that may not themselves be very new or different.

Assuming the advertisement gains the customer's attention, the ad must next communicate the information necessary to persuade the customer of the value proposition. A two-page magazine ad or a thirty-minute infomercial has plenty of space or time available to cover the important information, assuming that can be done in a way that will hold the customers' attention and keep them from turning the page or switching the channel. More often, the space and time available for the advertising message is much more limited—thirty seconds for the typical television spot, sixty seconds for a radio commercial, a fraction of a page in a newspaper. In that circumstance, the ad must at least communicate enough information to pique the customers' interest and perhaps direct them to another source (Web site, toll-free telephone number, dealer location) for additional detail.

Once the advertisement intended to communicate the value proposition has been developed, it should be evaluated to determine its probable effectiveness. A critical question at this point is whether the advertisement will truly appeal to the targeted customer group. Does the ad include the functional, emotional, or self-expressive benefits inherent in the value proposition? Does the ad use imagery and terminology familiar to the customer? Does the ad focus on the customer's interests and needs rather than those of the marketer? Is the explanation of those interests and needs clear, concise, complete, and convincing?

Developing advertisements that meet these criteria is far more difficult than it may sound. Many advertisements miss the mark, raising issues of little interest or importance or communicating a useful benefit but failing to link it to the brand. An advertisement where the situation is memorable, but the brand is not, has failed to convey the value being offered.

Advertising executions that meet the listed criteria can still be ineffective if they are placed in the wrong delivery vehicles and not seen by the desired customer group (or not seen by enough members of that group). An even bigger challenge for advertisements in general is to overcome customers' general dislike and distrust of advertising. Today's customers, very well aware of the intent of advertising, regard advertisements with some skepticism, even ads for brands they like and use. While advertising remains an important tool for communicating the value proposition and nurturing the customer-brand relationship, the challenges we have discussed throughout this text make it unlikely that any long-term relationship can be sustained through traditional media advertising alone.

Marketing Public Relations

The customer skepticism associated with advertising is one of the strongest arguments in favor of incorporating marketing public relations techniques into an effective message delivery campaign. Marketing public relations (MPR), like advertising, is a primarily long-term, brand-building communications technique. MPR involves activities in support of a brand focused on communicating with a variety of publics. The various publics or stakeholders on which public relations practitioners generally focus include groups similar to the customer groups we have identified earlier: end users, internal publics, influencers, and the like.

Marketing public relations is best thought of as a subset of the larger public relations function. One definition of public relations refers to "the management function that evaluates public attitudes, identifies the policies and procedures of an individual or organization with the public interest, and executes a program to earn public understanding and acceptance."[8] Much of that definition tracks directly with the principles we have advocated in building the customer-brand relationship.

Marketing public relations attempts to get media visibility for the brand by providing information to the media as the basis for news and feature stories. This is accomplished through such tools as written press releases, video news releases, company backgrounders, and fact sheets intended to pique the interest of reporters and editors. The perceived endorsement of the media vehicle carrying the resulting news item imparts credibility to the information, a sense of unbiased coverage that advertising can never provide the brand. Such news stories can create brand buzz and fuel positive word of mouth. Marketing public relations activities can make innovative functional benefits believable and foster a sense of trendiness for self-expressive benefit messages. A successful marketing public relations campaign may cost far less than a comparable advertising campaign, but deliver far greater impact.

Food marketing groups often have limited budgets, making marketing public relations particularly appealing. The success of a suddenly trendy food item is often based on a marketing public relations campaign. For example, pomegranate seeds began showing up in featured recipes in cooking magazines and on television cooking programs in part due to a focused public relations effort by POM Wonderful, a California company that is the largest pomegranate grower in the United States.[9] The company's public relations material included information on the health benefits of pomegranates, recipes for a range of food and beverage items, and even suggestions for decorating with pomegranates.

There is, of course, a downside to this news generation process. Reporters and editors do not, in most cases, accept public relations information without question. They first evaluate whether the information is of value to their audience at all, which leads to much public relations material being ignored. The material that does get past that first evaluation is then subject to editing and additional reporting. Many companies have provided facts and photographs as part of public relations press kits only to see them used in a news story that takes a negative slant on the company. The role of journalists as gatekeepers in marketing public relations is both the greatest challenge and greatest opportunity in using this technique as part of the brand communications campaign.

Public relations has much to offer in support of building customer-brand relationships beyond the strengths of marketing public relations. Public relations specialists also engage in employee communications through company newsletters, intranets, and similar communication forms. In many companies, it is the public relations function that takes the lead in developing community relations programs to foster a sense of civic engagement and neighborhood responsibility. Communications with investors and investment advisers are an important aspect of financial relations.

The greatest challenge facing public relations specialists is how to measure the effects of the public relations component of the campaign on brand success. There are at least two factors that make this difficult. The first is a challenge also faced by advertising, the long-term nature of most public relations activities. Measuring lagged effects—that is, effects and responses that occur sometime after the material has appeared—is difficult, and public relations practitioners and brand managers alike have struggled with this issue. The second challenge is that public relations, even more than advertising, tends to be most concerned with image building, which, as we have seen, is largely a perceptual process. Measuring perceptions is more time-consuming and more costly than many of the commonly used forms of campaign effectiveness assessment.

Modern conceptions of public relations focus heavily on building relationships. Public relations practice has evolved from historical models that emphasized press agentry and basic public information to two-way communication models. Two-way asymmetric public relations is an increasingly popular approach that uses research to identify and monitor public opinion. Asymmetric public relations does not just send out messages but tries to develop ones that actively inform the audience so informed consumer decision making can occur. The approach was developed by Edward L. Bernays, often considered the father of modern public relations. The two-way symmetric or interactive model of public relations also has research at its base but, as the name suggests, encourages dialogue and communication between the company and its publics.[10] Increasingly, public relations activities are a key component of brand communications.

Personal Selling

Personal selling differs from both advertising and public relations in that it does not use the media as an intermediary. Contact between the customer and the marketer is direct, either face-to-face or via telephone, email, or instant messaging. This direct contact greatly reduces or even eliminates misunderstood messages, incomplete information, or poor targeting. In keeping with our focus on relationships, the best salespeople are those who can establish quick rapport with customers and prospects by tailoring their messages specifically to the customer's interests and needs. Salespeople have an important role to play with all customer groups.

Personal selling to ultimate customer groups is much more common in business-to-business settings than in consumer marketing. The reason is not any decreased effectiveness of personal selling as a communications technique for consumer products, but instead prohibitive costs. The larger the prospective customer base, the less likely personal selling will play a major role in communications with ultimate customers. New technologies, however, are changing that historical reality. For example, customers who log on to Bank of America's Web site and appear to be having difficulty using the online banking function get a pop-up screen that allows the option of instant messaging with a Bank of America consultant. The consultant can troubleshoot for the customers, walking them through the steps to access the account or other information they need. Equally customer service and personal selling in its ability to introduce customers to aspects of online banking with which they were not previously familiar as well as promote the bank's other services, this use of technology can enhance the relationship between the customer and Bank of America.

A well-trained, effectively monitored sales force can provide ongoing, timely customer information that can be key to maintaining and enhancing brand relationships. Retail salespeople can report what items within the brand line are selling well and what concerns customers have with slower-moving items. Grocery product salespeople who are in regular contact with intermediaries can monitor competitive activity and intermediaries' responses to competitive efforts. While there are certainly costs in both money and time associated with this type of monitoring (establishing a relationship takes repeated personal contact), personal selling comes the closest of any of the traditional marketing communication techniques to truly establishing a relationship between the customer and the brand, so it is always worth evaluating as a means of delivering information about the brand to customers and prospective customers across all relevant customer groups.

PUSH COMMUNICATIONS FOR INCENTIVES

Sometimes, customers do not require any additional information about the brand. Instead, they need an incentive to move them to action. Or information may be necessary, but not enough by itself to generate the desired customer response. In those cases, the communication campaign must include an incentive. Incentives operate within a shorter time frame than messages, creating a measurable impact within days or even hours, rather than months or years. There are two primary types of traditional push communication generally associated with incentives, sales promotion and direct marketing.

Sales Promotion

Sales promotion activities create an incentive to buy the product by altering the price-value relationship. The price of the product or service can be lowered temporarily through sales promotion techniques such as coupons, rebates, off-invoice allowances, free goods, and

Exhibit 16.3 **Scrubbing Bubbles Promotion**

other promotion methods that reduce the cost to the buyer, be it the ultimate customer or an intermediary. Value-added sales promotion techniques include premium offers of a gift when the customer purchases the brand, contests or sweepstakes offering purchasers a chance at appealing prizes, spiffs (on-the-spot cash or gifts) for the sales force that reward the salesperson for promoting the "right" brand to the customer, and similar programs that promote the promise of getting something extra for purchasing the brand.

Sales promotion activities targeted at ultimate customers generally have one of three goals: encouraging trial among prospective customers; loading, or encouraging customers to purchase and inventory more units of the product than they would normally purchase; and encouraging repeated purchases through continuity programs. The first goal is an offensive measure to go after additional business; the second and third are more defensive in nature. Loading customers and encouraging loyalty both take customers out of the market for competitive brands, either in the short term with loading or over time with continuity programs. The offer from S.C. Johnson's Scrubbing Bubbles brand[11] shown in Exhibit 16.3 promotes both loading and purchase continuity; the $5 savings coupon for the Scrubbing Bubbles Automatic Shower Cleaner starter kit encourages the customer to buy this cleaning system while the

$1.50 savings coupon encourages loading on two refill packages; buying the system to start with should promote purchase continuity over time as more refills are needed.

Sales promotion activities targeted at intermediary customers also have three general goals: getting feature placements in the intermediary's own promotional materials, getting special displays within the intermediary's store or Web site, and holding onto or getting additional shelf space. Research among ultimate customers has shown that retail ad features and displays call extra attention to the brand and signal a price savings to the customer, whether or not that is in fact the case.[12] Additionally, sales data show that ad features and displays can have a very real and dramatic effect on brand sales.[13] As with the ultimate customer goal of trial, featuring and display goals are principally offensive in nature, while a goal of increased shelf space is defensive. More shelf space equates with both gaining greater visibility for the brand and keeping competitors out of that space. Whatever the primary goal, most brands build their sales promotion activities targeted to intermediaries around some sort of price reduction technique, knowing that the intermediary is likely to accept the offer where the greatest profit can be realized. And as noted in Chapter 5, sales promotion programs targeted at intermediaries can serve as a form of relationship building element themselves if the promotional programs are account-specific, helping the intermediary differentiate itself from others carrying the same brand.

Sales promotion activities tend to be most prevalent for brands with value propositions that are not particularly unique or differentiating. In those cases, the sales promotion incentive itself becomes the point of differentiation from competitive brands, although only in the short term. For those brands, sales promotion can quickly become an almost constant element of their communications with customer groups, as customers see no reason to choose the brand over parity competitors in the absence of an incentive offer. That is one very clear risk of a heavy reliance on sales promotion: training customers to expect the incentive discourages them from using the brand in its absence.

That is not to say that brands that offer a unique value proposition cannot also benefit from sales promotion. Sales promotion offers, particularly value-added offers, can call attention to the brand's differentiating benefits. In addition to offering traditional price-saving deals on various products in its line, Dove has used contests, including essay and photo contests, to complement its "Campaign for Real Beauty." This is Dove's effort to alter stereotypes of what constitutes female beauty and to empower women of all ages. Dove used its "Campaign for Real Beauty" Web site to feature contest winners and their winning entries, adding to the brand's perceptual value and underscoring the value proposition. In addition to cash prizes, winners received Dove products, strengthening relationships with the brand.[14]

As mentioned in the previous chapter, certain types of sales promotion programs can result in a long-term effect of the sales promotion in addition to the usual short-term results. Consumer franchise building sales promotion activities include sampling (the most effective means of generating brand trial), coupons that accompany informative messages about the brand, and demonstrations of the brand's use, recipes, and the like. These kinds of sales promotion activities have been shown to affect brand sales more than a year after the sales promotion has ended.[15]

While sales promotion incentives can encourage customer-brand relationships by rewarding customers for their patronage, there are also disadvantages to sales promotion beyond the danger of creating a dependence on deals. If customer database analysis or other assessment of customer brand knowledge has indicated that customers have negative attitudes toward the brand, sales promotion will be of little help. Saving money on a brand the customer does not like to start with is not a powerful incentive. Similarly, while sales promotion programs may help to slow a sales decline, they cannot turn that decline around. A steady decline in sales suggests either that there is something functionally wrong with the brand or that the brand has lost its relevance for customers. Sales promotion does not offer a solution to either of those problems.

Sales promotion is generally not good for brand image creation unless the image desired is that of a brand that is always "on special." Sales promotion tends to work best in conjunction with one or more of the message-focused forms of push communication, where the latter are used to establish the brand image while sales promotion provides the extra incentive needed to spark a behavioral response.

There is certainly a role for sales promotion in the process we have advocated throughout this text. The only caveat is to be sparing in its application. In relationship terms, brands that rely heavily or exclusively on sales promotion in their communication with customers are like the kid in school who is popular only because he does other students' homework for them or hands out gifts. It is not a relationship that can be sustained over time, and the benefit is largely one-sided.

Direct Marketing

In the context of push communications, the type of direct marketing discussed here is traditional direct marketing activities such as direct mail, catalogs, television infomercials, and telemarketing. The Direct Marketing Association has defined direct marketing as including direct ordering of products or services from the manufacturer or an intermediary, lead generation to encourage information seeking on the brand, and traffic generation to drive customers into a bricks-and-mortar store or to a Web site.[16]

Effective direct marketing relies on historical or previous customer behavioral information, preferably drawn from a database but also obtainable through custom research studies, to target brand offers more precisely than is possible with advertising or public relations efforts. Direct marketing activities are intended to provoke immediate, measurable responses from customers, and assessment of the technique's success is an important aspect of such efforts. The measurability and accountability of traditional direct marketing activities have contributed to sustained growth in direct marketing spending over many, many years.[17]

Direct marketing can be used for customer retention through loyalty programs such as the Kroger offers described in Chapter 3, which are delivered to customers via regular mail or email, depending on the customer's preference. Direct marketing can also be used by competitive brands to encourage trial, as in the Target program discussed in Chapter 15, where some of the coupons mailed to customers are for competitive brands in product categories the customer is known to use.

Direct marketers are constantly seeking additional prospects for their efforts or means to better target the customer group they are interested in influencing. List owners, brokers, and managers do a robust business providing names and contact information (mailing addresses, email addresses, and telephone numbers) for customers and prospective customers grouped by a variety of demographic, geographic, psychographic, and behavioral characteristics.

Lifestyle magazines rent their subscription lists, catalogs rent their buyer information, clubs make available their membership lists, hospitals publish lists of new parents; the sources of information are seemingly endless and, at least under current U.S. law, seemingly available to just about any marketer able to afford the price and effort to compile the information.

Once responses to the direct marketing program begin to come in and are amassed into a database, direct marketers segment their customers based on three factors associated with short-term, incentive-based thinking: recency, frequency, and monetary value (RFM analysis). (We discussed this topic in Chapter 3.) Recency analysis identifies the customer's last transaction with the direct marketer: when did that customer last purchase the brand? Frequency refers to responses over time: How often did the customer purchase the brand within a given time period? Monetary value assesses the amount of money the customer contributed to the brand and will vary based on factors such as whether a special incentive was being offered. The best customer, the customer meriting the most future communications attention, is the customer who bought recently, buys frequently, and spends a large amount of money relative to other customers.

To the extent that a marketer has information on individual customers, it just makes sense to incorporate direct marketing efforts into the communications mix. In doing so, however, it is critical to keep in mind that a strong relationship is based on trust. There are many privacy concerns associated with marketer use of customer data. The Direct Marketing Association monitors these concerns on a macro level and provides advice for its members on how to treat customer information. It is extremely important for each individual marketer to keep these concerns well in mind when developing and distributing communications to customers via direct marketing methods. Over-familiarity with the customer through too much personalization of messages and incentive offers can create the perception of the business equivalent of stalking, a situation that will send the customer running away from the brand, not toward it.

Push or Push Away?

All the marketing communication techniques we have discussed—advertising, marketing public relations, personal selling, sales promotion, and traditional direct marketing—are classified as push techniques because they are communications the marketer pushes out to the customer, whether the customer wants to hear that message or receive that incentive at the moment or not. The commercial that interrupts the building tension in a favorite television drama, the newspaper ad that forces the reader to turn to another page for the rest of the story, the Internet pop-up that covers the interesting Web site, the irritating magazine story about a designer's latest fashion offering, the sales rep who insists on talking to the doctor who is already forty-five minutes behind in patient appointments, the coupons for brands the customer will never buy that make the Sunday newspaper twice as large as it needs to be, the poorly targeted direct mail pieces that fill the mailbox, and the email offers that junk up the electronic in-box are all examples of marketers pushing their messages and incentives on customers who are not interested—or at least not interested right now. Yes, all of these traditional forms of communication activities are still effective to some extent, but most of them are less effective than they once were. One reason is overload: too many messages. Another reason is ineffective, poorly conceived value propositions that are not focused on customer needs. And still another reason is the increased sophistication of customers and technological changes that have put more and more power, especially the power of information, into the hands of the customer. It is the last situation in particular that necessitates looking at the role and potential of pull communications in the effort to build and sustain a relationship between the customer and the brand.

PULL COMMUNICATIONS

Unlike push communications, in which marketers put the message or incentive where they hope the customer will encounter it, pull communications involve situations that customers create themselves or actively seek out. The challenge, or requirement, lies in first determining what the critical pull venues are for the customer group in question and then making brand messages and incentives easily available in those venues.

The list of pull communications venues lengthens daily and includes many (but not all) applications of the Internet, event marketing, social networks, blogs, podcasts, mobile telephony, and the like. The primary point to keep in mind is that with pull communications, the customer is the driver, not the marketer.

Internet

From a pull communications perspective, the Internet includes information-based and direct sales Web sites, but not banners, pop-ups, pop-unders, interstitials, or other essentially traditional advertising forms or formats in this medium. Customers who access Web sites looking for information, either by going directly to the site or finding the site through a search engine, are intent on accessing the content they are interested in, not on having an electronic billboard get in their way.

It seems that almost every brand has recognized the value, and, indeed, the necessity, of providing brand information online. The best brand sites mix product information and lifestyle elements to flesh out the value proposition and keep customers returning to the site over time. This is true for sites that offer direct sales, those offering information only, and those concerned with traditional brand building. Amazon.com is known for the customization included on its site; regular customers get product recommendations keyed to their past search and purchasing behavior, offers for discounted shipping, and other features that reward regular interaction with the site and Amazon.[18] The Web site for Ragú sauces, constructed particularly for soccer moms, includes information and special offers for that group, positioning Ragú as a helpful, healthy part of that particular lifestyle.[19] (See Exhibit 16.4.)

Most marketers try to manage Internet traffic by using a variety of means to direct customers to the brand's site. These include putting the Web site URL in all traditional communication forms, using the various types of online advertising mentioned above to get the attention of online users, and paying search engines to highlight the brand. This last method has been of particular interest, fueling revenue growth for popular search sites such as Google, but some attitude survey research suggests that Web users are increasingly distrustful of search sites and prefer brand information from other sources, especially fellow consumers.[20]

Relevance and believability are critical considerations with all types of pull communications. Because these avenues are in the customers' control, it is the customers' values and perceptions that are most important. The Internet offers marvelous possibilities for informa-

Exhibit 16.4 **Ragú Web Page**

tion delivery, generally far better than traditional media. Customers who cannot be bothered to watch a thirty-second television commercial will go online to watch brand-based video content if they find the brand relevant in their lives.[21] Some brands, including Brawny Paper Towels, run entire video miniseries on their Web sites, bypassing traditional television to reach a smaller, but more interested, audience. The "Brawny Academy" took eight men nominated by their wives and put them through an eight-part retraining to improve their skills as helpful husbands. The concept was developed by Brawny's marketing communications agency, Fallon, which has had success with similar approaches for other clients.[22]

Social Networks

Social networks have been mentioned earlier in this text; in a 2007 survey, 55 percent of the members of "Generation C" (for content, creativity, consumption, and connected) said they belonged to at least one social network site.[23] Facebook, one of the most popular Web sites overall, has more than 16 million members.[24] However, social networks sites should not be thought of as offering mass audiences. Writing in *EContent*, Jessica Dye points out that for this group of customers, "their social networks are becoming simultaneously larger and narrower than ever. The entire globe is their new locale, and niche communities are the new mass audience."[25] Facebook, MySpace, and other social networks run multiple smaller networks, links established by the users themselves. The communication takes place within those smaller groups.

The overall size and positive word of mouth of these social networks have definitely captured marketer interest. Numerous brands and political candidates have established their own MySpace pages or created their own social network sites.[25] When successful, the use of social networks can generate strong buzz for the brand as customers make referrals to other customers. According to an article in *New Media Age*, "Users add brands' profile pages as friends, then, their friends do the same. Music videos and video ads pass round networks like wildfire, exposing brands to an attractive young demographic for relatively little investment."[27] Measuring the effect of a social network presence can be a challenge that has kept some marketers away from such sites.[28] A much greater risk, however, is the possibility of negative customer response to branded content and ads in social networks. A 2007 survey in the United Kingdom found that nearly half of respondents viewed advertising on social networks negatively and only 10 percent of respondents found such ads trustworthy.[29]

Virtual Worlds

Virtual worlds offer a space on the Internet where customers can interact with other people from around the world through self-designed avatars, the real customer's virtual image online. One of the largest and best known of the virtual worlds is Second Life. Second Life has more than 6 million participants, although just over 1 million tend to be active on the site on a monthly basis.[30]

Brands make use of Second Life in several ways. Kraft operates a virtual supermarket that carries only its brands; the supermarket's primary purpose is to showcase new products and offer online discussions with Kraft food experts.[31] Coca-Cola uses Second Life for customer contests, including designing a virtual vending machine.[32] Other firms have used Second Life to conduct customer research by encouraging participation in product design and to recruit prospective employees.[33]

Second Life and other virtual spaces are particularly popular with minority audiences. Hispanic consumers are heavier users of such spaces than the general population; Sprint uses Second Life to run a virtual concert series targeted at Hispanic audiences. Toyota developed its own virtual world, Mundo Yaris, to launch the Yaris model to the Hispanic community.[34]

Blogs

Short for "Web logs," blogs allow anyone with computer access to post thoughts, opinions, and whatever else they may want to share with anyone who cares to access that information. Brands can be praised or maligned through mentions in customer-generated blogs and in widely read blogs associated with traditional media reporters.[35] A number of companies offer blog-tracking services to help brand marketers track and respond to blog-based comments about their brands.[36]

Podcasts

Podcasting has not gained the penetration of blogs, social networks, or virtual worlds; in the United States, just 13 percent of customers listen to podcasts.[37] As a result, advertising revenue associated with podcasts continues to be low. But the possibility of linking brand messages with relevant, targeted audio content does hold promise. National Public Radio and ESPN are among many traditional providers repackaging content into podcasts. Podcast.net offers a directory of thousands of podcasts on a wide range of topics.[38]

Working With Consumer-Generated Media

Writing in *Advertising Age*, Philippe Guegan, strategy director for Agency.com, offers six suggestions for successful brand use of consumer-generated media such as social networks, blogs, and podcasts. His list summarizes some of the risks and opportunities we have noted with regard to these forms of pull communication.

1. "Make participation simple." Marketers cannot assume customers have either the technical skills or the time to participate in complicated programs.
2. "Target niche first, mass later." Guegan suggests starting small by focusing on the customers who have already established contact with the marketer through customer service or other channels, then expanding from there.
3. "Make it authentic, transparent." This is absolutely essential. As Guegan warns, "Ignore this cardinal rule and be prepared for consumer backlash of epic proportions."
4. "Make word-of-mouth relevant." The marketer should give customers a focus that will form the basis for the communication they generate. This focus should be the value proposition.
5. "Step up after going live." Success with consumer-generated media requires constant monitoring and quick response from the brand.
6. "Think beyond campaigns." Guegan argues that consumer-generated media offer useful possibilities for research and public relations applications.[39]

Event Marketing

A discussion of event marketing may seem out of place following our review of new media opportunities in pull communications. But events, while usually developed by brand marketers or created to attract brand support, fit our definition of pull communications because customers choose to attend and participate in the event. Events are to blogs and social networks what bricks-and-mortar stores are to online retailing, the physical manifestation of phenomena that are increasing available in the virtual world of online.

Event marketing is big business. "Events create a social setting for attendees and help raise attendees' involvement level; therefore, attendees are apt to be more receptive to marketing messages and images associated with the event than they are to those presented via other methods."[40] Brand marketers can either create their own events or sponsor existing events; sports sponsorships are particularly popular among marketers.

To promote its animated movie *Ratatouille,* Disney developed a cheese-themed event intended to attract children and families in conjunction with food festivals in ten U.S. cities. The event featured characters from the movie and also provided a venue for sampling food and video products from other marketers.[41] Sprint Nextel sponsors NASCAR's Nextel Cup and builds a variety of events and other promotions around that sponsorship.[42] Events link the brand to activities the customer enjoys, increasing the strength, favorability, and uniqueness of brand associations.

"WHAT HAPPENS HERE, STAYS HERE": APPLYING PUSH AND PULL COMMUNICATIONS

To conclude our discussion, we turn to a comprehensive example of the use of various push and pull communications to increase customer brand knowledge and convey an appealing value proposition. Beginning in 2004, a variety of marketing communications agencies collaborated with the Las Vegas Convention and Visitors Authority to develop a multiplatform communication campaign to increase tourism to Las Vegas.

Customer research indicated that Las Vegas equals escape for many people, a chance to do things they could not (and would not) do anywhere else.[43] The escape value proposition encompasses functional benefits (the various diversions Las Vegas offers that are not limited to gambling but include entertainment, dining, and shopping), emotional benefits (fun, release from cares, excitement, novelty), and self-expressive benefits (perhaps the heart of the "What Happens Here, Stays Here" campaign tagline). Research also indicated that while the gambling available in Las Vegas was well known, many people were not aware of the other activities the city had to offer.[44] Therefore, one goal for the campaign was to increase brand knowledge by informing targeted groups about Las Vegas's other functional benefits. The "Las Vegas Alibi" campaign was designed to focus on the functional benefits of visiting Las Vegas.

Push Communications for Las Vegas

The campaign used television advertising (executions developed for specific customer subsegments), print advertising, and Internet banners. Marketing public relations efforts included getting media mentions in a number of national newspapers, magazines, and news outlets. For example, the *Wall Street Journal* did a piece on the campaign, helping to reach a business traveler audience.[45] The campaign also used guerrilla marketing during major events such as the Super Bowl and Grammy Awards in order to reach customers attending those events as well as possibly get media attention.[46] Various venues in Las Vegas also offered sales promotion deals tied to key customer groups. The advertising and public relations campaign was developed by R&R Partners in Las Vegas.

Pull Communications for Las Vegas

The Las Vegas Convention and Visitors Authority worked with R&R Partners, who in turn involved an interactive agency, Critical Mass, to assist in development of two Web sites. VisitLasVegas.com, the consumer-oriented site, was designed to be the complete authority on all things related to Las Vegas travel. (See Exhibit 16.5 for the Vegas Alibi Kit.) The second Web site, LVCVA.com, was oriented toward influencers and intermediaries, including travel agents and meeting planners.[47] R&R Partners developed a Web strategy designed to use search engine placements, banners, email, and other techniques to drive traffic to the two Web sites.[48] The push campaign combined with the pull campaign worked especially well in generating word of mouth. The "What Happens Here, Stays Here" line was used by Jay Leno and Laura Bush, among others.[49]

Exhibit 16.5   **Vegas Alibi Kit Screen Shot**

Source: Las Vegas Convention and Visitors Authority.

Results

Visitors to Las Vegas increased by more than 400,000 from the period before the campaign; the strategy was created to fill new hotel rooms being developed as the campaign began, and it succeeded in doing so. Occupancy rates for Las Vegas hotels and resorts were much higher than the national average (85 to 90 percent in Las Vegas during 2004 compared to 59.2 percent nationally. Nearly 4 million people logged onto VisitLasVegas.com. A survey found that nearly three-quarters of people who saw the campaign were more interested in visiting Las Vegas as a result.[50] See Exhibit 16.6 for one of the print ads from the campaign.

Exhibit 16.6   **"We Tried Some Stuff" Ad**

Source: Las Vegas Convention and Visitors Authority.

Why was the Las Vegas campaign so effective? It was based on a thorough understanding of customer knowledge about the brand and identified a value proposition that incorporated functional, emotional, and self-expressive benefits. The value proposition effectively differentiated Las Vegas from the alternatives—other places offer gambling, there are fine restaurants, entertainment, and shopping elsewhere as well, but no other place offers the complete escape package available in Las Vegas. The delivery systems selected for the communications reached the campaign's targeted customer groups through a mix of appropriate channels. The value proposition was communicated through a mix of push and pull communications techniques, relying primarily on informational messages spiced with an air of fun and excitement. And the culminating success came when the tagline was embraced by customers and took on a life of its own. Pulling off all those challenges is never easy, but when a campaign like this works, it creates a relationship between the customer and the brand that is virtually competition-proof.

SUMMING UP

Before deciding on what combination of communication tools to use in building the customer-brand relationship, the brand communicator must first look at where the brand stands with the relevant customer group in terms of brand associations and the other dimensions of brand knowledge. Once that has been determined, the value proposition can be developed and then communicated through the appropriate mix of push and pull communication tools.

As the examples presented in this chapter show, most successful brand communication campaigns include a mix of push and pull communications. The selection of those elements must start with knowledge about the customer, a reminder that marketers must always look at the brand from the perspective of their customers and customer groups.

NOTES

1. K.L. Keller, "Conceptualizing, Measuring, and Managing Customer-Based Brand Equity," *Journal of Marketing* 57 (January 1993): 1–22.

2. Ibid., p. 3.

3. Ibid., p. 4.

4. Ibid.

5. Ibid.

6. Ibid., p. 5.

7. Ibid., p. 9.

8. H.F. Moore and B.R. Canfield, *Public Relations: Principles, Cases, and Problems*, 7th ed. (Burr Ridge, IL: Irwin, 1977), p. 5.

9. POM Wonderful, www.pomwonderful.com.

10. J.E. Grunig and T. Hunt, *Managing Public Relations* (New York: Holt, Rinehart & Winston, 1984).

11. Scrubbling Bubbles® is a registered trademark of S.C. Johnson & Son, Inc., used with permission.

12. J. Inman, L. McAlister, and W.D. Hoyer, "Promotion Signal: Proxy for a Price Cut?" *Journal of Consumer Research* 17 (June 1990): 74–81.

13. J.C. Totten, "Health and Beauty Aids: A Sharp Pencil Is Needed" (unpublished paper, Information Resources Inc., 1985).

14. Dove contest winners available at www.campaignforrealbeauty.com.

15. R.M. Prentice, "How to Split Your Marketing Funds Between Advertising and Promotion," *Advertising Age*, January 10, 1977, p. 49.

16. WEFA Group, *Economic Impact: U.S. Direct Marketing Today*, 4th ed. (Direct Marketing Association, 1998).

17. C. Krol, "DMA: Direct Helps Insulate Economy," *BtoB*, November 13, 2006, p. 13.

18. Amazon.com, www.amazon.com.

19. Ragú, www.eat.com.

20. *Marketing Week*, "Search Advertising: Searching for More Sales," April 5, 2007, p. 30.

21. S. Miller, "Can't Sit Through a :30? How About a 5-Minute Ad?" *Brandweek,* March 19, 2007, p. 7.

22. C. Hawley, "He Cooks, He Cleans . . . Fallon's Brawny Academy Helps Create the Perfect Man," *Boards*, August 2006, p. 10.

23. J. Dye, "Meet Generation C: Creatively Connecting Through Content," *EContent* 30, no. 4 (2007): 38–43.

24. Ibid.

25. Ibid., p. 40.

26. Ibid.

27. *New Media Age*, "Social Network Advertising: Making Friends," May 10, 2007, p. 19.

28. M. Shields, "Talk About the Passion," *Mediaweek*, April 16, 2007, p. 6.

29. *New Media Age*, "Half of Social Networkers Dismiss Adverts," May 3, 2007, p. 2.

30. *Marketing Week*, "Coca-Cola to Launch on Virtual World Second Life," April 19, 2007, p. 6.

31. B. Spethmann, "Kraft Launches Second Life Supermarket," *Promo Xtra*, May 7, 2007, www.promomagazine.com/retail/news/kraft_launches_second_life_supermarket_050707/index.html.

32. *Marketing Week*, "Coca-Cola."

33. P. Whitehead, "On a Mission to Second Life: What Are Companies Up To in There? Peter Whitehead Decided to Log On and Find Out," *Financial Times*, May 9, 2007, p. 5.

34. L.M. Ruiz-Velasco, "Latino Marketers and Agencies Set Out to Explore Virtual Worlds," *Advertising Age*, May 7, 2007, p. 36.

35. M. Conlin, "Web Attack: Nastiness Online Can Erupt and Go Global Overnight, and 'No Comment' Doesn't Cut It Anymore; Here's How to Cope," *Business Week,* April 16, 2007, p. 54.

36. Ibid.; A.O. Patrick, "Tapping Into Customers' Online Chatter: New Tools Will Track Critics, Fans on Blogs; The 'Seer' Trolls Web," *Wall Street Journal,* May 18, 2007.

37. H. Green, "Don't Quit Your Day Job, Podcasters; Grammar Girl Hit It Big, But So Far Few Others Have Been Able to Make the Shows Pay," *Business Week,* April 9, 2007, p. 72.

38. Podcast.net, www.podcast.net.

39. P. Guegan, "Keep It Simple, Honest, Focused," *Advertising Age*, April 23, 2007, p. 23.

40. A.G. Close, R.Z. Finney, R.Z. Lacey, and J.Z. Sneath, "Engaging the Consumer Through Event Marketing: Linking Attendees with the Sponsor, Community, and Brand," *Journal of Advertising Research* 46, no. 4 (2006): 420–433.

41. *Promo Xtra*, "Disney Hypes Up 'Ratatouille' Cheese Tour," May 15, 2007, http://promomagazine.com/eventmarketing/news/disney_hypes_ratatouille_cheese_tour_051507/.

42. B. Spethmann, "Nextel Revs NASCAR Sponsorship for Daytona 500," *Promo Xtra*, February 15, 2007, http://promomagazine.com/eventmarketing/news/nextel_revs_nascar_sponsorship_daytona_021507/.

43. R&R Partners, "Case Study: Only Vegas—Las Vegas Convention and Visitors Authority," www.rrpartners.com/work/case_study.cfm?xclient=73.

44. Harris Interactive Case Study, "What Happens Here, Stays Here: Las Vegas Alibi; A Campaign to Link the Brand's Benefits With Its Product Attributes," www.harrisinteractive.com/about/pubs/HI_Las VegasAlibi_Case_Study.pdf. The campaign won the ARF David Ogilvy Award for Excellence in Advertising Research in 2007; see www.harrisinteractive.com/about/awards_ARF.asp.

45. C. Binkley, "Family Trips: Taking the 'Sin' Out of Sin City," *Wall Street Journal,* October 8, 2005.

46. R&R Partners, "Case Study: Only Vegas."

47. Critical Mass, "Vegas Hits the Jackpot: The LVCVA Delivers a Truly Vegas Experience," http://beta.criticalmass.com/media/case_study_vegas.pdf.

48. Ibid.

49. M. Beirne, "Playing for Keeps," *Brandweek*, October 11, 2004, p. M6.

50. R&R Partners, "Case Study: Only Vegas."

CHAPTER 17

Next Steps in Building Customer-Brand Relationships

WHERE DO WE GO FROM HERE?

We have now reached the end of our journey through the planning, development, and application of a customer-brand value relationship program. When we started, some 300 pages earlier, we offered the premise that a new method of developing relationships with customers and prospects through various forms of marketing communication was needed. We have provided evidence throughout this text that (1) the marketplace has changed, (2) customers and prospects have changed, (3) media and delivery forms and systems have changed, (4) competitors have changed . . . in short, marketers and marketing communicators now find themselves in a radically different space everywhere in the world than was present a scant half dozen years ago. Those changes are not going to reverse themselves. Marketers will never be able to get back to what was once considered "normal," nor return to the old days when they knew fairly well what was likely to happen next. The marketplace of the late twentieth century, which they thought they understood, is gone, probably forever. Trying to hang onto the past is not a viable option for marketing organizations. The marketing and communication arena is only going to get more complex, more difficult, more changeable, and more perplexing in the future. On the positive side, the world of marketing communication is likely to be more interesting, more exciting, and more global, providing many more opportunities for growth and development than we have ever seen before. What is scary to some, others see as a golden opportunity. It simply depends on the view they take.

STARTING WITH CUSTOMERS AND PROSPECTS

What is clear among all these changes, however, is that all businesses, in all categories, in every market in the world will be driven by one primary factor: customers. And when we use the term *customers*, we mean all those people who not only buy but who influence the purchases of others, such as recommenders, suppliers, employees, and the media. That, of course, is a radically different definition of customers than simply focusing on the end user. But this expanded view of customers is what really differentiates the approach in *Building Customer-Brand Relationships* from traditional marketing communication.

Customers, no matter how they are defined, are the only people who matter, for they are the only ones who can say yes or no to communication activities and marketplace offerings. Having all the resources in the world and no customers is a losing proposition, no matter what the market, product category, or competitive framework. Customers are critical today and will only be more critical in the future.

Yet as important as customers are, as we have pointed out, too many organizations still know relatively little about their customers and even less about their prospects, thanks to the product focus that has dominated marketing and communication for the past several decades. Ever since the Four Ps were developed more than half a century ago, a concept that focused internally on what the organization wanted to do, not what customers wanted the organization to do, business managers have struggled to move from an internal to an external focus: that is, a focus on customers. This is, perhaps, the most difficult task of all, particularly for companies that have achieved marketplace success using the hoary concepts of the 1960s and 1970s. It worked then, so why will it not work now? But clearly the changes that have occurred have limited the potential for an inside-out view.

In this text, we have outlined, explained, and illustrated a new, externally oriented way to consider and focus on customers and prospects. We have offered a methodology based on putting the customer first; that is, on learning what customers and prospects want, need, and require and then trying to provide marketer-based solutions through product and service offerings. This is still a radically different way to think about what marketers and communicators do and how they do it. For example, from 1985 until 2004 the American Marketing Association (AMA) used a definition of marketing that made no mention of customers or customer relationships: "Marketing is the process of planning and executing the conception, pricing, promotion and distribution of goods, ideas and services to create exchanges that satisfy individual organizational goals." In 2004, the AMA redefined marketing by focusing on customers, relationships, and value: "Marketing is an organizational function and a set of processes for creating, communicating and delivering value to customers and for managing customer relationships in ways that benefit the organization and its stakeholders." It took the AMA nearly twenty years to make that change. Change is slow to come in marketing and marketing communication. Marketers advocate change but are slow to make those changes in their systems and processes.

What we discuss in this text is new—indeed, some will argue, revolutionary. But it is based on what we believe students and practitioners alike will need in order to develop effective programs in the twenty-first century.

While almost every company, organization, and manager claims to be, or aspires to be, customer-focused or customer-centric, very few are. And only a limited number of firms—for example, FedEx, UPS, IBM, USAA, and Tesco in the United Kingdom—have made the transition to this point. Others will follow, making the transition as their customers demand it. Quite simply, companies, organizations, and businesses are not organized to serve customers; they are organized to make and sell things . . . to anyone who could or would buy. This approach served sellers well in the past, but it also led to such oft-quoted phrases as "What's good for General Motors is good for the country" and "No one ever got fired for buying IBM"—ideas and approaches that put the marketer first, not the customer.

In this text, we have taken the position that the traditional method of developing marketing communications and delivering them primarily through outbound delivery systems is simply not sufficient in today's increasingly interactive marketplace. But simply shifting to new media forms, adopting new digital formats, or improving the organization's current pull communications approaches is not enough either. And it is certainly not the solution for the long term. Customers and consumers today live in the push and pull communication world we have described. Thus, the marketing communication question is not where or when to use pull to the exclusion of push or when to ignore pull systems and put more funding behind traditional outbound push programs. Instead, the challenge is how to use both together, in combination, mixing, matching, and managing the communication needs of both the company and the customers, simultaneously. Clearly, marketers need both push and pull because consumers use both, often indiscriminately and in many cases simultaneously.

More important, most customers move effortlessly from digital to analog and back again, from reading magazines to listening to their iPod, from mobile telephony to printed Yellow Pages, depending on what they believe will provide the current or long-term solutions they are seeking. Customers and consumers do not discriminate between marketing communication techniques and methodologies. They simply use what they think is best at the time. That means marketers must be less prone to relying on their favorite communication tools and become more oriented toward what customers want. Marketers may want to promote their product or service with a television commercial, but if customers prefer to obtain their information from a Web site, who do you think will win in this confrontation?

REEDUCATION IN MARKETING COMMUNICATION

The real challenge for all marketing communicators today is reeducation. Customers are far ahead of most marketers in the communication tools they use, how they use them, how they approach the marketplace, and the methods they use to solve their own, individual problems. Most marketers have been schooled in traditional, outbound media systems: newspapers, magazines, radio, television, outdoor billboards, and the like. Most marketing educational programs, whether colleges and universities or seminars and conferences, still focus on describing and illustrating one-way, outbound, push communication systems that are bound up in traditional media forms. Marketers still practice those linear, step-by-step approaches in their marketing communication programs—for example, first developing a television campaign, then adding a few promotional fillips and putting in a dash of PR—with little or no thought as to how consumers will access, receive, or process the information that the marketer is trying to deliver. This is still the common recipe for all too many marketing organizations today. For example, the linear planning process called AIDA (attention, interest, desire, action) has been around for almost 100 years. It might have made sense in the twentieth century, but it is hopelessly outdated and increasingly irrelevant in communicating with today's consumers.

Clearly, we need new views, new approaches, and new methodologies. In this book we have offered the integrated brand communication model (see Exhibit 17.1). Our approach features the three elements that marketing communication planners have available—customers, delivery, and content—all tied together with brand communication. We think this model is solid, focused, and, most of all, relevant for today's marketplace.

Exhibit 17.1   **Integrated Brand Communication Model**

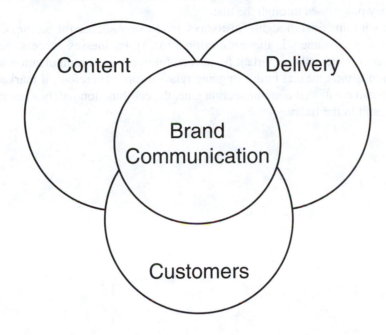

We will be the first to admit that building customer-brand relationships is not the only way to develop marketing communication programs in the beginning of the twenty-first century. There are certainly others. But we believe that the model we have presented accurately summarizes what needs to be done and in the most relevant sequence. Thus, we believe our approach is a very viable solution.

This need to think about how to send marketing messages and, at the same time, respond to consumer requests complicates marketing communication planning. It requires multitasking at the highest level for the organization, a capability that generally has not been well developed in marketing firms although customers mastered this art years ago.

Building customer-brand relationships is a tough, complicated job, yet, at the same time, it simplifies what needs to be done and the requirements involved. It requires a better understanding of customers than most organizations presently have. It means a shift from message and incentive distribution to an understanding of media delivery and message and incentive consumption—by the customer or prospect, not by the media form used. It encourages, or rather demands, measurement and accountability by marketing communication managers, two areas that they have unfortunately neglected in their haste to develop the next great, award-winning, creative, outbound, communication breakthrough.

In short, the new marketplace demands new tools, new approaches, new methodologies, and, most of all, new thinking. We have tried to supply as many of those concepts and approaches as time and space would allow. But we have not covered the spectrum by any means. Many of the new approaches are still developing and some are even yet to be envisioned. In short, this text is a work in progress, with some areas fairly clear and well developed, and others still in the nascent developmental stage. Hopefully, readers have been able to discern which is which as they progressed through the text.

So we end with this final thought. Customers drive every successful business. Knowing and understanding customers is therefore critical to any businesses success. Knowledge about customers is especially important for successful two-way communication with them. Communication is the glue that builds ongoing relationships. Therefore, if marketers know customers and can create that communication glue, the combination will bind them together for mutual benefit in the future.

Index

About the Authors

Don E. Schultz is Professor Emeritus-in-Service of Integrated Marketing Communications at Northwestern University. He has a BBA from Oklahoma, an MA and a PhD from Michigan State University, and fifteen years of industry experience. Author of eighteen books and more than a hundred articles, he is a regular columnist for *Marketing News* and *Marketing Management* and the founding editor of *Journal of Direct Marketing*.

Beth E. Barnes is a professor in the integrated strategic communication program and director of the School of Journalism and Telecommunications at the University of Kentucky. She previously taught at Syracuse University, Penn State University, Northwestern University, and Miami (Ohio) University. She has worked in advertising on both the client and agency sides of the business and in public relations. She teaches the introductory course in integrated strategic communication at Kentucky.

Heidi F. Schultz is a consultant, author, and lecturer specializing in the area of brands, branding, and integrated marketing communication. She teaches branding in the graduate program of the Integrated Marketing Communications department of the Medill School, Northwestern University, and conducts guest lectures on these topics at universities in Asia, Australia, and Europe. She previously was the publisher of *Chicago* magazine.

Marian Azzaro joined the faculty of Roosevelt University in 1999 and is now a tenured professor teaching marketing, advertising, and media planning classes. She also serves Roosevelt as the head of its graduate IMC program. Before joining Roosevelt, she enjoyed a successful twenty-year career in business, spending ten years in advertising media planning and then, after earning her MBA, moving into brand management and marketing communications. She is the lead author of the media-planning textbook, *Strategic Media Decisions*.